Autodesk AutoCAD 2017 and Inventor 2017 Tutorial

Tutorial Books

For Technical Support, contact us at:
online.books999@gmail.com

Table of Contents

Part 2: Autodesk Inventor Basics Contents

INTRODUCTION

AutoCAD is the industry leader among all CAD products. It is the most widely used CAD software. The commands and concepts introduced by AutoCAD are utilized by other systems. As a student, learning AutoCAD provides you with a greater advantage as compared to any other CAD software.

Autodesk Inventor as a topic of learning is vast, and having a wide scope. It is package of many modules delivering a great value to enterprises. It offers a set of tools, which are easy-to-use to design, document and simulate 3D models. Using this software, you can speed up the design process and reduce the product development costs.

This book provides a step-by-step approach for users to learn Autodesk Inventor and AutoCAD. It is aimed for those with no previous experience CAD. Each chapter has components explained with the help of real world models.

Scope of this book

This book is written for students and engineers who are interested to learn AutoCAD and Autodesk Inventor for designing mechanical components and assemblies, and then create drawings.

Part-I

- **Chapter 1**, "Introduction to AutoCAD 2015", gives an introduction to AutoCAD. The user interface and terminology are discussed in this chapter.

- **Chapter 2**, "Drawing Basics", explores the basic drawing tools in AutoCAD. You will create simple drawings using the drawing tools.

- **Chapter 3**, "Drawing Aids", explores the drawing settings that will assist you in creating drawings.

- **Chapter 4**, "Editing Tools", covers the tools required to modify drawing objects or create new objects using the existing ones.

- **Chapter 5**, "Multi View Drawings", teaches you to create multi view drawings standard projection techniques.

- **Chapter 6**, "Dimensions and Annotations", teaches you to apply dimensions and annotations to a drawing.

- **Chapter 7**, "Parametric Tools", teaches you to create parametric drawings. Parametric drawings are created by using the logical operations and parameters that control the shape and size of a drawing.

- **Chapter 8**, "Section Views", teaches you to create section views of a component. A section view is the inside view of a component when it is sliced.

- **Chapter 9**, "Blocks, Attributes and Xrefs", teaches you to create Blocks, Attributes and Xrefs. Blocks are group of objects in a drawing that can be reused. Attributes are notes, or values related to an object. Xrefs are drawing files attached to another drawing.

- **Chapter 10**, "Layouts and Annotative Objects", teaches you create layouts and annotative objects. Layouts are the digital counterparts of physical drawing sheets. Annotative objects are dimensions, notes and so on which their sizes with respect to drawing scale.

- **Chapter 11**, "Templates and Plotting", teaches you create drawing templates and plot drawings.

- **Chapter 12**, "3D Modeling Basics", explores the basic tools to create 3D models.

- **Chapter 13**, "Solid Editing Tools", covers the tools required to edit solid models and create new objects by using the existing ones.

- **Chapter 14**, "Creating Architectural Drawings", introduces you to architectural design in AutoCAD. You will design a floor plan and add dimensions to it.

Part-II

- **Chapter 1** introduces Autodesk Inventor. The user interface and terminology are discussed in this chapter.

- **Chapter 2** takes you through the creation of your first Inventor model. You create simple parts.

- **Chapter 3** teaches you to create assemblies. It explains the Top-down and Bottom-up approaches for designing an assembly. You create an assembly using the Bottom-up approach.

- **Chapter 4** teaches you to create drawings of the models created in the earlier chapters. You will also learn to place exploded views, and part list of an assembly.

- **Chapter 5:** In this chapter, you will learn additional modeling tools to create complex models.

- **Chapter 6** introduces you to Sheet Metal modeling. You will create a sheet metal part using the tools available in the Sheet Metal environment.

- **Chapter 7** teaches you create Top-down assemblies. It also introduces you create mechanisms by applying joints between the parts.

- **Chapter 8:** teaches you to apply dimensions and annotations to a 2D drawing.

Chapter 1: Introduction to AutoCAD 2017

In this chapter, you will learn about:

- **AutoCAD user interface**
- **Customizing user interface**
- **Important AutoCAD commands**

Introduction

AutoCAD is legendary software in the world of Computer Aided Designing (CAD). It has completed 34 years by the 2016. If you are a new user of this software, then the time you spend on learning this software will be a wise investment. If you have used previous versions of AutoCAD, you will be able to learn the new enhancements. I welcome you to learn AutoCAD using this book through step-by-step examples to learn various commands and techniques.

System requirements

The following are system requirements for running AutoCAD smoothly on your system.

- Microsoft Windows 8/8.1, Windows 7, Windows 10.
- Minimum Intel® Pentium® 4 or AMD Athlon™ 64 processor.
- 2 GB of RAM (3GB Recommended) for 32-bit.
- 4GB of RAM (8GB Recommended) for 64-bit.
- Resolution 1024x768 (1600x1050 or higher recommended) with True Color.
- 6 GB of free space for installation.
- Windows display adapter capable of 1024x768 with True Color capabilities. DirectX® 9 or DirectX 11 compliant card recommended.
- Windows Internet Explorer 9.0 or later.
- .NET Framework Version 4.5

Starting AutoCAD 2017

To start **AutoCAD 2017**, double-click the **AutoCAD 2017** icon on your Desktop (or) click **Start > All apps > AutoCAD 2017 > AutoCAD 2017**.

AutoCAD user interface

When you double-click the AutoCAD 2017 icon on the desktop, the AutoCAD 2017 initial screen will appear.

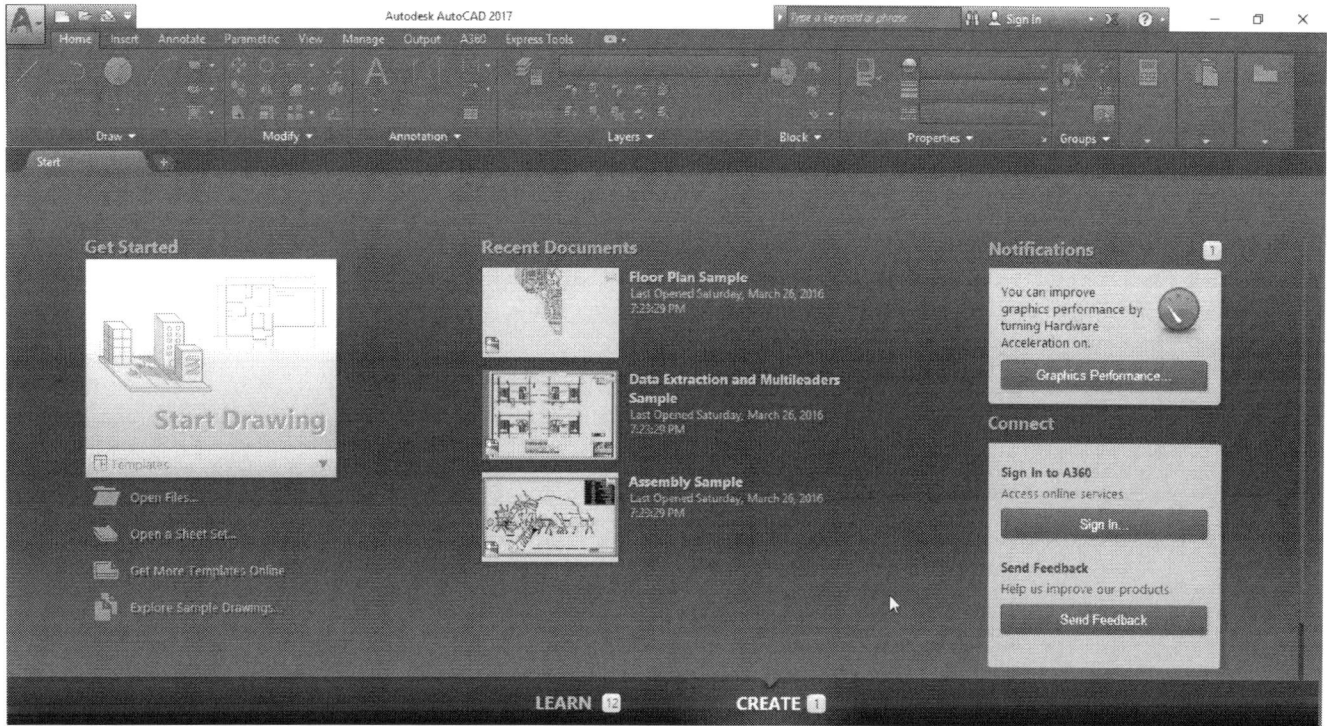

On the Initial Screen, click Start Drawing to open a new drawing file. The drawing file consists of a graphics window, ribbon, menu bar, toolbars, command line, and other screen components, depending on the workspace that you have selected.

Changing the Color Scheme

AutoCAD 2017 is available in two different color schemes: **Dark** and **Light**. You can change the color scheme by using the **Options** dialog. Click the right mouse button and select **Options** from the shortcut menu. On the **Options** dialog, click the **Display** tab and select an option from the **Color Scheme** drop-down.

Workspaces in AutoCAD

There are three workspaces available in AutoCAD: **Drafting & Annotation**, **3D Basics**, and **3D Modeling**. By default, the **Drafting & Annotation** workspace is activated. You can create 2D drawings in this workspace. You can also activate other workspaces by using the **Workspace** drop-down on the top-left corner or the **Workspace Switching** menu on the lower-right corner of the window.

Drafting & Annotation Workspace

This workspace has all the tools to create a 2D drawing. It has a ribbon located at the top of the screen. The ribbon is arranged in a hierarchy of tabs, panels, and tools. Panels such as **Draw**, **Modify**, and **Layers** consist of tools which are grouped based on their usage. Panels in turn are grouped into various tabs. For example, the panels such as **Draw**, **Modify**, and **Layers** are located in the **Home** tab.

3D Basics and 3D Modeling Workspaces

These workspaces are used to create 3D models. You will learn more about these workspaces in Chapter 12. The other components of the user Interface are discussed next.

Application Menu

The **Application Menu** appears when you click on the icon located at the top left corner of the window. The **Application Menu** consists of a list of self-explanatory menus. You can see a list of recently opened documents or a list of currently opened documents by clicking the **Recent Documents** and **Open Documents** buttons, respectively. The Search Bar is used to search for any command. You can type any keyword in the search bar and find a list of commands related to it.

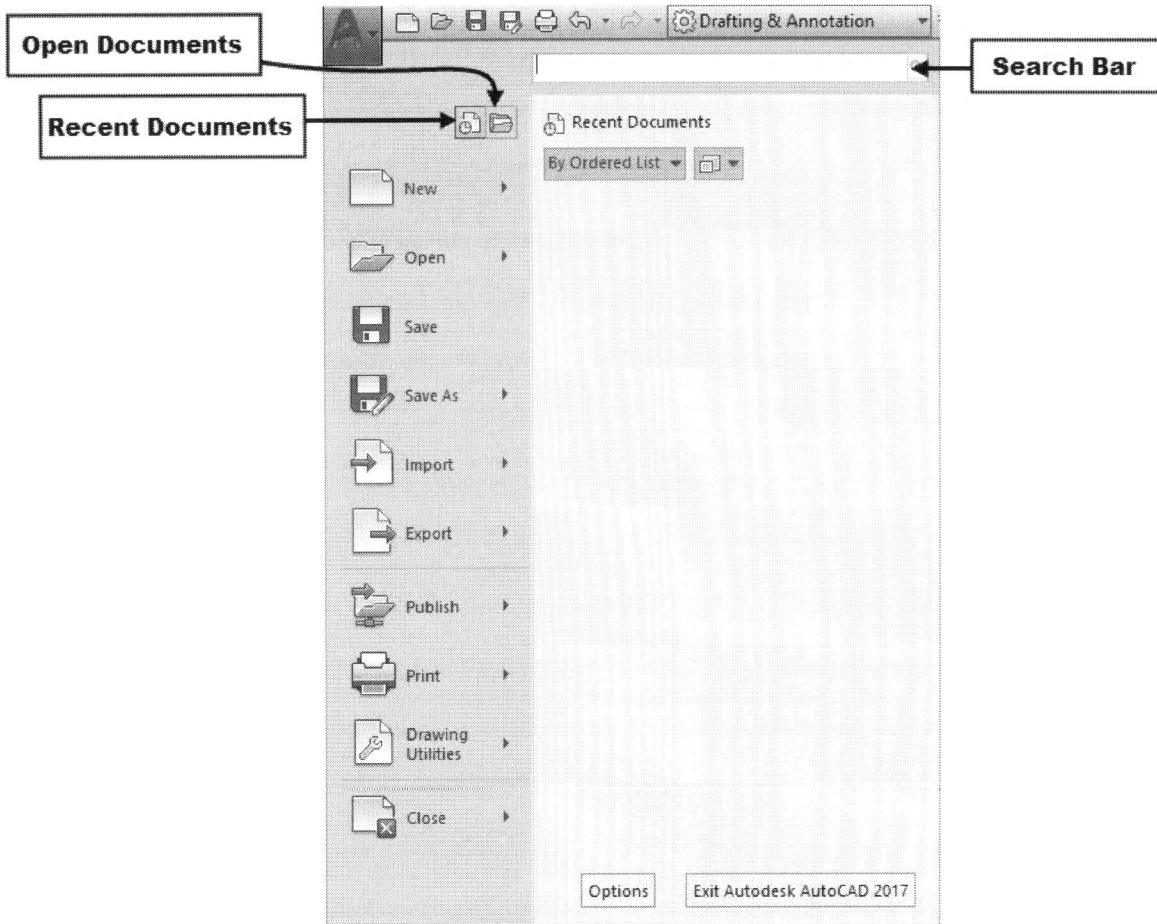

Quick Access Toolbar

This is located at the top left corner of the window and helps you to access commands, quickly. It consists of commonly used commands such as **New**, **Save**, **Open**, **Save As**, and so on.

File tabs

File tabs are located below the ribbon. You can switch between different drawing files by using the file tabs. Also, you can open a new file by using the + button, easily.

Graphics Window

Graphics window is the blank space located below the file tabs. You can draw objects and create 3D graphics in the graphics window. The top left corner of the graphics window has **In-Canvas Controls**. Using these controls, you can set the orientation and display style of the model.

ViewCube

The ViewCube allows you to navigate in the 3D Modeling and 2D drafting environments. Using the ViewCube, you can set the orientation of the model. For example, you can select the top face of the ViewCube to set the orientation to Top. You can click the corner points to set the view to Isometric.

Navigation Bar

The Navigation Bar contains navigation tools such as **Steering wheel, Pan, Zoom, Orbit,** and **ShowMotion**.

Command line

The command line is located below the graphics window. It is very easy to execute a command using the command line. You can just type the first letter of a command and it lists all the commands starting with that letter. This helps you to activate commands very easily and increases your productivity.

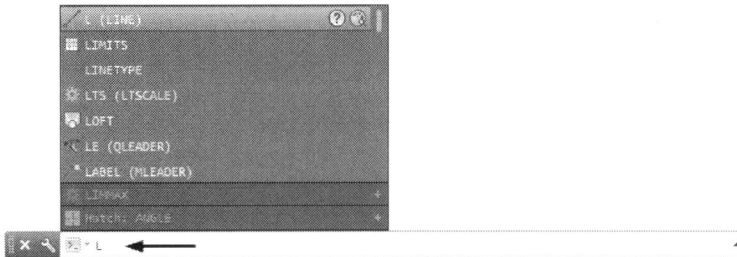

Also, the command line shows the current state of the drawing. It shows various prompts while working with any command. These prompts are series of steps needed to successfully execute a command. For example, when you activate the LINE command, the command line displays a prompt, "Specify the first point". You need to click in the graphics window to specify the first point of the line. After specifying the first point, the prompt, "Specify next point or [Undo]:" appears. Now, you need to specify the next point of the line. It is recommended that you should always have a look at the command line to know the next step while executing a command.

System Variables

System variables control the behavior of various functions and commands in AutoCAD. Usually, the system variables have two or more values. You can control a system variable value from the command line. For example, the MIRRTEXT system variable controls the direction of text when you mirror it. The 0 value retains the text direction when you mirror it. Whereas, the 1 value reverses the text direction when you mirror it.

In AutoCAD, you can also control the system variables by using the **System Variable Monitor** dialog. Type SYSVARMONITOR in the command line and press Enter to open this dialog. A list of system variables, which are monitored by default appears on the dialog. You can know the function of a system variable by clicking the **Help** icon located next to it. You can change a system variable value in the **Preferred** column of the dialog. The **Status** column shows a yellow triangle if you have changed the default value of a system variable. The **Enable balloon notification** option shows a balloon on the status bar, if you changed any system variable value. You can click the **Reset All** button to restore the default values of system variables.

You can monitor more system variables by clicking the **Edit List** button. Next, on the **Edit System Variable List** dialog, select a system variable from the **Available system variables** list, and click the **Add** (>>) button. You can also remove system variables from the Monitored system variables list by selecting them and clicking the **Remove** (<<) button. Click **OK** on both the dialogs after changing the values.

Status Bar

Status Bar is located at the bottom of the AutoCAD window. It contains many buttons which help you to create a drawing very easily. You can turn ON or OFF these buttons just by clicking on them. Some buttons are hidden by default. You can display more buttons on the status bar by clicking the **Customization** button at the bottom right corner and selecting the options from the menu. The buttons available on the status bar are briefly discussed in the following section.

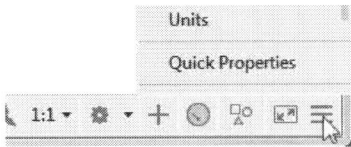

Button	Description
6627.2412, 525.0753, 0.0000 **Coordinates**	This button is hidden by default. You can show it by using the **Customization** menu. It displays the drawing coordinates when you move the pointer in the graphics window. You can turn OFF this button by clicking on it.
Infer Constraints	This icon automatically creates constraints when you draw objects in the graphics window. Constraints are logical operations which control the shape of a drawing. You can turn it ON or OFF by clicking on it.
Snap Mode (F9)	The Snap mode aligns pointer only with the Grid points. When you turn ON this button, the pointer will be able to select only the Grid points.
Grid Display (F7)	It turns the Grid display ON or OFF. You can set the spacing between the grid lines by clicking the drown arrow next to the Snap Mode

	button and selecting the **Snap Settings** option. You can use grid lines along with the Snap Mode to draw objects easily and accurately.
Ortho Mode (F8)	It turns the Ortho Mode ON or OFF. When the Ortho Mode is ON, only horizontal or vertical lines can be drawn.
Polar Tracking (F10)	This icon turns ON or OFF the Polar Tracking. When the Polar Tracking is turned ON, you can draw lines easily at regular angular increments, such as 5, 10, 15, 23, 30, 45, or 90 degrees. You will notice that a trace line is displayed when the pointer is at a particular angular increment. You can set the angular increment by clicking the down arrow next to this button and selecting the required angle.
isoplane Left / isoplane Top / isoplane Right **Isometric Drafting**	This icon is used to switch between planes while drawing isometric views. The grid lines are also displayed if the Grid Mode is turned ON. The orientation of the grid lines change based on the selected isoplane option.
Object Snap (F3)	This icon turns ON or OFF the Object Snap mode. When this mode is turned ON, you can easily select the key points of objects such as endpoints, midpoint, and center point and so on.

3D Object Snap (F4)	This icon turns ON or OFF the 3D Object Snap. The 3D Object Snap is used to select the key points of 3D objects.
Object Snap Tracking (F11)	This icon is used to turn ON or OFF the Object Snap Tracking mode. When this mode is turned ON, you can easily select points by using the trace lines originating from the key points.
Dynamic UCS (F6)	This icon turns ON/OFF the Dynamic UCS. When the Dynamic UCS is turned ON, you can draw and create objects on any face of a 3D Model, dynamically.
Dynamic Input (F12)	This icon turns ON or OFF the Dynamic Input mode. When this mode is turned ON, a dynamic input box is attached to the pointer along with a prompt. You can directly enter a value in the dynamic input box. You can use Dynamic Input in place of command line.

Show/Hide Lineweight	This icon turns ON or OFF the lineweight. Line weight is the thickness of objects. You can set the thickness of objects by specifying the lineweight. If the Lineweight is turned OFF, the objects are displayed with the default thickness. Lineweight ON Lineweight OFF
Transparency	This icon turns ON or OFF the transparency of an object. You can set the transparency using the Layer Properties Manager. Transparency ON Transparency OFF
Quick Properties	This button is used to display some important properties of a selected object.
Selection Cycling	This icon turns ON or OFF the Selection Cycling. Selection Cycling is very useful while selecting overlapped objects. Turn ON the selection cycling and click on the overlapping objects. Select the required object from the Selection list.

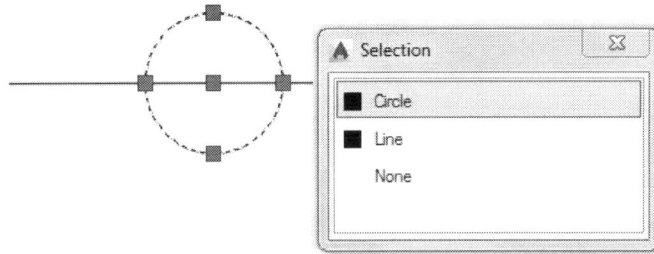

✛ **Annotation Monitor**	This icon turns the Annotation Monitor ON or OFF. The Annotation Monitor checks whether the annotations are attached to their respective objects. When an annotation is not attached to any object, it displays an error message.

MODEL **Model or Paper Space**	This icon switches between the Model space and Paper space. Model space is used to create drawings and Paper space is used to print drawings.

1:1 ▾ **Annotation Scale**	This icon controls the size of annotative objects. Annotative objects are dimensions, texts, notes and other objects which can be sized as per the drawing scale.

Annotation Visibility	This icon displays annotative objects that are not created in the current scale.
AutoScale	This icon resizes the annotative objects as per the new drawing scale.
Annotation Scale	This icon changes the annotation scale of objects.
Workspace Switching	This icon changes the workspace.
Hardware Acceleration On/Off	This icon increases or decreases the graphics speed.
Isolate Objects	This icon hides or isolates objects in a drawing. If you hide an object, it will be hidden and all the other objects in the drawing will be visible. If you isolate an object, the other objects in the drawing will be hidden and the selected object will be visible.
Lock UI	This icon locks the toolbars, panel, tool palettes and other User Interface elements at their current position. Click the down arrow next to this icon to view the options to lock the user interface.

Menu Bar

Menu Bar is not displayed by default. However, you can display the Menu Bar in other workspaces by clicking on the down-arrow located at the right side of the Quick Access Toolbar and selecting the **Show Menu Bar** option. The Menu Bar is located at the top of the window just below the title bar. It contains various menus such as File, Edit, View, Insert, Format, Tools, Draw, Dimensions, Modify, and so on. Clicking on any of the word on the Menu Bar displays a menu. The menu contains various tools and options. There are also sub-options available on the menu. These sub-options are displayed if you click on an option with an arrow. If you click on an option with (...), a dialog will appear.

Changing the display of the Ribbon

You can change the display of the ribbon by clicking the arrow button located at the top of it. The ribbon can be displayed in three different modes as shown below.

Ribbon Minimized to panels

Minimize to panel titles

Minimized to tabs

You can use the GALLERYVIEW system variable to hide or show galleries on the ribbon. The system variable value 1 displays a gallery for dimension styles, blocks, table styles, and mleader styles. The value 0 hides the gallery view.

Gallery

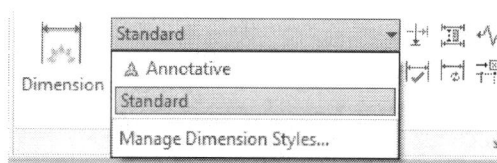

Drop-down

Dialogs and Palettes

Dialogs and Palettes are part of AutoCAD user interface. Using a dialog or a palette, you can easily specify many settings and options at time. Examples of dialogs and palettes are as shown below.

Dialog box

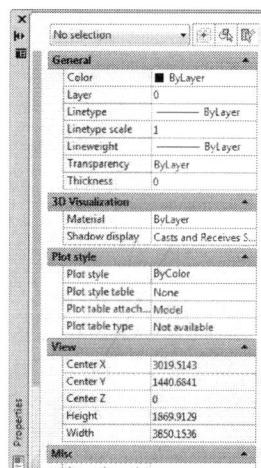

Palette

Tool Palettes

Tool Palettes provide you with another way of selecting tools and placing objects. You can display Tool Palettes by clicking **View > Palettes > Tool Palettes** on the ribbon. A Tool Palette is similar to a palette except that it has many palettes grouped in the form of tabs. You can select tools from the Tool Palettes as well as drag and place objects (blocks) into the drawing. You can also create a new Tool Palette and add frequently used tools and objects to it.

Shortcut Menus

Shortcut Menus appear when you right-click in the graphics window. AutoCAD provides various shortcut menus in order to help you access tools and options very easily and quickly. There are various types of shortcut menus available in AutoCAD. Some of them are discussed next.

Right-click Menu

This shortcut menu appears whenever you right-click in the graphics window without activating any command or selecting any object.

Select and Right-click menu

This shortcut menu appears when you select an object from the graphics window and right-click. It consists of editing and selection options.

Command Mode shortcut menu

This shortcut menu appears when you activate a command and right-click. It shows options depending upon the active command. The shortcut menu below shows the options related to the RECTANGLE command.

Right-click Menu

Select and Right-click menu

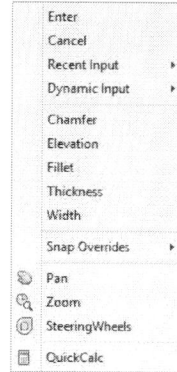

Command Mode shortcut menu

Grip shortcut menu

This shortcut menu is displayed when you select a grip of an object, move the pointer and right-click. It displays various operations that can be performed using grip.

Selection Window

A selection window is used to select multiple elements of a drawing. You can select multiple elements by using two types of selection windows. The first type is a rectangular selection window. You can create this type of selection window by defining its two diagonal corners. When you define the first corner of the selection window on the left and second corner on the right side, the elements which completely fall under the selection window will be selected.

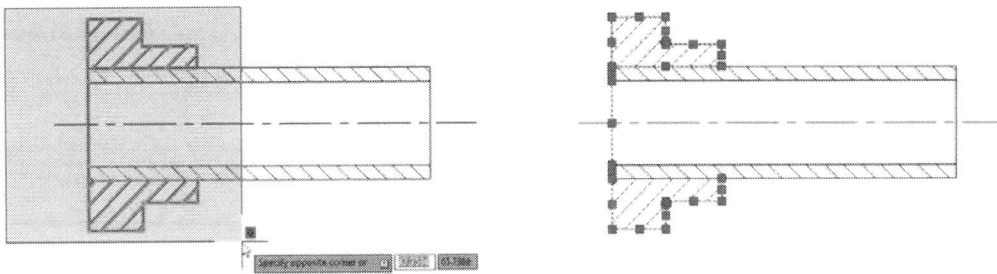

However, if you define the first corner on the right side and second corner of the left side, the elements, which fall completely or partially under the selection window, will be selected.

The second type of selection window is the Lasso. Lasso is an irregular shape created by clicking and dragging the pointer across the elements to select. If you drag the pointer from the left to right, the elements falling completely under the lasso will be selected.

If you drag the pointer from right to left, the elements, which fall completely or partially under the lasso, will be selected.

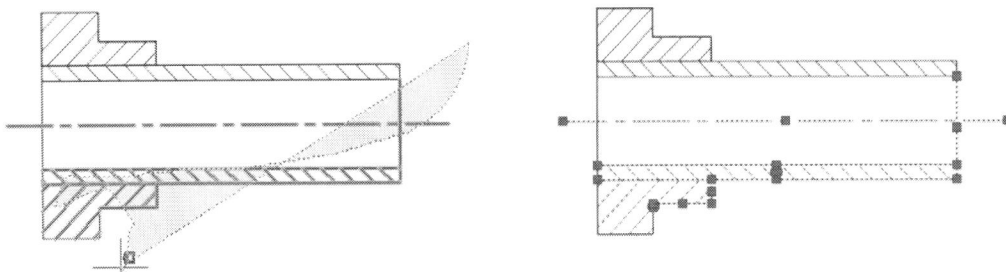

Starting a new drawing

You can start an AutoCAD document by using the **Get Started** section or by using the **Select template** dialog.

Get Started Section on the Initial Screen

To start a new drawing, click Create at the bottom of the initial screen, and then select a template from **Get Started > Templates** drop-down.

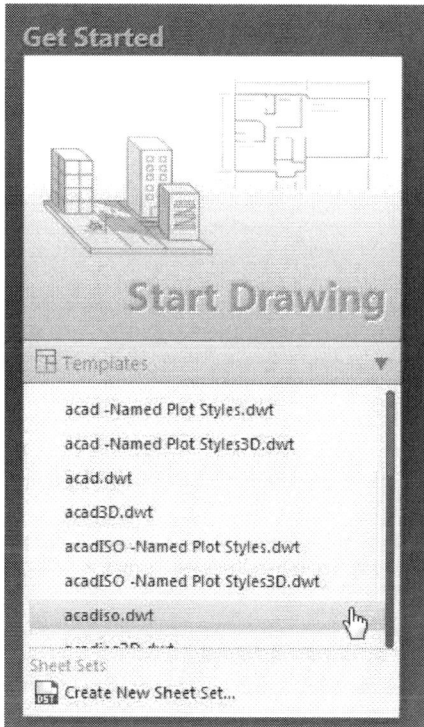

The Select Template dialog

To start a new drawing, click the **New** button on anyone of the following:

- Quick Access Toolbar
- **Application Menu**

The **Select Template** dialog appears when you click the **New** button. In this dialog, select the **acad.dwt** (inch units) or **acadiso.dwt** (metric units) template for creating a 2D drawing. Select the **acad3D.dwt** or **acadiso3D.dwt** template for creating 3D models.

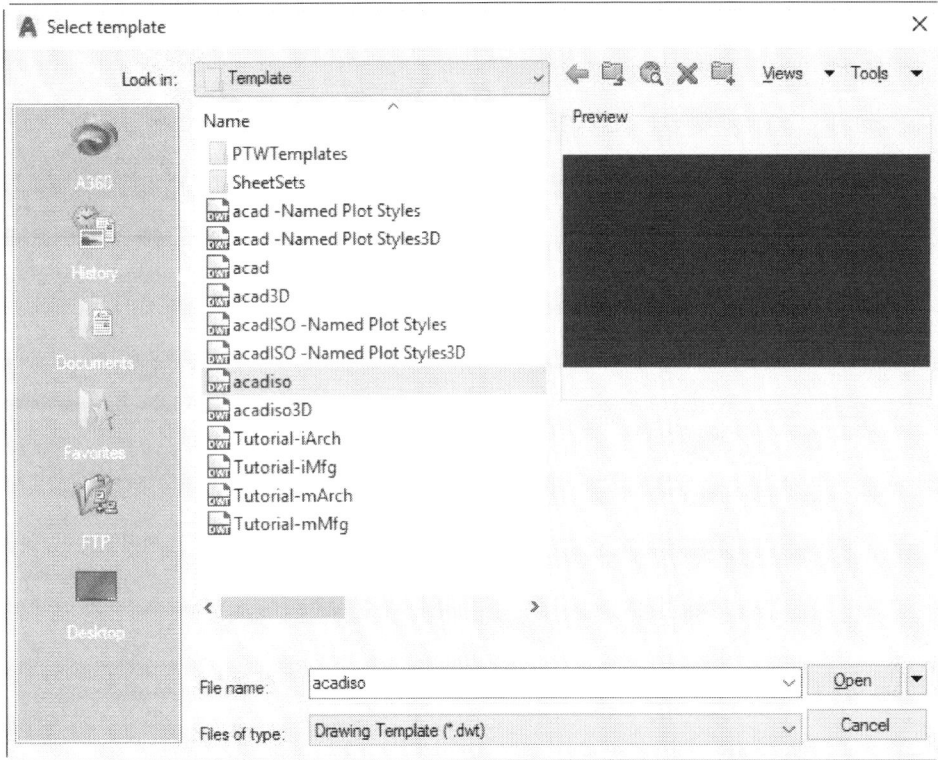

Help

Press F1 or type a keyword in the Search bar located at the top right corner of the window to get help for any topic. On the Autodesk AutoCAD 2017 –Help window, click the Find option next to the topic; an animated arrow appears on the window showing the tool location.

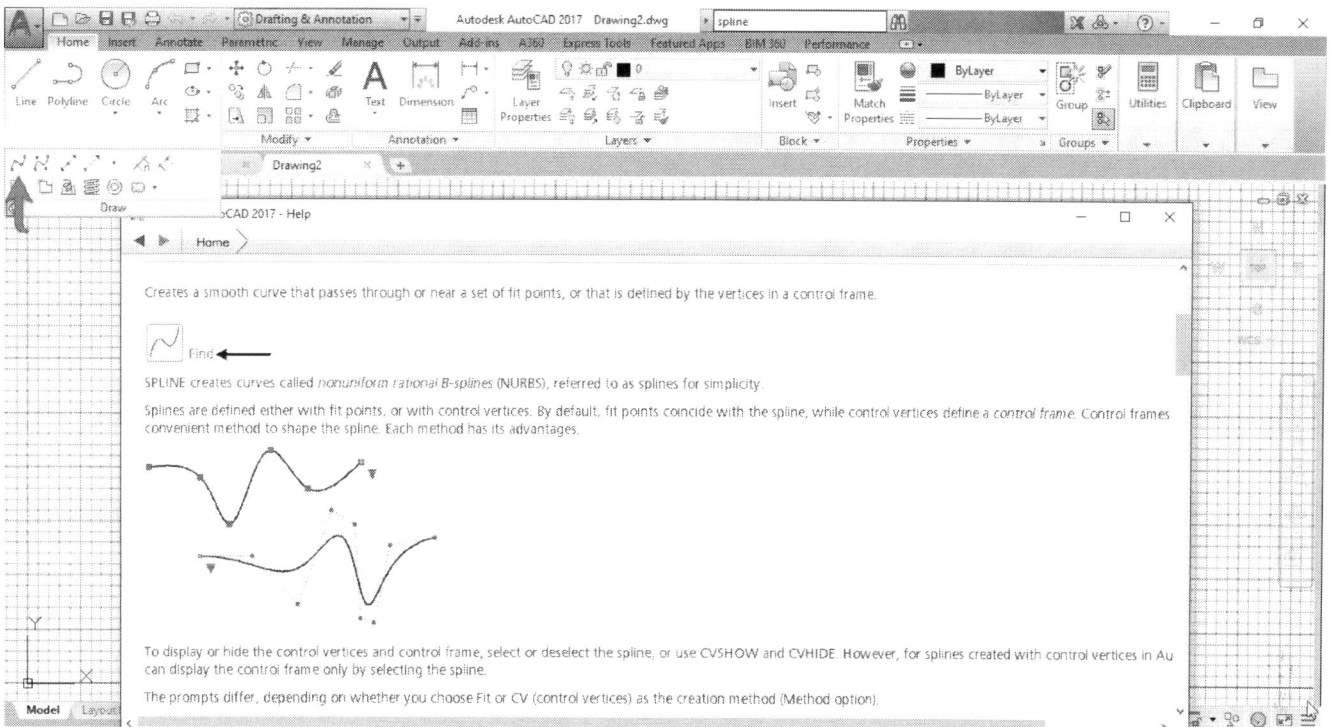

Command List

Various commands in AutoCAD are given in the table below:

Command	Alias	Description
APPLOAD		Activates the **Load/Unload Applications** dialog.
ADCENTER	**DC**	Opens the **DesignCenter** palette.
ALIGN	**AL**	Used to align objects with other objects.
ARC	**A**	Used to create an arc.
AREA		Displays the area of a selected closed object.
ARRAY	**AR**	Creates Rectangular, Path or Polar 2D arrays.

ASE		Displays the **dbConnect Manager** palette.
ATTDEF	ATT	Displays the **Attribute Definition** dialog.
ATTEDIT	ATE	Used to edit Attributes.
AUDIT		Used to check and fix errors.
AUTOCONSTRAIN		Used to apply constraints automatically.
AUTOPUBLISH		Used to create a DWF file.
BACTION	AC	Used to add an action to a dynamic block. This command is available in Block Editor.
BLOCK		Used to create a block.
BMAKE	B	Used to create a block.
BMPOUT		Used to create a Raster image out of the drawing.
BOUNDARY	BO	Used to create a hatch boundary.
BREAK	BR	Used to break an object.
CAL		Used to calculate mathematical expressions.
CHAMFER	CHA	Used to create chamfers.

CHPROP	CH	Changes the properties of a selected object.
CIRCLE	C	Used to create a circle.
COLOR	COL	Displays the **Select Color** dialog.
COPYTOLAYER		Used to copy objects from one layer to another.
COPY	CO	Used to copy objects inside a drawing.
COPYCLIP		Used to copy objects from one drawing to another.
CUSTOMIZE		Used to customize tool palettes.
DDEDIT	ED	Used to edit a note or annotation.
DIMSTYLE	D	Used to create or modify a dimension style.
DDMODIFY		Displays the Properties palette.
DELCONSTRAINT		Used to delete constraints.
OSNAP	OS	Used to set **Object Snap** settings.
DDPTYPE		Used to set the point style and size.
VIEW	V	Used to save views by names.

DGNEXPORT		Used to export the drawing to Microstation (DGN) format.
DGNIMPORT		Used to import a Microstation (DGN) format file.
DIMCONSTRAINT	**DCON**	Used to apply dimensional constraints to objects.
DIMLINEAR	**DLI**	Used to create a linear dimension.
DIMALIGNED	**DAL**	Used to create an aligned dimension.
DIMARC	**DAR**	Used to dimension the arc length.
DIMRADIUS	**DIMRAD**	Used to create at radial dimension.
DIMJOGGED	**JOG**	Used to create a jogged dimension.
DIMDIAMETER	**DIMDIA**	Used to create a diameter dimension.
DIMANGULAR	**DAN**	Used to create an angular dimension.
DIMORDINATE	**DOR**	Used to create ordinate dimension.
DIMCONTINUE	**DIMCONT**	Used to create continuous dimensions from an existing one.
DIMBASELINE	**DIMBASE**	Used to create baseline dimensions.

DIMINSPECT		Used to create an inspection dimension.
-DIMSTYLE		Update a dimension according the dimension style.
DIMSPACE		Used to adjust space between dimensions.
DIMBREAK		Used to break the extension line of a dimension when it intersects with another dimension.
DIMOVERRIDE		Used to override the system variables of a selected dimension.
DIMCENTER		Used to create a center mark of a circle.
DIMEDIT	DIMED	Used to edit a dimension.
DIMTEDIT	DIMTED	Used to edit the dimension text.
DIMDISASSOCIATE		Disassociates a dimension from the object.
DIST	DI	Used to measure the distance between two points.
DISTANTLIGHT		Used to create distant light.
DIVIDE	DIV	Places evenly spaced objects on a line segment
DONUT	DO	Used to create a donut.

DVIEW		Used to get the aerial view of a drawing.
DXBIN		Used to open a DXB file.
DXFIN		Used to open a DXF file.
DXFOUT		Used to save a file in DXF format.
ELLIPSE	EL	Used to create an ellipse.
ERASE	E	Used to erase objects.
EXIT		Used to close AutoCAD.
EXPLODE	X	Used to explode or ungroup objects.
EXPLORER		Displays Windows Explorer.
EXPORT	EXP	Used to export data.
EXTEND	EX	Used to extend an object up to another.
FILLET	F	Used to create a fillet at the corner.
FILTER		Used to set object selection filters.
GEOMCONSTRAINT	GCON	Used to apply geometric constraints.

GRADIENT		Used to apply gradient to a closed area.
GROUP	G	Used to group objects.
HATCH	H	Used to apply hatch to a closed area.
HATCHEDIT	HE	Used to edit hatch.
HELP		Display the Help window.
HIDE	HI	Changes the Visual Style to Hidden.
ID		Displays the coordinate values of a selected point.
IMAGE, IMAGEATTACH	IM	Used to attach an Image reference.
IMAGEADJUST	IAD	Used to adjust images.
IMAGECLIP		Used to crop an image.
IMPORT		Used to import other forms of CAD data.
INSERT	I	Used to insert a block.
INSERTOBJ		Used to insert an object into the drawing.
ISOPLANE	CTRL+E	Used to set the current isometric plane.

JOIN	J	Used to join end points of two linear or curved objects.
LAYCUR		The Layer of the selected objects will be made current.
LAYER	LA	Used to create a new layer and modify its properties.
LAYFRZ		Used to freeze the layer of a selected object.
LAYISO		Isolates the layer of a selected object.
LAYOUT		Used to modify layouts.
LAYOFF		Used to turn off the layer of a selected object.
LAYON		Used to turn ON all the layers.
LAYOUTWIZARD		Displays the Create Layout dialog.
LENGTHEN	LEN	Used to increase the length of an object.
LIMITS		Used to set the drawing limits.
LIMMAX		Used to set the maximum limit of a drawing.
LINE	L	Used to create a line.
LINETYPE	LT	Used to set the linetype.

LIST	LI	Lists the properties of a selected object in the text window.
LOAD		Imports the shapes that can be used by the SHAPE command.
LTSCALE	LTS	Used to set the linetype scale.
MEASURE	ME	Used to place points or blocks at measured intervals on an object.
MENU		Used to load a customization file.
MENULOAD		Used to load or unload a customizable file.
MIRROR	MI	Used to create a mirror image of an object.
MLEDIT		Used to edit a multiline.
MLINE	ML	Used to create multiple parallel lines.
MLSTYLE		Used to create and modify a multiline style.
MOVE	M	Used to move selected objects.
MSLIDE		Used to create slide out of a drawing.
MSPACE	MS	Used to switch from paper space to model space.

MSTRETCH		Used to stretch multiple objects at a time.
MTEXT	MT or T	Used to write text in multiple lines.
MVIEW	MV	Used to create and modify viewports.
MVSETUP		Used to set drawing specifications for printing purpose.
NEW	CTRL+N	Used to open a new file.
NOTEPAD		Used to edit file in Notepad.
OFFSET	O	Creates a parallel copy of a selected object at a specified distance.
OOPS		Used to undo the ERASE command.
OPEN		Used to open an existing file.
OPTIONS	OP	Used to set various options related to the drawing.
ORTHO		Turns ON/OFF the Ortho Mode.
OSNAP	OS	Used to the **Object Snap** settings.
PAGESETUP		Used to specify the printing properties of a layout.
PAN	P	Used to drag a drawing to view its different portions.

PARAMETER	PAR	Used to assign expressions to a dimensional constraint.
PBRUSH		Opens the **Windows Paint** application.
PEDIT	PE	Used to edit polylines.
PLINE	PL	Used to create a polyline. A polyline is a single object which can have continuous lines and arcs.
PLOT	CTRL+P	Used to plot a drawing.
POINT	PO	Used to place a point in the drawing.
POLYGON	POL	Used to create a polygon.
PREVIEW	PRE	Used to preview the plotted drawing.
PROPERTIES	PR	Displays the **Properties** palette.
PSOUT		Used to create a postscript file.
PURGE	PU	Used to remove the unwanted data from the drawing.
QDIM		Used to create a quick dimension.
QSAVE		Used to save the current drawing.
QUICKCALC	QC	Displays the QuickCalc calculator.

QUIT		Used to close the current drawing session.
RAY		Used to create a line that starts from a selected point and extends up to infinity.
RECOVER		Used to repair and open the damaged files.
RECOVERALL		Used to repair a damaged file along with the attached external references.
RECTANG		Used to create a polyline rectangle.
REDEFINE		Used to restore an AutoCAD command which has been overridden.
REDRAW	R	Refreshes the current viewport.
UNDEFINE		Used to override an existing command with a new one.
REDO		Used to cancel the previous UNDO command.
REDRAWALL	RA	Refreshes all the viewports in a drawing.
REGEN	RE	Regenerates the current viewport of a drawing.
REGENALL	REA	Regenerates all the viewports of a drawing.
REGION	REG	Convert the area enclosed by objects into a region.

RENAME	**REN**	Used to rename blocks, viewports, dimension styles and so on.
REVCLOUD		Used to highlight a portion of drawing by creating a cloud around it.
RIBBON		Displays the ribbon.
RIBBONCLOSE		Hides the ribbon.
SAVE	**CTRL+S**	Saves the currently opened drawing.
SAVEAS		Saves the drawing with another name and location.
SAVEIMG		Used to save a rendered output file.
SCALE	**SC**	Used to increase or decrease the size of a drawing.
SCRIPT	**SCR**	Used to load a script file. A script is used to run various commands in a sequential manner.
SETVAR	**SET**	Used to list or change a system variable.
SHAPE		Used to insert a shape into a drawing.
SHELL		Used to enter MS-DOS commands.
SKETCH		Used to draw freehand sketches.

SOLID	**SO**	Used to create filled triangles or quadrilaterals.
SPELL	**SP**	Used to check the spelling of a text.
SPLINE	**SPL**	Used to create a spline (curved object).
SPLINEDIT	**SPE**	Used to edit a spline.
STATUS		Used to display the details of a drawing such as limits, model space usage, layers and so on.
STRETCH	**S**	Used to stretch objects.
STYLE	**ST**	Used to create or modify the text style.
TABLET	**TA**	Allows using a tablet for creating drawings.
TBCONFIG		Used to customize user interface.
TEXT		Used to enter text in the drawing.
THICKNESS	**TH**	Used to set a thickness value to 2D objects.
TOLERANCE		Used to apply geometric tolerances to the drawing.
TOOLBAR	**TO**	Used to customize toolbars.
TRIM	**TR**	Used to trim unwanted portions of an object.

UCS		Used to specify the location of the user coordinate system.
UNDO	CTRL+Z (or) U	Used to undo the last operation.
UNITS	UN	Set the units of the drawing
VIEW		Used to save and restore model space, layout, and preset views.
VPLAYER		Used to control the layer visibility in paper space.
VPORTS		Used to create multiple viewports in model space of paper space.
VSLIDE		Used to show an image slide file.
WBLOCK	W	Used to convert a block into a drawing.
WMFIN		Used to import a Windows Metafile. This file contains drawing data and image data. But only drawing data is imported.
WIPEOUT		Used to wipeout a portion of the drawing.
WMFOPTS		Used to specify options for importing a Windows Metafile.
WMFOUT		Used to save objects as Windows Metafile.

XATTACH	**XA**	Used to attach a drawing as an external reference.
XLINE	**XL**	Used to create construction lines. Construction lines extend to infinity and help in drawing objects.
XREF	**XR**	Used to attach a drawing as an external reference.
ZOOM	**Z**	Used to Zoom in or out of a drawing.

3D Commands

Command	Shortcut	Description
3DARRAY	**3A**	Used to create three-dimensional arrays of an objects.
3DALIGN	**3AL**	Used align 3D objects.
3DFACE	**3F**	Used to create three sided or four 3D surface.
3DMESH		Used to create freeform 3D mesh.
3DCORBIT		Used to rotate a view in the 3D space with continuous motion.
3DDISTANCE		Used to control the distance.
3DEDITBAR		Used to add and edit control vertices on a NURBS surface or spline.

3DFLY		Used to view the 3D model as if you are flying through.
3DFORBIT		Used to freely rotate a view in 3D space.
3DMOVE	**3M**	Used to move the objects in 3D space.
3DORBIT	**3DO**	Used to rotate the view constrained along horizontal or vertical axis.
3DORBITCTR		Used to set the center for rotating view in 3D space.
3DPAN		Used to pan the 3D models horizontally or vertically. This is used when working in perspective view.
3DPOLY	**3P**	Used to create a 3D polyline.
3DPRINT	**3DP**	Used to print the model in 3D (plastic prototype).
3DROTATE		Used to rotate 3D objects in 3D space.
3DSCALE	**3S**	Used to increase or decrease the size of 3D object along the X, Y, Z directions.
3DSIN		Used to import a 3ds Max file.
3DDWF		Export the 3D model to a 3D DWF file.

3DWALK	Used to view the 3D model as if you are walking through it.
ANIPATH	Used to create an animation when you are navigating through the model.
BOX	Used to create a 3D box.
CONE	Used to create a 3D cone.
CONVERTOLDLIGHTS	Used to convert lights created in previous releases to the current format.
CONVERTOLDMATERIALS	Used to convert old materials to new format
CONVTONURBS	Used to convert a surface to NURBS. You can edit can easily edit a NURBS by using control vertices displayed on it.
CONVTOSOLID	Used to convert 3D meshes, polylines and circles to 3D solids.
CONVTOSURFACE	Used to convert objects to surfaces.
CVADD	Used to add control vertices to a NURBS surface or spline.
CVREMOVE	Used to remove control vertices from a NURBS surface or spline.

CVHIDE		Used to hide the control vertices of a NURBS surface or splines,
CVSHOW		Used to display the control vertices of a NURBS surface or splines.
CVREBUILD		Used to rebuild the control vertices of a NURBS surface.
CYLINDER		Used to create a 3D Cylinder.
EDGESURF		Used to create a mesh surface from four adjacent edges.
EXTRUDE	EXT	Used to extrude a closed region or polyline.
FILLETEDGE		Used to blend an edge of a 3D object.
FLATSHOT		Used to create a 2D representation of a 3D model.
FREEPOINT		Used to create point light that emits light in all directions.
FREESPOT		Used to create a spot light without any target.
HELIX		Used to create a helical or spiral curve.
INTERFERE		Used to create a 3D solid at the interference point of the various solid objects.

INTERSECT	IN	Used to create a 3D solid at the intersection portion of solid.
LIGHT		Used to create a light.
LIGHTLIST		Displays the lights available in the current 3D model.
LOFT		Used to create 3D solid or surface between various cross sections.
MATERIALS		Displays the Material Browser.
MATERIALASSIGN		Used to assign a material to the model.
MATERIALMAP		Used to the control the texture.
MATERIALATTACH		Used to associate materials with layers.
MESH		Used to create 3D mesh objects.
MESHREFINE		Used to refine the mesh of 3D mesh objects.
MESHSMOOTH		Used to increase the smoothness of mesh objects.
MIRROR3D		Used to mirror 3D objects in 3D space.
OFFSETEDGE		Used to create a parallel copy of an edge at a specified distance.

PFACE		Used to create a 3D Polyface mesh by specifying vertices.
PLAN		Displays the top view of the 3D model.
PLANESURF		Used to create a planar surface.
POINTLIGHT		Used to create point light that emits light in all directions.
PRESSPULL		Used to extrude or subtract material.
PYRAMID		Used to create a pyramid.
-RENDER		Used to specify settings for rendering.
RENDERCROP		Used to render a rectangular portion of a 3D model.
RENDERENVIRONMENT		Used to control visual properties rendered image.
RENDEREXPOSURE		Used to control the lighting of a rendered image.
RENDERONLINE		Used to render an image in Autodesk 360 (cloud).
RENDERPRESETS		Used to specify preset values for rendering an image.
RENDERWIN		Displays the render window.
REVOLVE	REV	Used to create a revolved solid.

REVSURF		Used to create a revolved surface.
RMAT		Displays the Material Browser.
RPREF	**RPR**	Used to specify advanced render settings.
SECTION	**SEC**	Used to create section plane in a 3D model.
SLICE	**SL**	Used to slice a 3D model.
SOLPROF		Create a profile from a 3D model in a paper space.
SOLIDEDIT		Used to edit faces and edges of a 3D solid.
SPACETRANS		Used to calculate equivalent model space and paper space distance.
SPHERE		Used to create a 3D sphere.
SPOTLIGHT		Used to create a spotlight that emits light like a torch.
STLOUT		Used to export a file to STL format.
SUNPROPERTIES		Displays the Sun properties palette.
SURFBLEND	**BLENDSRF**	Used to create a continuous blend surface between two surfaces.

SURFEXTEND	Used to lengthen a surface up to another surface.
SURFEXTRACTCURVE	Used to create Isoline curves on a surface, solid, or a face in U and V directions.
SURFFILLET	Used to create a surface fillet between two surfaces.
SURFOFFSET	Used to create parallel surface at a specified distance.
SURFNETWORK	Used to create a surface from various curves in U and V directions.
SURFPATCH	Used to create a surface using the edges forming a closed loop.
SURFSCULPT	Used to create a closed surface by trimming and combining the surfaces that form a region together.
SURFTRIM	Used to trim portions of a surface at intersections with other surfaces.
SURFUNTRIM	Used to untrim the trimmed surface.
SWEEP	Used to create 3D solid or surface by sweeping a profile along a path.
TABSURF	Used to create a mesh from an line or curve swept along a straight path

TORUS	**TOR**	Used to create a torus.
UNION	**UNI**	Used to combine various solids into one.
VISUALSTYLES		Used to create and modify visual styles.
VPOINT		Used to set the viewing direction of the 3D model.
WEDGE	**WE**	Used to create a wedge shape.
XEDGES		Used to create a 3D wireframe from a 3D solid.

Chapter 2: Drawing Basics

In this chapter, you will learn to do the following:

- Draw lines, rectangles, circles, ellipses, arcs, polygons, and polylines
- Use the Erase, Undo and Redo tools
- Draw entities using the absolute coordinate points
- Draw entities using the relative coordinate points
- Draw entities using the tracking method

Drawing Basics

This chapter teaches you to create simple drawings. You will create these drawings using the basic drawing tools. These tools include **Line**, **Circle**, **Polyline**, and **Rectangle** and so on and they are available in the **Draw** panel of the ribbon, as shown below. You can also activate these tools by typing them in the command line.

Drawing Lines

You can draw a line by specifying its start point and end point using the **Line** tool. However, there are various methods to specify start and end of a line. These methods are explained in the following examples.

Example 1 (using the Absolute Coordinate System)

In this example, you will create lines by specifying points in the absolute coordinate system. In this system, you specify the points with respect to the origin (0, 0). A point will be specified by entering its X and Y coordinates separated by a comma, as shown in figure below.

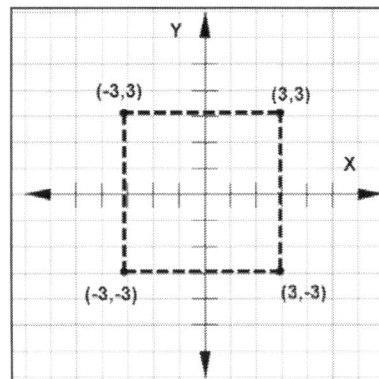

- Start AutoCAD 2017 by clicking the **AutoCAD 2017** icon on your desktop.
- On the Welcome screen, click **Start Drawing > Templates > acadISO-Named Plot Styles.dwt**. This starts a new drawing using the ISO template.
- Click **Zoom > Zoom All** on the **Navigation Bar**; the entire area in the graphics window will be displayed.

line. This creates a rectangle, as shown below.

- Turn OFF the **Grid Display** by pressing the F7 key.
- Click the **Customization** button on the status bar, and then select **Dynamic Input** from the flyout. This displays the **Dynamic Input** icon on the status bar.

- Turn OFF the **Dynamic Input** icon. You will learn about **Dynamic Input** later in this chapter.

- To draw a line, click **Home > Draw > Line** on the ribbon, or enter **LINE** or **L** in the command line.
- Type **50, 50** and press ENTER.
- Type **150, 50** and press ENTER.
- Type **150,100** and press ENTER.
- Type **50,100** and press ENTER.
- Select the **Close** option from the command

- Click **Save** on the **Quick Access Toolbar**.

- Save as **Line-example1.dwg**.
- Close the file.

Example 2 (using Relative Coordinate system)

In this example, you will draw lines by defining its end points in the relative coordinate system. In the relative coordinate system, you define the location of a point with respect to the previous point. For this purpose, the symbol, '@' is used before the point coordinates. This symbol means that the coordinate values are defined in relation with the previous point.

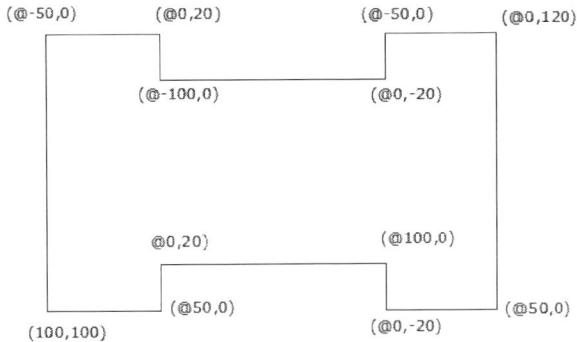

- Click **New** on the **Quick Access Toolbar**.

- Select the **acadISO-Named Plot Styles** template. Click **Open**.

- Type-in **Z** in the command line to activate the **ZOOM** command.

- Click the **All** option in the command line. This displays the entire area in the graphics window.

- Turn OFF the **Grid** icon on the status bar.

- Turn OFF the **Dynamic Input** mode, if active.

- Click **Home > Draw > Line** on the ribbon, or enter **LINE20** or **L** in the command line.

- Type **100,100** and press ENTER. This defines the first point of the line.

- Type **@50,0** and press ENTER.

- Type **@0,20** and press ENTER.

- Type **@100,0** and press ENTER.

- Type **@0,-20** and press ENTER.

- Type **@50,0** and press ENTER.

- Type **@0,120** and press ENTER.

- Type **@-50,0** and press ENTER.

- Type **@0,-20** and press ENTER.

- Type **@-100,0** and press ENTER.

- Type **@0,20** and press ENTER.

- Type **@-50,0** and press ENTER.

- Select the **Close** option from the command line.

- Save the file as **Line-example2.dwg**.

- Close the file.

Example 3 (using Polar Coordinate system)

In the polar coordinate system, you define the location of a point by entering two values: distance from the previous point and angle from the zero degrees. You enter the distance value along with the @ symbol and angle value with the < symbol. You have to make a note that AutoCAD measures the angle in anti-clockwise direction.

Drawing Task

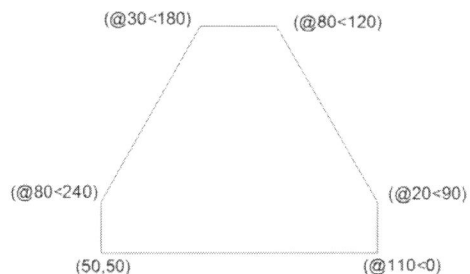

- Open a new file using the **acadISO-Named Plot Styles.dwt** template.

- Click **Zoom > Zoom All** on the **Navigation Bar**.

- Turn OFF the **Grid** icon on the status bar.

- Turn OFF the **Dynamic Input** mode, if active.
- Click **Home > Draw > Line** on the ribbon, or enter **LINE** or **L** in the command line.
- Type **50,50** and press **Enter** key.
- Type **@110<0** and press ENTER.
- Type **@20<90** and press ENTER.
- Type **@80<120** and press ENTER.
- Type **@30<180** and press ENTER.
- Type **@80<240** and press ENTER.
- Select the **Close** option from the command line.
- Save the file as **Line-example3.dwg**.
- Close the file.

Example 4 (using Direct Distance Entry)

In the direct distance entry method, you draw a line by entering its distance and angle values. You use the **Dynamic Input** mode in this method.

- Open a new file using the **acadISO-Named Plot Styles.dwt** template.
- Turn OFF the **Grid** and **Snap Mode** icons on the Status Bar.
- Click **Zoom > Zoom All** on the **Navigation Bar**.
- Activate the **Dynamic Input** icon on the Status Bar.

- Click **Home > Draw > Line** on the ribbon, or enter **LINE** or **L** in the command line.
- Define the first point of the line by typing 50,50 and pressing ENTER.
- Move the pointer horizontally toward right and type-in 150 in the length box.
- Press the TAB key and type 0 as angle. Next, press ENTER.

- Move the pointer vertically upwards and type-in 100 as length.
- Press the TAB key and type 90 as angle. Next, press ENTER.
- Move the pointer horizontally toward left and type 50.
- Press the TAB key and type 180 as angle. Next, press ENTER.
- Move the pointer vertically downwards and type 20.
- Press the TAB key and type 90 as angle. Next, press ENTER.
- Move the pointer horizontally toward left and type 50.
- Press the TAB key and type 180 as angle. Next, press ENTER.
- Move the pointer vertically downwards and type 40.

- Press the TAB key and type 90 as angle. Next, press ENTER.
- Move the pointer horizontally toward left and type 50.
- Press the TAB key and type 180 as angle. Next, press ENTER.
- Click the **Close** option in the command line.
- Save and close the file.

Erasing, Undoing and Redoing

- Draw the sketch similar to the one shown below using the **Line** tool.

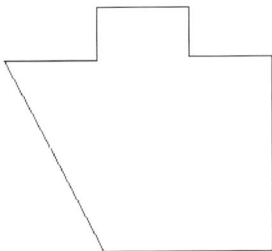

- Click **Home > Modify > Erase** on the ribbon or Enter **ERASE** or **E** in the command line.

- Select the lines shown below and press ENTER. This erases the lines.

- Click the **Undo** button on the **Quick Access Toolbar**. This restores the lines.

- Click the **Redo** button on the **Quick Access Toolbar**. This erases the lines again.

- Type **E** in the command line and press the SPACEBAR; the **ERASE** command will be activated.
- Drag a selection lasso as shown below and press ENTER; the entities will be erased.

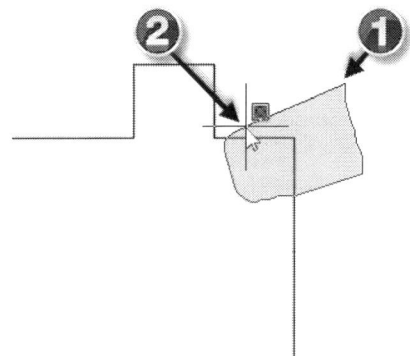

Drawing Circles

The tools in the **Circle** drop-down on the **Draw** panel can be used to draw circles. You can also type-in the **CIRCLE** command in the command line and create circles. There are various methods to create circles. These methods are explained in the following examples.

Example 1(Center, Radius)

In this example, you will create a circle by specifying its center and radius value.

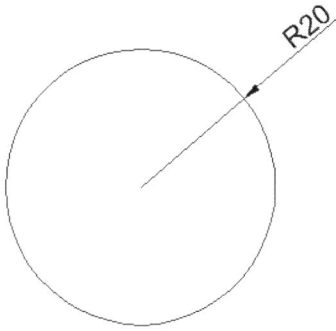

- Click **Home > Draw > Circle > Center, Radius** on the ribbon.
- Select an arbitrary point in the graphics window to specify the center point.
- Type 20 as the radius and press ENTER.

Example 2(Center, Diameter)

In this example, you will create a circle by specifying its center and diameter value.

- Click **Home > Draw > Circle > Center, Diameter** on the ribbon. The message, "Specify center point for circle or [3P/2P/Ttr (tan tan radius)]:" appears in the command line.
- Pick a point in the graphics window, which is approximately horizontal to the previous circle.

Center point

- Type 40 as the diameter and press ENTER; the circle will be created.

Example 3(2-Point)

In this example, you will create a circle by specifying two points. The first point is to specify the location of the circle and the second defines the diameter.

- Click the down arrow next to the **Object Snap** icon on the status bar. A flyout appears. The options in this flyout are called Object Snaps. You will learn about these Object Snaps later in Chapter 3.
- Activate the **Center** option, if it is not already active.
- Now, you will create a circle by selecting the center points of the previous circles.

- Click **Home > Draw > Circle > 2-Point** on the ribbon. The message, "Specify first end point of circle's diameter:" appears in the command line.
- Select the center point of the left side circle; the message, "Specify second end point of circle's diameter:" appears in the command line.
- Select the center point of the right side circle; the circle will be created a shown below.

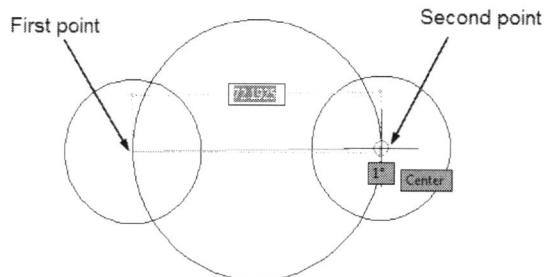

First point

Second point

Example 4(3-Point)

In this example, you will create a circle by specifying three points. The circle will pass through these three points.

- Open a new file.
- Use the **Line** tool and create the drawing shown in figure below. The coordinate points are also given in the figure.

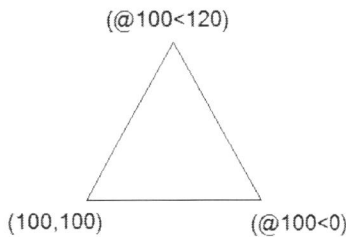

(@100<120)

(100,100)   (@100<0)

- Click **Home > Draw > Circle > 3-Point** on the ribbon.
- Select the three vertices of the triangle; a circle will be created passing through the selected points.

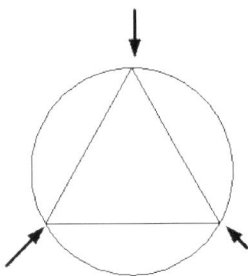

Example 5 (Tan, Tan, Radius)

In this example, you will create a circle by selecting two objects, and then specifying the radius of the circle. This creates a circle tangent to the selected objects.

- Click **Home > Utilities > Measure > Radius** on the ribbon. The message, "Select arc or circle: "appears in the command line.
- Select the circle passing through the three

vertices of the triangle; the radius and diameter values of the circle will be displayed above the command line.

Circle selected

Select arc or circle:
Radius = 57.7350
Diameter = 115.4701
MEASUREGEOM Enter an option [Distance Radius Angle

- Click **Home > Utilities > Quick Calculator** on the ribbon; the **Quick Calculator** appears.
- Type-in **57.7350** in the **Quick Calculator**.
- Click the **/** button and then the **2** button on the **Number Pad**.
- Click the **=** button; the value **28.8675** is displayed in the value box.

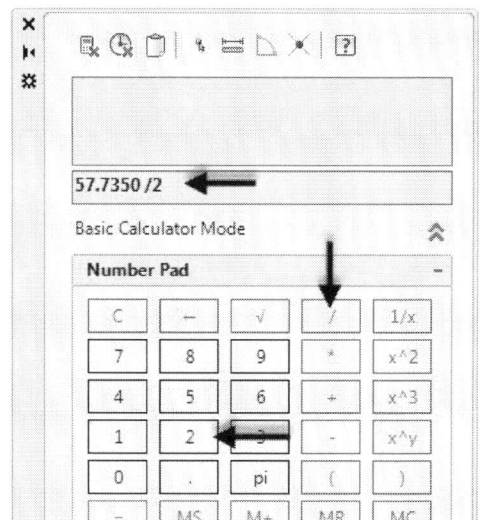

57.7350 /2

Basic Calculator Mode

Number Pad

C	—	√	/	1/x
7	8	9	*	x^2
4	5	6	+	x^3
1	2		-	x^y
0	.	pi	(	)
=	MS	M+	MR	MC

- Click **Home > Draw > Circle > Tan, Tan,**

Radius on the ribbon; the message, "Specify point on object for first tangent of circle:" appears in the command line.

- Select the horizontal line of the triangle; the message, "Specify point on object for second tangent of circle:" appears in the command line.

- Select anyone of the inclined lines; the message, "Specify radius of circle" appears in the command line.

- Click the **Paste value to command line** button on the **Quick Calculator**; the value **28.8675** will be pasted in the command line.

- Press ENTER to specify the radius; the circle will be created touching all three sides of the triangle.

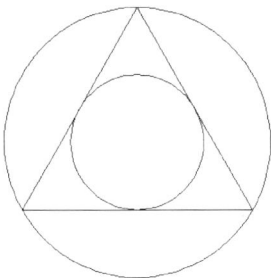

- Save and close the file.

Example 6 (Tan, Tan, Tan)

In this example, you will create a circle by selecting three objects to which it will be tangent.

- Click the **Open** button on the **Quick Access Toolbar**; the **Select File** dialog appears.

- Browse to the location of **Line-example3.dwg** file and double-click on it; the file will be opened.

- Click **Home > Draw > Circle > Tan, Tan, Tan** on the ribbon.

- Select the bottom horizontal line of the drawing.

- Select the two inclined lines. This creates a circle tangent to the selected lines.

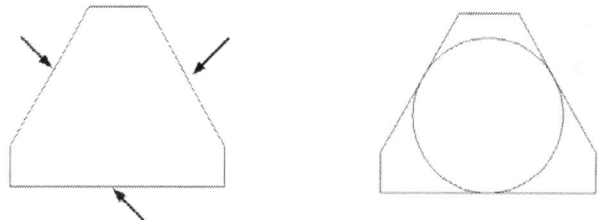

- Save and close the file.

Drawing Arcs

An arc is a portion of a circle. The total angle of an arc will always be less than 360 degrees, whereas the total angle of a circle is 360 degrees. AutoCAD provides you with eleven ways to draw an arc. You can draw arcs in different ways by using the tools available in the **Arcs** drop-down of the **Draw** panel.

The usage of these tools will depend on your requirement. Some methods to create arcs are explained in the following examples.

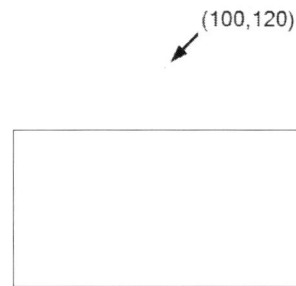

Example 1 (3-Point)

In this example, you will create an arc by specifying three points. The arc will pass through these points.

- Open the **Line-example1.dwg** file.
- Expand the **Draw** panel in the **Home** tab and select the **Multiple Points** tool.

- Type 100,120 in the command line and press ENTER. This places a point above the rectangle.

(100,120)

- Click the down arrow next to the **Object Snap** icon on the status bar, and then select the **Node** option from the menu.

- Click **Home > Draw > Arc > 3-Point** on the ribbon. The message, "Specify start point of arc or [Center]:" appears in the command line.

- Select the top left corner of the rectangle.

- Select the point located above the rectangle.

- Select the top right corner of the rectangle; the three-point arc will be created.

Example 2 (Start, Center, End)

In this example, you will draw an arc by specifying its start, center and end points. The first two points define the radius of the arc and third point defines its included angle.

- Click **Home > Draw > Arc > Start, Center, End** on the ribbon. The message, "Specify start point of arc or [Center]:" appears in the command line.

The included angle of the arc is measured in the counter-clockwise direction. Press and hold the Ctrl key, if you want to reverse the direction.

- Pick an arbitrary point in the graphics window to define the start point of an arc. The message, "Specify center point of arc:" appears.
- Pick a point to define the radius of the circle. You can also type-in the radius value and press ENTER; the message, "Specify end point of arc or [Angle/chord Length]:" appears.
  You will notice that, as you move the pointer, the included angle of the arc changes.
- Pick a point to define the included angle of the arc. You can also type the angle value and press ENTER.

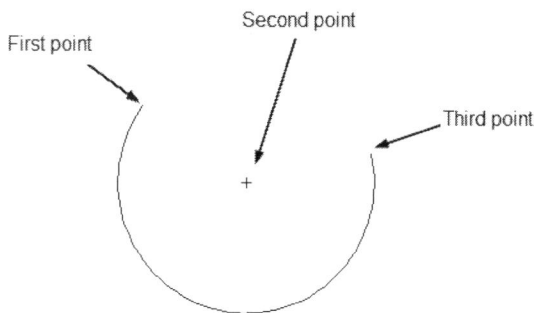

Example 3 (Start, End, Direction)

- Use the **Line** tool and create the drawing shown in figure below. The dimensions are also given in the figure.

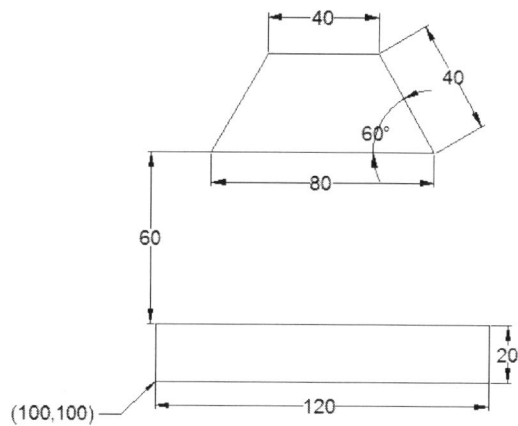

- Click **Home > Draw > Arc > Start, End, Direction** on the ribbon.
- Select the start and end points of the arc as shown in figure.
- Move the pointer vertically downward and click to specify the direction.

- Likewise, create another arc.

Drawing Polylines

A Polyline is a single object that consists of line segments and arcs. It is more versatile than a line as you can assign a width to it. In the following example, you will create a closed polyline.

Example 1

- Activate the **Ortho Mode** on the Status Bar.

- Click **Home > Draw > Polyline** on the ribbon or enter **PLINE** or **PL** in the command line; the message, "Specify start point:" appears in the command line.

- Select an arbitrary point in the graphics window.

- Move the pointer horizontally toward right and type 100. Next, press ENTER.

- Select the **Arc** option from the command line.

- Move the pointer vertically upward and type **50**. Next, press ENTER.

- Select the **Line** option from the command line.

- Move the pointer horizontally toward left and type **50**. Next, press ENTER.

- Move the pointer vertically upward and type **50**. Next, press ENTER.

- Select the **Arc** option from the command line.

- Move the pointer horizontally toward left and type **50**. Next, press ENTER.

- Select the **CLose** option from the command line.

Now, when you select a line segment from the sketch, the whole sketch will be selected. This is because the polyline created is a single object.

Drawing Rectangles

A rectangle is a four sided single object. You can create a rectangle by just specifying its two diagonal corners. However, there are various methods to create a rectangle. These methods are explained in the following examples.

Example 1

In this example, you will create a rectangle by specifying its corner points.

- Open a new file.

- Click **Home > Draw > Rectangle** on the ribbon, or enter **RECTANG** or **REC** in the command line; the message, "Specify first corner point or [Chamfer/Elevation/Fillet/Thickness/Width]:" appears in the command line.

- Pick an arbitrary point in the graphics window; the message "Specify other corner point or [Area/Dimensions/Rotation]:" appears in the command line.

- Move the pointer diagonally toward right and click to create a rectangle.

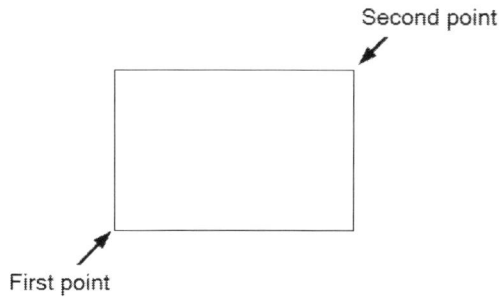

Second point

First point

Example 2

In this example, you will create a rectangle by specifying its length and width.

200

400

- Click **Home > Draw > Rectangle** on the ribbon, or enter **RECTANG** or **REC** in the command line.

- Specify the first corner of the rectangle by picking an arbitrary point in the graphics window.

- Follow the prompt sequence given next:

  Specify other corner point or [Area/Dimensions/Rotation]: Select the **Dimensions** option from the command line

  Specify length for rectangles: Type **400** and press ENTER.

  Specify width for rectangles: Type **200** and press ENTER.

  Specify other corner point or [Area/Dimensions/Rotation]: Move the

pointer upward and click to create the rectangle.

Example 3

In this example, you will create a rectangle by specifying its area and width.

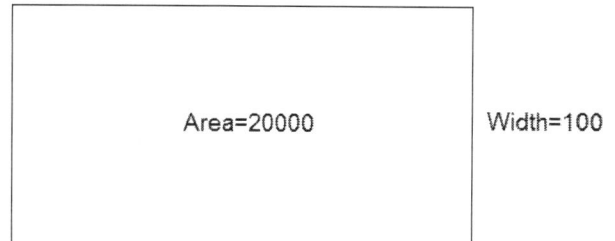

Area=20000   Width=100

- Click **Home > Draw > Rectangle** on the ribbon, or enter **RECTANG** or **REC** in the command line.

- Specify the first corner of the rectangle by picking an arbitrary point.

- Follow the prompt sequence given next:

  Specify other corner point or [Area/Dimensions/Rotation]: Select the **Area** option from the command line

  Enter area of rectangle in current units: Type **20000** and press ENTER.

  Calculate rectangle dimensions based on [Length/Width] <Length>: Select the **Width** option from the command line.

  Enter rectangle width: Type **100** and press ENTER; the length will be calculated automatically.

Example 4

In this example, you will create a rectangle with chamfered corners.

- Click **Home > Draw > Rectangle** on the ribbon, or enter **RECTANG** or **REC** in the command line.
- Follow the prompt sequence given next:

  Specify first corner point or [Chamfer/Elevation/Fillet/Thickness/Width]: Select the **Chamfer** option from the command line.

  Specify first chamfer distance for rectangles: Type **20** and press ENTER.

  Specify second chamfer distance for rectangles: Type **20** and press ENTER.

  Specify first corner point or [Chamfer/Elevation/Fillet/Thickness/Width]: Click at an arbitrary point in the graphics window to specify the first corner.

  Specify other corner point or [Area/Dimensions/Rotation]: Move the pointer diagonally toward right and click to specify the second corner.

Example 5

In this example, you will create a rectangle with rounded corners.

- Click **Home > Draw > Rectangle** on the ribbon, or enter **RECTANG** or **REC** in the command line.
- Follow the prompt sequence given next:

  Specify first corner point or [Chamfer/Elevation/Fillet/Thickness/Width]: Select the **Fillet** option from the command line.

  Specify fillet radius for rectangles: Type **50** and press ENTER.

  Specify first corner point or [Chamfer/Elevation/Fillet/Thickness/Width]: Click at an arbitrary point in the graphics window to specify the first corner.

  Specify other corner point or [Area/Dimensions/Rotation]: Move the pointer diagonally toward right and click to specify the second corner.

Example 6

In this example, you will create an inclined rectangle.

- Click **Home > Draw > Rectangle** on the ribbon, or enter **RECTANG** or **REC** in the command line.
- Specify the first corner of the rectangle by picking an arbitrary point.

- Follow the prompt sequence given next:

  Specify other corner point or [Area/Dimensions/Rotation]: Select the **Rotation** option from the command line.
  Specify rotation angle or [Pick points]: Type **60** and press ENTER.
  Specify other corner point or [Area/Dimensions/Rotation]: Enter **400** and press TAB and then **300** in the Dynamic Input boxes.

Drawing Polygons

A Polygon is a single object having many sides ranging from 3 to 1024. In AutoCAD, you can create regular polygons having sides with equal length. There are two methods to create a polygon. These methods are explained in the following examples.

Example 1

In this example, you will create a polygon by specifying the number of sides, and then specifying the length of one side.

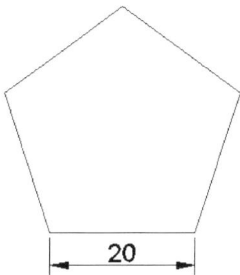

- Click **Home > Draw > Polygon** on the ribbon.

- Follow the prompt sequence given next.

  Enter number of sides <4>: Type **5** and press **ENTER**.
  Specify center of polygon or [Edge]: Select the **Edge** option from the command line.
  Specify first endpoint of edge: Select an arbitrary point.
  Specify second endpoint of edge: Type **20** and press **ENTER**.

Example 2

In this example, you will create a polygon by specifying the number of sides, and drawing an imaginary circle (inscribed circle). The polygon will be created with its corners located on the imaginary circle. You can also create a polygon with the circumscribed circle. A circumscribed circle is an imaginary circle which is tangent to all the sides of a polygon.

- Type **POL** in the command line and press ENTER; the **POLYGON** command will be activated.
- Follow the prompt sequence given next:

Enter number of sides <5>: Type **8** and press **ENTER**.

Specify center of polygon or [Edge]: Select an arbitrary point

Enter an option [Inscribed in circle/Circumscribed about circle] <C>: Select the **Inscribed in circle** option from the command line.

Specify radius of circle: Type **20** and press ENTER; a polygon will be created with its corners touching the imaginary circle.

Drawing Splines

Splines are non-uniform curves, which are used to create irregular shapes. In AutoCAD, you can create splines by using two methods: **Spline Fit** and **Spline CV**. These methods are explained in the following examples:

Example 1: (Spline Fit)

In this example, you will create a spline using the **Spline Fit** method. In this method you need to specify various points in the graphics window. The spline will be created passing through the specified points.

- Start a new drawing file.
- Use the **Line** tool and create a sketch similar to the one shown below.

- Expand the **Draw** panel in the **Home** tab and select the **Spline Fit** button; the message, "Specify first point or [Method/Knots/Object]:" appears in the command line.

- Select the lower-left corner of the sketch; the message, "Enter next point or [start Tangency/toLerance]:" appears in the command line.
- Select the top-left corner point of the sketch.
- Similarly, select the top-right and lower-right corners; a spline will be attached to the pointer.
- Press ENTER to create the spline.

Example 2: (Spline CV)

In this example, you will create a spline by using the **Spline CV** method. In this method, you will specify various points called control vertices. As you specify the control vertices, imaginary lines are created connecting them. The spline will be drawn tangent to these lines.

- Expand the **Draw** panel in the **Home** tab and select the **Spline CV** button.

- Select the four corners of the sketch in the same sequence as in the earlier example.

- Press ENTER; a spline with control vertices will be created.

Example 2:

- Create a polyline, as shown.

- Activate the **Spline CV** button.
- Select **Object** from the command line.
- Select the polyline and press Enter.

Drawing Ellipses

Ellipses are also non-uniform curves, but they have a regular shape. They are actually splines created in a regular closed shape. In AuoCAD, you can draw an ellipse in three different ways by using the tools available in the **Ellipse** drop-down of the **Draw** panel. The three different ways to draw ellipses are explained in following examples.

Example 1 (Center)

In this example, you will draw an ellipse by specifying three points. The first point defines the center of the ellipse. Second and third points define the two axes of the ellipse.

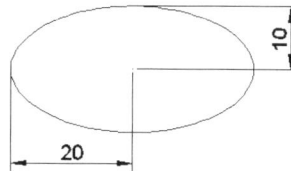

- Click **Home > Draw > Ellipse > Center** on the ribbon; the message, "Specify center of ellipse:" appears in the command line.
- Select an arbitrary point in the graphics window; the message, "Specify endpoint of axis:" appears in the command line.
- Move the pointer horizontally and type 20. Next, press ENTER; the message, "Specify distance to other axis or [Rotation]:" appears in the command line.
- Type 10 and press ENTER; the ellipse will be created.

Example 2 (Axis, End)

In this example, you will draw an ellipse by specifying three points. The first two points define the location and length of the first axis. The third point defines the second axis of the ellipse.

- Activate the **Dynamic Input** on the status bar, if it is not active.
- Click **Home > Draw > Ellipse > Axis, End** on the ribbon.
- Select an arbitrary point to specify an axis endpoint.
- Type **50** as length of the first axis and press TAB.
- Type **60** as angle and press ENTER.
- Type **10** as radius of the second axis and press ENTER; the ellipse will be created inclined at 60-degree angle.

Example 3 (Elliptical Arc)

In this example, you will draw an elliptical arc. To draw an elliptical arc, first you need to define the location and length of the first axis. Next, define the radius of the second axis; an ellipse will be displayed. Now, you need to define the start angle of the elliptical arc. The start angle can be any angle between 0 and 360. After defining the start angle,

you need to specify the end angle of the elliptical arc.

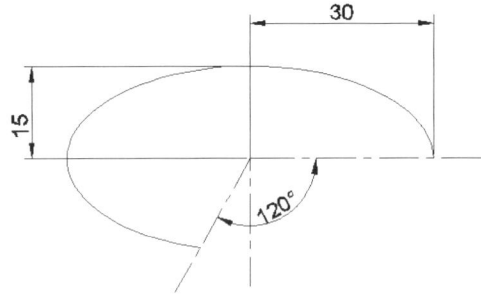

- Turn on the **Ortho Mode** on the Status bar.

- Click **Home > Draw > Ellipse > Elliptical Arc** on the ribbon.
- Select an arbitrary point to specify an axis endpoint.
- Move the pointer horizontally toward left and type **60**. Next, press ENTER to specify the axis length.
- Move the pointer upward and type 15. Next, press ENTER to specify the length of another axis.
- Type **0** and press ENTER to specify the start angle.
- Type **240** and press ENTER to specify the end angle.

Exercises

Chapter 3: Drawing Aids

In this chapter, you will learn to do the following:

- **Use Grid and Snap**
- **Use Ortho Mode and Polar Tracking**
- **Use Object Snaps and Object Snap Tacking**
- **Create Layers and assign properties to it**
- **Zoom and Pan drawings**

Drawing Aids

This chapter teaches you to define the drawing settings, which will assist you to easily create a drawing in AutoCAD. Most drawing settings can be turned on or off from the status bar. You can also access additional drawing settings by right-clicking on the button located on the status bar.

Setting Grid and Snap

Grid is the basic drawing setting. It makes the graphics window appear like a graph paper. You can turn ON the grid display by clicking the **Grid** icon on the status bar or just pressing **F7** on the keyboard.

Snap is used for drawing objects by using the intersection points of the grid lines. When you turn the Snap Mode ON, you will be able to select only grid points. In the following example, you will learn to set the grid and snap settings.

Example:

Upper limit (80,50)
Lower limit (0,0)

- Click **Application Menu > New**; the **Select Template** dialog appears.
- Select the **acadISO-Named Plot Styles** template. Click **Open**.
- On the Status bar, click the down arrow next to the **Snap Mode** icon and select **Snap Settings**. The **Drafting Settings** dialog appears.
- Click the **Snap and Grid** tab on the dialog.
- Set **Grid X spacing** to **10** and press TAB key; the **Grid Y spacing** is updated with the same value.
- Set **Major line every** to **10**.

- Select the **Snap On** check box.
- Make sure that **Snap X spacing** and **Snap Y spacing** is set to **10**.

- Make sure that the **Grid snap** option is selected in the **Snap type** group.

- Click **OK** on the dialog.
- Activate the **Grid** ⊞ icon on the Status Bar.

Setting the Limits of a drawing

You can set the limits of a drawing by defining its lower-left and top-right corners. By setting Limits of a drawing, you will define the size of the drawing area. In AutoCAD, limits are set to some default values. However, you can redefine the limits to change the drawing area as per your requirement.

- Type **Limits** at the command line and press ENTER.

- Press ENTER to accept the lower limit as 0,0. Now, you need to define the upper limit.
- Type 80,50 and press ENTER key.
- On the Navigate Bar, click **Zoom > Zoom All**; the graphics window will be zoomed to the limits.

Setting the Lineweight

Line weight is the thickness of the objects that you draw. In AutoCAD, there is a default lineweight assigned to objects. However, you can set a new lineweight. The method to set the lineweight is explained below.

- On the Status bar, click the **Customization** ≡ option, and then select **LineWeight** from the flyout. This shows the **LineWeight** icon on the status bar.

- Activate the **Show/Hide Lineweight** ≣ icon located on the status bar.

- Right click on the **Show/Hide Lineweight** icon, and then select **Lineweight Settings**. The **Lineweight Settings** dialog appears.

- On the **Lineweight Settings** dialog, select **0.40** mm from the **Default** drop-down.
- Click **OK**.
- Type L in the command line and press ENTER.
- Type 10,10 and press ENTER to define the first point.
- Move the pointer horizontally toward right and click on the sixth grid point from the first point.
- Move the pointer vertically upwards and select the third grid point from the second point.

- Move the pointer horizontally toward left and select the second grid point from the previous point.
- Move the pointer vertically downwards and select the grid point next to the previous point.
- Move the pointer horizontally toward left and select the second grid point from the previous point.
- Move the pointer vertically upwards and select the grid point next to the previous point.
- Move the pointer horizontally toward left and select the second grid point from the previous point.
- Right-click and select **Close**.

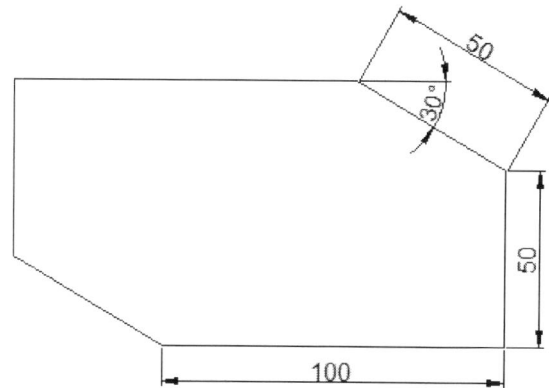

- Save and close the file.

Using Ortho mode and Polar Tracking

Ortho mode is used to draw orthogonal (horizontal or vertical) lines. Polar Tracking is used to constrain the lines to angular increments. In the following example, you will create a drawing with the help of Ortho Mode and Polar Tracking.

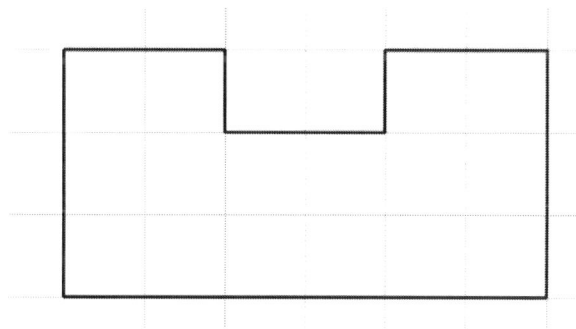

- Open a new AutoCAD file.
- Deactivate the **Grid Display** and **Snap Mode** icons on the status bar.
- Click the **Ortho Mode** icon on the status bar.
- Click **Zoom All** on the **Navigation Bar**.
- Click the **Line** button on the **Draw** panel.
- Select an arbitrary point to define the starting point.
- Move the pointer toward right, type 100 and press ENTER; you will notice that a horizontal line is created.
- Move the pointer upwards, type 50 and press ENTER; you will notice that a vertical line is created.
- Click the **Polar Tracking** icon on the status bar.

- Click the down arrow next to the **Polar tracking** icon, and select **30** from the menu.

You will notice a track line at 30-degree increments when you rotate the pointer.

- Move the pointer and stop when the tooltip displays <150 angle value.

- Type 50 and press ENTER when the tooltip displays <150°.
- Move the pointer toward left.
- Type 100 and press ENTER when the tooltip displays <180°.
- Move the pointer downward.
- Type 50 and press ENTER when the tooltip displays <270°.
- Right-click and select **Close**.

Using Layers

Layers are like a group of transparent sheets that are combined into a complete drawing. The figure below displays a drawing consisting of object lines and dimension lines. In this example, the object lines are created on the 'Object' layer, and dimensions are

created on the layer called 'Dimension'. You can easily turn-off the 'Dimension' layer for a clearer view of the object lines.

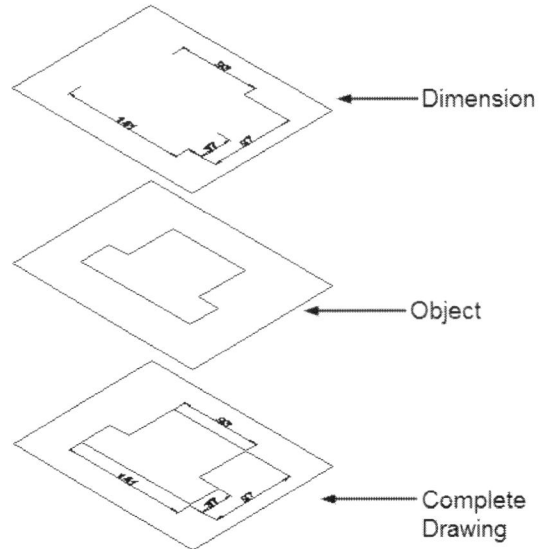

Layer Properties Manager

The **Layer Properties Manager** is used to create and manage layers. To open **Layer Properties Manager**, click **Home > Layers > Layer Properties** on the ribbon or enter **LA** in the command line.

The components of the **Layer Properties Manager** are shown below. The **Tree View** section is used for displaying layer filters, group, or state information. The **List View** section is the main body of the **Layer Properties Manager**. It lists the individual layers that currently exist in the drawing.

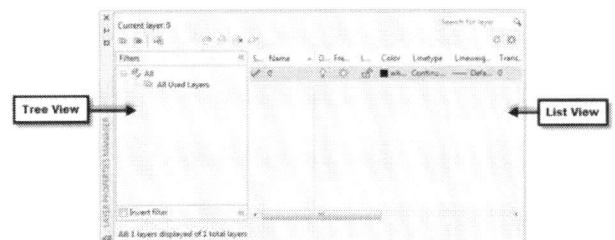

The **List View** section contains various properties. You can set layer properties and perform various operations in the **List View** section. A brief explanation of each layer property is given below.

Status –Shows a green check when a layer is set to current.

Name - Shows the name of the layer.

On – Used to turn on/off the visibility of a layer. When a layer is turned on, it shows a yellow light-bulb. When you turn off a layer, it shows a grey light-bulb.

Freeze/Thaw – It is used to freeze the objects of a layer so that they cannot be modified. Also, the visibility of the object is turned off.

Lock/Unlock- It is used to lock the layer so that the objects on it cannot be modified.

Color – It is used to assign a color to the layer.

Linetype – It is used to assign a linetype to the layer.

Lineweight – It is used to define the lineweight (thickness) of objects on the layer.

Transparency – It is used to define the transparency of the layer. You set a transparency level from 0 to 90 for all objects on a layer.

Plot Style – It is used to override the settings such as color, linetype, and lineweight while plotting a drawing.

Plot – It is used to control which layer will be plotted.

New VP Freeze – It is used to create and freeze a layer in any new viewport.

Description – It is used to enter a detailed description about the layer.

Creating a New Layer

You can create a new layer by using anyone of the following methods:

1. Click the **New Layer** button on the **Layer Properties Manager**; a new layer with the name 'Layer1' appears in **Name** field. Next, enter the name of the layer in the **Name** field.

2. Right-click in the **Name** field and select **New Layer** from the shortcut menu.

3. Select an existing layer, and then type ENTER or comma (,).

Making a layer current

If you want to draw objects on a particular layer, then you have to make it current. You can make a layer current using the methods listed below.

1. Select the layer from the List view and click the **Set Current** button on the **Layer Properties Manager**.

2. Double-click on the **Name** field of the layer.

3. Right-click on the layer and select **Set current**.

4. Select the layer from the **Layer** drop-down of the Layer panel.

5. Click the **Make Current** button on the **Layers** panel. Next, select an object; the layer related to the selected object will become current.

Deleting a Layer

You can delete a layer by using anyone of the following methods:

1. Click the **Delete Layer** button or press ALT+D.

   Current layer: 0

2. Right-click in the **Name** field and select **Delete Layer** from the shortcut menu.

You will learn more about layers in later chapters. You can find an example related to layers in the **Offset** tool section of chapter 4.

Using Object Snaps

Object Snaps are important settings that improve your performance and accuracy while creating a drawing. They allow you to select keypoints of objects while creating a drawing. You can activate the required Object Snap by using the **Object snap** shortcut menu. Press and hold the SHIFT key and right-click to display this shortcut menu. Note that the object snaps can be used only when a drawing command is active.

↪ Temporary track point
⌐ From
  Mid Between 2 Points
  Point Filters   ›

  3D Osnap   ›

╱ Endpoint
╱ Midpoint
✕ Intersection
✕ Apparent Intersect
--- Extension

⊙ Center
▣ Geometric Center
◈ Quadrant
○ Tangent

⊥ Perpendicular
∥ Parallel
∘ Node
Ɔ Insert
⁄∘ Nearest
▓ None

ℕ Osnap Settings...

The functions of various Object Snaps are explained next.

Endpoint: Snaps to the endpoints of lines and arcs.

Midpoint: Snaps to the midpoint of a line.

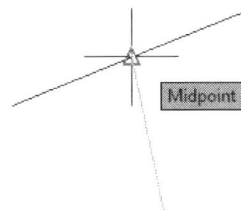

Intersection: Snaps to the intersections of objects.

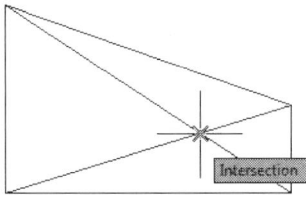

Apparent Intersection: Snaps to the projected intersection of two objects in 3D space.

Extension: Creates a temporary extension line when the pointer passes through the endpoints of a line or an arc. You can pick points along the temporary extension lines.

Center: Snaps to the centers of circles and arcs.

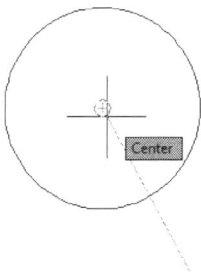

Geometric Center: Snaps to the center point of a closed geometry created by a single object such as polyline, rectangle or polygon.

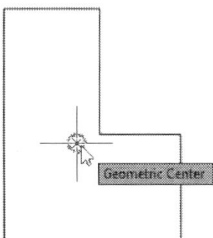

Quadrant: Snaps to four key points located on a circle.

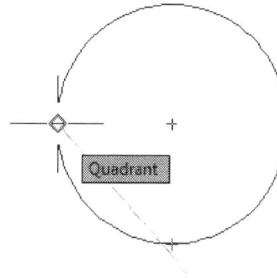

Tangent: Snaps to the tangent points of arcs and circles.

Perpendicular: Snaps to a perpendicular location on an object.

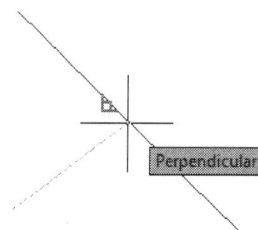

Parallel: It is used to draw an object parallel to another object.

Node: Snaps to points of dimension` lines, text objects, dimension text and so on.

Insert: Snaps to the insertion point of blocks, shapes and text.

Nearest: Snaps to the nearest point found along any object.

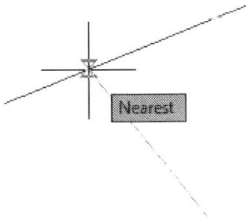

None: Deactivates Object Snap.

Temporary Track Point: It is used to locate a point by using trace lines from a reference point.

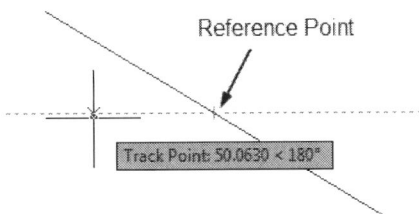

From: Locates a point at a specified distance and direction from a selected reference point.

Midpoint Between 2 Points: Snaps to the middle point of two selected points.

Running Object Snaps

Previously, you have learned to select Object Snaps from the shortcut menu. However, you can make Object Snap modes available continuously instead of selecting them every time. You can do this by using the **Running Object Snaps**. To use the Running Object Snaps, click the down arrow next to the **Object Snaps** button on the status bar and select the required object snap from the menu.

✓ ✓ Endpoint
  ✓ Midpoint
✓ ◎ Center
  ◻ Geometric Center
  ○ Node
  ◇ Quadrant
✓ ✕ Intersection
✓ --- Extension
  ⊡ Insertion
  ⊥ Perpendicular
  ○ Tangent
  ⟋ Nearest
  ✕ Apparent Intersection
  ∥ Parallel

Object Snap Settings...

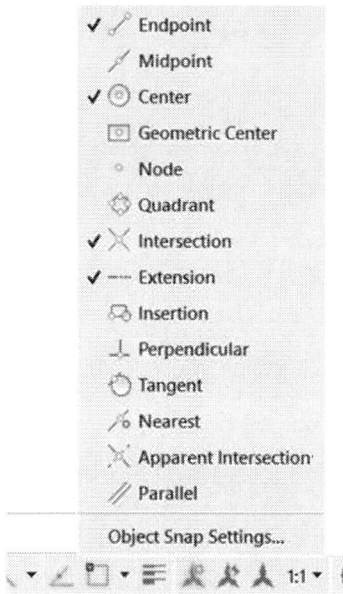

You can also select the **Object Snap Settings** option from the menu to open the **Drafting Settings** dialog. In this dialog, you can select the required Object Snaps by selecting check boxes.

Cycling through Object Snaps

After setting the Running Object Snap settings, AutoCAD displays object snaps depending on the

shape of the object. However, you can cycle through the object snaps by pressing the TAB key. In the following example, you will learn to cycle through different object snaps.

Example:

- Click the down arrow next to the **Object Snap** button and select the **Object Snap Settings** option; the **Drafting Settings** dialog appears. Select the **Select All** check box and click the **OK** button.

- Draw the objects as shown below.

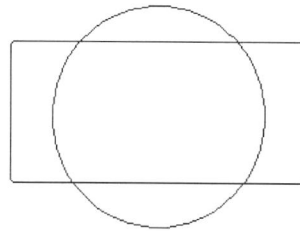

- Click the **Circle** button on the **Draw** panel.
- Place the pointer on the drawing. Press the TAB key; you will notice that the object snaps change.

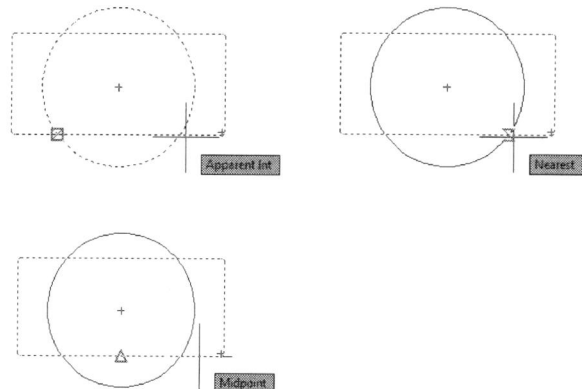

- Click when the **Center** snap is displayed and draw a circle.

Using Object Snap Tracking

Object Snap tracking is the movement of pointer along the trace lines originating from the keypoints of objects. Object Snap Tracking works only when the **Object Snap** mode is turned on. In the following example, you will learn to use Object Snap Tracking for creating objects.

Example:

- Select the **Object Snap Tracking** button from the Status bar.

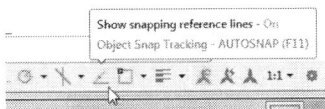

  (OR)

- Open the **Drafting Settings** dialog and click the **Object Snap** tab.
- Select the **Object Snap Tracking On** check box.

- Click **OK**.
- Use the **Line** tool and draw the objects as shown below.

- Press the ENTER key twice to start drawing lines from the last point.
- Move the pointer and place it on the endpoint of the lower horizontal line.

- Move the pointer above; you will notice the trace line, as shown below.

- Click on the trace line to create an inclined line.
- Snap the pointer to the endpoint of the lower horizontal line and click.

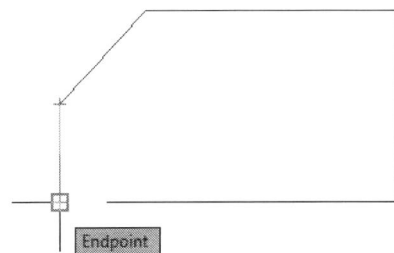

- Right-click and select **Enter**.

- Click the **Circle** button on the **Draw** panel of the ribbon.

- Place the pointer over the lower endpoint of the inclined line and move horizontally; you will notice that a trace line is displayed.

- Place the pointer on the midpoint of the lower horizontal line; a vertical trace line is displayed from the midpoint of the horizontal line as show below.

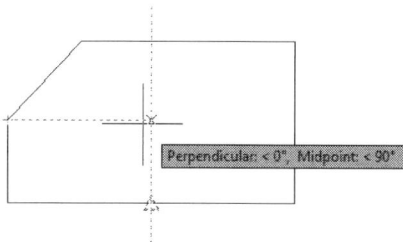

- Click at the point where the horizontal and vertical trace lines intersect. Next, create a circle as shown below.

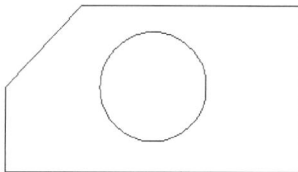

Using Zoom tools

Using the zoom tools, you can magnify or reduce a drawing. You can use these tools to view the minute details of a very complicated drawing. The Zoom tools can be accessed from the Navigation Bar, Command line, and Menu Bar.

Navigation Bar

Menu Bar

Zooming with the Mouse Wheel

Zooming using the mouse wheel is one of the easiest methods.

- Roll the mouse wheel forward to zoom into a drawing.

- Roll the mouse wheel backwards to zoom out of the drawing.

- Press the mouse wheel and drag the mouse to pan the drawing.

Using Zoom Extents

Using the **Zoom Extents** tool, you can zoom to the extents of the largest object in a drawing.

- Click **Zoom Extents** on the Navigation Bar.
- You can also double-click on the mouse wheel to zoom to extents.

Using Zoom-Window

Using the **Zoom-Window** tool, you can define the area to be magnified by selecting two points representing a rectangle.

- Click **Zoom > Zoom Window** on the Navigation Bar.
- Create a window by selecting the first and second corner; the area covered by the window will be magnified.

First Point

Second Point

Using Zoom-Previous

After magnifying a small area of the drawing, you can use the **Zoom-Previous** tool to return to the previous display.

- Click **Zoom > Zoom Previous** on the Navigation Bar.

Using Zoom-Realtime

Using the **Zoom-Realtime** tool, you can zoom in or zoom out of a drawing dynamically.

- Click **Zoom > Zoom Realtime** on the **Navigation Bar**; the pointer is changed to a magnifying glass with plus and minus symbols.
- Press and hold the left mouse button and drag the mouse forward to zoom into the drawing.
- Drag the mouse backward to zoom out of the drawing.

Using Zoom-All

The **Zoom All** tool is used to adjust the drawing space to the limits set by using the LIMITS command.

- Click **Zoom > Zoom All** on the **Navigation Bar**; the drawing will be zoomed to its limits.

Using Zoom Dynamic

With the **Zoom Dynamic** tool, you can zoom to a particular portion of a drawing by using a viewing box.

- Click **Zoom Dynamic** on the **Navigation Bar**; the drawing will be zoomed to its limits. In addition, a viewing box is attached to the pointer.

- Click and drag the pointer to define the size of the viewing box.

- Left-click and move the pointer to the area to be zoomed.

- Click the right mouse button. The area covered by the viewing box is magnified.

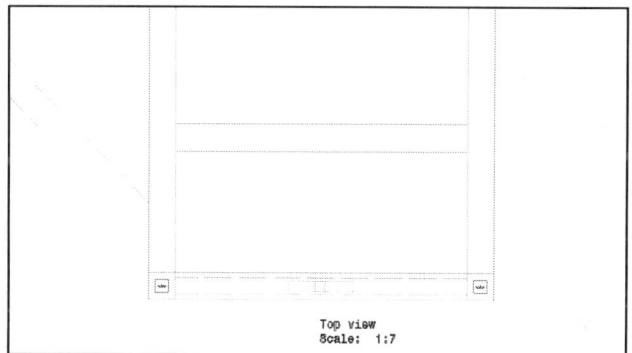

Using Zoom-Scale

Using the **Zoom-Scale** tool, you can zoom in or zoom out of a drawing by entering zoom scale factors directly from your keyboard.

- Click **Zoom > Zoom Scale** on the Navigation Bar. The message, "**Enter a scale factor (nX or nXP)**" appears in the command line.
- Enter the scale factor 0.25 to scale the drawing to 25% of the full view.
- Enter the scale factor 0.25X to scale the drawing to 25% of the current view.

- Enter the scale factor 0.25XP to scale the

  drawing to 25% of the paper space.

Using Zoom-Center

Using the **Zoom Center** tool, you can zoom to an area of the drawing based on a center point and magnification value.

- Click **Zoom > Zoom Center** on the Navigation

  Bar; the message, "**Define Center point**"

  appears in the command line.

- Select a point in the drawing to which you want

  to zoom in; the message, "**Enter magnification**

  or height" appears in the command line.

- Enter 10X in the command line to magnify the

  location of point by ten times.

Using Zoom-Object

Using the **Zoom Object** tool, you can magnify a

portion of the drawing by selecting one or more

objects.

- Click **Zoom > Zoom Object** on the Navigation

  Bar.

- Select one or more objects from the drawing and

  press ENTER; the objects will be magnified.

Using Zoom-In

Using the **Zoom In** tool, you can magnify the

drawing by a scale factor of 2.

- Click **Zoom > Zoom-In** on the Navigation Bar;

  the drawing is magnified to double.

Using Zoom-Out

The **Zoom-out** tool is used to de-magnify the display

screen by a scale factor of 0.5.

Panning Drawings

After zooming into a drawing, you may want to

view an area which is outside the current display.

You can do this by using the **Pan** tool.

- Click **Pan** on the Navigation Bar.

- Press and hold the left mouse button and drag

  the mouse; a new area of the drawing, which is

  outside the current view, is displayed.

Exercises

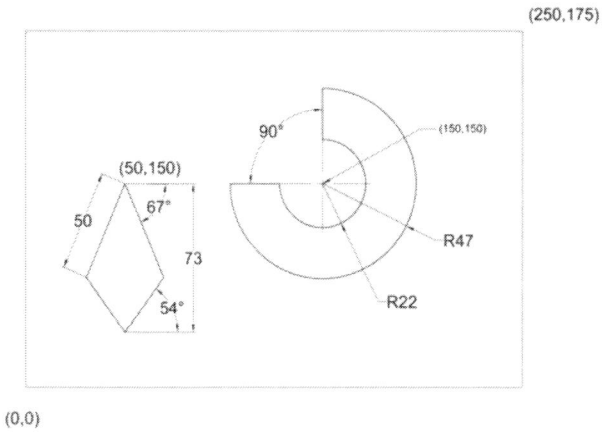

Chapter 4: Editing Tools

In this chapter, you will learn the following tools:

- The **Move** tool
- The **Copy** tool
- The **Rotate** tool
- The **Scale** tool
- The **Trim** tool
- The **Extend** tool
- The **Fillet** tool
- The **Chamfer** tool
- The **Mirror** tool
- The **Explode** tool
- The **Stretch** tool
- The **Polar Array** tool
- The **Offset** tool
- The **Path Array** tool
- The **Rectangular Array** tool

Editing Tools

In previous chapters, you have learned to create some simple drawings using the basic drawing tools. However, to create complex drawings, you may perform various editing operations. The tools to perform the editing operations are available in the **Modify** panel on the **Home** ribbon. You can click the down arrow on this panel to find more editing tools. Using these editing tools, you can modify existing objects or use existing objects to create new or similar objects.

The Move tool

The **Move** tool moves a selected object(s) from one location to a new location without changing its orientation. To move objects, you must activate this tool and select the objects from the graphics window. After selecting the objects, you must define the 'base point' and the 'destination point'.

Example:

- Create the drawing as shown below.

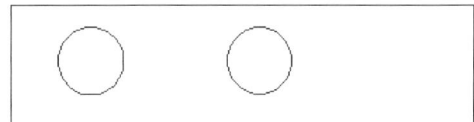

- Click **Home > Modify > Move** on the ribbon, or enter **M** in the command line.
- Click on the circle located at the right-side, and then right-click to accept the selection.
- Select the center of the circle as the base point.
- Make sure that the **Ortho Mode** is activated.
- Move the pointer toward right and pick a point as shown below. This moves the circle to the new location.

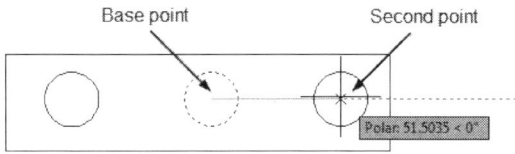

Base point   Second point

Polar 51.5035 < 0°

The Copy tool

The **Copy** tool is used to copy objects and place them at a required location. This tool is similar to the **Move** tool, except that object will remain at its original position and a copy of it will be placed at the new location.

Example:

- Draw two circles of 80 mm and 140 mm diameter, respectively.

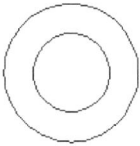

- Click **Home > Modify > Copy** on the ribbon or enter **CO** in the command line.
- Select the two circles, and then right-click to accept the selection.
- Select the center of the circle as the base point.
- Make sure that the **Ortho Mode** is active.
- Move the pointer toward right.
- Type 200 and press ENTER.
- Select **Exit** from the command line. This creates a copy of the circles at the new location.

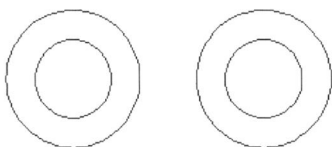

The Rotate tool

The **Rotate** tool rotates an object or a group of objects about a base point. Activate this tool and select the objects from the graphics window. After selecting objects, you must define the 'base point' and the angle of rotation. This rotates the object(s) about the base point.

- Click **Home > Modify > Rotate** on the ribbon or enter **RO** in the command line.
- Select the circles as shown below, and then right-click to accept.

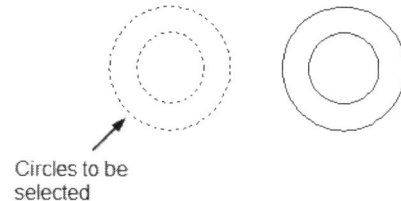

Circles to be selected

- Select the center of the other circle as the base point.

Point to be selected

Center

- Select the **Copy** option from the command line.
- Type -90 as the rotation angle and press ENTER.

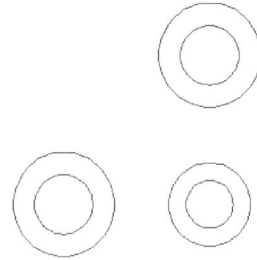

The Scale tool

The **Scale** tool changes the size of objects. It reduces or enlarges the size without changing the shape of an object.

- Click **Home > Modify > Scale** on the ribbon or enter **SC** in the command line.
- Select the circles as shown below and right-click to accept the selection.

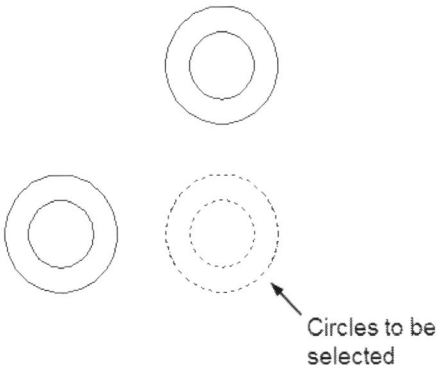

Circles to be selected

- Select the center point of the selected circles as the base point.
- Type 0.8 as the scale factor and press ENTER.

- Likewise, scale the circles located at the top to 0.7.

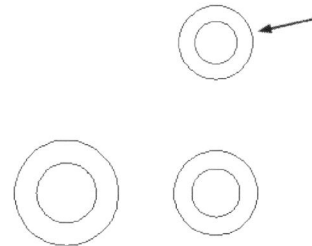

- Click **Home > Draw > Circle > Tan, Tan, Radius** on the ribbon.
- Select the two circles shown below to define the tangent points.

- Type 150 as the radius of the circle and press ENTER.

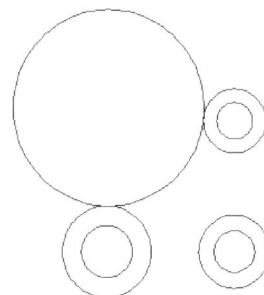

- Likewise, create other circles of radius 100 and 120.

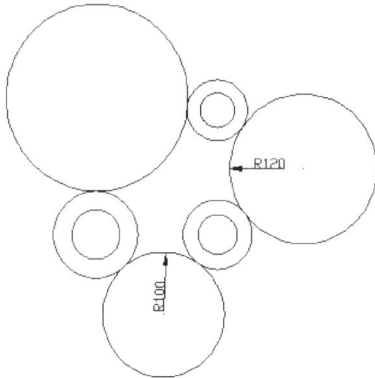

The Trim tool

When an object intersects with another object, you can remove its unwanted portion by using the **Trim** tool. To trim an object, you must first activate the **Trim** tool, and then select the cutting edge (intersecting object) and the portion to be removed. If there are multiple intersection points in a drawing, you can simply select the **select all** option from the command line; all the objects in the drawing objects will act as 'cutting edges'.

- Click **Home > Modify > Trim** on the ribbon or enter **TR** in the command line.
  Now, you must select the cutting edges.
- Press ENTER to select all the objects as the cutting edges.
  Now, you must select the objects to be trimmed.
- Select the large circles one by one; the circles will be trimmed.

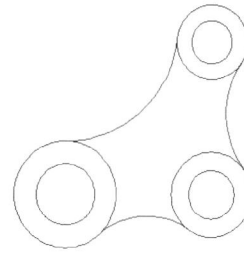

- Likewise, trim the other circles as shown below.

- Save and close the drawing.

The Extend tool

The **Extend** tool is similar to the **Trim** tool but its use is opposite of it. This tool is used to extend lines, arcs and other open entities to connect to other objects. To do so, you must select the boundary up to which you want to extend the objects, and then select the objects to be extended.

- Start a new drawing.
- Create a sketch as shown below using the **Line** tool.

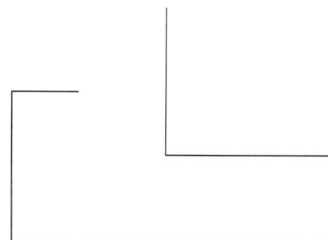

- Click **Home > Modify > Trim > Extend** on

the ribbon or enter **EX** in the command line.

- Select the vertical line as the boundary edge. Next, right-click.

- Select the horizontal open line. This will extend the line up to the boundary edge.

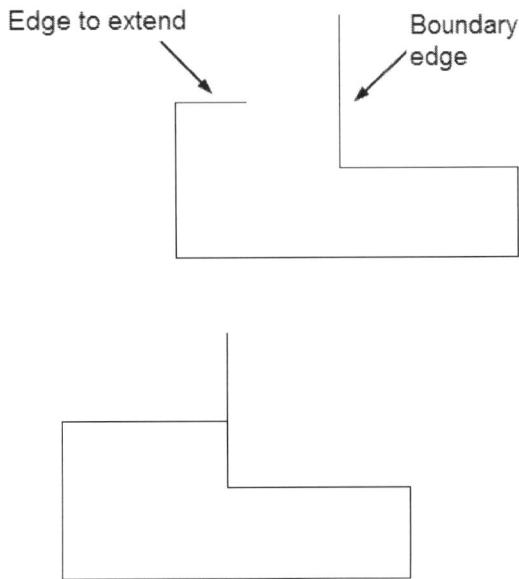

Before   After

The Fillet tool

The **Fillet** tool converts the sharp corners into round corners. You must define the radius and select the objects forming a corner. The following figure shows some examples of rounding the corners.

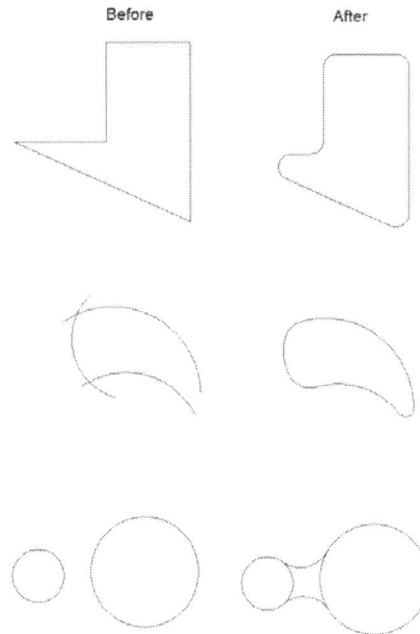

- Start a new drawing.
- Type **Limmax** in the command line and press ENTER.
- Set the maximum limit to 100,100 and press ENTER.
- Click **Zoom All** on the Navigation Bar.
- Click **Home > Draw > Polyline** on the ribbon.
- Define the start point as 20, 50.
- Draw the lines as shown below.

- Right-click and select **Enter**.
- Click **Home > Modify > Fillet** on the ribbon or enter **F** in the command line.

- Select the **Radius** option from the command line.
- Type **5** and press ENTER.
- Select the vertical and horizontal lines, as shown below.

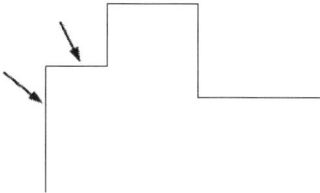

- Notice that a fillet is created.

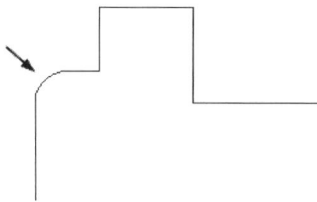

The Chamfer tool

The **Chamfer** tool replaces the sharp corners with an angled line. This tool is similar to the **Fillet** tool, except that an angled line is placed at the corners instead of rounds.

- Click **Home > Modify > Fillet > Chamfer** on the ribbon or enter **CHA** in the command line.

- Follow the prompt sequence given next:

Select first line or [Undo/Polyline/Distance/Angle/Trim/mEthod/ Multiple]: Select the **Distance** option from the command line.

Define first chamfer distance <0.0000>: Enter **8** as the first chamfer distance and press ENTER.

Define second chamfer distance <8.0000>: Press ENTER to accept 8 as the second chamfer distance.

Select first line or [Undo/Polyline/Distance/Angle/Trim/mEthod/ Multiple]: Select the vertical line on the right-side.

Select second line or shift-select to apply corner or [Distance/Angle/Method]: Select the horizontal line connected to the vertical line.

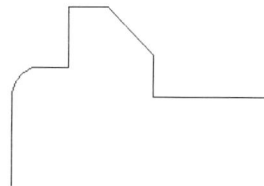

The Mirror tool

The **Mirror** tool creates a mirror image of objects. You can create symmetrical drawings using this tool. Activate this tool and select the objects to mirror, and then define the 'mirror line' about which the objects will be mirrored. You can define the mirror line by either creating a line or selecting an existing line.

- Click **Home > Modify > Mirror** on the ribbon or enter **MI** in the command line.

- Select the drawing by clicking on it, and then press Enter.

- Select the first point of the mirror line as shown below.

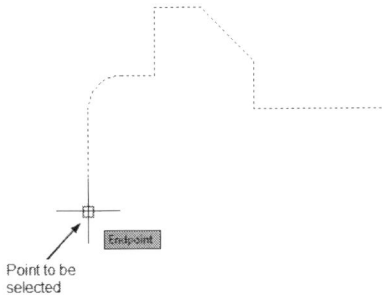

- Make sure that the **Ortho Mode** on the status bar is active.

- Move the pointer toward right and click.

- Select the **No** option from the command line to retain the source objects.

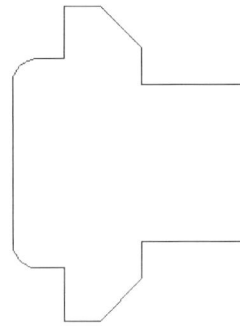

- Click **Home > Draw > Arc > Start, End, Direction** on the ribbon.

- Select the start point of the arc as shown.

- Select the end point of the arc as shown.

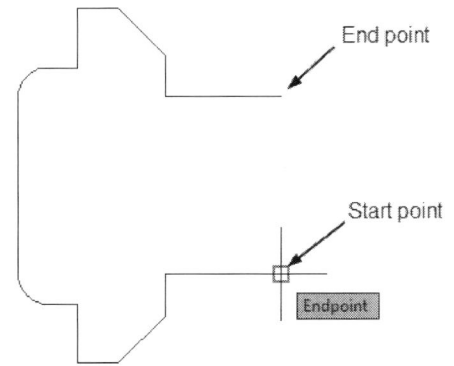

- Make sure that the **Ortho Mode** is active.

- Move the pointer toward right and click.

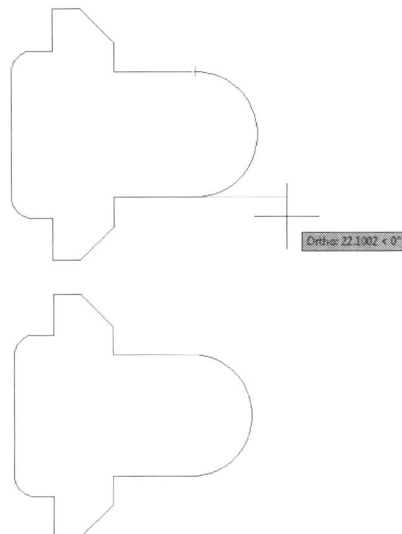

The Explode tool

The **Explode** tool explodes a group of objects into individual objects. For example, when you create a drawing using the **Polyline** tool, it acts as a single object. You can explode a polyline or rectangle or any group of objects using the **Explode** tool.

- Click on the portion of the drawing created using the **Polyline** tool; you will notice that the complete polyline is selected as a single object.

- Click **Home > Modify > Explode** on the ribbon or enter **X** in the command line.
- Select the polylines from the drawing.

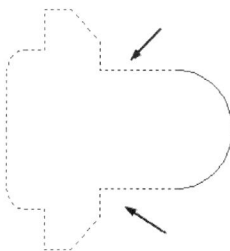

- Press ENTER; the polyline is exploded into individual objects.

Now, you can select the individual objects of the polyline.

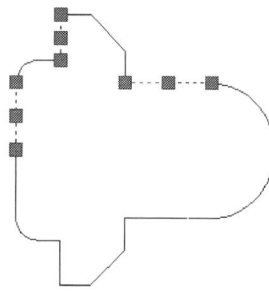

The Stretch tool

The **Stretch** tool lengthens or shortens drawings or parts of drawings. Note that you cannot stretch circles using this tool. In addition, you must select the portion of the drawing to be stretched by dragging a window.

- Click **Home > Modify > Stretch** on the ribbon or enter **STRETCH** in the command line.
- Create a crossing window to select the objects of the drawing.

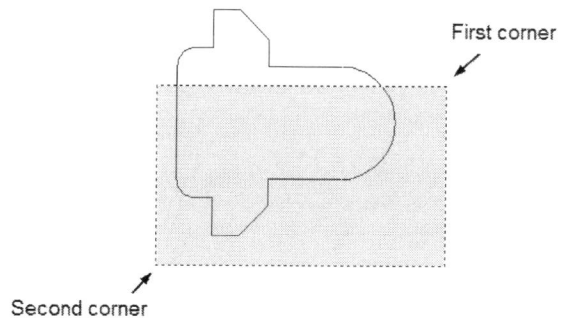

First corner

Second corner

- Press ENTER (or) right-click to accept the selection.
- Select the base point as shown below.

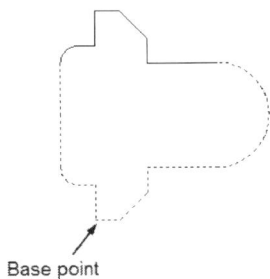

Base point

- Move the pointer downward and click to stretch the drawing.

- Save and close the file.

The Polar Array tool

The **Polar Array** tool creates an arrangement of objects around a point in a circular form.

The following example shows you to create a polar array.

- Create two concentric circles of 140 and 50 diameters.

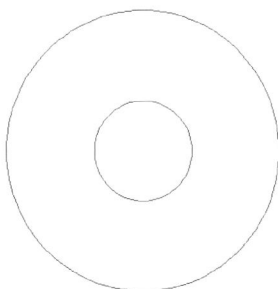

- Type **C** in the command line and press ENTER.

- Press and hold the Shift key, right-click and select **Quadrant** from the shortcut menu.
- Select the quadrant point of the circle as shown below.

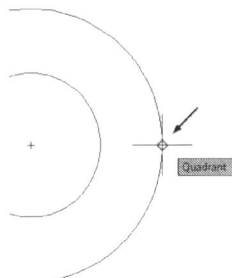

- Type 30 as radius and press ENTER.

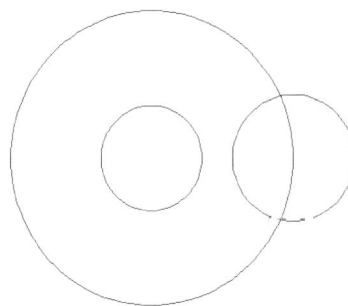

- Click **Home > Modify > Trim** on the ribbon.
- Select the large circle as the cutting edge and right-click.
- Select the circle on the quadrant as the object to be trimmed.

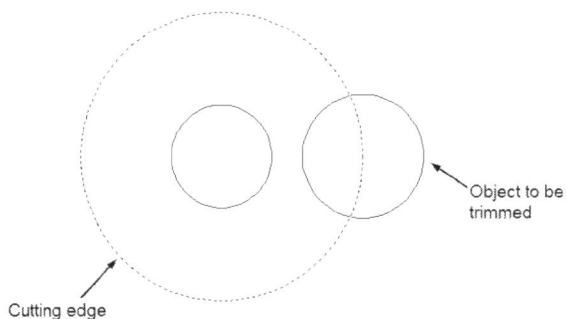

Object to be trimmed

Cutting edge

- Press Enter.
- Click **Home > Modify > Array > Polar Array** on the ribbon or **ARRAYPOLAR** in

the command line.

- Select the arc created after trimming the circle. Next, right-click to accept the selection.

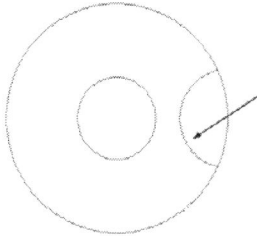

- Make sure that **Object Snap** is activated.
- Select the center of the large circle as the center of the array; the **Array Creation** tab appears in the ribbon.
- In the **Items** panel of the **Array Creation** tab, set the **Items** value to 4.

Notice that the **Rotate Items** button is active in the **Properties** panel of the **Array Creation** tab. This rotates the objects of the polar array. If you deactivate this button, the polar array is created without rotating the objects as shown in figure.

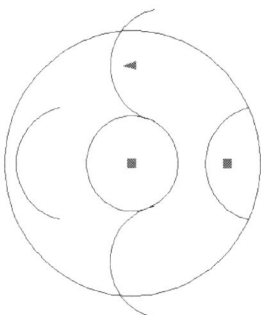

In addition, the **Associative** button is active by default. This ensures that you can edit the array after creating it.

- Make sure that the **Associative** and the **Rotate Items** buttons are active. Next, click the **Close Array** button on the ribbon.

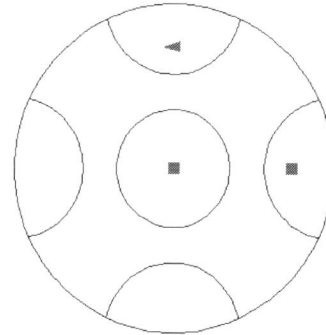

- Click the **Trim** button on the **Modify** panel.
- Press ENTER to select all objects as cutting edges.
- Trim the unwanted portions as shown below.

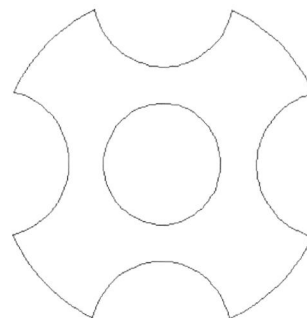

The Offset tool

The **Offset** tool creates parallel copies of lines, polylines, circles, arcs and so on. To create a parallel copy of an object, first you must define the offset distance, and then select the object. Next, you must define the side in which the parallel copy will be placed.

- Create the drawing shown below using the **Polyline** tool. Do not add dimensions.

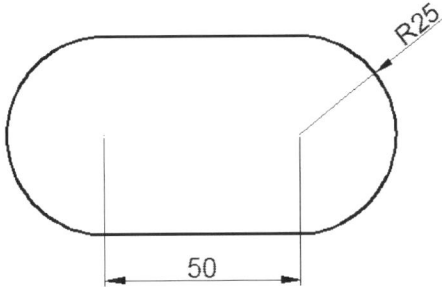

- Click **Home > Modify > Offset** on the ribbon or enter **O** in the command line.
- Type **20** as the offset distance and press ENTER.
- Select the polyline loop.
- Click outside the loop to create the parallel copy.

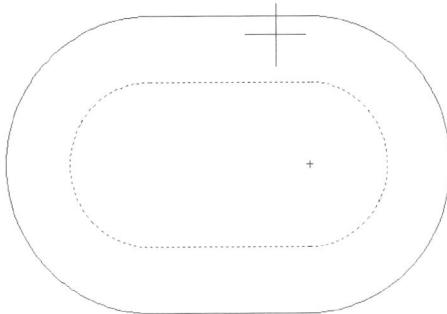

- Click **Home > Layers > Layer Properties** on the ribbon (or) type **LA** in the command line; the **Layer Properties Manager** appears.
- Click the **New layer** button on the **Layer Properties Manager**. Enter **Centerline** in the **Name** field.

- Click the **Set current** icon. This activates the new layer.
- Click in the **Linetype** field of the current layer; the **Select Linetype** dialog appears.

- On the **Select Linetype** dialog, click the **Load** button; the **Load or Reload Linetypes** dialog appears.

- Select the **CENTER2** Linetype from this dialog. Click **OK**. This adds the linetype to the **Select Linetype** dialog.

- Select the **CENTER2** linetype from the **Select Linetype** dialog and click **OK**.
- Close the **Layer Properties Manager**.
- Click the **Offset** button on the **Modify** panel.
- Select the **Layer** option from the command line.
- Select the **Current** option from the command line; this ensures that the offset entity will be created with the currently active layer properties. If you select the **Source** option, the offset entity will be created with the properties of the source object.
- Type **10** as the offset distance and press ENTER.
- Select the outer loop of the drawing.
- Move the pointer inwards and click to create the offset entity.

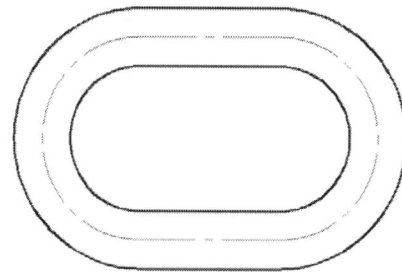

- Click on the **Layer** drop-down on the **Layer** panel of the ribbon.
- Select the **0** layer from the drop-down.

- Create a circle of 12 mm diameter.

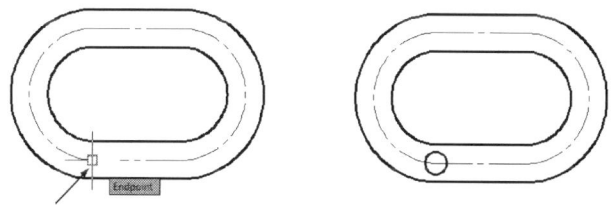

The Path Array tool

The **Path Array** tool creates an array of objects along a path (line, polyline, circle, helix, spline, and so on).

- Click **Home > Modify > Array > Path Array** on the ribbon or enter **ARRAYPATH** in the command line.
- Select the circle and right-click.
- Select the centerline as the path; the preview of the path array appears.

- Click the **Divide** method on the **Properties** panel. Now, you must enter the number of items in the path array.

  If you select the **Measure** method, you must enter the distance between the items in the path array.

- Set the Items count to 12.

Notice that the **Align Items** button is active by default. As a result, the items are aligned with the path. If you deactivate this button, the items will not be aligned with the path.

With the Align Items button active   Align Items button Inactive

- Click the **Close Array** button.

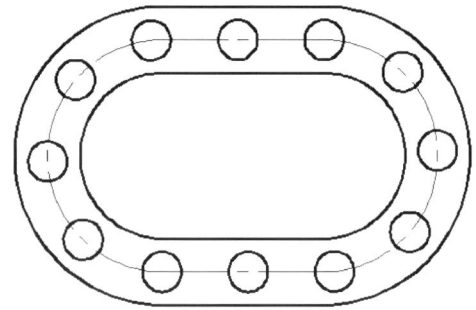

- Save and close the file.

The Rectangular Array tool

The **Rectangular Array** tool creates an array of objects along the X and Y directions.

- Open a new AutoCAD file and draw the sketch shown below. Do not add dimensions

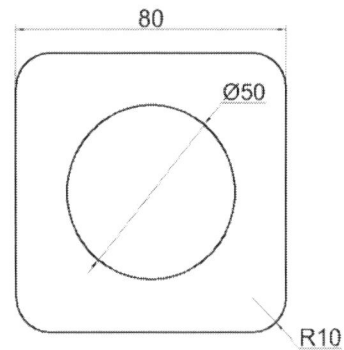

- Draw a circle of 10mm diameter concentric to the fillet.

- Click **Home > Modify > Array > Rectangular Array** on the ribbon or enter **ARRAYRECT** in the command line.

- Select the small circle and right-click; a rectangular array with default values appears.

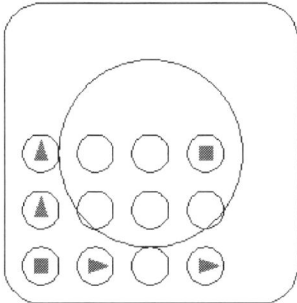

In addition, the **Array Creation** tab appears.

- Set the **Columns** count to 2.
- Set the **Rows** count to 2.
- Set the **Between** value in the **Columns** panel to 60.
- Set the **Between** value in the **Rows** panel to 60.

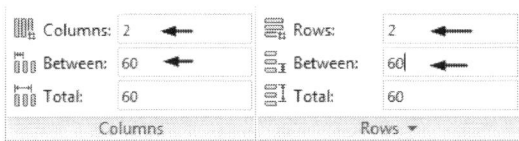

- Click **Close Array** on the ribbon.

Editing Using Grips

When you select objects from the graphics window, small squares appear on them. These squares are called grips. You can use these grips to stretch, move, rotate, scale, and mirror objects, change properties, and perform other editing operations. Grips displayed on selecting different objects are shown below.

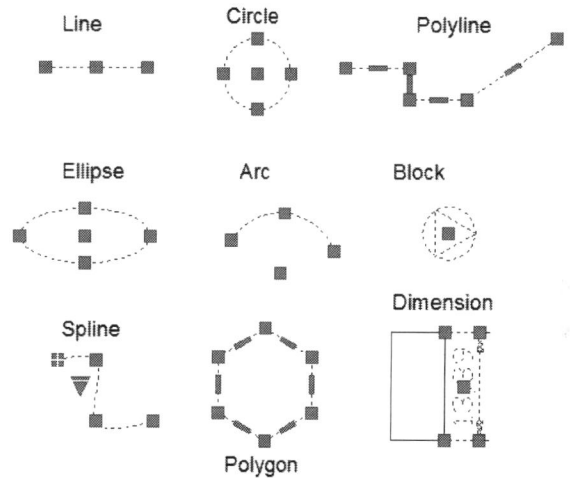

The following table gives you the details of the editing operations that can be performed when you select and drag grips.

Object	Grip	Editing Operation
Circle	Grip on circumference	**Scale**: Select anyone of the grips on the circumference and move the pointer to scale a circle.

		Ortho: 25.2044 < 0°
	Center point grip	**Move**: Select the center grip of the circle and move the pointer.
Arc	Grip on circumference	**Stretch**: Select the grip on the circumference and move the pointer.
	Center point grip	**Move**: Select the center grip of the arc and move the pointer.
Line	Midpoint Grip	**Move**: Select the Midpoint grip and move the pointer

	Endpoint Grip	**Stretch/Lengthen**: Select an endpoint grip and move the pointer.
Polylines, Rectangles, Polygons	Corner Grips	**Stretch**: Select the corner grips and move the pointer. **Add/Remove Vertex**: Place the pointer on the corner grip and select Add Vertex/Remove Vertex.
	Midpoint Grips	**Convert to Arc**: Place the pointer on the midpoint grip and select **Convert to Arc**.

Convert to Line: Place the pointer on the midpoint grip of a polyline arc and select **Convert to Line**.

Ellipse	Center Grip	**Move**: Select the center grip and move the pointer.
	Grips on circumference	**Stretch**: Select a grip on circumference and move the pointer.
Spline	Fit Points	**Stretch**: Select a grip on the spline and move the pointer.

Add/Remove Fit Point: Place the pointer on a fit point and select **Add Fit Point** or **Remove Fit Point**.

Stretch Vertices: Select the control vertices of a CV spline and move the pointer.

Control Vertices

Add/Remove Vertices: Place the pointer on a control vertex and select **Add Vertex** or **Remove Vertex**.

Refine Vertices: Place the pointer on a control vertex and select **Refine Vertices**.

Modifying Rectangular Arrays

You can use grips to edit rectangular arrays dynamically. Various array editing operations using grips are given next.

Moving a Rectangular array

- Create a rectangular array as shown below.

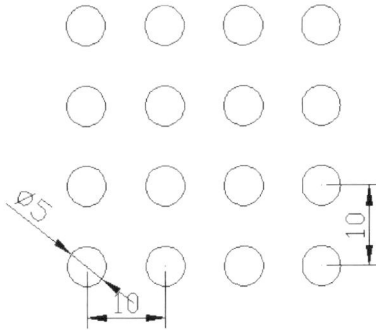

- Select the array; you will notice that grips are displayed on it.
- Select the grip located at the lower left corner and move the array, as shown below.

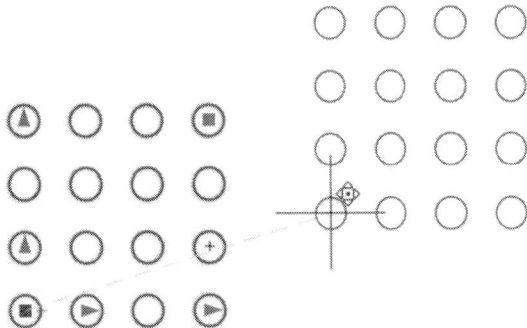

Adding/Removing Level to a Rectangular array

- Place the pointer on the lower left grip of the rectangular array; a shortcut menu appears.
- Select **Level Count** from the shortcut menu; the message, "**Specify number of levels**" appears in the command line.
- Type 3 and press ENTER.

- Click the **Home** button near the ViewCube to view the levels.

- Change the view to Top view by using the In-Canvas controls.

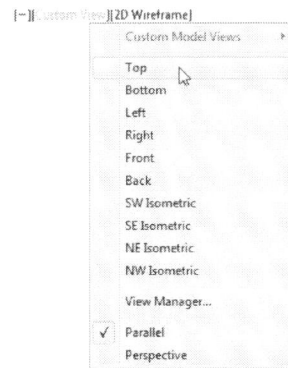

Changing the Column and Row Count

- To change the column and row count, place the pointer on the top right corner grip; a shortcut menu appears.
- Select **Row and Column Count** from the shortcut menu; the message, "**Specify number of rows and columns**" appears in the command line.
- Type **5** in the command line and press ENTER; the number of rows and columns are changed to 5.
- If you only want to change the column count; place the pointer on the lower right corner grip of the array.

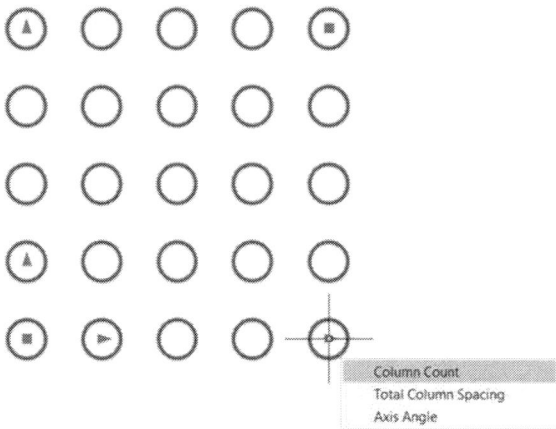

- Select **Colum Count** from the shortcut menu.
- Next, enter the number of columns or drag the pointer and click.

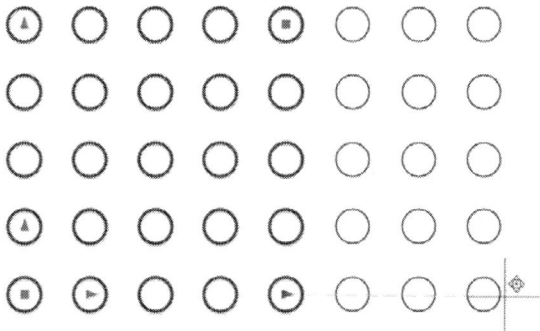

- To change the row count only, click the top left corner grip and drag the pointer. You can also enter the row count in the command line.

Changing the Column and Row Spacing

- To change the total column and row spacing, place the pointer on the top right corner grip and select **Total Row and Column Spacing** from the shortcut menu.

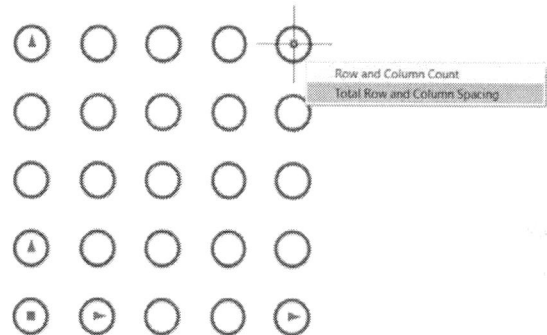

- Type 80 in the command line; the spacing between the columns and rows is adjusted to fit the total length.

- To change the total column spacing only, place the pointer on the lower right corner grip and select **Total Column Spacing** from the shortcut menu.

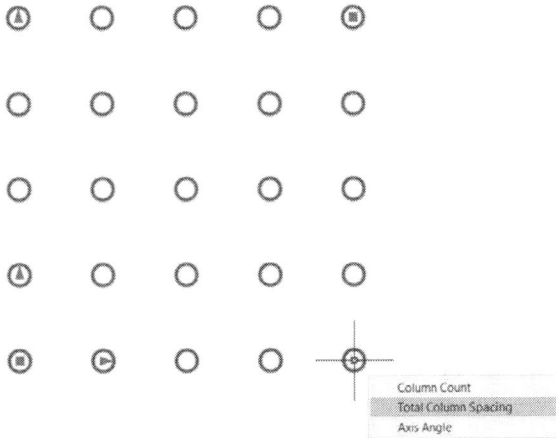

| Column Count |
| Total Column Spacing |
| Axis Angle |

- Next, enter the total column distance or drag the pointer and click.

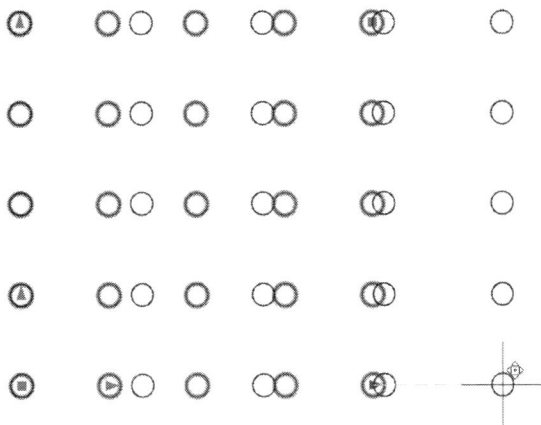

- If you want to change the distance between the individual columns, click the second column grip and drag the pointer.

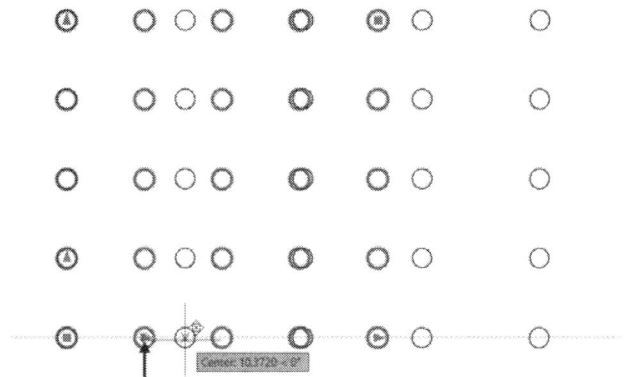

Center: 10.3720 < 0°

- You can also enter the distance in the command line.
- Likewise, you can change the total row spacing and distance between the individual rows by using the grips shown below.

Total row spacing

Distance between rows

Changing the Axis Angle of the Rectangular Array

- To change the Axis angle of the rows, place the pointer on the lower right corner grip and select **Axis angle** from the shortcut menu.

- Type the angle and press ENTER. Note that the angle is calculated from the first column of the array. For example, if you enter 60 as the axis angle, the rows will be inclined by 60 degrees from the first column.

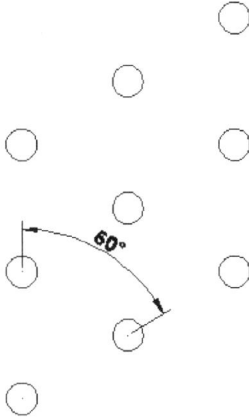

- Likewise, you can change the axis angle of the columns by using the top left corner grip.

Editing the Source Item of the Rectangular Array

- Create a rectangular array as shown below.

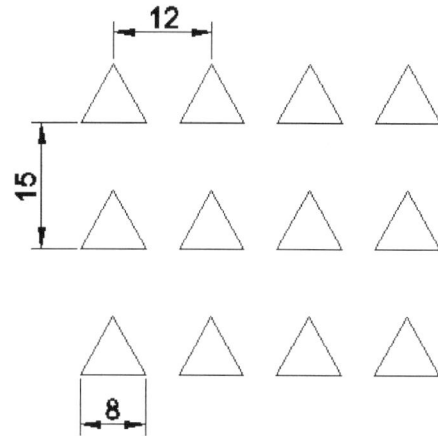

- Select the rectangular array; the **Array** tab appears in the ribbon.

- Click the **Edit Source** button on the **Option** panel; the message, "**Select item in array**" message appears in the command line.

- Select the lower left triangle of the rectangular array; the **Array Editing State** message box appears.

- Click **OK**; the array editing state is activated.

- Draw a circle and trim the unwanted portion as shown below.

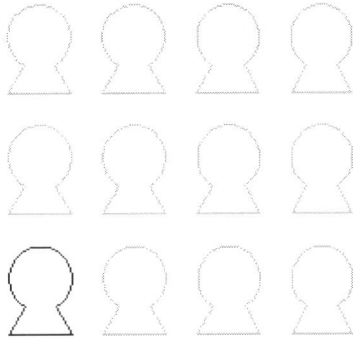

- Click **Save Changes** on the **Edit Array** panel of the ribbon.

Modifying Polar Arrays

Similar to editing rectangular arrays, you can also edit a polar array by using grips. Various array editing operations using grips are given next.

Changing the Radius of a Polar array

- Create the polar array, as shown in figure.

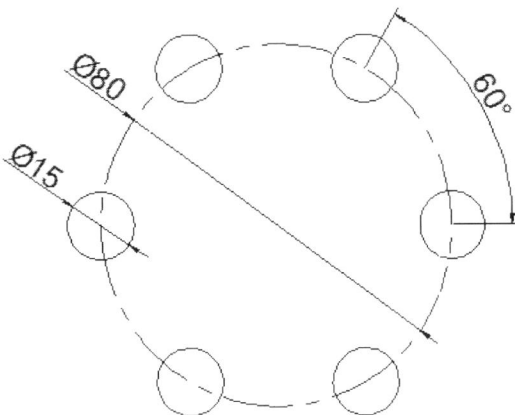

- Select the polar array; grips will be displayed on it.
- Place the pointer on the base grip, as shown in figure.
- Select **Stretch Radius** from the shortcut menu.

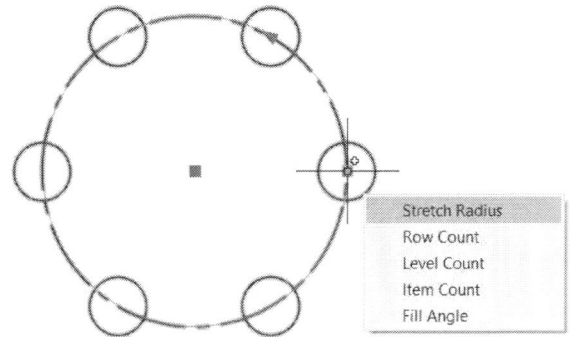

- Move the pointer outward or inward and click. You can also enter a new radius value of the polar array.

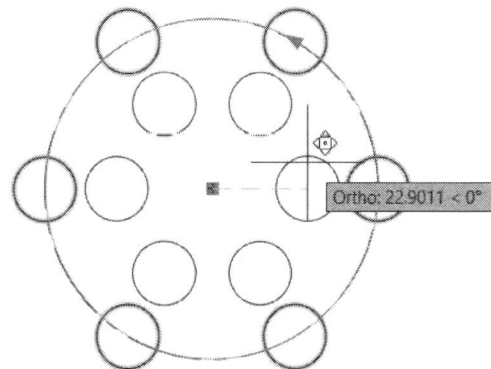

Changing the Row Count of a Polar array

- Place the pointer on the base grip of the array and select **Row Count** from the shortcut menu.
- Move the pointer outward and click. You can also enter the number of the rows in the command line.

- Next, move the pointer and click. You can also enter the total row spacing value in the command line.
- To change the distance between the individual rows, click the second row grip and move the pointer outward. You can also enter the distance in the command line.

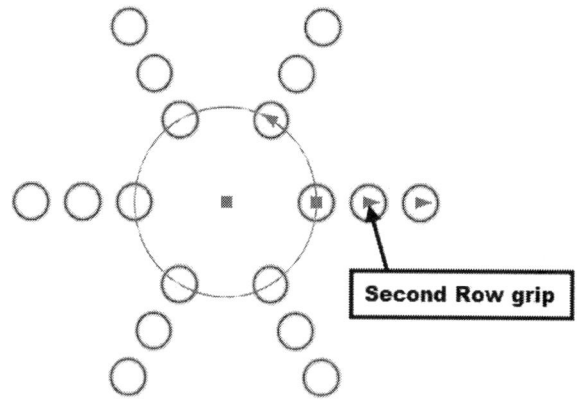

- You can again change the **Row Count** by using the last row grip.

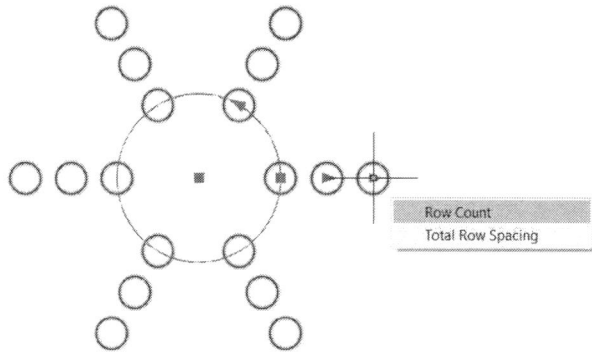

Second Row grip

Changing the Angle between the Items

- To change the angle between the items, click the second radial grip and enter the new angle value.

Changing the Row Spacing

- To change the total row spacing, place the pointer on the last row grip and select **Total Row Spacing**.

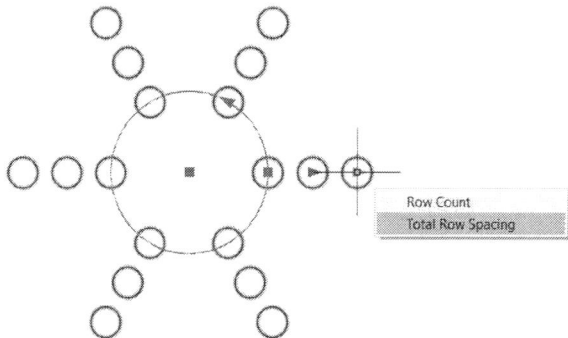

The Second radial grip

Changing the Fill angle of the array

- The default fill angle of a polar array is 360 degrees. To change the fill angle, place the pointer on the base grip and select **Fill Angle** from the shortcut menu.

- Enter a new value for the fill angle or drag the pointer and click.

Changing the Item count of a Polar array

- Select the polar array and enter a new item count in the **Items** box of the **Array** ribbon.

Revision Clouds

Revision clouds are used to highlight the areas in a drawing. You can create revision clouds using three different tools.

Example 1:

- Start a new drawing using the acadISO template.

- On the ribbon, click **Annotate > Markup > Revision Cloud > Rectangular**.

- Select **Arc Length** from the command line.

- Type 3 and press Enter to specify the minimum arc length.

- Type 5 and press Enter to specify the maximum arc length.

- Specify the first and second corners of the revision cloud. You can also select the Object option, and select an object from the graphics window. The selected object will be converted into a revision cloud.

- Select the revision cloud and notice the grips. You can use the midpoint grip to stretch or add new vertices to the revision cloud.

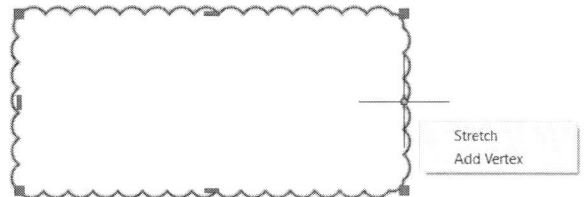

You can use the corner point grip to stretch, add, or remove vertices.

Example 2:

- On the ribbon, click **Annotate > Markup >**

  Revision Cloud > Polygonal .
- Select **Style** from the command line.
- Select **Calligraphy** from the command line.
- Specify the corners of the revision cloud and press Enter.

- On the ribbon, click **Annotate > Markup >**

  Revision Cloud > Freehand .
- Specify the start point of the revision cloud.
- Move the pointer around the area to be highlighted.
- Move the pointer onto the start point to close the cloud.

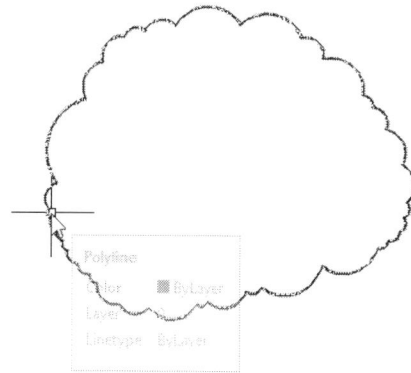

Example 3:

Exercises

400

350

300

550

450

497

R75

15 HOLES Ø15
EQUI-SPACED

R50

R100

Chapter 5: Multi View Drawings

In this chapter, you will learn to create:

- **Orthographic Views**
- **Auxiliary Views**
- **Named Views**

Multi view Drawings

To manufacture a component, you must create its engineering drawing. The engineering drawing consists of various views of the object, showing its true shape and size so that they can be clearly dimensioned. This can be achieved by creating the orthographic views of the object. In the first section of this chapter, you will learn to create orthographic views of an object. The second section introduces you to auxiliary views. The auxiliary views clearly describe the features of a component, which are located on an inclined plane or surface.

Creating Orthographic Views

Orthographic Views are standard representations of an object on a sheet. These views are created by projecting an object onto three different planes (top, front, and side planes). You can project an object by using two different methods: **First Angle Projection** and **Third Angle Projection**. The following figure shows the orthographic views that will be created when an object is projected using the **First Angle Projection** method.

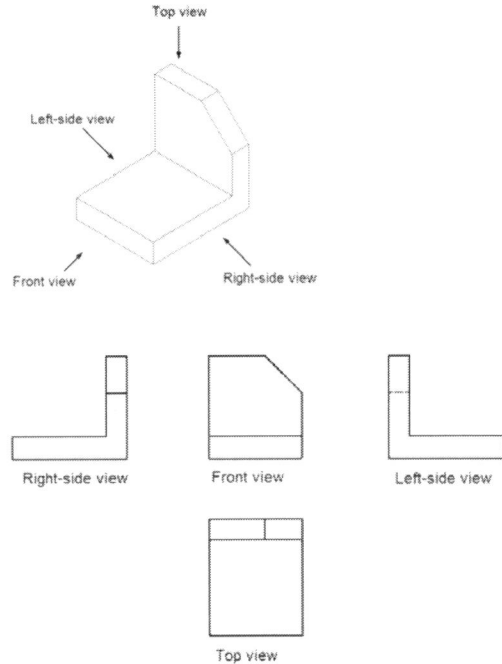

The following figure shows the orthographic views that will be created when an object is projected using the **Third Angle Projection** method.

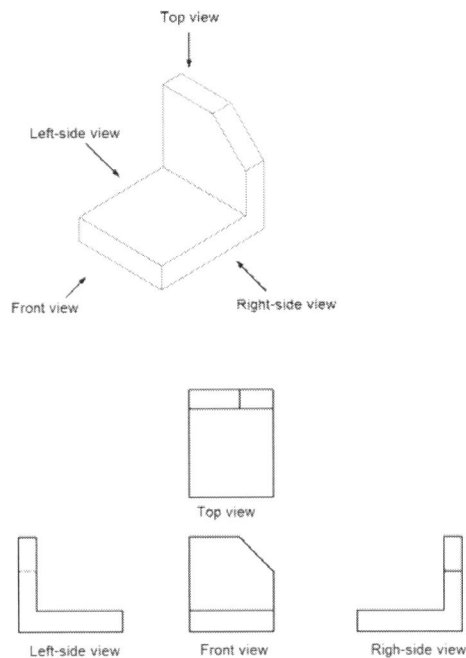

Example:

In this example, you will create the orthographic views of the part shown below. The views will be created by using the **Third Angle Projection** method.

- Open a new drawing using the **acadISO – Named Plot Styles.dwt** template.
- Click the **Layer Properties** button on the **Layers** panel; the **Layer Properties Manager** appears.
- Click the **New Layer** button on the **Layer Properties Manager** to create new layers.
- Create two new layers with the following properties.

Layer Name	Lineweight	Linetype
Construction	0.00 mm	Continuous
Object	0.30 mm	Continuous

- Right-click on the **Construction** layer and select **Set current**.
- Close the **Layer Properties Manager**.
- Activate the **Ortho Mode** icon on the status bar.
- Click **Zoom > Zoom All** on the Navigation Bar.

  Next, you need to draw construction lines. They are used as references to create actual drawings. You will create these construction lines on the **Construction** layer so that you can hide them when required.

- Click **Home > Draw > Construction** line on the ribbon or enter **XLINE** in the command line.

- Click anywhere in the lower left corner of the graphics window.
- Move the pointer upward and click to create a vertical construction line.
- Move the pointer toward right and click to create a horizontal construction line.
- Press ENTER to exit the tool.
- Click the **Offset** button on the **Modify** panel.
- Type 100 as the offset distance and press ENTER.
- Select the vertical construction line.

- Move the pointer toward right and click to create an offset line.
- Right-click and select **Enter** to exit the **Offset** tool.
- Press the SPACEBAR on the keyboard to start the **Offset** tool again.
- Type 75 as the offset distance and press ENTER.
- Select the horizontal construction line.
- Move the pointer above and click to create the offset line.
- Press ENTER to exit the **Offset** tool.
- Likewise, create other offset lines as shown below.

- Activate the **Object** layer.

Now, you must create object lines.

- Click the **Line** button on the **Draw** panel.

- Create an outline of the front view by selecting the intersection points between the construction lines.

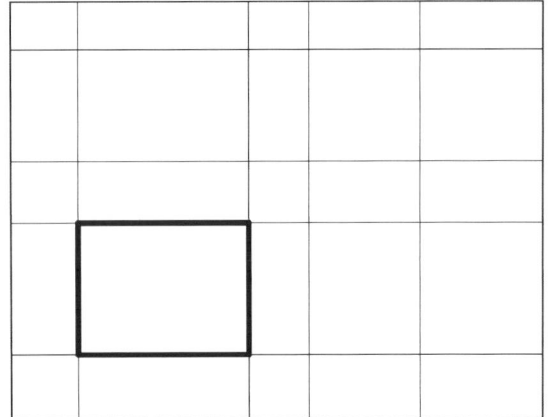

- Right-click and select **Enter** to exit the **Line** tool.
- Activate the **Show/Hide Lineweight** button on the status bar.
- Likewise, create the outlines of the top and side views.

Next, you must turn off the **Construction** layer.

- Click on the **Layer** drop-down in the **Layers panel**.

- Click the light-bulb of the **Construction** layer; the layer will be turned off.

- Use the **Offset** tool and create two parallel lines on the front view, as shown below.

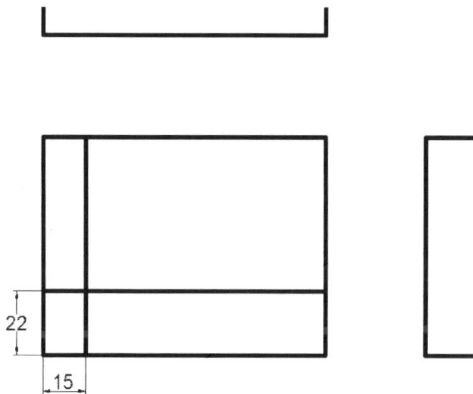

- Use the **Trim** tool and trim the unwanted lines of the front view as shown below.

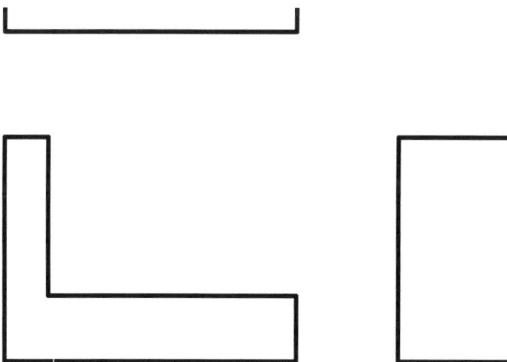

- Use the **Offset** tool to create the parallel line as shown below.

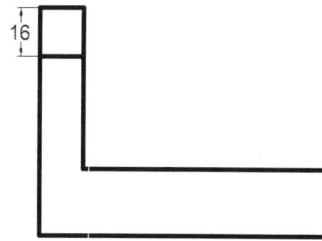

- Use the **Offset** tool and create offset lines in the Top view as shown below.

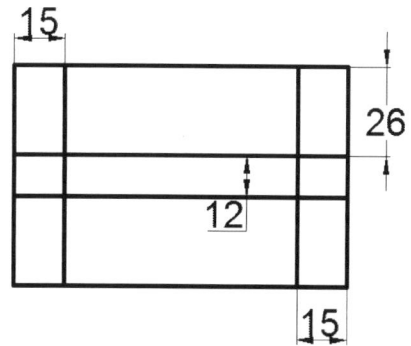

- Use the **Trim** tool and trim the unwanted objects.

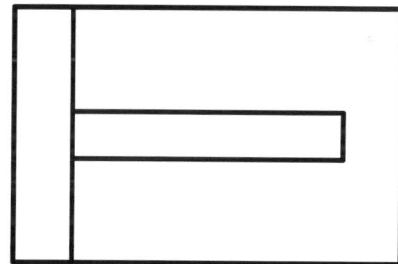

- Create other offset lines and trim the unwanted portions as shown below.

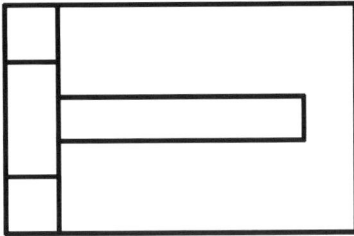

- Deactivate the Ortho Mode icon on the status bar.
- Click the **Line** button on the **Draw** panel.
- Press and hold the SHIFT key and right-click. Select the **From** option.

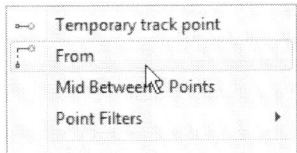

- Select the endpoint of the line in the front view as shown below.

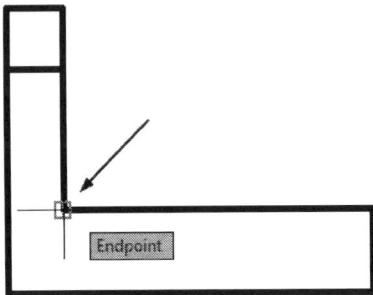

- Move the pointer on the vertical line and enter **40** in the command line; the first point of the line is specified at a point 40 mm away from the endpoint. Also, a rubber band line will be attached to the pointer.
- Move the pointer onto the endpoint on the top view as shown below.

- Move the pointer vertically downward; you will notice the track lines.
- Move the pointer near the horizontal line of the front view and click at the intersection point as shown below. Press ENTER to exit the tool.

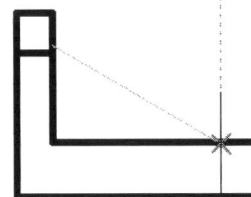

Next, you must create the right side view. To do this, you must draw a 45- degree miter line and project the measurements of the top view onto the side view.

- Click on the **Layer** drop-down in the **Layers** panel.

- Click the light-bulb icon of the **Construction** layer; the **Construction** layer is turned on.
- Select the **Construction** layer from the **Layer** drop-down to set it as the current layer.
- Draw an inclined line by connecting the intersection points of the construction lines as shown below.

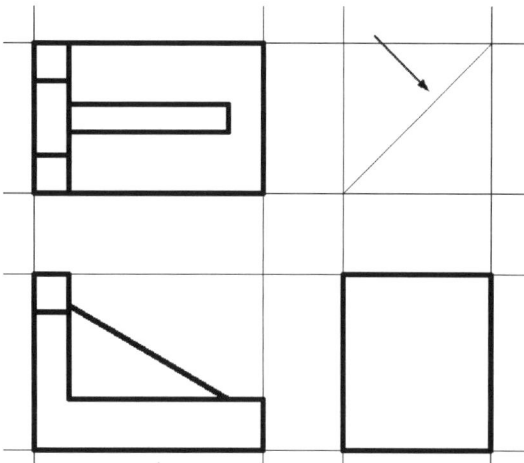

- Click the **Construction Line** button on the **Draw** panel.
- Select the **Hor** option from the command line and create the projection lines as shown below.

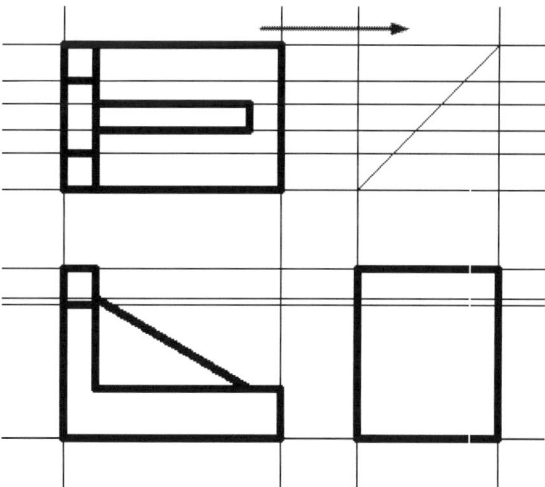

- Right-click to exit the **Construction Line** tool.
- Press ENTER and select the **Ver** option from the command line.
- Create the vertical projection lines as shown below.
- Use the **Trim** tool trim the extend portions of the construction lines.

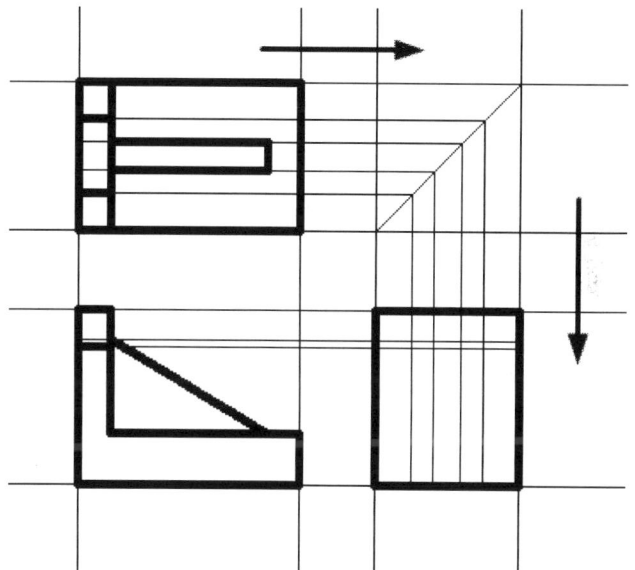

- Set the **Object** layer as current.
- Click the **Offset** button on the **Modify** panel.
- Select the **Through** option from the command line.
- Select the lower horizontal line of the side view.

- Select the end point on the front view as shown below.

- Click **Exit** in the command line.
- Use the **Line** tool and create the objects in the side view as shown below.

- Turn off the **Construction** layer by clicking on the light-bulb of the **Construction** layer.
- Trim the unwanted portions on the right side view.

The drawing after creating all the views is shown below.

- Save the file as **ortho_views.dwg**. Close the file.

Creating Auxiliary Views

Most of the components are represented by using orthographic views (front, top and/or side views). But many components have features located on inclined faces. You cannot get the true shape and size for these features by using the orthographic views. To see an accurate size and shape of the inclined features, you must create an auxiliary view. An auxiliary view is created by projecting the component onto a plane other than horizontal, front or side planes. The following figure shows a component with an inclined face. When you create orthographic views of the component, you will not be able to get the true shape of the hole on the inclined face.

Object   Orthographic Views

To get the actual shape of the hole, you must create an auxiliary view of the object as shown below.

Auxiliary view

Example:

In this example, you will create an auxiliary view of the object shown below.

Ø35 THRU

- Open a new AutoCAD file.
- Create four new layers with the following properties.

Layer Name	Lineweight	Linetype
Construction	0.00 mm	Continuous
Object	0.50 mm	Continuous
Hidden	0.30 mm	HIDDEN
Centerline	0.30 mm	CENTER

- Select the **Construction** layer from the **Layer** drop-down in the **Layers** panel.
- Create a rectangle at the lower left corner of the graphics window, as shown in figure.

- Select the rectangle and click the **Copy** button on the **Modify** panel.
- Select the lower left corner of the rectangle as the base point.
- Make sure that the **Ortho mode** is activated.
- Move the pointer upward and type **25** in the command line. Next, press ENTER.
- Press ESC to exit the **Copy** tool.

- Click the **Rotate** button on the **Modify** panel and select the copied rectangle. Press ENTER to accept.
- Select the lower right corner of the rectangle as the base point.
- Type 45 as the angle and press ENTER.

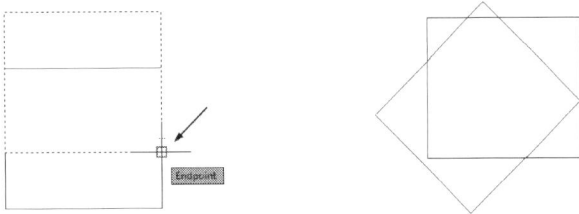

- Create another rectangle approximately 60 mm above the previous one.

The rectangle located at the top is considered as top view and the below one is the front view.

- Click the **Explode** button on the **Modify** panel and select the newly created rectangle. Next, right-click to explode the rectangle.
- Use the **Offset** tool and offset the vertical lines of the rectangle.

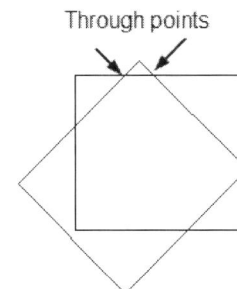

- Select the **Object** layer from the **Layer** drop-down in the **Layers** panel.

- Create the object lines in the front and top views as shown below.

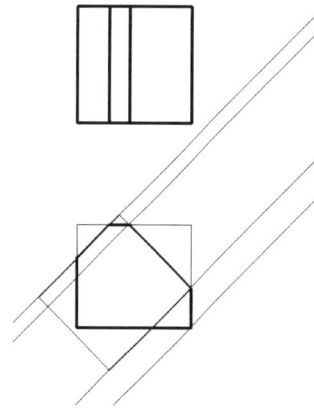

- Select the **Construction** layer from the **Layers** panel.
- Click the **Construction Line** button on the **Draw** panel.
- Select the **Offset** option from the command line. Next, select the **Through** option.
- Select the inclined line on the front view. Next, select the intersection point as shown below.

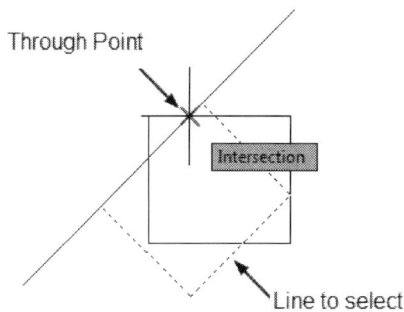

Through Point

Intersection

Line to select

- Likewise, create other construction lines as shown below.

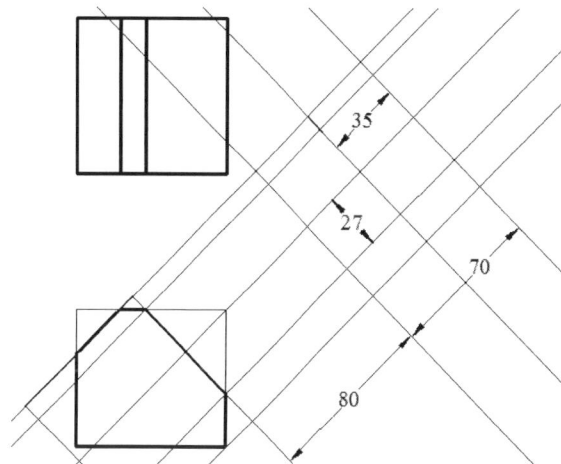

- Create other construction lines as shown below.

- Set the **Object** layer as current layer. Next, create the object lines using the intersection points between the construction lines.
- Use the **Circle** tool and create a circle of 35 mm diameter.

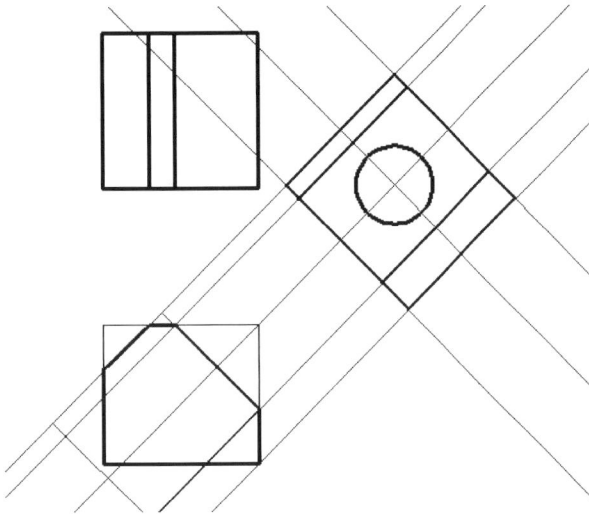

- Set the **Construction** layer as current layer. Create projection lines from the circle.
- Create the other object lines, hidden lines, and center lines, as shown below.

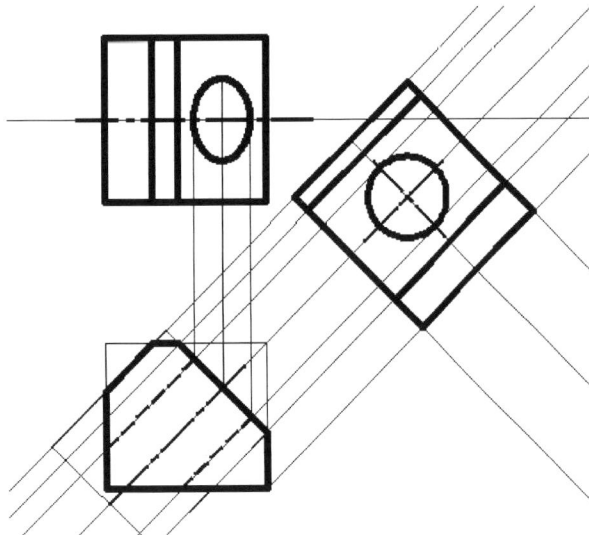

- The drawing after hiding the **Construction** layer is shown next.
- Save the file as auxiliary_views.dwg.

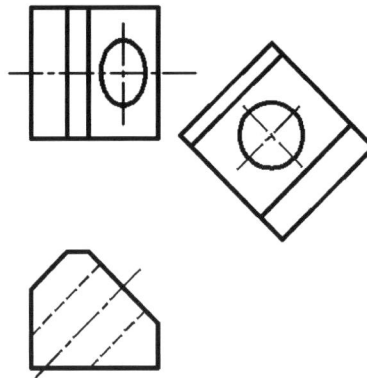

Creating Named views

While working with a drawing, you may need to perform numerous zoom and pan operations to view key portions of a drawing. Instead of doing this, you can save these portions with a name. Then, restore the named view and start working on them.

- Open the **ortho_views.dwg** file.
- Click the **View** tab on the ribbon.
- Click the right mouse button on the ribbon and select **Show Panels > Views**. This displays the **Views** panel on the ribbon.
- To create a named view, click **View > Views > View Manager** on the ribbon; the **View Manager** dialog appears.

- Click the **New** button on the **View Manager** dialog; the **New View/Shot Properties** dialog appears.

- Select the **Define Window** option from the **Boundary** section of the **New View/Shot Properties** dialog.

- Create a window on the front view, as shown below.

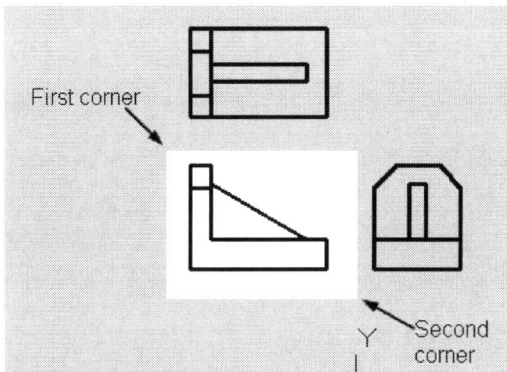

- Press ENTER to accept.

- Enter **Front** in the **View name** box.

- Click **OK** on the **New View/Shot Properties** dialog.

- Likewise, create the named views for the top and right views of the drawing.

- To set the **Top** view to current, select it from the **Views** tree and click the **Set Current** button on the dialog. Next, click **OK** on the **View Manager** dialog; the **Top** view will be zoomed and fitted to the screen.

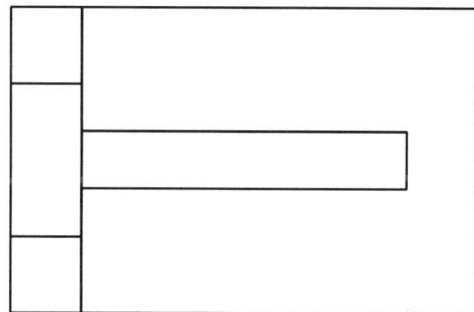

- Save and close the file.

Exercise 1

Create the orthographic views of the object shown below.

Create the orthographic and auxiliary views of the object shown below.

Exercise 2

Create the orthographic views of the object shown

below.

Exercise 4

Create the orthographic and auxiliary views of the object shown below.

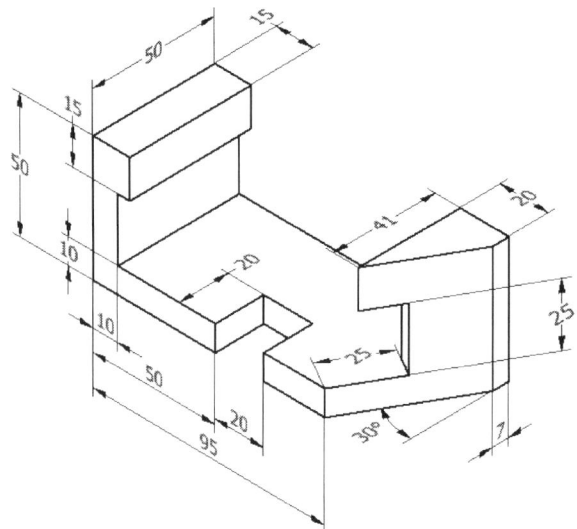

Exercise 3

Chapter 6: Dimensions and Annotations

In this chapter, you will learn to do the following:

- **Create Dimensions**
- **Create Dimension Style**
- **Add Leaders**
- **Create Centerlines**
- **Add Dimensional Tolerances**
- **Add Geometric Tolerances**
- **Edit Dimensions**

Dimensioning

In previous chapters, you have learned to draw shapes of various objects and create drawings. However, while creating a drawing, you also need to provide the size information. You can provide the size information by adding dimensions to the drawings. In this chapter, you will learn how to create various types of dimensions. You will also learn about some standard ways and best practices of dimensioning.

Creating Dimensions

In AutoCAD, there are many tools available for creating dimensions. You can access these tools from the Ribbon, Command line, and Menu Bar.

The following table gives you the functions of various dimensioning tools.

Tool	Shortcut	Function
Dimension	DIM	This tool creates a dimension based on the selected geometry.

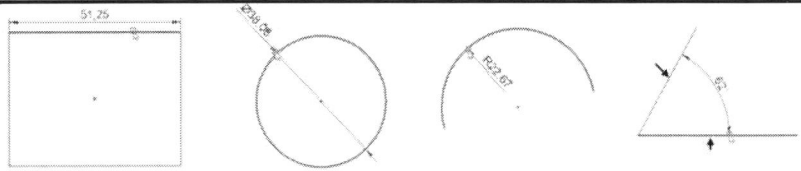

- Click **Annotate > Dimensions > Dimension** on the ribbon.
- Select a line, move the pointer, and click to create the linear dimension.
- Select a circle, move the pointer, and click to position the diameter dimension.
- Select an arc, move the pointer, and click to position the radial dimension.
- Place the pointer on the arc, type L, and press Enter. Select the arc and click to position the arc length dimension.
- Place the pointer on the arc, type A, and press Enter. Select the arc and click to position the angle of the arc.
- Select two non-parallel lines and position the angular dimension between them.

Likewise, you can create other types of dimensions using the **Dimension** tool.

Linear	DLI	This tool creates horizontal and vertical dimensions. - Click **Annotate > Dimensions > Dimension** drop-down> **Linear** on the ribbon. - Select the first and second points of the dimension. - Move the pointer in horizontal direction to create a vertical dimension (or) move in the vertical direction to create a horizontal dimension. - Click to position the dimension.

Aligned	DAL	This tool creates a linear dimension parallel to the object.

14,46

- Click **Annotate > Dimensions > Dimension** drop-down > **Aligned** on the ribbon.
- Select the first and second points of the dimension line (or) press Enter and select the line.
- Move the pointer and click to position the dimension.

Arc Length	DAR	It dimensions the total or partial length of an arc.

28,5   49,21

- Click **Annotate > Dimensions > Dimension** drop-down > **Arc Length** on the ribbon.
- Select an arc from the drawing.
- If you want to dimension only a partial length of an arc, select **Partial** option from the command line. Next, select the two points on the arc.
- Move pointer and click to position the dimension.

Continue	DCO	It creates a linear dimension from the second extension line of the previous dimension.

15   20   30

- Create a linear dimension by selecting the first and second points.

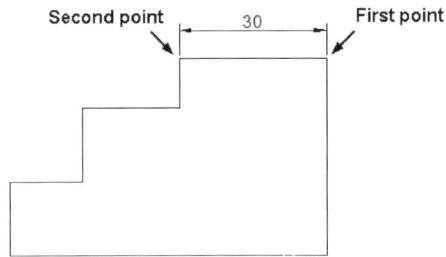

- Click **Annotate > Dimensions > Continue** on the ribbon; a chain dimension is attached to the pointer.

- Select the third and fourth points of the chain dimension.

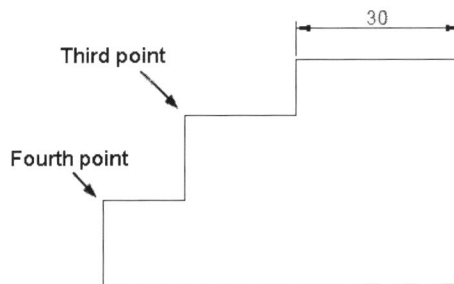

- Position the chain dimension. Next, right-click and select **Enter**.

	DBA	It creates dimensions by using the previously created dimension, as shown below.
Baseline		

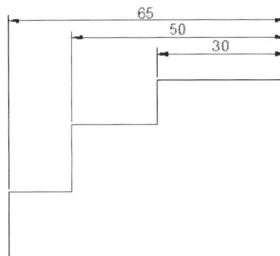

- Create a linear dimension by selecting the first and second points.

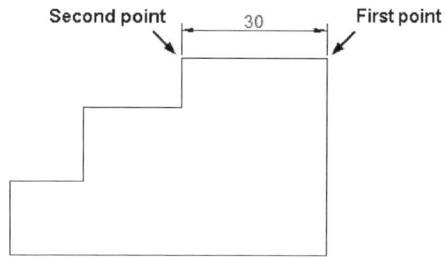

- Click **Annotate > Dimensions > Continue > Baseline** on the ribbon.
- Select the base dimension.
- Select the third and fourth point of the baseline dimension. Next, right-click and select **Enter**.

DAN	It creates an angular dimension.	
Angular		

- Click **Annotate > Dimensions > Dimension** drop-down **> Angle** on the ribbon.
- Select the first line and second line.
- Move the pointer and position the angle dimension.
- To create an angle dimension on an arc, select the arc and position the dimension.

		• To create an angle dimension on a circle, select two points on the circle and position the angle dimension. 121° 168°
Diameter	DIA	It adds a diameter dimension to a circle or an arc. Ø2 Ø3 • Click **Annotate > Dimensions > Dimension** drop-down> **Diameter** on the ribbon. • Select a circle or an arc and position the dimension.
Radius	DRA	It adds a radial dimension to an arc or circle. R18 R11
Jogged	DJO	It creates jogged dimensions. A jogged dimension is created when it is not possible to show the center of an arc or circle. R2 • Click **Annotate > Dimensions > Dimension** drop-down > **Jogged** on the ribbon. • Select an arc or circle. • Select a new center point override.

		• Locate the dimension and the jog location.
		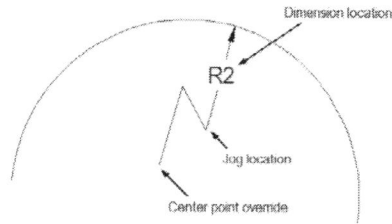
Dimension, Dimjogline ∿	DJL	It creates a jogged linear dimension. 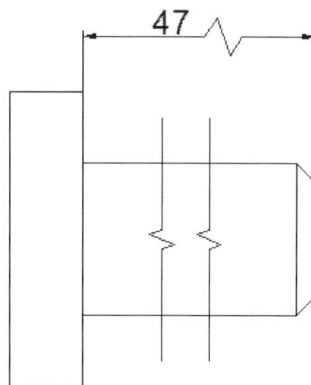 • Click **Annotate > Dimensions > Dimension, Dimjogline** on the ribbon. • Select the linear dimension to add a jog. • Define the location of the jog on the dimension.
Center Mark	CENTERMARK	It adds a center mark to a circle or an arc. 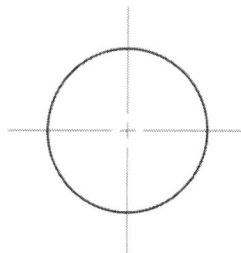 • Click **Annotate > Centerlines > Center Mark** on the ribbon. • Select an arc or a circle; the center mark will be positioned at its center.
Centerline	CENTERLINE	It creates a centreline between two lines. The centreline has the associative property. It changes with the position of the lines • Click **Annotate > Centerlines > Centerline** on the ribbon.

- Select two lines which are parallel or non-parallel to each other; a centreline is created between them.

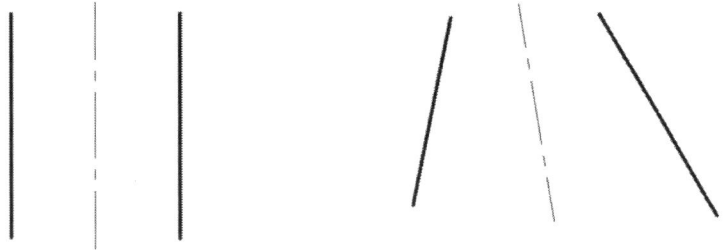

- Change the position of the lines; the centreline also changes.

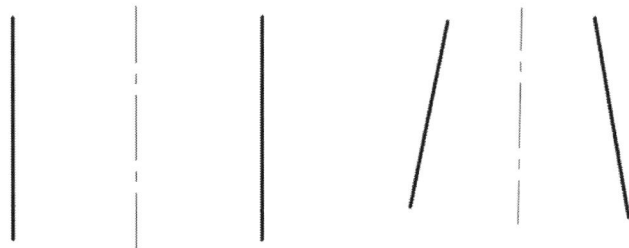

| | DOR | It creates ordinate dimensions based on the current position of the User Coordinate System (UCS). |

Ordinate

40

(Y-Coordinate Value)   20

20   57

(X-Coordinate Value)

- Click **Annotate > Dimensions > Dimension** drop-down > **Ordinate** on the ribbon.

- Select the point of the object.

- Move the pointer in the vertical direction and click to position the X-Coordinate value.

- Move the pointer in the horizontal direction and click to position the Y-Coordinate value.

Quick Dimension ⊡	QDIM	It dimensions one or more objects at the same time. • Click **Annotate > Dimensions > Quick Dimension** on the ribbon. • Select one or more objects from a drawing. • Right-click and position the dimensions.
Adjust Space ⊡		It is used to adjust the space between dimensions.
	DIMSPACE	• Click **Annotate > Dimensions > Adjust Space** on the ribbon. • Select the base dimension from which the other dimensions are to be adjusted. • Select the dimensions to adjust. • Right-click to accept. • Enter the space value or select the **Auto** option; the dimensions will be adjusted with respect to the base dimension.
Break ⊢	DIMBREAK	It adds breaks to a dimension, extension, and leader lines.

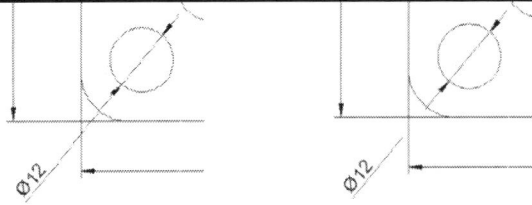

- Click **Annotate > Dimensions > Break** on the ribbon.
- Select the dimension to add a break.
- Select the cutting object. This breaks the dimension by the cutting object.
- Right-click to exit the tool.

| | DIMINSPECT | It creates an inspection dimension. The inspection dimension describes how frequently the dimension should be checked during inspection process to ensure the quality of the component. |

Inspect

- Click **Annotate > Dimensions > Inspect** on the ribbon; the **Inspection Dimension** dialog appears.

- Click the **Select dimensions** button on the dialog and select the dimension to apply the inspection rate.
- Right-click to accept.
- Select the shape of the inspection from the **Shape** section.
- Enter the **Inspection rate**. 100% means that the value will be checked every time during the inspection process. 50% means half the times.
- If required, select the **Label** check box and enter the inspection label.
- Click **OK**.

Example:

In this example, you will create the drawing as shown in figure and add dimensions to it.

- Create four new layers with the following settings.

Layer	Lineweight	Linetype
Construction	0.00 mm	Continuous
Object	0.50 mm	Continuous
Hidden	0.30 mm	HIDDEN2
Dimensions	Default	Continuous

- Set the maximum limit of the drawing to 100,100.
- Click **Zoom All** on the **Navigation Bar**.
- Create the drawing on the **Object** and **Hidden** layers.

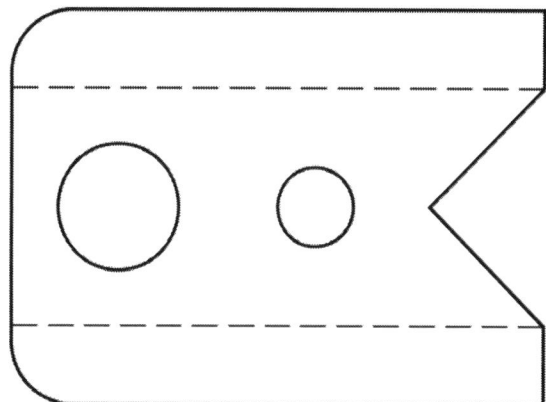

- Select the **Dimensions** layer from the **Layer** drop-down in the **Dimensions** panel.

Creating a Dimension Style

The appearance of the dimensions depends on the dimension style that you use. You can create a new dimension style using the **Dimension Style Manager** dialog. In this dialog, you can specify various settings related to the appearance and behaviour of dimensions. The following example helps you to create a dimension style.

- Expand the **Annotation** panel on the **Home** ribbon tab and click **Dimension Style**.

The **Dimension Style Manager** dialog appears.

The basic nomenclature of dimensions is given below.

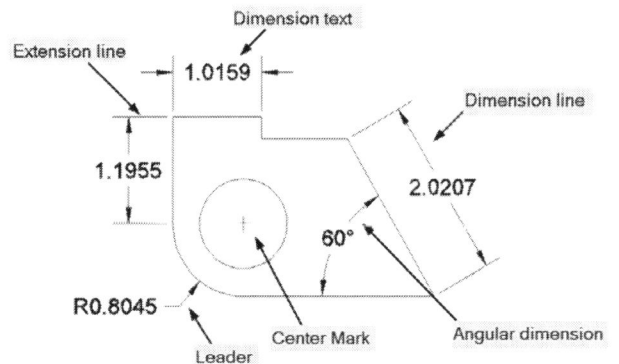

By default, the **ISO-25** or the **Standard** dimension style is active. If the default dimension style does not suit the dimensioning requirement, you can create a new dimension style and modify the nomenclature of the dimensions.

- To create a new dimension style, click the **New** button on the **Dimension Style Manager** dialog; the **Create New Dimension Style** dialog appears.
- In the **Create New Dimension Style** dialog, enter **Mechanical** in the **New Style Name**.
- Select **ISO-25** from the **Start With** drop-down and click **Continue**.

- In the **New Dimension Style** dialog, click the **Primary Units** tab.
- Ensure that the **Unit Format** is set to **Decimal**.
- Set **Precision** to **0**.
- Select **Decimal separator > '.'(Period)**.

Study the other options in the **Primary Units** tab. Most of them are self-explanatory.

- Click the **Text** tab.
- Ensure that the **Text height** is set **2.5**.
- In the **Text placement** section, set the **Vertical** and **Horizontal** values to **Centered**.
- Select **Text alignment > Horizontal**.

Study the other options in the **Text** tab. These options let you to change the appearance of the dimension text.

- Click the **Lines** tab on the dialog.
- In this tab, notice the two options in the **Extension lines** section: **Extend beyond dim lines** and **Offset from origin**.

- Set **Extend beyond dim lines** and **Offset from origin** to **1.25**.
- Set the **Baseline spacing** in the **Dimension lines** section to **5**.

Study the different options in this tab. The options in this tab are used to change the appearance and behaviour of the dimension lines and extension lines.

- Click the **Symbols and Arrows** tab and set **Arrow size** to 3 and **Center Marks** to 3.

- Select the **Line** option in the **Center marks** section.

Notice the different options in this tab. The options in this tab are used to change the appearance of the arrows and symbols. Also, you can set the appearance of the center marks and centrelines of circles and arcs.

- Click **OK** to accept the settings.
- Click **Set Current** on the **Dimension Style Manager** dialog; the **Mechanical** dimension style will be set as current.
- Click **Close** to close the dialog.

- On the **Annotate** tab of the ribbon, click

  Centerlines > Center Mark .

- Select the circles from the drawing to apply the center mark to them.

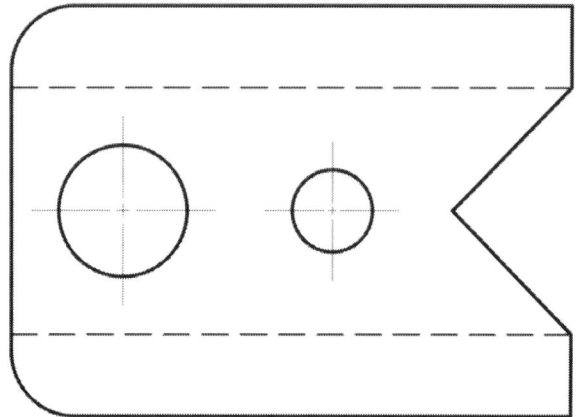

- On the ribbon, click **Annotate >**

  Dimensions > Dimension .

- Make sure that the **Object Snap** icon is turned on the status bar.

- Select the lower right corner of the drawing.

- Select the endpoint of the center mark of the small circle; the dimension is attached to the pointer.

- Move the pointer vertical downwards and position the dimension, as shown below.

- Select the **Baseline** option from the command line.
- Select the right extension line of the linear dimension; a dimension is attached to the pointer.
- Select the endpoint of the center mark of the large circle; another dimension is attached to the pointer.
- Select the lower left corner of the drawing.
- Press ENTER twice.

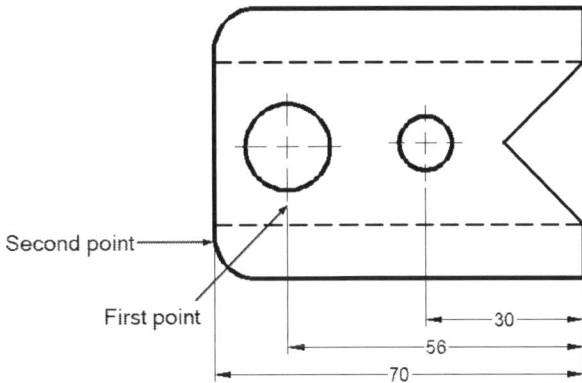

- Select the **Angular** option from the command line.
- Select the two angled lines of the drawing and position the angle dimension.
- Select the large circle and position the diameter dimension.
- Likewise, select the small circle and position the dimension.
- Select the fillet located at the top left corner; the radial dimension is attached to the pointer.
- Select **Mtext** from the command line and type **2X** and press SPACEBAR.
- Click in the graphics window to update the dimension text.

- Next, position the radial dimension at 45 degrees.
- Likewise, apply the other dimensions, as shown.
- Save and close the drawing.

Adding Leaders

A leader is a thin solid line terminating with an arrowhead at one end and a dimension, note, or symbol at the other end. In the following example, you will learn to create a leader style, and then create a leader.

Example 1:

- Draw a square of 24 mm side length.
- Create a circle of 10.11 mm diameter at center of the square.

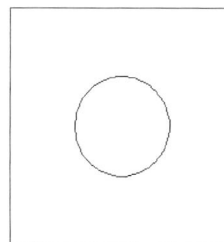

- Click **Home > Draw > Arc > Center, Start, Angle** on the ribbon.

- Select the center point of the circle.
- Move the pointer horizontally toward right.
- Type 6 as the radius and press ENTER.
- Type 270 as the included angle and press ENTER.

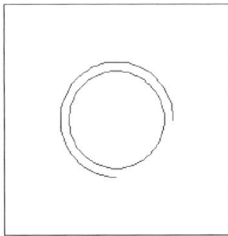

- On the **Home** tab of the ribbon, expand **Annotation** panel and click **Multileader Style** icon; the **Multileader Style Manager** appears.

- In the **Multileader Style Manager** dialog, click the **New** button; the **Create New Multileader Style** dialog appears.

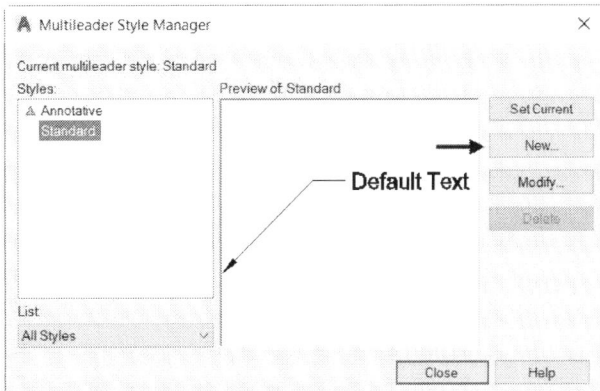

- In the **Create New Multileader Style** dialog, enter **Hole callout** in the **New style name** box and select **Standard** from the **Start with** drop-down.

- Click **Continue**; the **Modify Multileader Style** dialog appears.
- Click the **Leader Format** tab and set the **Arrowhead Size** to **2.5**.

Also, notice the other options in this tab. They are used to set the appearance of the multileader lines and the arrow head.

- Click the **Leader Structure** tab and set the **Landing distance** to **5**.

- Click the **Content** tab and set the **Text height** to **2.5**.

The other options in this tab are used to define the appearance of the text or block that will be attached at the end of the leader line.

- Click **OK** on the **Modify Multileader Style** dialog.

- Click **Set Current** on the **Multileader Style Manager** dialog.

- Click **Close** to close the dialog.

- Click **Annotate > Leaders > Multileader** on the ribbon.

- Click the down arrow next to the **Polar tracking** button on the status bar and select **45** from the menu.

- Activate the **Polar tracking** button on the status bar.

- Select a point in the first quadrant of the arc.

- Move the pointer in the top right direction and click to create the leader.

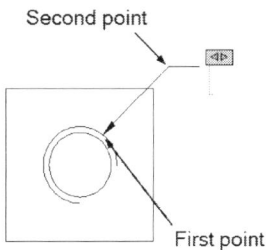

- Type **M12x1.75 – 6H 16** in the text editor. Next, you must insert the depth symbol before 16.

- Position the pointer before 16 and click the **Symbol** button on the **Insert** panel of the **Text Editor** ribbon; a menu appears.

- Click **Other** on the menu; the **Character Map** dialog appears.

- In the **Character Map** dialog, select **GDT** from the **Font** drop-down.

- Select the Depth symbol from the fonts table.

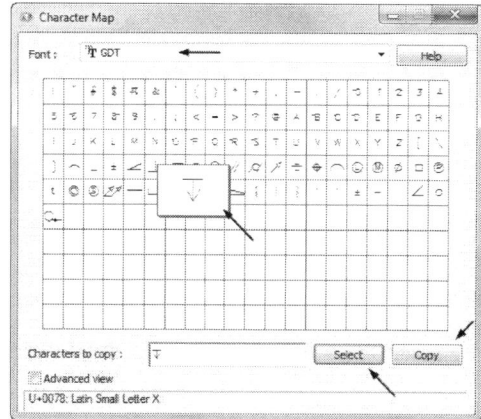

- Click **Select** and **Copy** buttons.

- Close the **Character Map** dialog.

- Right-click and select **Paste**; the depth symbol is pasted in the text editor.

- Adjust the spacing so that the complete text is in one line.

- Click in the graphics window.

Adding Dimensional Tolerances

During the manufacturing process, the accuracy of a part is an important factor. However, it is impossible to manufacture a part with the exact dimensions. Therefore, while applying dimensions to a drawing we provide some dimensional tolerances, which lie within acceptable limits. The following example shows you to add dimension tolerances in AutoCAD.

Example:

- Create the drawing, as shown below. Do not add dimensions to it.

- Create a new dimension style with the name **Tolerances**.
- In the **New Dimension Styles** dialog, click the **Tolerances** tab.
- In the **Tolerances** tab, set the **Method** as **Deviation**.
- Set **Precision** as **0.00**.
- Set the **Upper Value** and **Lower Value** to **0.05**.
- Set the **Vertical position** as **Middle**.
- Specify the following settings in the **Primary Units**, **Text**, and **Symbols and Arrows** tab:

    Primary Units tab:
    Unit format: Decimal
    Precision: 0.00
    Decimal Separator: '.'Period

Text tab:
Text Height: 2.5
Text placement: Centered
Text alignment: Horizontal

Symbols and Arrows tab:
Arrow Size: 2.5
Center Marks: Line

- Click **OK** on **New Dimension Styles** dialog.
- Click **Set Current** and **Close** on the **Dimension Style Manager** dialog.
- Apply dimensions to the drawing.

Geometric Dimensioning and Tolerancing

Earlier, you have learned how to apply tolerances to the size (dimensions) of a component. However, the dimensional tolerances are not sufficient for manufacturing a component. You must give tolerance values to its shape, orientation and position as well. The following figure shows a note which is used to explain the tolerance value given to the shape of the object.

Note: The vertical face should not taper over 0.08 from the horizontal face

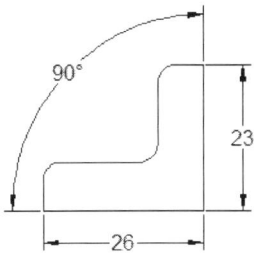

90°

23

26

In this figure, the vertical face to which the tolerance frame is connected, must be within two parallel planes 0.08 apart and perpendicular to the datum reference (horizontal plane).

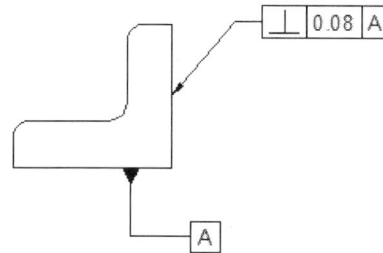

⟂ | 0.08 | A

A

Providing a note in a drawing may be confusing. To avoid this, we use Geometric Dimensioning and Tolerancing (GD&T) symbols to specify the tolerance values to shape, orientation and position of a component. The following figure shows the same example represented by using the GD&T symbols.

The Geometric Tolerancing symbols that can be used to interpret the geometric conditions are given in the table below.

Purpose		Symbol
To represent the shape of a single feature.	Straightness	⎯
	Flatness	▱
	Cylindricity	⌭
	Circularity	○
	Profile of a surface	⌒

	Profile of a line	
To represent the orientation of a feature with respect to another feature.	Parallelism	
	Perpendicularity	
	Angularity	
To represent the position of a feature with respect to another feature.	Position	
	Cocentricity and coaxiality	
	Run-out	
	Total Run-out	
	Symmetry	

Example 1:

In this example, you will apply geometric tolerances to the drawing shown below.

- Create the drawing as shown below.

- Click **Annotate > Dimensions > Tolerance** on the ribbon; the **Geometric Tolerance** dialog appears.

- In the **Geometric Tolerance** dialog, click the upper box of the **Sym** group. The **Symbol** dialog appears.

- In the **Symbol** dialog, click the **Perpendicularity** symbol. The symbol appears in the **Sym** group.

- Click in the top left box in the **Tolerance 1** group. The diameter symbol appears in the box.
- Enter .05 in the box next to the diameter symbol.

- Enter **A** in the upper box of the **Datum 1** group.

- Click **OK** and position the **Feature Control frame** as shown below.

Next, you must add the datum reference.

- On the **Home** ribbon tab, expand the **Annotation** panel and click **Multileader Style** .
- Click the **New** button.
- On the **Create New Multileader Style** dialog, type **Tolerance** in the **New Style name** box, and click **Continue**.
- Click the **Leader Format** tab and select **Arrowhead > Symbol > Datum triangle filled**.
- Set the **Size** to 2.5.
- On the **Leader Structure** tab, set **Maximum leader points** to **2**.
- Click the **Content** tab and select **Multileader type > Block**.
- Select **Source block > Box**.
- Set the **Scale** value to 0.75.
- Click **OK**, **Set Current**, and **Close**.
- On the **Home** ribbon tab, click **Annotation > Multileader** .

- Specify the first and second points of the datum reference as shown.
- On the **Edit Attributes** dialog, set type **A** in the **Enter tag number** box.
- Click **OK**.

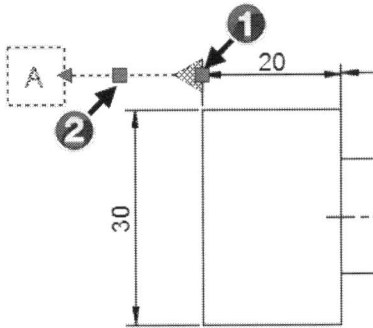

Editing Dimensions by Stretching

In AutoCAD, the dimensions are associative to the drawing. If you modify a drawing, the dimensions will be modified, automatically. In the following example, you will stretch the drawing to modify the dimensions.

`

Example:

- Create the drawing as shown below and apply dimensions to it.

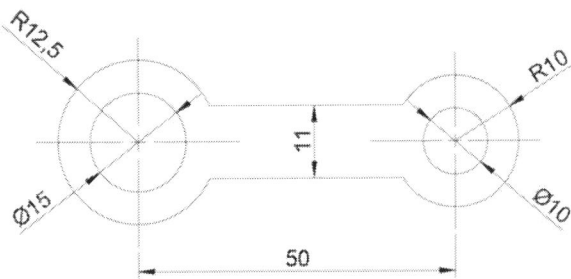

- Click **Home > Modify > Stretch** on the ribbon.
- Drag a window and select the right-side circles and the horizontal lines.

- Right-click and select the center point of the right-side circles.
- Move the pointer to stretch the drawing; you will notice that the horizontal dimension also changes.
- Type **30** and press ENTER; the horizontal dimension is updated to 80.

Modifying Dimensions by Trimming and Extending

In earlier chapters, you have learned to modify drawings by trimming and extending objects. In the same way, you can modify dimensions by trimming and extending. The following example shows you to modify dimensions by this method.

Example:

- Create a drawing as shown below and add dimensions to it.

- Click **Home > Modify > Trim** on the ribbon.
- Select the horizontal edge as shown in figure and right-click to accept.

- Select the vertical dimension with the value 18. This trims the dimension up to the selected edge.

- Press ESC.
- Click **Home > Modify > Trim > Extend** on the ribbon.
- Select the vertical edge as the boundary, as shown below. Next, right-click to accept.

- Select the horizontal dimension with the value 10. This will extend the dimension up to the selected boundary.
- Press Esc.

Using the DIMEDIT command

The **DIMEDIT** command can be used to modify dimension. Using this command, you can add text to a dimension, rotate the dimension text and extension lines or reset the position of the dimension text.

Example 1: (Adding Text to the dimension)

- Type **DED** in the command line and press ENTER.
- Select the **New** option from the command line; a text box appears.
- Enter **TYP** in the text box and press the SPACEBAR.

- Left-click and select the dimension with value 10.

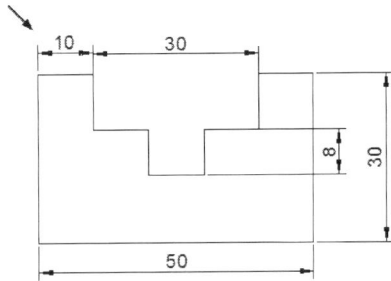

- Press ENTER; the dimension text will be changed.

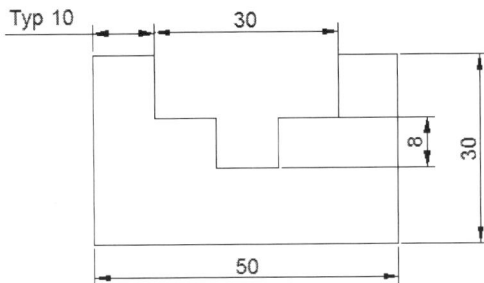

Example 2: (Rotating the dimension text)

- Enter **DED** in the command line and select the **Rotate** option; the message, "Specify angle for dimension text" appears in the command line.

- Type **30** and press ENTER.
- Select the dimension with the value 50 and right-click. The angle of the dimension text is changed to 30 degrees. Note that the angle is measured from the horizontal axis (X-axis).

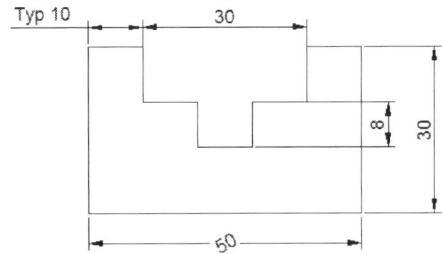

Using the Update tool

The **Update** tool is used to update a dimension with the currently active dimension style. For example, if you have created a new dimension style, you can apply it to an already existing dimension using the **Update** tool. The following example shows you to update a dimension.

- Type **D** in the command line and press ENTER; the **Dimension Style Manager** dialog appears.
- In the **Dimension Style Manager** dialog, select **Standard** from the **Styles** list and click **Modify**.
- In the **Modify Dimension Style** dialog, set the **Text height** to **2.5**.
- Click the **Text Style** button; the **Text Style** dialog appears.

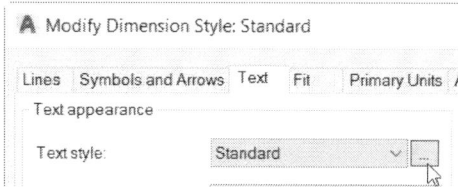

- In the **Text Style** dialog, change the **Font Style** to **Italic**.

- Click **Apply** and close the **Text Style** dialog.

- Click **OK** on the **Modify Dimension Style** dialog.

- Click **Close** on the **Dimension Style Manager** dialog.

- In the **Dimensions** panel, set the dimension style to **Standard**.

- Click the **Update** button on the **Dimensions** panel.

- Select the horizontal dimension with the value 30. Next, right-click; the dimension will be updated with the current the dimension style.

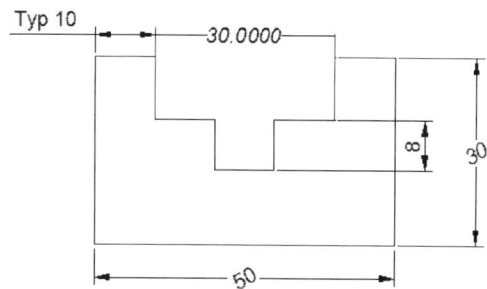

Using the Oblique tool

The **Oblique** tool is used to incline the extension lines of a dimension. This tool is very useful while dimensioning the isometric drawings. It can also be used in 2D drawings when the dimensions overlap with each other.

Example:

In this example, you will create an isometric drawing and add dimensions to it. Next, you will use the **Oblique** tool to change the angle of the dimension lines.

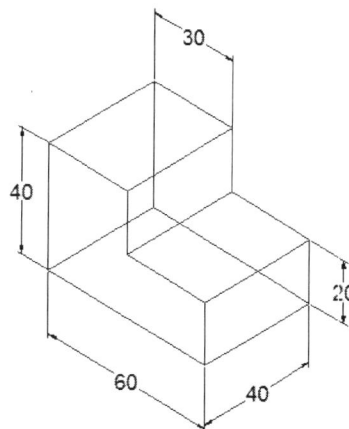

154

- Type-in **DS** in the command line, and then press Enter.
- On the **Drafting Settings** dialog, click the **Snap and Grid** tab.
- In the **Drafting Settings** dialog, set **Snap type** to **Isometric snap** and click **OK**.

Snap type
- Grid snap
- Rectangular snap
- Isometric snap ←
- PolarSnap

- Turn on the **Snap Mode** and the **Ortho Mode**. Also, turn on the **Dynamic Input**.
- Click **Zoom All** on the Navigation Bar.
- Type **L** in the command line and press ENTER.
- Click at a random point and move the pointer vertically.
- Type 40 in the command line and press ENTER; a vertical line will be created.
- Move the pointer toward right; you will notice that an inclined line is attached to the pointer.

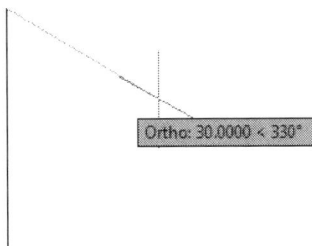

Ortho: 30.0000 < 330°

- Type 30 and press ENTER; an inclined line is drawn.

- Move the pointer toward downward and click when the tooltip shows 20<270.

Ortho: 20.0000 < 270°

- Move the pointer toward right and click when the tooltip displays 30 < 330.
- Move downward and click when the tooltip shows 20 < 270.
- Move the pointer toward left and click on the start point of the sketch.
- Right-click select **Enter**.

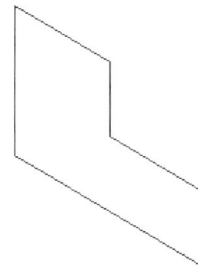

- Turn off the **Ortho Mode**.
- Create a selection window and select all the objects of the sketch.
- Right-click and select **Copy-Selection** from the shortcut menu.
- Select the lower left corner point as the base point.

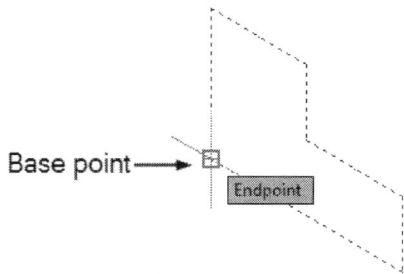

- Move the pointer toward right and click when the tooltip shows 40 < 30.
- Right-click and select **Enter**.

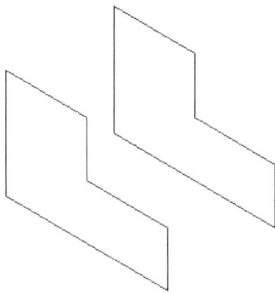

- Use the **Line** tool and connect the endpoints of the two sketches.

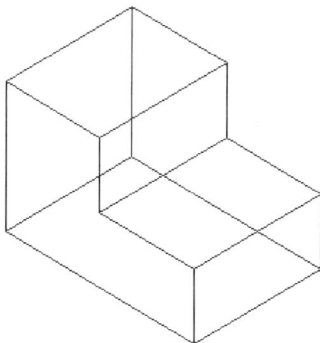

- Deactivate the ISODRAFT and the Snap Mode icons on the Status bar.
- Use the dimensioning tools and apply dimensions to the sketch.

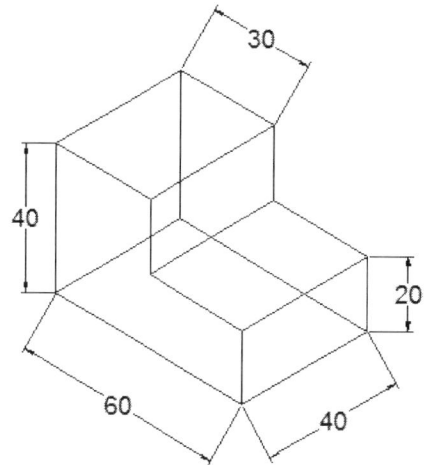

- Expand the **Dimensions** panel on the **Annotate** ribbon tab and click the **Oblique** button.

- Select the vertical dimensions and right-click to accept; the message, "**Enter obliquing angle**" appears in the command line.

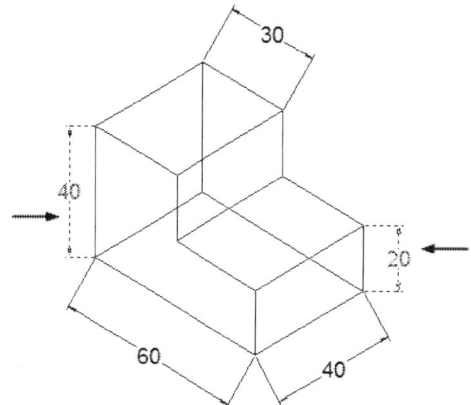

- Type 150 as the oblique angle and press ENTER; the dimensions are oblique as shown below.

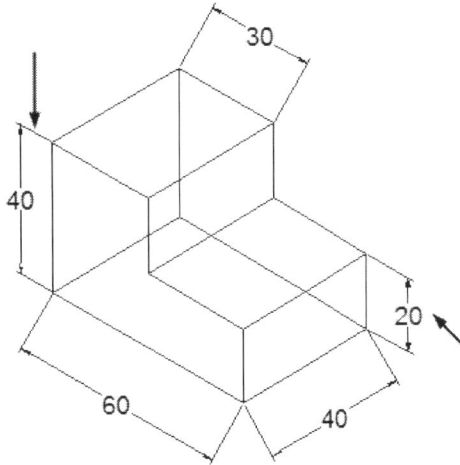

- Again, click the **Oblique** tool on the **Dimensions** panel and select the aligned dimensions. Next, right-click to accept.

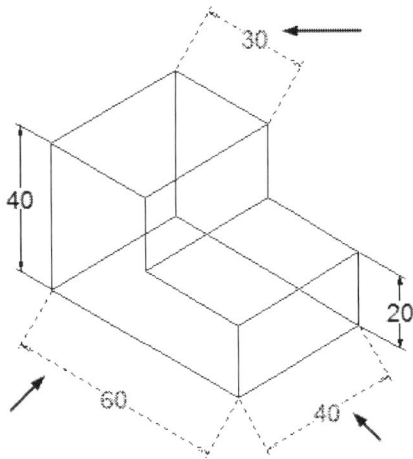

- Type 90 as the oblique angle and press ENTER; the dimensions will be oblique as shown below.

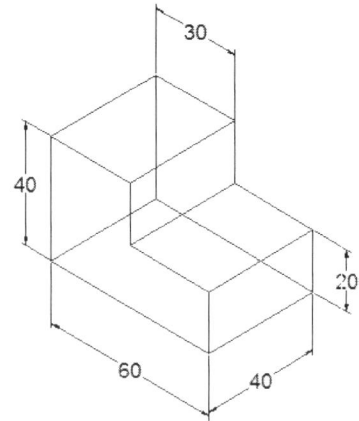

Editing Dimensions using Grips

In Chapter 4, you have learned to edit objects using grips. In the same way, you can edit dimensions using grips. The editing operations using grips are discussed next.

Example 1: (Stretching the Dimension)

- Select the dimension to display grips on it.
- Select the endpoint grip of the dimension.
- Next, move the pointer and select a new point; the dimension value will be updated, automatically.

- You can also stretch angular or radial dimensions.

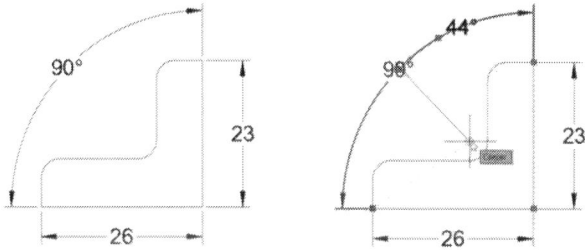

Example 2: (Moving the Dimension)

- To move a linear dimension, select the middle grip and move the pointer.

- Likewise, you can move the angular and radial dimensions.

Example 3: (Modifying the Dimension text)

- Select the dimension and position the pointer on the middle grip; a shortcut menu appears as shown below.

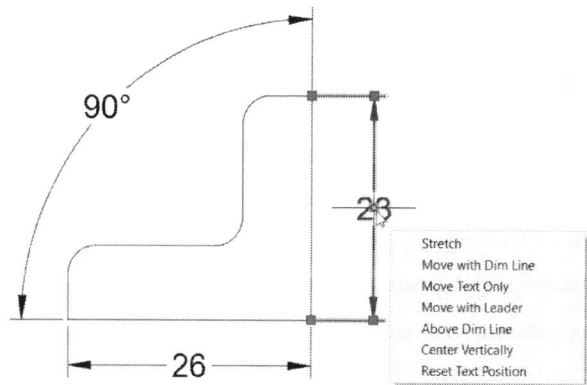

The options in the menu are self-explanatory. You can perform the required operation by selecting the corresponding option.

- Likewise, position the pointer on the endpoint of the dimension line and select the required option from the menu.

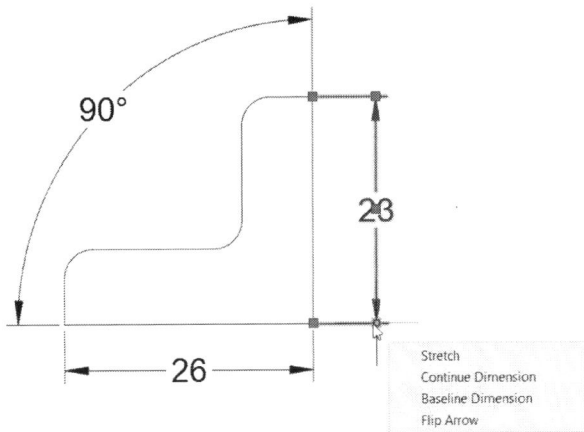

Modifying Dimensions using the Properties palette

Using the **Properties** palette, you can modify the dimensional properties such as text, arrow size, precision, linetype, lineweight, and so on. The **Properties** palette comes in handy when you want to modify the properties of a particular dimension only.

Example:

- Create the drawing shown in figure and apply dimensions to it.

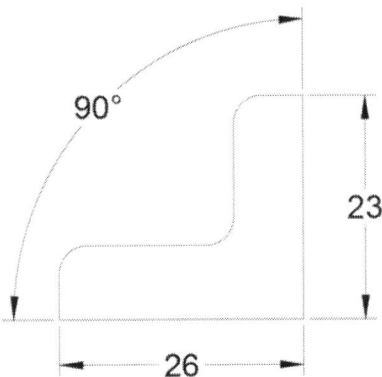

- Select the vertical dimension and right-click.
- Select **Properties** from the shortcut menu; the **Properties** palette appears.

- In the **Properties** palette, under the **Lines & Arrows** section, set the **Arrow size** to **2**.

- Under the **General** section, set **Color** to **Blue**.

- Set the **Ext line offset** value to **1.25**.
- Scroll down to the **Text** section and set **Text height** to **2**.

- Close the **Properties** palette; you will notice that the properties of the dimension are updated as per the changes made.

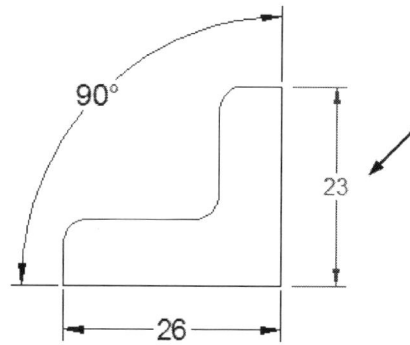

Matching Properties of Dimensions or Objects

In the previous section, you have learned to change the properties of a dimension. Now, you can apply these properties to other dimensions by using the **Match Properties** tool.

- Click **Home > Properties > Match Properties** on the ribbon or type **MA** and press ENTER; the message, "Select source object" appears in the command line.

- Select the vertical dimension from the drawing; the message, "Select destination object(s) or [Settings]:" appears in the command line.

- Select the **Settings** option from the command line; the **Property Settings** dialog appears.

In this dialog, you can select the settings that can be applied to the destination dimensions or objects. By default, all the options are selected in this dialog.

- Click **OK** on the **Property Settings** dialog. Next, you must select the destination objects.

- Select the other dimensions from the drawing; the properties of the source dimension are applied to other dimensions.

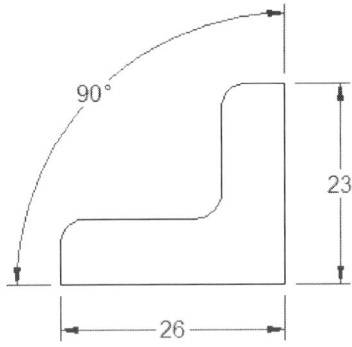

90°

23

26

- Right-click and select **Enter**.

Exercise 1

Create the drawing shown below and create hole callouts for different types of holes. Assume missing dimensions.

Exercise 2

Create the following drawings and apply dimensions and annotations. The Grid Spacing X= 10 and Grid Spacing Y=10.

Exercise 3

Create the drawing shown below. The Grid spacing is 10 mm. After creating the drawing, apply dimensional tolerances to it. The tolerance specifications are given below.

Method: Limits
Precision: 0.00
Upper Value: 0.05
Lower Value: 0.05

Chapter 7: Parametric Tools

In this chapter, you will learn to do the following:

- **Apply Geometric and Dimensional Constraints**
- **Create Equations using the Parameter Manager**
- **Create Inferred Constraints**

Parametric Tools

Parametric tools are one of the main advancements in CAD/CAM/CAE. Using the parametric tools, you can define the shape and size of a drawing by applying relations and dimensions between the objects. You can also use equations in place of dimensions. Changing one parameter of an equation would change the entire shape and size of the drawing. This makes it easy to modify the design.

The parametric tools can be accessed from the Ribbon, Command line, and Menu Bar.

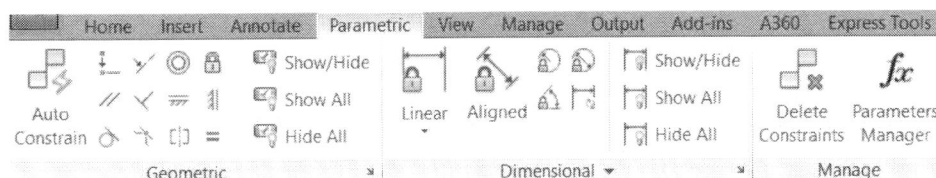

Geometric Constraints

Geometric Constraints are used to control the shape of a drawing by applying geometric relationships between the objects. For example, you can apply the **Tangent** constraint to make a line tangent to a circle. You can use the **Equal** constraint to make two lines equal in length.

The following table shows various geometric constraints and their functions.

Constraint	Function
Coincident	It is used to constraint a point to lie on another point or an object. • Click **Parametric > Geometric > Coincident** on the ribbon. • Select a point on a line or arc. • Select a point on another object; the two points will coincide with each other. First point Second point
Collinear	It is used to constraint a line along another line. The lines are not required to touch each other. Second object First obiect • Click **Parametric > Geometric > Collinear** on the ribbon. • Select the first line and the second line; the second line will be made collinear with the first line.
Concentric	It is used to make the center points of arcs, circles or ellipses coincident. First circle Second circle

- Click **Parametric > Geometric > Concentric** on the ribbon.
- Select a circle or arc from the drawing.
- Select another circle or arc; the second circle will be concentric with the first circle.

| ⚌ **Equal** | It is used to make two objects equal. For example, if you select two circles, the diameter of the two circles will become equal. If you select two lines, the length of the two lines will be equal. |

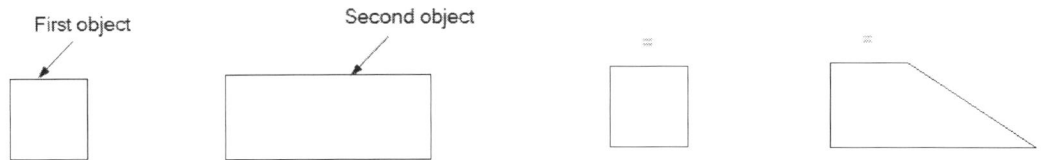

First object   Second object

- Click **Parametric > Geometric > Equal** on the ribbon.
- Select two objects from the drawing; the second object will be made equal to the first object.

| ☰ **Horizontal** | It is used to make a line horizontal. You can also make two points lie along the horizontal axis. |

Line selected

- Click **Parametric > Geometric > Horizontal** on the ribbon.
- Select a line to make it horizontal.
- If you want to make points horizontal, select the **2Points** option from the command line and select the two points.

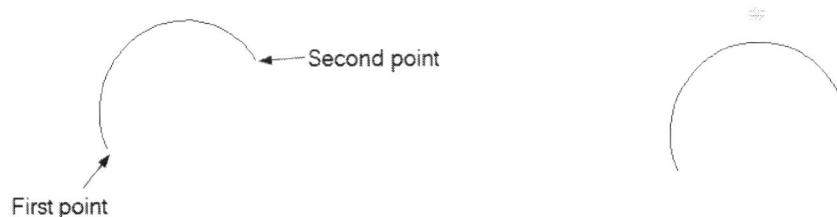

Second point

First point

| ⌿ **Vertical** | It is used to make a line vertical. You can also make two points vertical. |
| | • Click **Parametric > Geometric > Vertical** on the ribbon. |

	• Select a line to make it vertical. • You can also use the **2Points** option to make two points vertical.
🔒 Fix	It is used to fix a point or an object at a particular location. • Click **Parametric > Geometric > Fix** on the ribbon. • Select a point to make it fixed at its location. • You can also use the **Objects** option to select objects from the drawing.
Perpendicular	It is used to make two lines perpendicular to each other. Second object First object • Click **Parametric > Geometric > Perpendicular** on the ribbon. • Select two lines from the drawing; the second line is made perpendicular to the first line.
Smooth	It is used to make a spline continuous with another spline or arc. First point Second point • Click **Parametric > Geometric > Smooth** on the ribbon. • Select a spline curve.

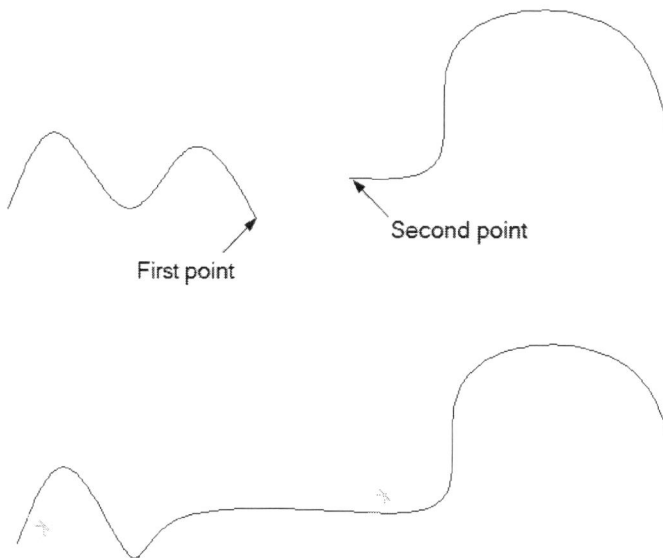

- Select another spline or arc; the first curve will become continuous with the second curve.

// **Parallel**	It is used to make two lines parallel to each other.	

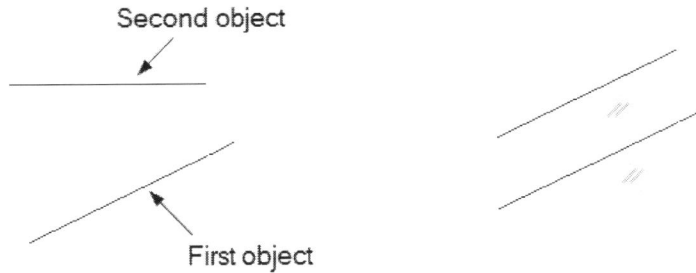

Second object

First object

- Click **Parametric > Geometric > Parallel** on the ribbon.
- Select two lines from the drawing; the second line is made parallel to the first line.

⊏⊐ **Symmetric**	It is used to make two objects symmetric about a line. The objects will have same size, position and orientation about a line.	

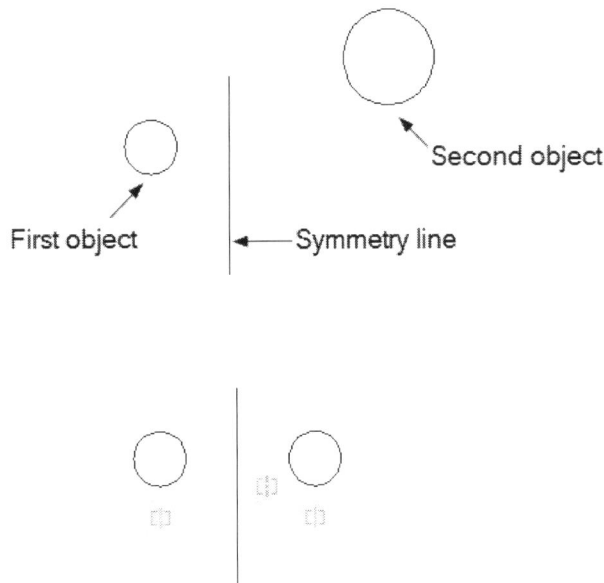

Second object

First object — Symmetry line

- Click **Parametric > Geometric > Symmetric** on the ribbon.
- Select two objects from the drawing.
- Select the symmetry line; the objects will be made symmetric about the selected line.
- You can also use the **2Points** option to make two points symmetric about a line.

◌ **Tangent**	It is used to make an arc, circle, or line tangent to another arc or circle.	

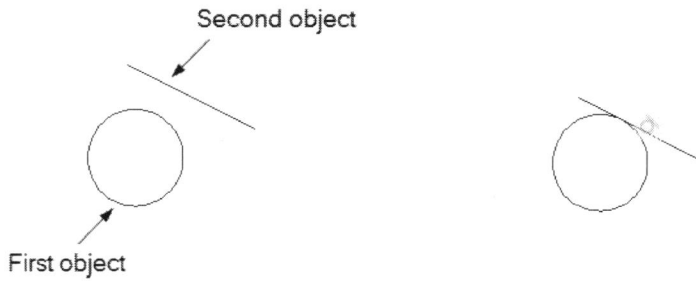

Second object

First object

- Click **Parametric > Geometric > Tangent** on the ribbon.
- Select a circle, arc, or line.
- Select another circle, arc, or line; the second object will be tangent to the first object.

Auto Constrain

The **Auto Constrain** tool is used to apply constraints to the objects, automatically.

- Click **Parametric > Geometric > Auto Constrain** on the ribbon.
- Select the **Settings** option from the command line; the **Constraint Settings** dialog appears.

- In this dialog, select the constraints that you want to apply. You can also select the **Tangent objects must share an intersection point** and **Perpendicular objects must share an intersection point** options.
- Click **OK**.
- Select multiple objects by clicking on them or by dragging a selection window.

> - Right-click and select **Enter**; geometric constraints are applied to the objects based on their geometric condition.

Example:

In this example, you will create the following drawing by using the drawing and parametric tools.

- Open a new AutoCAD file.
- Create two circles and a line as shown in figure.

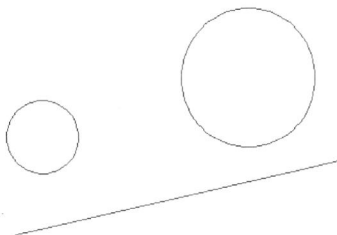

- Click **Parametric > Geometric > Horizontal** on the ribbon.
- Select the line to make it horizontal.

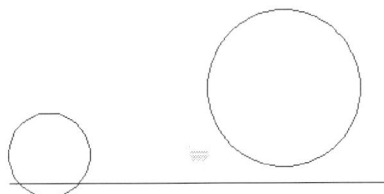

- Press the SPACEBAR and select the **2Points**

option from the command line.

- Select the large circle and the small circle; the center points of the two circles will be horizontal.

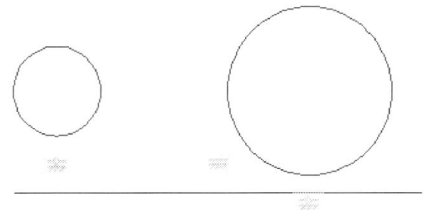

- Create four lines as shown below.

- Click the **Coincident** button on the **Geometric** panel and select the two endpoints of the lines as shown below; the endpoints will be made coincident.

- Click the **Auto Constrain** button on the **Geometric** panel and select the four lines as shown below.

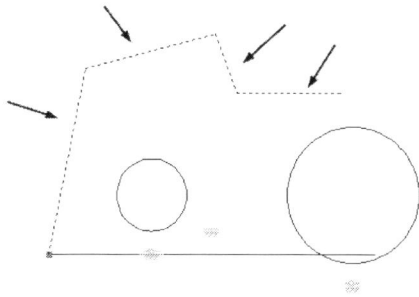

- Right-click and select **Enter**; constraints are applied to the selected objects, automatically.

- Click the **Vertical** button on the **Geometric** panel and select the line as shown below; the line will become vertical.

- Use the **Parallel** tool and make the two lines parallel, as shown below.

- Use the **Perpendicular** tool and make the two lines perpendicular, as shown below.

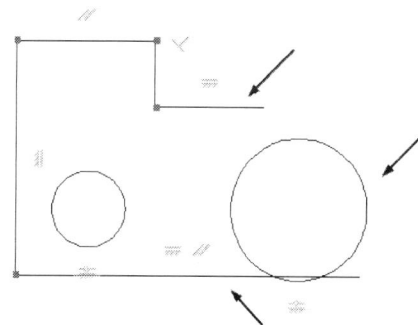

- Use the **Tangent** tool and make the two horizontal lines tangent to the large circle, as shown below.

- Click the **Coincident** button on the **Geometric** panel.
- Select the **Object** option from the command line and select the large circle.
- Select the endpoint of the lower horizontal line to make it coincident with the circle.

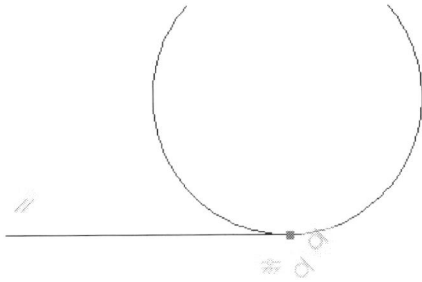

- Likewise, apply the **Coincident** constraint between the large circle and the upper horizontal line.

- Use the **Trim** tool and trim the unwanted portion of the circle.

Also, you will notice that the **Tangent** and **Coincident** constraints have been deleted. These constraints were the properties of the trimmed portion of the circle. As a result, constraints are also deleted along with the trimmed portion.

- Click the **Auto Constrain** button on the **Geometric** panel.
- Drag a window around the arc and horizontal lines.
- Right-click and select **Enter**; the **Tangent** and **Coincident** constraints are applied between the arc and the horizontal lines.

Dimensional Constraints

Dimensional constraints are applied to a drawing after applying the Geometric constraints. They are used to control the size and position of the objects in a drawing. You can apply the dimensional constraints using the tools available in the **Dimensional** panel of the **Parametric** ribbon.

- Click the inclined arrow on the **Dimensional** panel; the **Constraint Settings** dialog appears.
- On the **Constraints Settings** dialog, set **Dimension name format** to **Name**.

- Click the **OK** button.
- Click **Parametric > Dimensional > Linear** on the ribbon.

- Select the two endpoints of the lower horizontal line; the dimensional constraint is attached to the pointer.

- Place the dimension constraint and left click.

- Similarly, apply linear dimensions to other lines as shown below.

You will notice that when you try to apply dimensional constraint to the horizontal line connected to the arc, the **Dimensional Constraints** message box appears. It shows that the dimension will over-constrain the geometry. In an over-constrained geometry, there are conflicting dimensions or relations or both. Click the **Cancel** button on the **Dimensional Constraints** message box.

- Click the **Diameter** button on the **Dimensional** panel and apply the diameter dimension to the circle located on the left side.

- Click the **Radius** button on the **Dimensional** panel and apply the radial dimension to the arc.

Creating equations using the Parameters Manager

Equations are relations between the dimensional constraints. Look at the drawing given below. In this drawing, all the dimensions are controlled by the diameter of the hole. In AutoCAD, you can create this type of relations between dimensions very easily using the **Parameter Manager** palette.

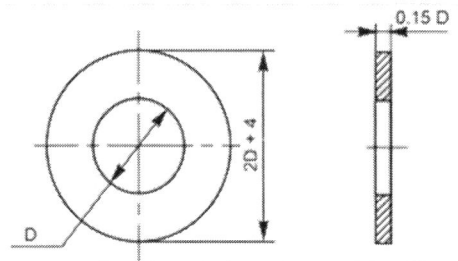

- Click the **Parameters Manager** button on the **Manage** panel; the **Parameters Manager** palette appears.

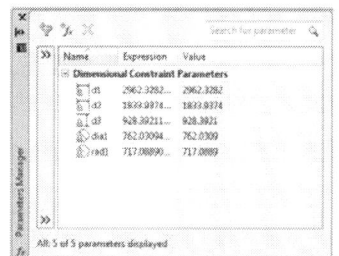

- Double-click in the box next to the **dia1** and enter **50**.

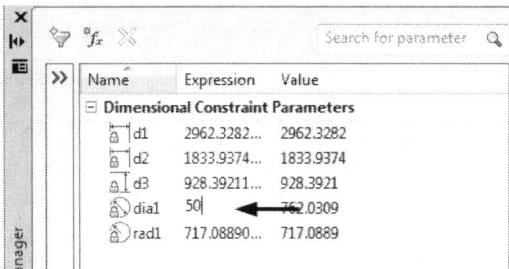

- Likewise, change the values of the other dimensions as shown below.

You will notice that the circle is placed outside the loop.

- Click **Zoom All** on the **Navigation Bar** to view the circle.

Creating Inferred Constraints

The Infer Constraints button helps you to create constraints automatically. With this button active on the status bar, you can automatically create constraints while drawing a sketch.

- On the status bar, click the **Customization** button and select **Infer Constraints** from the flyout. This adds the **Infer Constraints** button to the status bar.
- Activate the **Infer Constraints** button on the status bar.

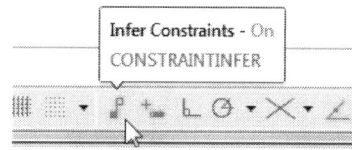

- Click the **Fillet** button on the **Modify** panel of the **Home** ribbon.
- Select the **Radius** option from the command line and enter **50** as the radius.
- Create a fillet at the lower left corner of the sketch.

You will notice that **Tangent** and **Coincident** constraints are applied, automatically.

- Click the **Concentric** button on the **Geometric** panel.
- Select the circle located outside the loop and the fillet; they both will be concentric.

- Use the **Radius** tool from the **Dimensional** panel and apply the radius dimensional constraint to the fillet.

- Open the **Parameters Manager** palette and modify the **rad2** value to **3/2*dia1**.

Name	Expression	Value
⊟ **Dimensional Constraint Parameters**		
🔒 d1	3*dia1+100	250
🔒 d2	3*dia1	150
🔒 d3	3*dia1/2	75
🔒 dia1	50	50
🔒 rad1	2*dia1	100
🔒 rad2	3/2*dia1 ◄──	75

- To hide all the Geometric Constraints, click the **Hide All** button on the **Geometric** panel.

- Similarly, click **Hide All** on the **Dimensional** panel to hide all the dimensional constraints.

- To modify the size of the drawing, change the value of **dia1** in the **Parameters Manager** window; you will notice that all the values will be changed, automatically.

- Save and close the file.

Exercise 1

In this exercise, you need to create the drawing shown in figure and apply geometric and dimensional constraints to it.

Exercise 2

In this exercise, you need create the drawing as shown below and apply geometric and dimensional constraints to it. Also, create relations between dimensions in the **Parameter Manager**.

Chapter 8: Section Views

In this chapter, you will learn to:

- **Create Section Views**
- **Set Hatch Properties**
- **Use Island Detection tools**
- **Create text in Hatching**
- **Edit Hatching**

Section Views

In this chapter, you will learn to create section views. You can create section views to display the interior portion of a component that cannot be shown clearly by means of hidden lines. This can be done by cutting the component using an imaginary plane. In a section view, section lines, or cross-hatch lines are added to indicate the surfaces that are cut by the imaginary cutting plane. In AutoCAD, you can add these section lines or cross-hatch lines using the **Hatch** tool.

The Hatch tool

The **Hatch** tool is used to generate hatch lines by clicking inside a closed area. When you click inside a closed area, a temporary closed boundary will be created using the PLINE command. The closed boundary will be filled with hatch lines, and then it will be deleted.

Example 1:

In this example, you will apply hatch lines to the drawing as shown in figure below.

- Open a new AutoCAD file.
- Create four layers with the following properties.

- Create the drawing as shown below. Do not apply dimensions.

- Select the **Hatch lines** layer from the **Layer** drop-down.

- Click **Home > Draw > Hatch** on the ribbon, or enter **H** in the command line; the **Hatch Creation** tab appears in the ribbon.

- Select **ANSI31** from the **Pattern** panel of the **Hatch Creation** ribbon tab.

- Click in the four regions of the drawing, as shown below.

- Click the **Close Hatch Creation** button on the ribbon.

Example 2:

In this example, you will create the front and section views of a crank.

- Create five layers with the following settings:

Layer	Lineweight	Linetype
Construction	0.00 mm	Continuous
Object	0.30 mm	Continuous
Centerline	0.00 mm	CENTER
Hatch lines	0.00 mm	Continuous
Cutting Plane	0.30 mm	PHANTOM

- Activate the **Construction** layer and create construction lines, as shown.

- Set the **Object** layer as current and create draw circles, as shown below.

Ø36 Ø80

Ø64

Ø120

- Switch to **Construction** layer and create construction lines as shown.

40 30

- Switch to **Object** layer and create two lines as shown.

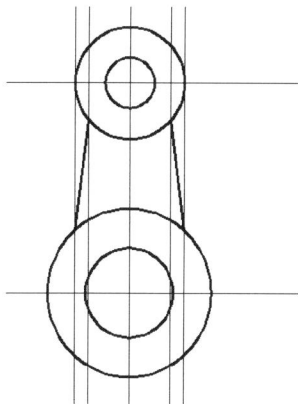

- On your own, create other objects on the front view as shown.

- On your own, create the objects of the section view, as shown below.

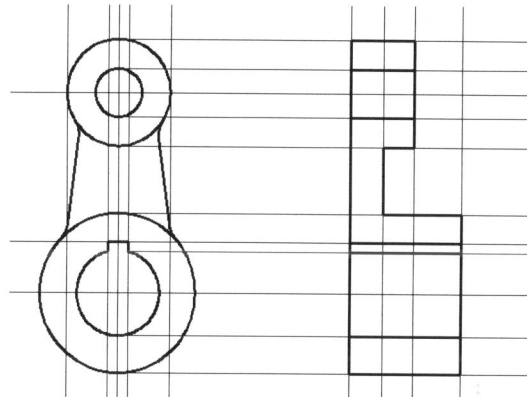

R20

16 R20

38

- On your own, create the objects of the section view, as shown below.

- Set the **Centerlines** layer as current and create center marks and centrelines.

- Set the **Cutting Plane** layer as current.
- Click the **Polyline** button on the **Draw** panel and pick a point below the front view, as shown.

- Select the **Width** option from the command line.

- Type 0 as the starting width and press ENTER.

- Type 10 as the ending width and press ENTER.

- Move the pointer horizontally toward right and enter 20.

- Again select the **Width** option from the command line.

- Set the starting and ending width to 0.

- Move the pointer horizontally and click when trace lines are displayed, as shown below.

- Move the pointer vertically up and click.

- Move the pointer toward left and click when trace lines are displayed from the endpoint of the lower horizontal line.

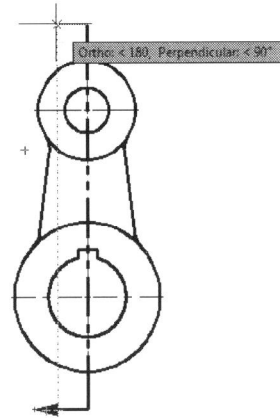

- Create another arrow by changing the width of the polyline. Deactivate the tool.

- Activate the **Hatch lines** layer.

- Type **H** in the command line and press ENTER.

- Select the **seTtings** option from the command line; the **Hatch and Gradient** dialog appears.

- Click in the **Swatch** box under the **Type and pattern** group; the **Hatch Pattern Palette** dialog appears.

- Click the **ANSI** tab, select **ANSI31** from the dialog, and then click **OK**.

- Set the **Scale** value to **2**.

- Click the **Add Pick Points** button from the **Boundaries** group and click in Region 1, Region 2 and Region 3.

- Press ENTER to create hatch lines.

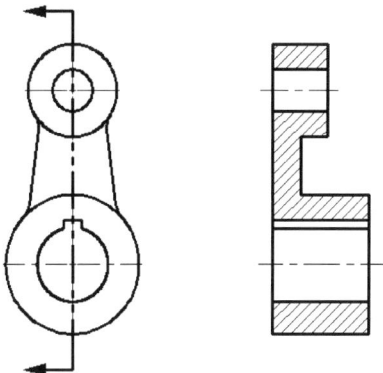

- Save the drawing as **Crank.dwg** and close.

Setting the Properties of Hatch lines

You can set the properties of the hatch lines such as angle, scale, transparency in the **Properties** panel of the **Hatch Creation** ribbon.

Example:

- Create four layers with the following settings.

Layer	Lineweight	Linetype
Construction	0.00 mm	Continuous
Object	0.30 mm	Continuous
Centerline	0.00 mm	CENTER2
Hatch lines	0.00 mm	Continuous

- Create the following drawing in different layers. Do not apply dimensions.

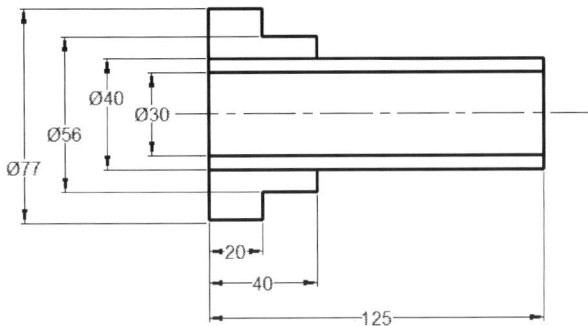

- Type **H** and press ENTER; the **Hatch Creation** tab appears in the ribbon.
- Select the **Pattern** option from the **Hatch Type** drop-down in the **Properties** panel.

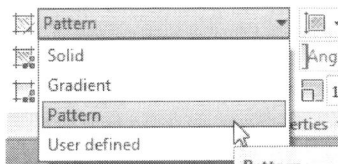

You can also select a different hatch type such as Solid, Gradient, and User defined.

- Select **ANSI31** from the **Pattern** panel.
- Select **Blue** from the **Hatch Color** drop-down.

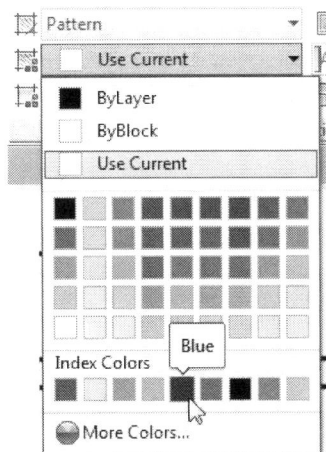

- Expand the **Properties** panel and set the **Hatch Layer Override** to **Hatch lines**.

- Click the **Pick Points** button from the **Boundaries** panel.

- Pick points in the outer areas of the drawing as shown below.

- Adjust the **Hatch Pattern Scale** to **1.5**; you will notice that the distance between the hatch lines changes.

- Click **Close Hatch Creation** button on the **Close** panel.

- Press the SPACEBAR to activate the HATCH command again.
- Change the **Hatch Angle** value to **90** in the **Properties** panel.

- Pick points in the area as shown below.

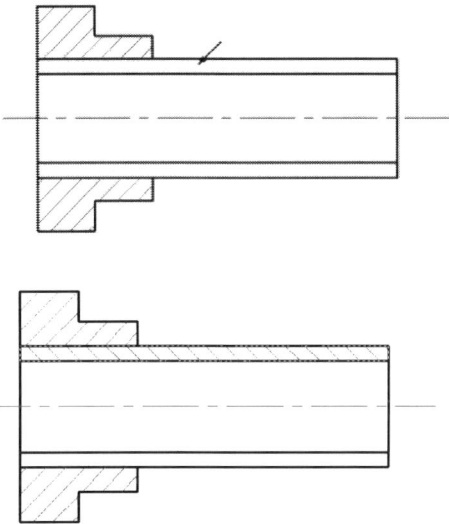

On zooming into the hatch lines, you may notice that they are not aligned properly. This is because the **Use Current Origin** button activated in the **Origin** panel. As a result, the origin of the drawing will act as the origin of the hatch pattern. However, you can change the origin of the hatch pattern.

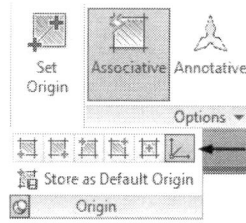

- Click **Set Origin** button on the **Origin** panel.
- Set the origin point as shown below

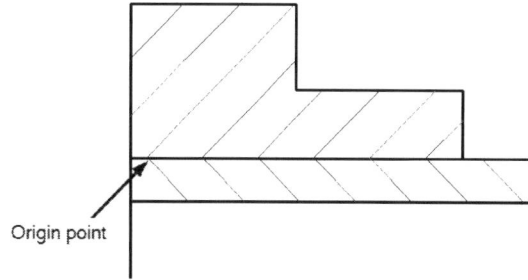

Origin point

- Click **Close Hatch Creation**.
- Activate the **Hatch** tool and click **Match Properties > Use source hatch origin** on the **Options** panel.

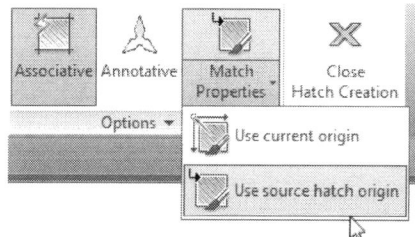

The **Match Properties** tools are used to create new hatch lines by using the properties of an existing one. The **Use source hatch origin** tool will create a new hatching using the origin of the source.

- Select the source hatching, as shown in figure.
- Pick a point in the empty area as shown below.

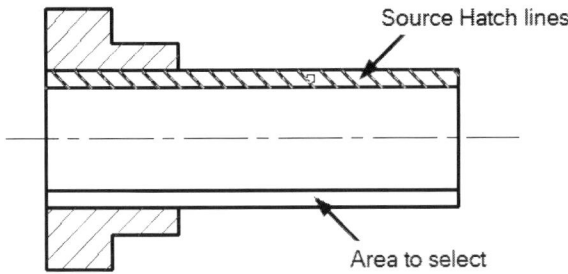

Source Hatch lines

Area to select

New hatch lines are created using the properties and origin of the source hatching.

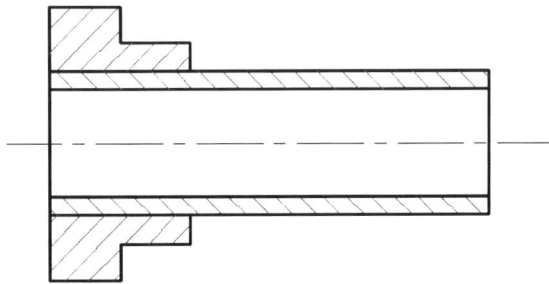

- Save and close the file.

Island Detection tools

While creating hatch lines, the island detection tools help you to detect the internal areas of a drawing.

Example:

- Create the drawing as shown below. Do not apply dimensions.

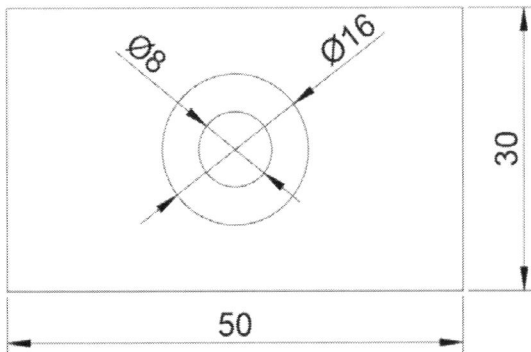

- Click **Home > Draw > Hatch** on the ribbon.

- Select **ANSI31** from the **Pattern** panel.

- Expand the **Options** panel and select the **Normal Island Detection** tool.

- Pick a point in the area outside the large circle; you will notice that the area inside the small circle is detected automatically. Also, hatch lines are created inside the small circle.

- Press **Enter**.

- Click **Undo** on the **Quick Access Toolbar**.

- Activate the **Hatch** tool and select **ANSI31** from the **Pattern** panel.

- Expand the **Options** panel and select **Outer Island Detection** option.

- Pick a point in the area outside the large circle and press ENTER; you will notice that hatch lines are created only outside the large circle. The **Outer Island Detection** tool will enable you to create hatch lines only in the outermost level of the drawing.

- Repeat the process using the **Ignore Island Detection** tool. You will notice that the internal loops are ignored while creating the hatch lines.

Text in Hatching

You can create hatching without passing through the text and dimensions.

- Create a drawing as shown in figure.

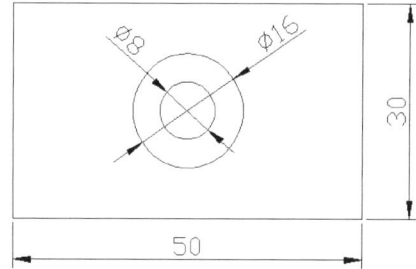

- Click **Home > Annotation > Multiline Text** on the ribbon.

- Specify the first and second corner of the text editor, as shown below.

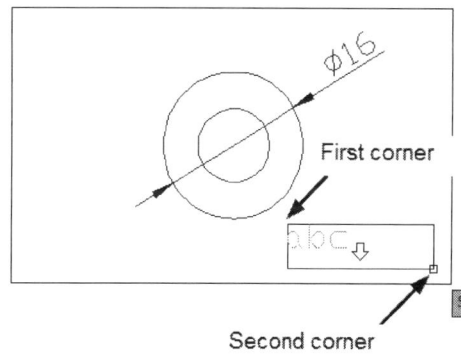

- Select **Arial** from the **Font** drop-down of the **Formatting** panel.

- Ensure that **Text Height** is set to **2.5**.

- Type **AutoCAD** in the text editor. Left-click in the empty space of the graphics window.

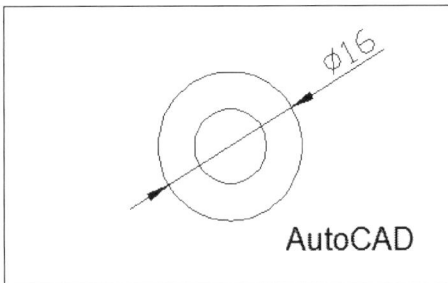

- Activate the **Hatch** tool and select the **Normal Island Detection** option from the **Options** panel.
- Pick a point in the area covered by the outside boundary and press ENTER; hatch lines are created.

  You will notice that hatch lines do not pass through the text and dimension.

Editing Hatch lines

You can edit a hatch by using the **Edit Hatch** tool or simply selecting the hatch.

- To edit a hatch using the **Edit Hatch** tool, expand the **Modify** panel of the **Home** ribbon and select the **Edit Hatch** tool.

- Select the hatch from the drawing, the **Hatch Edit** dialog appears. The options in this dialog are same as that available in the **Hatch Creation** ribbon. Expand this dialog by clicking the **More Options** button located at the bottom right corner.

The expanded dialog will display more options as shown below. The options in this dialog are same as that available in the

Hatch Creation tab.

- Edit the options in the **Hatch Edit** dialog and click the **OK** button; the hatch pattern will be modified.

Exercise 1

Create the half section view of the object shown below.

A-A

Exercise 2

In this exercise, the top, front, and right side views of an object are given. Replace the front view with a section view. The section plane is given in the top view.

Chapter 9: Blocks, Attributes and Xrefs

In this chapter, you will learn to do the following:

- **Create and insert Blocks**
- **Create Annotative Blocks**
- **Explode and purge Blocks**
- **Use the Divide tool**
- **Use the DesignCenter and Tool Palettes to insert Blocks**
- **Insert Multiple Blocks**
- **Edit Blocks**
- **Create Blocks using the Write Block tool**
- **Define and insert Attributes**
- **Work with Xrefs**

Introduction

In this chapter, you will learn to create and insert Blocks and Attributes in a drawing. You will also learn to attach external references to a drawing. The first part of this chapter deals with Blocks. A Block is a group of objects combined and saved together. You can later insert it in drawings. The second part of this chapter deals with Attributes. An Attribute is an intelligent text attached to a block. It can be any information related to the block such as description, part name, and value and so on. The third part of the chapter deals with the Xrefs (external references). External references are drawing files, images, PDF files attached to a drawing.

Creating Blocks

To create a block, first you need to create shapes using the drawing tools and use the BLOCK command to convert all the objects into a single object. The following example shows the procedure to create a block.

Example 1

- Create the drawing as shown below. Do not apply dimensions. Assume the missing dimensions.

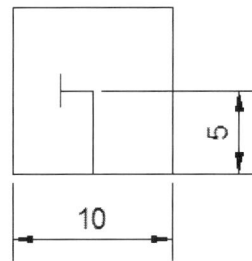

- Click **Insert > Block Definition > Create Block** on the ribbon; the **Block Definition** dialog appears.

- Enter **Target** in the **Name** field.
- Click the **Select Objects** button on the dialog. Drag a window and select all the objects of the drawing.
- Right-click to accept; the dialog appears again.

  You can choose to retain or delete the objects after defining the block. The **Retain** option under the **Objects** section retains the objects in the graphics window after defining the block. The **Convert to Block** option deletes the objects and displays the block in place of them. The **Delete** option completely deletes the objects from the graphics window.
- Select the **Delete** option under the **Objects** section.
- Click the **Pick point** button on the dialog.
- Select the midpoint of the left vertical line. The selected point will be the insertion point when you insert this block into a drawing.

You can also add description to the block in the **Description** box. In addition to that, you can set the behaviour of the block such as scalability, annotative and explode ability using the options in the **Behavior** section. The options in the **Settings** area can be used to set the units of the block and link a website or other files with the block.

- Uncheck the **Scale uniformly** option (for this example).
- Click **OK** on the dialog; the block will be created and saved in the database.

Inserting Blocks

After creating a block, you can insert it at the desired location inside the drawing using the INSERT command. The procedures to insert blocks are explained in following examples.

Example 1

- Click **Insert > Block > Insert > Target** on the ribbon.

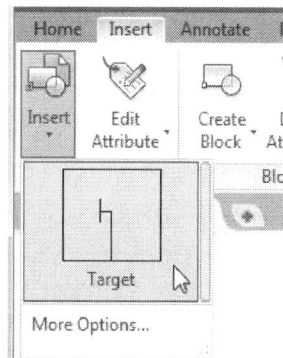

- Pick a point in the graphics window to place the block.

Example 2 (Scaling the block)

- On the ribbon, click **Insert > Block > Insert > More Options**; the **Insert** dialog appears.
- Select **Target** from the **Name** drop-down. You can use the options in the **Scale** section to scale the block. The **Uniform Scale** option can be used to scale the block uniformly. You can uncheck this option to specify the scale factor separately in the X, Y and Z boxes. If you check the **Specify On-screen**

option, the block can be scaled dynamically in the graphics window.

- Check the **Specify On-screen** option and uncheck the **Uniform Scale** option in the **Scale** section.

- Click **OK**; the block is attached to the pointer.

- Pick a point in the graphics window; the message, "Enter X scale factor, specify opposite corner, or [Corner/XYZ]:" appears in the command line. In addition, as you move the pointer, the block automatically scales.

- Type 3 and press ENTER; the message, "Enter Y scale factor <use X scale factor>:" appears.

- Type 2 as the Y scale factor and press ENTER; the block will be scaled, as shown below.

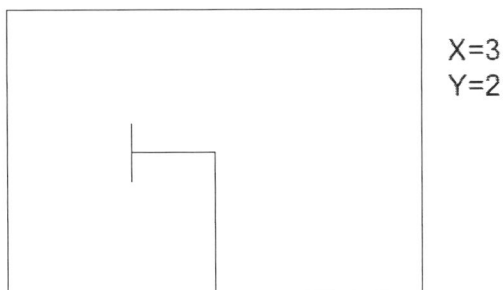

X=3
Y=2

Example 3 (Rotating the block)

- Click **Home > Block > Insert > More Options** on the ribbon; the **Insert** dialog appears.

- Select **Target** from the **Name** drop-down.

- Uncheck the **Specify On-screen** option in the **Scale** section and check the **Uniform**

scale option.

The options in the **Rotation** section are used to rotate the block. You can enter the rotation angle in the **Angle** box. You can dynamically rotate the block by selecting the **Specify On-screen** option.

- Check the **Specify On-screen** option in the **Rotation** section.

- Click **OK** and pick a point in the graphics window; the message, "Specify rotation angle <0>:" appears in the command line. As you rotate the pointer, the block also rotates. You can dynamically rotate the block and pick a point to orient the block at an angle or type a value and press ENTER to specify the angle.

- Type **45** and press **ENTER**; the block will be rotated by **45** degrees.

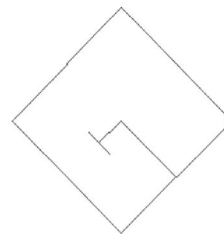

- Save and close the drawing file.

Creating Annotative Blocks

Annotative blocks possess the annotative properties. They will be scaled automatically depending upon the scale of the drawing sheet. The procedure to create and insert annotative blocks is explained in the following example.

Example:

- Create the drawing a shown in figure. Assume the missing dimensions.

- Click **Insert > Block Definition > Create Block** on the ribbon; the **Block Definition** dialog appears.
- Enter **Turbine Driver** in the **Name** field.
- Click the **Select Objects** button on the dialog. Create a window and select all the objects of the drawing. Right-click to accept the selection.
- Select the **Delete** option under the **Objects** section.
- Click the **Pick Point** button and select the midpoint of the left vertical line.

- Check the **Annotative** option under the **Behavior** section. Click the **OK** button on the dialog.
- Activate the **Automatically Add Scale to Annotative Objects** button located at the right-side of the Status Bar.

- Set the **Annotation Scale** to **1:10**.

- Click **Insert > Block > Insert > More Options**.
- Uncheck the **Specify On Screen** option under the **Rotation** section.
- Click **Name > Turbine Driver** on the **Insert** dialog.
- Click **OK**.
- Pick a point in the graphics window; the block will be inserted with the scale factor 1:10.
- Click **Zoom All** on the **Navigation Bar** to view the block.
- Change the **Annotation Scale** to **1:2**; you will notice that the block is automatically scaled to **1:2**.

Exploding Blocks

When you insert a block into a drawing, it will be considered as a single object even though it consists of numerous individual objects. At many times, you may require to break a block into its individual parts. Use the **Explode** tool to break a block into its individual objects.

- To explode a block, click **Home > Modify > Explode** on the ribbon or type EXPLODE in the command line and press ENTER.

- Select the block and press ENTER; the block will be broken into individual objects. You can select the individual objects by clicking on them.

Using the Purge tool

You can remove the unused blocks and other unwanted drawing data from the database using the **Purge** tool.

- To delete the unused data, click **Application Menu > Drawing Utilities > Purge**; the **Purge** dialog appears.

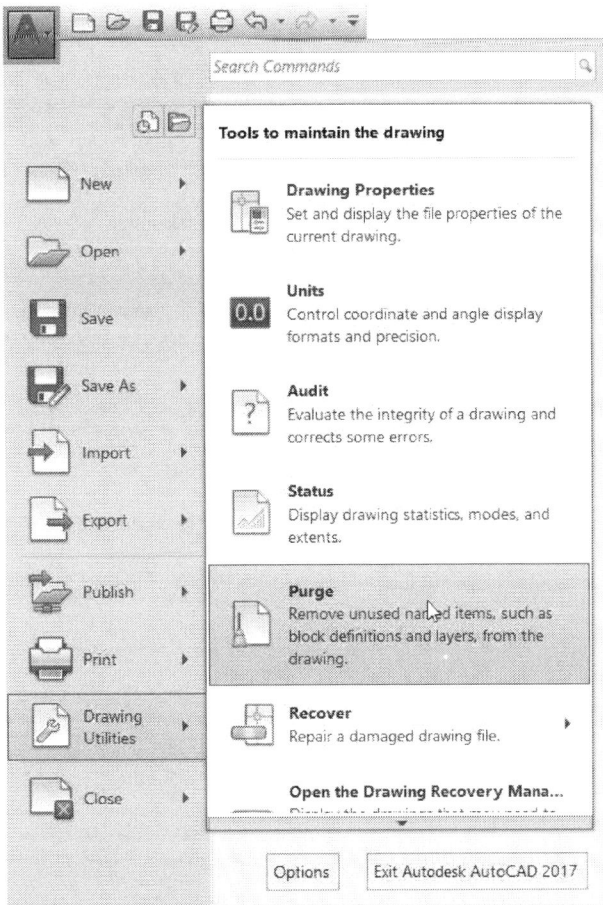

- To remove unwanted blocks from the database, expand the **Blocks** tree and select the blocks.

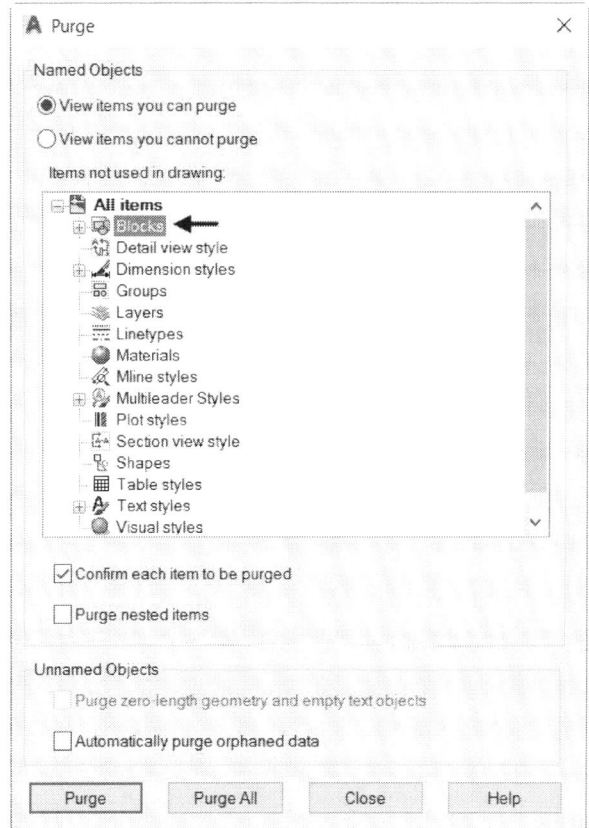

- Click the **Purge** button on the dialog; the **Purge – Confirm Purge** message box appears.

- Click **Purge this item** to delete the item from the database.

- Click **Close** on the **Purge** dialog.

Using the Divide tool

The **Divide** tool is used to place number of instances of an object equally spaced on a line segment. You can also place blocks on a line segment. The following example shows you to divide a line using the **Divide** tool.

Example:

- Create the object, as shown in figure.

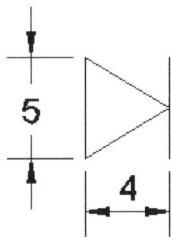

- Create a block with the name **Diode**. Specify the midpoint of the left vertical line as the base point.
- Create a line of 50 mm length and 45 degrees inclination.
- Expand the **Draw** panel in the **Home** tab and click the **Divide** button.

- Select the line segment; the message, "Enter the number of segments or [Block]:" appears.
- Select the **Block** option from the command line; the message, "Enter name of block to insert" appears.
- Type **Diode** and press ENTER; the message,

"Align block with object? [Yes/No] <Y>:" appears.

- Select the **Yes** option; the message, "Enter the number of segments:" appears.
- Type **5** and press ENTER; the line segment will be divided into five segments and four instances of blocks will be placed.

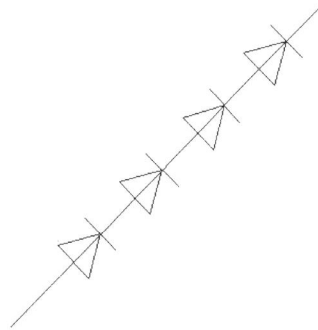

- Trim the unwanted portions, as shown below.

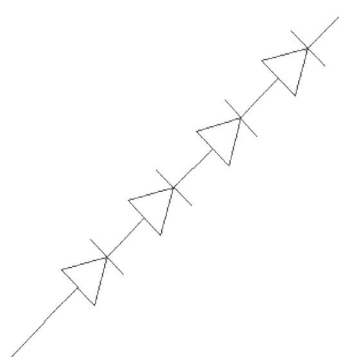

Renaming Blocks

You can rename blocks at any time. The procedure to rename blocks is discussed next.

- On Menu bar, click **Format > Rename** or type **RENAME** in the command line and press ENTER; the **Rename** dialog appears.

- In the **Rename** dialog, select **Blocks** from the **Named Objects** list.
- Select the block to be named from the **Items** list and enter a new name in the **Rename To** box.

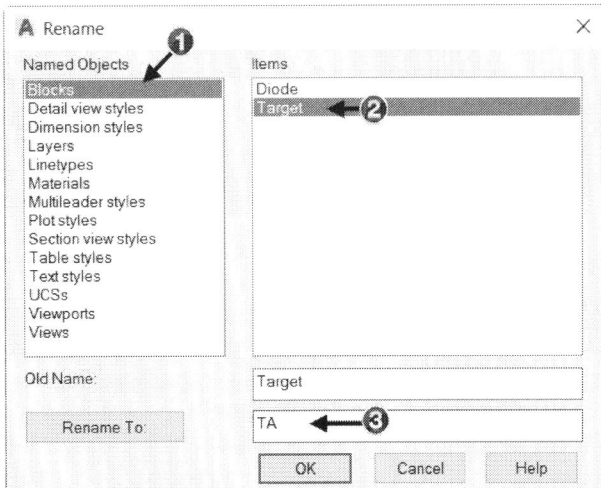

- Click **OK**; the block will be renamed.

Inserting Blocks in a Table

You can insert blocks in a table and fit inside the table cells. Note that you cannot insert Annotative blocks in a table. The following example shows you to insert a block in a table.

Example:

- Create three blocks as shown below.

INT   Lamp   Signal

- On the ribbon, click **Annotate > Tables > Table**.

- On the **Insert table** dialog, specify the values, as shown below.

- Click **OK** and define the insertion point of the table.
- Type-in values in the table cells, as shown below.

Electronic/Electrical Symbols	
Symbol	Name
	INT
	Lamp
	Signal

- Select the first cell in the **Symbol** row and right-click.
- Select **Insert > Block** from the shortcut menu; the **Insert a Block in a Table Cell** dialog appears.

Match Cell		
Remove All Property Overrides		
Data Link...		
Insert	▶	Block...
Edit Text		Field...
Manage Content ...		Formula ▶
Delete Content	▶	

- In the **Insert a Block in a Table Cell** dialog, select **INT** from the **Name** drop-down.
- Set **Overall cell alignment** to **Middle Center**.

Electronic/Electrical Symbols	
Symbol	Name
	INT
	Lamp
	Signal

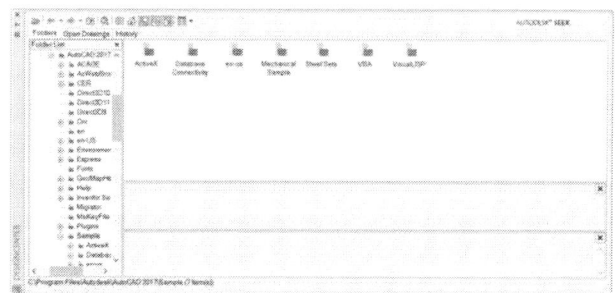

Using the DesignCenter

DesignCenter is one of the additional means by which you can insert blocks and drawings in an effective way. Using the DesignCenter, you can insert blocks created in one drawing into another drawing. You can display the DesignCenter by clicking **View > Palettes > DesignCenter** on the ribbon (or) entering **DC** in the command line. The following example shows you to insert blocks using the DesignCenter.

- Click **OK**; the **INT** symbol will be placed in the selected cell.

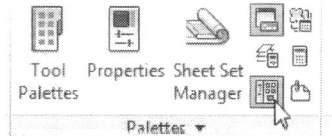

Electronic/Electrical Symbols	
Symbol	Name
	INT
	Lamp
	Signal

- Likewise, insert the other symbols in the corresponding cells.

Example:

- Open a new drawing file.
- Create the following symbols and convert them into blocks.

NPN

Ø8

5

1.5

Resistor

PNP

3

5

Capacitor

R2   Ø8

Lamp

1

8

Earth

Variable Resistor

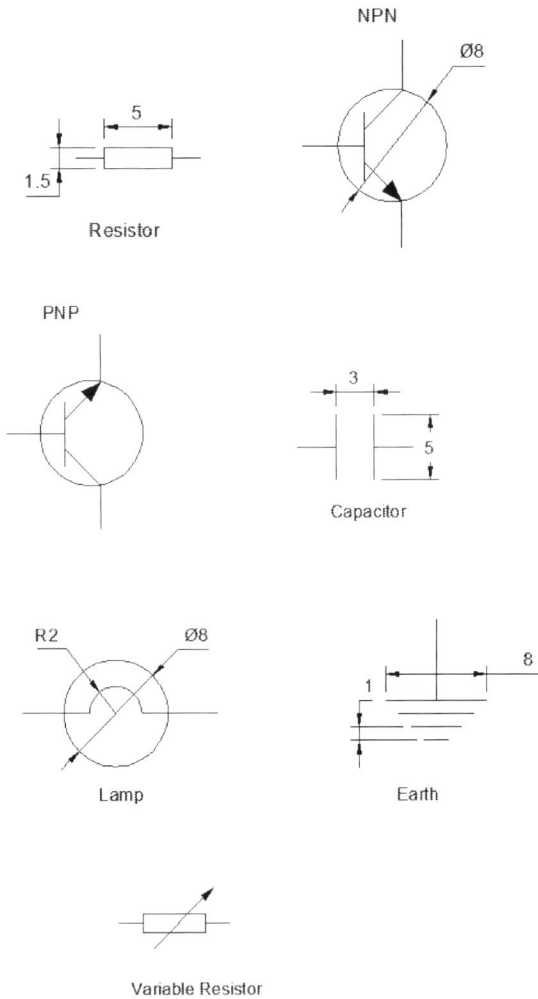

- Save the file as **Electronic Symbols.dwg**. Close the file.
- Open a new drawing file.
- Set the maximum limit of the drawing to 100,100. Click **Zoom All** on the Navigation Bar.
- Click **View > Palettes > DesignCenter** on the ribbon; the **DesignCenter** palette appears.
- In the **DesignCenter** palette, browse to the location of the **Electronic Symbols.dwg** file using the **Folder List**. Select the file and double-click on the **Blocks** icon; all the

blocks present in the file will be displayed.

- Drag and place the blocks in the graphics window.

You can also insert blocks by activating the **Insert** dialog.

- Use the **Move** and **Rotate** tools and arrange the blocks, as shown below.

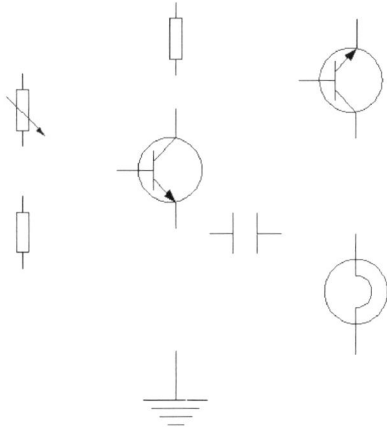

- Close the **DesignCenter** palette.

- Use the **Line** tool and complete the drawing, as shown below.

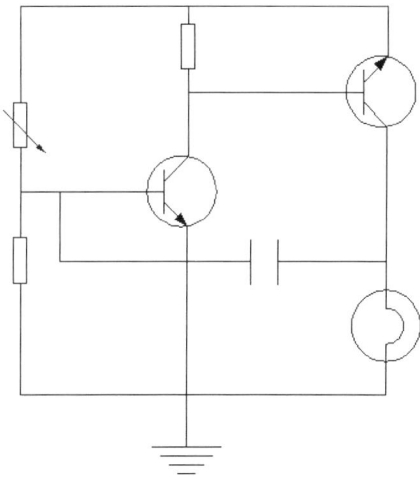

Using Tool Palettes

You can arrange blocks, dimensions, hatch patterns and other frequently used tools in Tool Palettes. Similar to the **DesignCenter** palette, you can drag and place various features from Tool Palettes into the drawing. You can display the Tool Palettes by clicking **View > Palettes > Tool Palettes** on the

ribbon or entering **TOOLPALETTES** in the command line.

There are many palettes arranged in the Tool Palettes window. You can display more palettes by clicking the lower left corner of the Tool Palettes and selecting the required palettes.

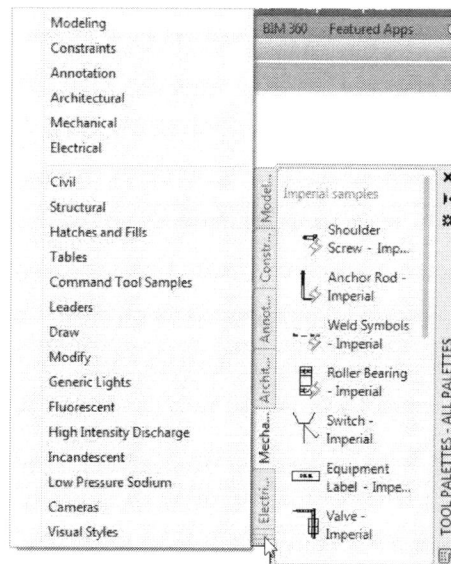

There are many blocks available in the **Architectural**, **Mechanical**, **Electrical**, Civil, and **Structural** palettes. You can drag and place blocks from these palettes. You can also right-click on a block and perform various operations using the shortcut menu displayed as shown in figure.

Creating a New Tool Palette

- Right-click on the Tool Palette and select **New Palette** from the shortcut menu; a new palette is added to Tool Palettes.
- Enter **Electronic Symbols** as the name.

You can also create a new tool palette using the **Customize** dialog.

- Right-click on Tool Palettes and select **Customize Palettes**; the **Customize** dialog appears.
- In the **Customize** dialog, right-click in the **Palettes** list and select **New Palette**.

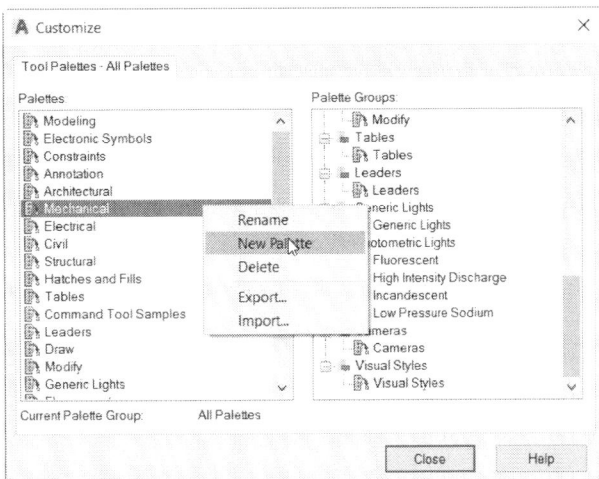

- Enter the name of the palette and click the **Close** button.

Adding Blocks to a Tool Palette

- Open the **DesignCenter** palette and select the **Electronic Symbols.dwg** file from the **Folders** list; the blocks available in the selected file appear.
- Drag the blocks from the **DesignCenter** and place them in the Tool Palette.

You can also create a new tool palette from a drawing consisting of blocks.

- In the **DesignCenter** palette, select the **Electronic symbols.dwg** file from **Folder List**.
- Right-click and select **Create Tool Palette**; a new palette will be created from the drawing file.

In the Tool Palette, you can group blocks depending on their function.

- Right-click on the **Tool Palette** and select **Add Separator**; a separator will be added.

- Right-click and select **Add Text**. Enter the name of the group.

Inserting Multiple Blocks

You can insert multiple instances of a block at a time by using the **MINSERT** command. This command is similar to the **ARRAY** command. The following example explains the procedure to insert multiple blocks at a time.

Example:

- Create a two blocks as shown below.

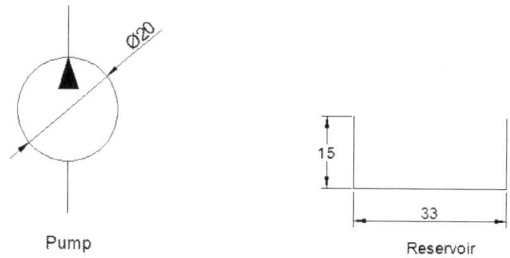

Pump   Reservoir

- Type **MINSERT** in the command line and press ENTER; the message, "Enter block name or [?]:" appears.

- Type **Pump** and press ENTER; the Pump is attached to the pointer.

- Pick a point in the graphics window.

- Enter 1 as the scale factor.

- Enter 0 as the rotation angle; the message, "Enter number of rows (---) <1>:"appears.

- Enter 1 as the row value; the message, "Enter number of columns (| | |) <1>:" appears.

- Enter 4 as the column value; the message, "Specify distance between columns (| | |):" appears.

- Type 60 and press ENTER; the pumps will be inserted as shown below.

- Likewise, insert the reservoirs and create lines as shown below.

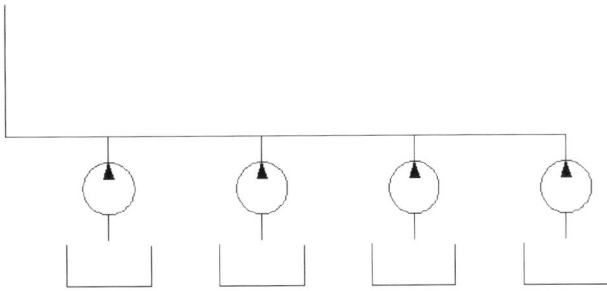

Editing Blocks

During the design process, you may need to edit blocks. You can easily edit a block using the **Block Editor** window. As you edit a block, all the instances of it will be automatically updated. The procedure to edit a block is discussed next.

- Click **Insert > Block Definition > Block Editor** on the ribbon; the **Edit Block Definition** dialog appears.

- In the **Edit Block Definition** dialog, select **Pump** from the list and click **OK**; the **Block Editor** window appears.

- Click **Home > Draw > Polyline** on the ribbon and draw a polyline, as shown below.

- Click **Close Block Editor** on the **Close** panel.

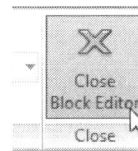

- In the **Block – Changes Not Saved** dialog, click **Save the changes to Pump**.

All the instances of the block will be updated automatically.

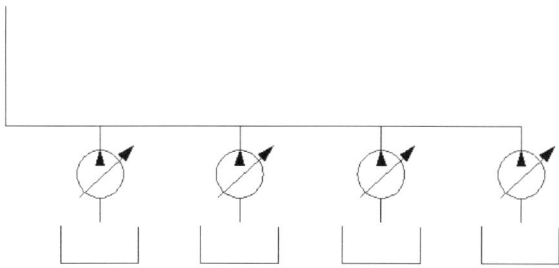

Using the Write Block tool

Using the **Write Block** tool, you can create a drawing file from a block or objects. You can later insert this drawing file as a block into another drawing. The procedure to create a drawing file using blocks is discussed in the following example.

Example:

- Start a new drawing file and create two blocks, as shown below.

Gate Valve   Orifice

- Insert the blocks and create the drawing, as shown below.

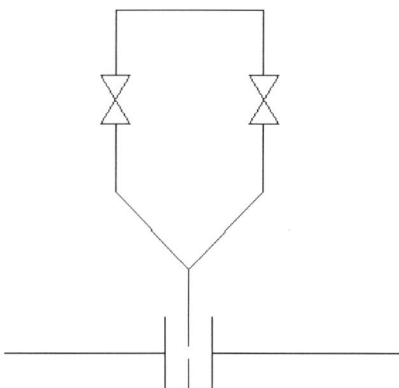

- Expand the **Block Definition** panel and select the **Set Base point** button.

- Select the endpoint of the lower horizontal line as shown.

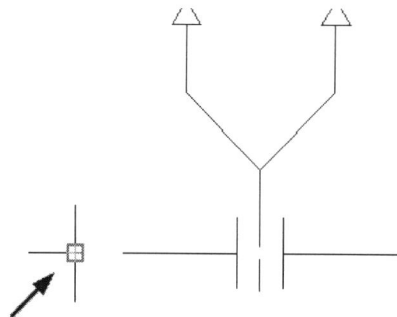

- Click **Insert > Block Definition > Write Block** on the ribbon; the **Write Block** dialog appears.

In the **Write Block** dialog, you can select three different types of sources (Block, entire drawing, or objects) to create a block. If you select the **Block** option, you can select blocks present in the drawing from the drop-down.

- Select the **Entire drawing** option.
- Specify the location of the file and name it as **Tap-in line**.

- Click the **OK** button.
- Close the drawing file.
- Open a new drawing file, and then type **I** in the command line and press ENTER; the **Insert** dialog appears.
- Click the **Browse** button and go to the location of the **Tap-in Line** file.
- Select **Tap-in line** from the **Name** drop-down and click **OK**.

- Pick a point in the graphics window to insert the block.
- Press Enter to accept 0 as the angle of rotation.

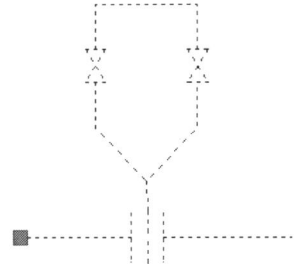

Defining Attributes

An attribute is a line of text attached to a block. It may contain any type of information related to a block. For example, the following image shows a Compressor symbol with an equipment tag. The procedure to create an attribute is discussed in the following example.

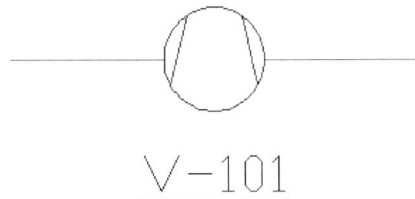

Example 1:

- Open a new drawing file.
- Create the symbols, as shown below.

R55

69

89

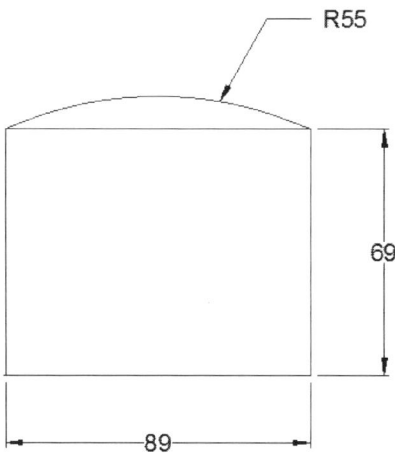

- Click **Insert > Block Definition > Define Attributes** on the ribbon; the **Attribute Definition** dialog appears.

- The options in the **Mode** group of the **Attribute Definition** dialog define the display mode of the attribute. If you check the **Invisible** option, the attribute will be invisible. The **Constant** option makes the value of the attribute constant. You cannot change the value. The **Verify** option prompts

you to verify after you enter a value. The **Preset** option can be used to set a predefined value for the attribute. The **Lock position** option fixes the position of the attribute to a selected point. The **Multiple lines** option allows typing the attribute value in a single or multiple lines.

- Ensure that the **Lock position** option is selected.

The options in the **Attribute** group define the values of the attribute. The **Tag** box is used to enter the label of the attribute. For example, if you want to create an attribute called RESISTANCE, you must type **Resistance** in the **Tag** box. The **Prompt** box defines the prompt message that appears after placing the block. The **Default** box defines the default value of the attribute.

- In the **Attribute Definition** dialog, enter **Valvetag** in the **Tag** box.

The **Text Settings** options define the display properties of the text such as style, height and so on. Observe the other options in this dialog. Most of them are self-explanatory.

- Enter **5** in the **Text Height** box.
- Set the **Justification** to **Middle** and click **OK.**
- Specify the location of the attribute as shown below.

VALVETAG

VALVETAG

EQUIPMENTTAG

Insertion point

- Click the **Create Block** button on the **Block Definition** panel; the **Block Definition** dialog appears.
- On the dialog, click the **Select objects** button.
- Drag a window, select the control valve symbol, and attribute. Press ENTER.
- Select the **Delete** option from the **Objects** group.
- Click the **Pick Point** button under the **Base point** group and select the point, as shown below.

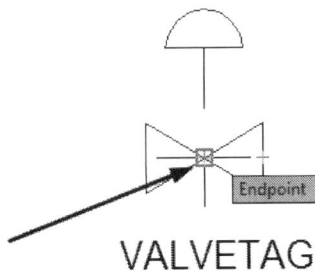

VALVETAG

- Enter **Control Valve** in the **Name** box and click **OK**.
- Likewise, create **Equipmenttag** attribute and place inside the tank symbol.
- Create a block and name it as **Tank**.

- Also, create a block of the nozzle symbol and name it **Nozzle**.

Insertion point

Inserting Attributed Blocks

You can use the INSERT command to insert the attributed blocks into a drawing. The procedure to insert attributed blocks is discussed next.

- On the ribbon, click **Insert > Block > Insert > Tank**.
- Click in the graphics window to define the insertion point. The **Edit Attributes** dialog appears.
- Enter **TK-001** in the **EQUIPMENTTAG** field and click **OK**; the block will be placed along with the attribute.

- Likewise, place control valves, as shown below.

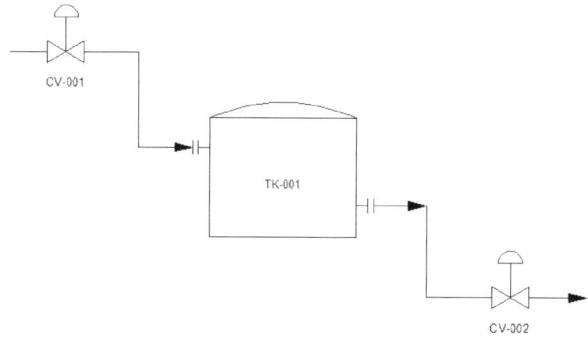

- Place the nozzles on the tank, as shown below.

- Use the **Polyline** tool and connect the control valves and tank.

Working with External references

In AutoCAD, you can attach a drawing file, image or pdf file to another drawing. These attachments are called External References (Xrefs). They are dynamic in nature and update automatically when changes are made to them. In the following example, you will learn to attach drawing files to a drawing.

Example 1:

- Create the drawing shown below.

- Type **BASE** in the command line and press ENTER.
- Select the midpoint of the vertical line as the base point.

- Save the drawing as **Crank pin.dwg**

- Create another drawing as shown below.

- Use the **Set Base Point** tool and specify the base point, as shown below.

- Save the drawing as **Nut.dwg** and close it.

- Open the **Crank.dwg** file created in Chapter 8.

- Click **Insert > Reference > Attach** on the ribbon; the **Select Reference file** dialog appears.

- Browse to the location of the **Crankpin.dwg**

and double-click on it; the **Attach External Reference** dialog appears.

Some of the options available in this dialog are similar to that in the **Insert** dialog, such as the insertion point, scale, and rotation angle of the external reference.

- Accept the default settings in this dialog and click **OK**; the crank pin will be attached to the pointer.

- Select the point on the section view as shown below.

- z

- In the **External References** palette, open the **Attach** drop-down and select the **Attach DWG** option; the **Select References file** dialog appears.

- Browse to the location of the **Nut.dwg** and double-click on it; the **Attach External Reference** dialog appears.
- In the **Attach External Reference** dialog, enter **90** in the **Angle** box under the **Rotation** group and click **OK**.
- Select the insertion point on the section view as shown below.

Fading an Xref

You can change the fading of Xref by using the Xref fading slider available in the expanded **Reference** panel.

- Expand the **Reference** panel of the **Insert** ribbon and use the **Xref fading** slider to adjust the fading.

Clipping External References

You can hide the unwanted portion of an external reference by using the **Clip** tool.

- Click **Insert > Reference > Clip** on the ribbon; the message, "Select Object to clip" appears in the command line.

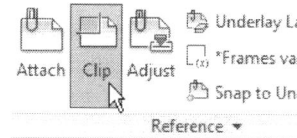

- Select the **Nut.dwg** from the graphics window.
- Select the **New boundary** option from the command line.
- Select the **Rectangular** option from the command line.
- Draw a rectangle as shown below; only the front view of the nut is visible and the top view is hidden. Also, the clipping frame is visible.

- To hide the clipping frame, type XCLIPFRAME in the command line

- Type 0 and press ENTER.
- You can also hide the frame by clicking
  Modify > Object > External reference >
  Frame on the Menu Bar.

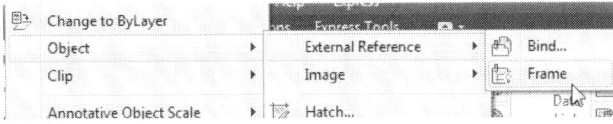

- Attach another instance of the **Nut.dwg** file.
- Use the **Rotate** and **Move** tools to position
  the top view as shown below.

- Use the **Clip** tool and clip the Xref.

Editing the External References

AutoCAD allows you to edit the external references
in the file to which they are attached. You can also

edit them by opening their drawing file. The
procedure to edit an external reference is discussed
next.

- To edit an external reference, expand the
  Reference panel and click the **Edit**
  Reference button.

- Select **Nut** from the drawing; the **Reference**
  Edit dialog appears
- Click **OK** to get into the reference editing
  mode.
- In the drawing, you will notice that the
  centerlines of the nut are overlapping on the
  centerlines of the crank. Delete the
  centerlines and center marks of the nut.
- Click **Save changes** on the **Edit Reference**
  panel; the **AutoCAD** message box appears.

- Click **OK**.

Adding Balloons

- Click **Annotate > Leader > Multileader Style Manager** (inclined arrow) button on the ribbon; the **Multileader Style Manager** dialog appears.

- Click the **New** button on the dialog.

- In the **Create New Multileader Style** dialog, enter **Balloon Callout** in the **New Style name** box and click **Continue**.

- In the **Modify Multileader Style** dialog, click the **Content** tab and set the **Multileader type** to **Block**.

- Under **Block Options**, set the **Source block** to **Circle**.

- Set the **Scale** to **3**.

- Click **Leader Format** tab and set the Arrowhead **Size** to 8.

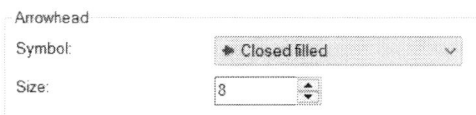

- Click **OK** and set the **Balloon Callout** style as current.

- Click **Close**.

- Click **Annotate > Leader > Multileader** on the ribbon.

- Click the down arrow next to the **Polar Tracking** icon on the status bar and select **45** from the menu. Activate the **Polar Tracking**.

- Select a point on the section view of the crank.

- Move the pointer along the polar trace lines and click; the **Edit Attributes** dialog appears.

- In the **Edit Attributes** dialog, enter 1 in the **Enter tag number** field.

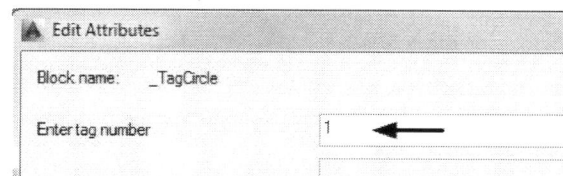

- Click **OK**; the balloon will be created.

- Likewise, create other balloons.

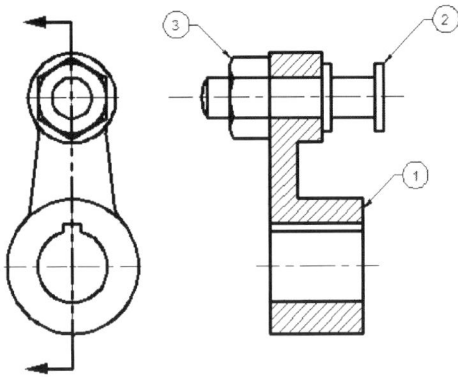

Creating Part List

- Click **Annotate > Table > Table Style** on the ribbon; the **Table Style** dialog appears.

- In the **Table Style** dialog, click the **New** button; the **Create New Table Style** dialog appears,

- In the **Create New Table Style** dialog, enter **Part List** in the **Name** box. Click **Continue**; the **New Table Style** dialog appears.

- Click the **Text** tab and set the **Text height** to **10**.

- Select the **Header** option from the **Cell Styles** drop-down and set the **Text height** to **10**.

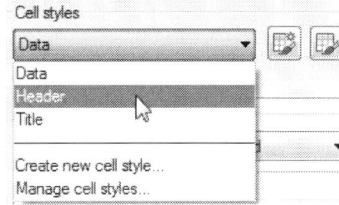

- Click **OK**.

- In the **Table Style** dialog, select the **Part List** style and click **Set current**.

- Close the dialog.

- Click the **Table** button on the **Tables** panel; the **Insert table** dialog appears.

- Ensure that the **Table style** is set to **Part List**.

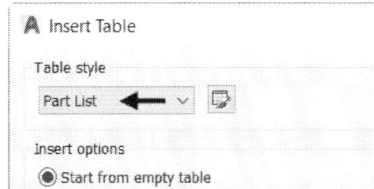

- Under the **Set cell Styles** group, set the **First row cell style** to **Header**.

- Set the **Second row cell style** and **All other row cell styles** to **Data**.

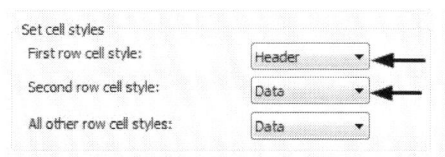

- Set the number of **Columns** to **4** and **Column width** to **65**.

- Set the Data rows and Row height to 2 and 1, respectively.

- Click **OK** and place the table at the lower

right corner of the graphics window.

- Enter **PART No., NAME, MATERIAL, QTY** in the first row of the **Part list** table. Use the **TAB** key to navigate between the cells.

- Click **Close Text Editor** button on the ribbon.

- Click on anyone of the edges of the table; you will notice that grips are displayed on it. You can edit the table using these grips.

- Click and drag the square grip below the MATERIAL cell; the width of the cell will be changed.

- Click and drag the triangular grip located at the bottom left corner of the table; the height of the rows will be increased uniformly.

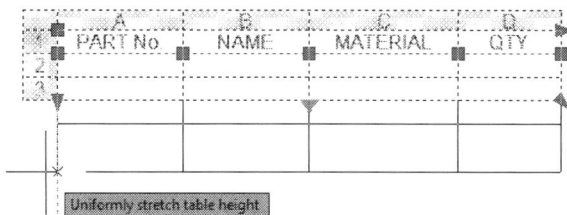

- Click in the second cell of the first column; the **Table Cell** ribbon appears. You can use this ribbon to modify the properties of the table cell.

- Click the **Insert Below** button on the **Rows** panel; a new row will be added to the cell.

- Click in the top left corner cell of the table.

- Press and hold the SHIFT key and click in the lower right corner of the table; all the cells in the table will be selected.

- In the **Table Cell** ribbon, click **Cell Styles > Alignment > Middle Center**; the data in all the cells will appear in the middle center of the cells.

- Double-click in the cell below the **PART No.;** the text editor will be activated.
- Enter the following data in the cells. Use the TAB to navigate between the cells.

PART No.	NAME	MATERIAL	QTY
1	Crank	Forged Steel	1
2	Crank pin	45C	1
3	Nut	MS	1

Exercise

Chapter 10: Layouts & Annotative Objects

In this chapter, you will learn to do the following:

- **Create Layouts**
- **Specify the Paper space settings**
- **Create Viewports in Paper space**
- **Change Layer properties in Viewports**
- **Create Title Block on the layout**
- **Use Annotative objects in Viewports**

Drawing Layouts

There are two workspaces in AutoCAD: The Model space and the Paper space. In the Model space, you create 2D drawings and 3D models. You can even plot drawings from the model space. However, it is difficult to plot drawings at a scale or if a drawing consists of multiple views arranged at different scales. For this purpose, we use Layouts or paper space. In Layouts or paper space, you can work on notes and annotations and perform the plotting or publishing operations. In Layouts, you can arrange a single view or multiple views of a drawing or multiple drawings by using Viewports. These viewports display drawings at specific scales on layouts. They are mainly rectangular in shape but you can also create circular and polygonal viewports. In this chapter, you will learn about viewports and various annotative objects.

Working with Layouts

Layouts represent the conventional drawing sheet. They are created to plot a drawing on a paper or in electronic form. A drawing can have multiple layouts to print in different sheet formats. By default, there are two layouts available: Layout 1 and Layout 2. You can also create new layouts by clicking the plus (+) symbol next to the layout. Next, select **New layout** from the shortcut menu. In the following example, you will create two layouts, one representing the ISO A1 (841 X 594) sheet and another representing the ISO A4 (210 X 297) sheet.

Example:

- Open a new drawing file.
- Create layers with the following settings:

Layer	Linetype	Lineweight
Construction	Continuous	Default
Object Lines	Continuous	0.6mm
Hidden Lines	Hidden	0.3 mm
Center Lines	CENTER	Default
Dimensions	Continuous	Default
Title Block	Continuous	1.2mm
Viewport	Continuous	Default

- Create the drawing, as shown next. Do not add dimensions.

- Click the **Layout 1** tab at the bottom of the graphics window.

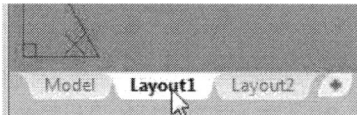

You will notice that a white paper is displayed with the viewport created, automatically. The components of a layout are shown in figure below.

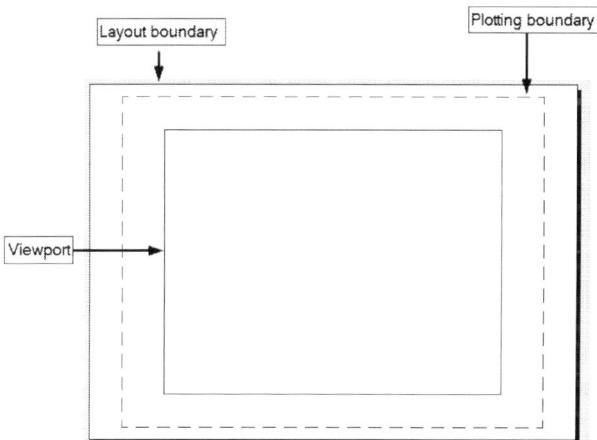

- Click **Output > Plot > Page Setup Manager** on the ribbon; the **Page Setup Manager** dialog appears.

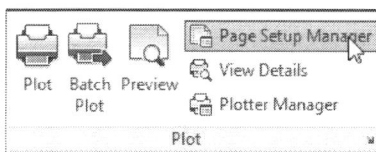

- In the **Page Setup Manager** dialog, click the **Modify** button; the **Page Setup –Layout1**

dialog appears.

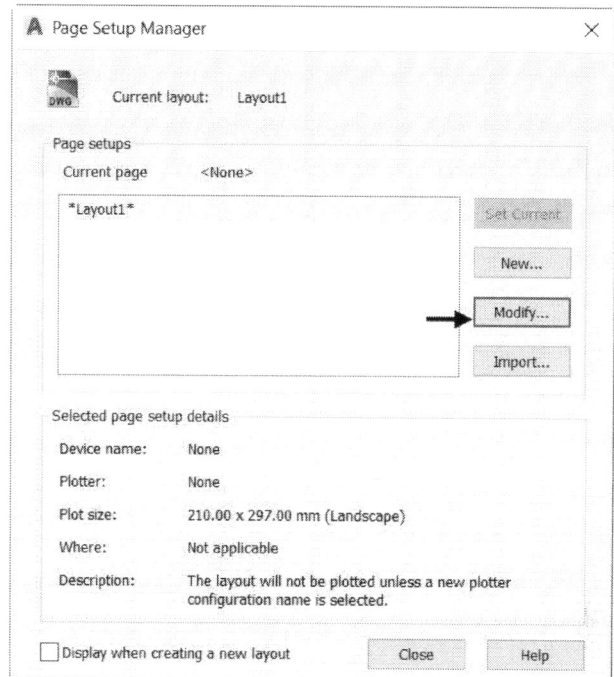

- In the **Page Setup** dialog, select **DWG to PDF.pc3** from the **Name** drop-down under the **Printer/Plotter** group.
- Set the **Plot Style table** to **acad.stb**.
- Set the **Paper size** to **ISO A1 (841.00 x 594.00 MM)**. Set the **Plot scale** to **1:1**.

- Click **OK**, and then click **Close** on the **Page Setup Manager** dialog.
- Click the **Layout2** tab below the graphics window.
- Double-click on the **Layout1** tab and enter **ISO A1**; the **Layout1** is renamed.
- Similarly, rename the **Layout2** to **ISO A2**.
- Click **Layout > Layout > Page Setup** on the ribbon; the **Page Setup Manager** dialog appears.
- Select **ISO A4** from the list.
- Click the **Modify** button on the dialog.
- In the **Page Setup** dialog, select the **DWG to PDF.pc3** plotter and select **acad.stb** from the **Plot style table** drop-down.
- Set the **Paper size** to **ISO A4 (210 x 297 MM)** and **Scale** to **1:1**.
- Set **Drawing Orientation** as **Portrait** and click **OK**; you will notice that the size of the Layout is changed to A4 size.
- Close the **Page Setup Manager** dialog.

Creating Viewports in the Paper space

The viewports that exist in the paper space are called floating viewports. This is because you can position them anywhere in the layout and modify their shape size with respect to the layout.

Creating a Viewport in the ISO A4 layout

- Open the **ISO A4** layout, if not already open.
- Select the default viewport that exists in the **ISO A4** layout.

- Press the DELETE key; the viewport will be deleted.
- Click **Layout > Layout Viewports > Rectangular** on the ribbon.

- Create the rectangular viewport by picking the first and second corner points, as shown in figure.

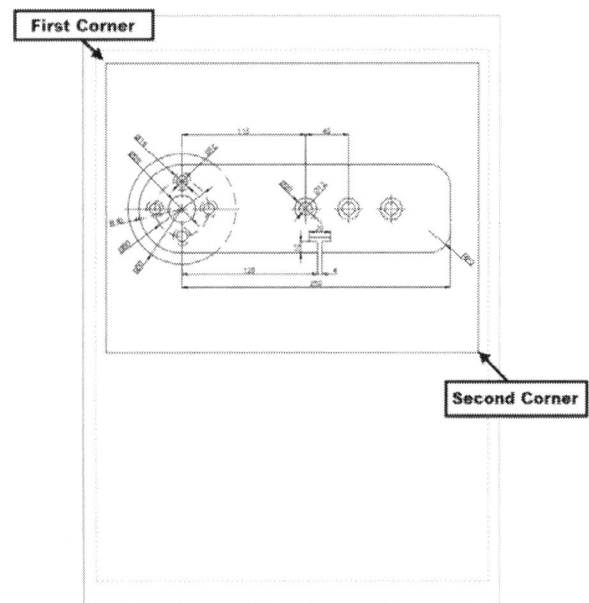

- Click the **PAPER** button on the status bar; the model space inside the viewport will be activated. In addition, the viewport frame will become thicker when you are in model space.

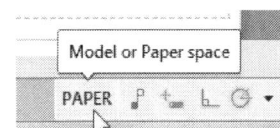

- Click the **Viewport Scale** button and select **1:2** from the menu; the drawing will be zoomed out.

- Use the **Pan** tool and position the drawing in the center of the viewport.
- After fitting the drawing inside the viewport, you can lock the position by clicking the **Lock/Unlock Viewport** button on the status bar.

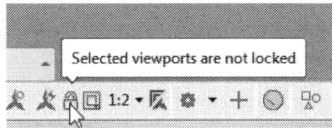

After locking the viewport, you cannot change the scale or position of the drawing.

- Click the **MODEL** button on the status bar to switch back to paper space.

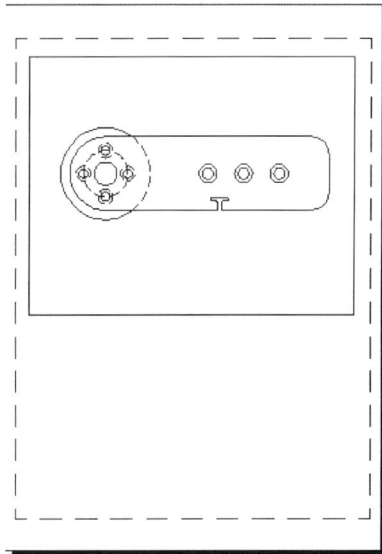

- Select the viewport frame and modify the viewport using the grips, as shown below.

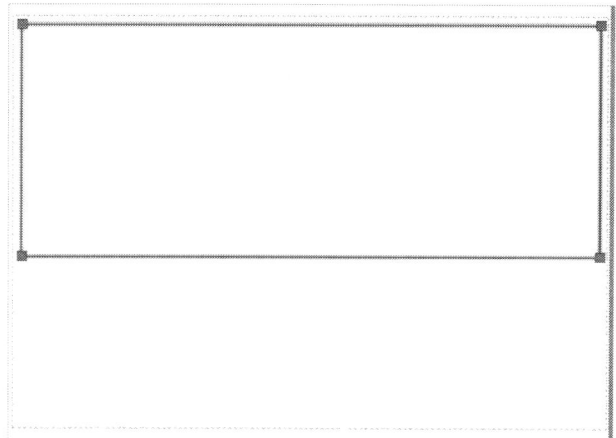

- Double-click inside the viewport to switch to the model space.
- Use the **Zoom** and **Pan** tools and drag the drawing to the center of the viewport.
- Click the **Viewport Scale** button and select the **2:1** from the menu.
- Use the **Pan** tool and position the drawing, as shown in figure.
- Click the **Lock/Unlock Viewport** button on the status bar.
- Double-click outside the viewport to switch to the paper space.
- Use the **Circle** tool and create a 180 mm diameter circle on the layout, as shown below.

Creating Viewports in the ISO A1 layout

- Click the **ISO A1** tab below the graphics window.

- Click **Layout > Layout Viewports > Viewport drop-down > Object** on the ribbon.

- Select the circle from the layout; it will be converted into a viewport.

- Double-click in the circular viewport to switch to the model space.
- Click the **Viewport Scale** button on the status bar and select **4:1** from the menu; the drawing will be zoomed in to its center.
- Use the **Pan** tool and adjust the drawing, as shown below.

- Click the **Lock** button on the **Layout Viewports** panel.

- Select the circular viewport and press ENTER; the drawing inside the viewport will be locked. Now, you cannot zoom or pan the drawing.

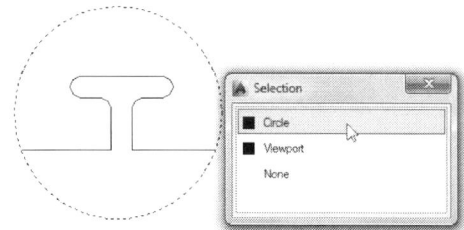

- Click **Output > Plot > Preview** on the ribbon; the plot preview will be displayed. You will notice that the viewport frames are also displayed in the preview.

- Press ESC to close the preview window.

To hide viewport frames while plotting a drawing, follow the steps given below.

- Type **LA** in the command line to open the **Layer Properties Manager**.
- In the **Layer Properties Manager**, create a new layer called **Hide Viewports** and make it current.
- Deactivate the plotter symbol 🖨 under the **Plot** column of the **Hide Viewports** layer; the object on this layer will not be plotted.
- Close the **Layer Properties Manager**.
- Click the **Home** tab on the ribbon and expand the **Layers** panel.
- Click the **Change to Current Layer** button on the **Layers** panel.

- Select the viewports in the **ISO A1** layout and press ENTER; the viewport frames will become unplottable. To check this, click the **Preview** button on the **Plot** panel; the plot preview will be displayed as shown below.

- Close the preview window.

Changing the Layer Properties in Viewports

The layer properties in viewports are not related to the layer properties in model space. You can change the layer properties in viewports without any effect in the model space.

- Double-click inside the larger viewport to activate the model space.
- Type **LA** in the command line to open the **Layer Properties Manager**.
- In the **Layer Properties Manager**, click the icon in the **VP Freeze** 🔲 column of the **Hidden** layer; the hidden lines will disappear in the viewport, as shown below.

- Double-click outside the viewport to switch to paper space.
- Click the **Model** tab below the graphics window; you will notice that the hidden lines are retained in the model space.

Creating the Title Block on the Layout

You can draw objects on layouts to create a title block, borders and viewports. However, it is not recommended to draw the actual drawing on layouts. You can also create dimensions on layouts.

Example1:

- Click the **ISO A1** layout tab.
- Set the **Title Block** layer as current.

- Click the **Rectangle** button on the **Draw** panel.
- Pick a point at the lower right corner of the layout.
- Select the **Dimensions** option from the command line.
- Specify the length of the rectangle as **820** and width as **550**.
- Click in the upper area of the layout; a rectangular border will be created.
- Create a title block at the lower right corner, as shown below.

- Create attributes and place them inside the title, as shown below.

- Use the **Create Block** tool and convert it into a block.
- Use the **Insert** tool and insert it at the lower right corner of the layout.
- Save the drawing file as **Viewports-Example.dwg**.

Working with Annotative Dimensions

In AutoCAD, you create drawings at their actual size. However, when you scale a drawing to fit inside a viewport, the size of the dimensions will not be scaled properly. For example, in the following figure, the first viewport is scaled to 1:2 and the second viewport is scaled to 1:1. The dimensions in the first viewport appear much smaller. You can fix this problem by applying the Annotative property to dimensions.

- Open the **Viewports-Example.dwg**, if not already opened.
- Set the **Dimensions** layer as current.
- Type **D** in the command line and press ENTER.
- In the **Dimension Style Manager**, click the **New** button.

- In the **Create New Dimension Style** dialog, enter **New style name** as **Dim_Anno** and select the **Annotative** check box. Click **Continue**.

- Set the following settings in the **New Dimension Style** dialog.

  Lines tab: Offset from origin-1.25

  Symbols and Arrows tab: Arrow size -2.5, Center Marks-Line.

  Text tab: Text height – 2.5, Text placement - Vertical-Centered, Text alignment - Horizontal

  Primary Units tab: Units Format – Decimal, Precision – 0, Decimal separator – '.'period

- In the **Fit** tab, ensure that the **Annotative** check box is selected.

- Click **OK** on the **New Dimension Style** dialog; you will notice that the **Dim_Anno** style is listed in the **Dimension Style Manager**. Also, the annotation symbol is displayed next to it. This indicates that all dimensions created using this style will have annotative property. Click on the **Close** button.

- Activate the **Dimension** tool and set the Annotation Scale to **1:1**. Click **OK**.

- Create a linear dimension as shown below.

- Activate **Automatically add scales to annotative objects when the annotation scale changes** on the status bar.

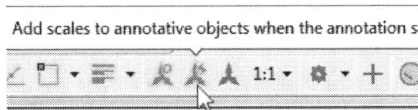

- Set the **Annotation Scale** to **1:2**; the size of the dimension will automatically increase by two times.

Example 2:

- Ensure that the **Annotation Scale** is set to **1:2** and create another linear dimension as shown in figure.

- Click the **ISO A4** layout in which the viewport scale is set to 1:2; you will notice that the dimensions are scaled with respect to the viewport.

- Click the **ISO A1** layout; you will notice that the dimensions are not displayed in the 2:1 viewport. To display dimensions in the 2:1 viewport, you need to add 2:1 scale to dimensions.

- Click the **Model** tab below the graphics window to switch to the model space.
- Click **Annotate > Annotation Scaling > Add/Delete Scales** on the ribbon.

- Select the dimensions from the graphics window and right-click; the **Annotation Object Scale** dialog appears. In this dialog, the **Object Scale list** shows the scales applied to the selected dimensions. You need to add 2:1 scale to the dimensions so that they will be visible in the 2:1 viewport.

- To add a new scale to the dimensions, click

the **Add** button; the **Add Scales to Object** dialog appears.

- Select the **2:1** scale from the list and click **OK**; the scale will be added to **Object Scale list**.
- Click **OK** on the **Annotation Object Scale** dialog.
- Click the **ISO A1** layout; the dimensions are displayed in both 2:1 and 1:2 viewports.

- Similarly, create other dimensions as shown below. Add 2:1 and 1:2 scales to dimensions and check the drawing in two different layouts.

Scaling Hatches relative to Viewports

While working in layouts, you may also need to scale the hatch with respect to the viewport scale. The following figure shows a drawing in two different viewports 1:2 and 1:1. The hatch in the left viewport is smaller than that in right side viewport. You can correct this problem by using the **Relative to Paper Space** option.

- Double-click inside a viewport; the model space will be activated.
- Select the hatch patterns from the drawing; the **Hatch Editor** tab appears.
- In the **Hatch Editor** tab, expand the **Properties** panel and select the **Relative to Paper Space** button.

- Click the **Close Hatch Editor** button; you will notice that the hatch will be scaled with respect to the viewport scale. Double-click outside the viewport to switch to the paper space.

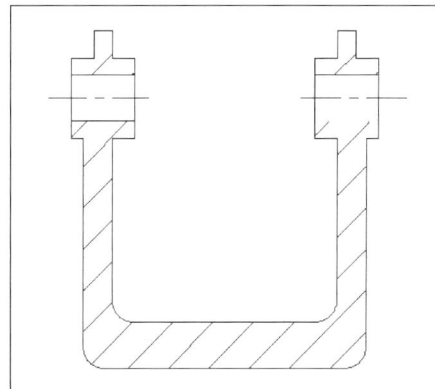

Working with Annotative Text

Annotative property can also be assigned to text. The annotative text will be scaled with respect to the viewport scale.

- Open the **Viewports-Example.dwg**, if not already opened.
- Click **Annotate > Text > Text Style** on the ribbon; the **Text Style** dialog appears.

- Click the **New** button on the **Text Style** dialog; the **New Text Style** dialog appears.

- Enter **Text_Anno** as the **Style name** and click **OK**.

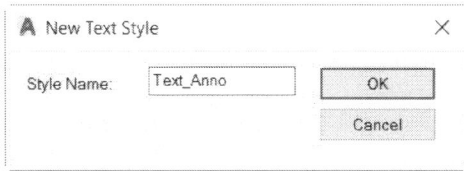

- Select the **Text_Anno** style from the **Styles** list.

- Set **Font Name** to **Arial** and select the **Annotative** check box.

- Set **Paper Text Height** to **2.5** and **Width Factor** to **1**.

- Click **Apply** and **Close**.

- Select **1:1** from the **Viewport Scale** menus at the status bar.

- Click **Annotate > Text > Multiline Text** on the ribbon.

- Specify the first corner of the text editor by picking an arbitrary point.

- Select the **Justify** option from the command line; the command line displays:

```
Specify opposite corner or [Height/Justify/Line spacing/Rotation/St
A - MTEXT Enter justification [TL TC TR ML MC MR BL BC BR] <TL>:
```

- Select the **MC** option from the command line.

- Move the pointer toward right and specify the second corner of the text editor.

- Type **All dimensions are in mm** and click the **Close Text Editor** button on the **Close** panel.

- Move the text and place at the bottom left corner of the drawing as shown below. You can also add a frame to the text. Right-click on it and select **Properties**. On the **Properties** palette, under the **Text** section, set **Text Frame** to **Yes**.

- View the drawing in the **ISO A4** layout; you will notice that the text is not displayed. This is because the text is set to 1:1 scale.

- On the status bar, click the **Show annotation objects** button.

The text is visible in the ISO A4 layout.

- Save the drawing as **Layout Example.dwg** and close.

Exercise 1

Create the drawing, as shown below. After create the drawing, perform the following tasks:

- Create a layout of A3 size and then create a viewport.

- Set the viewport scale to 1:2.

- Set the scale of the dimensions and hatch lines with respect to the viewport.

Chapter 11: Templates and Plotting

In this chapter, you will learn to do the following:

- **Configure Plotters**
- **Create Plot Style Tables**
- **Use Plot styles**
- **Create Templates**
- **Plot/Print the drawing**

Plotting Drawings

Plotting is the process of producing a physical copy of the drawing using a printer or plotter. The printer may be directly connected to an AutoCAD workstation or on the network of workstations. Although the process of plotting is very simple, it is important to know how to establish communication between AutoCAD and the plotter. In this chapter, you will learn to connect a plotter with AutoCAD, define plotting style, and produce professional prints of drawings. You will also learn to print and publish drawings in digital format.

Configuring Plotters

It is assumed that you have connected plotter to your workstation and installed the drivers related to it. Even after doing so, you need to set a connection between the plotter and AutoCAD. You can

establish this connection by using the Add-plotter wizard. The following example explains the procedure to connect a plotter to AutoCAD.

Example:

- Start AutoCAD 2017.
- Click **Application Menu > Print > Manage Plotters** or type PLOTTERMANAGER in the command line; the **Plotters** folder will be opened, as shown below. All the configured plotters are displayed in this folder.

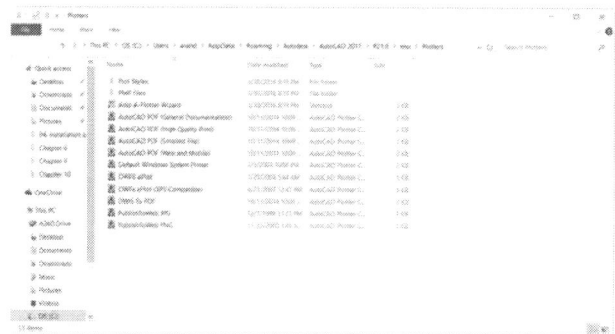

- In the **Plotters** folder, double-click on the **Add-A-Plotter Wizard** icon; the **Add Plotter – Introduction** page appears.
- Click the **Next** button; the **Add Plotter – Begin** page appears. In this page, there are three options that allow you to setup a plotter: **My Computer**, **Network Plotter Server**, and **System Printer**. These options are explained on the dialog itself, as shown below.

- Select the **System Printer** option and click **Next**; the **System Printer** page appears. A list of printers installed on your workstation is displayed.

- From the list, select the required printer and click **Next**; the **Import** page appears.
- Click the **Next** button; the **Plotter Name** page appears.
- Type name of the plotter in the **Plotter Name** box and click **Next**; the **Finish** page appears. You can edit the configuration of the plotter by using the **Edit Plotter Configuration** button.

If you click the **Edit Plotter Configuration** button, the **Plotter Configuration Editor** dialog appears. In this dialog, you can modify the default settings of the plotter. The **Calibrate Plotter** button is used to test the plotter.

- Click the **Finish** button; a new plotter will be added to the **Plotters** folder.

Creating Plot Style Tables

Plot styles determine the final look of the plotted drawing. They are used to override the layer properties such as color, linetype, lineweight and so on when the drawing is printed. After configuring a plotter, you need to create a plot style. There are two types of the plot styles: **Color-dependent** and **Named** plot style. **Color-dependent** plot styles are assigned based on the object color, whereas the **Named** plot styles are assigned based on layer or by object.

- On the **Application Menu**, click **Print > Manage Plot styles** or type STYLESMANAGER in the command line; the **Plot Styles** folder appears.

- Double-click on the **Add-A-Plot Style Table Wizard** icon; the **Add Plot Style Table** dialog appears. Read the information on this dialog and click **Next**.

- Select the **Start from Scratch** option and click **Next**.

- Select the **Named Plot Style Table** option and click **Next**.

- Enter **Sample** in the **File name** box and click Next; the **Finish** page appears.

- Click the **Plot Style Table Editor** button; the **Plot Style Table Editor** dialog appears.

- Click the **Add Style** button available at the bottom left of the dialog; a new style named **Style 1** is added.

- Enter **PS1** in the **Name** box.

- Select **Black** from the **Color** drop-down.

- Set the **Screening** value to 70. The screening factor will fade objects in the printed output. A 20% screening factor will result in more fading of objects than a 50% screening factor.

- Click **Save & Close** on the **Plot Style Table Editor** dialog.

- Click **Finish** to close the **Add Plot Style Table** dialog; the **Sample** plot style will be added to the **Plot Style** folder.

Using Plot Styles

In AutoCAD, the Color-Dependent Plot style is used by default. In order to use the newly created plot style, you need to specify a setting in the **Options** dialog.

- Right-click in the graphics window and select **Options**; the **Options** dialog appears.

- Select the **Plot and Publish** tab in the

Options dialog and click the **Plot Style Table Settings** button; the **Plots Style Table settings** dialog appears.

- Select the **Use named plot styles** option from the dialog.
- Select **Sample.stb** from the **Default plot style table** drop-down.
- Select **PS1** from the **Default plot style for layer 0** drop-down.
- Set the **Default plot style for objects** to **ByLayer**.

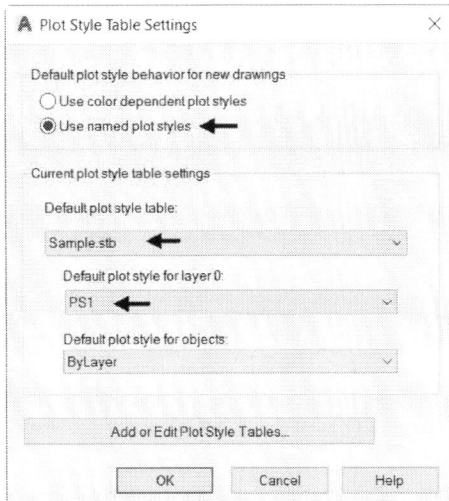

- Click **OK** twice to close both the dialogs.
- Close the drawing file by clicking the **Close** button located at the top-right corner.

- Click **NO** on the **AutoCAD** alert message.
- Click the **New** button on the **Quick Access Toolbar**; the **Select Template** dialog appears.
- Select **Open > Open with no Template – Metric** from the bottom right corner of the dialog; a drawing file will be opened.

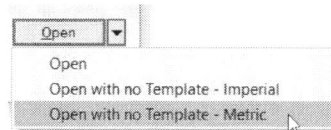

- Open the **Layers Properties Manager** and create the layers contained in the table below:

Layer	Linetype	Lineweight	Plot Style
Construction	Continuous	Default	PS1
Object	Continuous	0.7 mm	PS1
Hidden Lines	Hidden	0.3 mm	PS1
Center Lines	CENTER	0.25 mm	PS1
Dimensions	Continuous	0.25 mm	PS1
Section Lines	Continuous	0.5 mm	PS1
Cutting Plane	Phantom	0.6mm	PS1
Title Block	Continuous	1mm	PS1
Viewport	Continuous	0.25 mm	PS1
Text	Continuous	Default	PS1
Title block text	Continuous	Default	PS1

- Click the **Layout 1** tab to activate the paper space.
- Click **Output > Plot > Page setup Manager** on the ribbon; the **Page Setup Manager** dialog appears.
- Click **Modify** on the **Page Setup** Manager; the **Page Setup** dialog appears.
- Under the **Printer/plotter** group, select the plotter that you have configured to your workstation.
- Set the **Paper Size** to **A3** and **Drawing orientation** to **Landscape**.
- Click **OK** and **Close** to exit both the dialogs.
- Draw a title block in the paper space, as shown below.

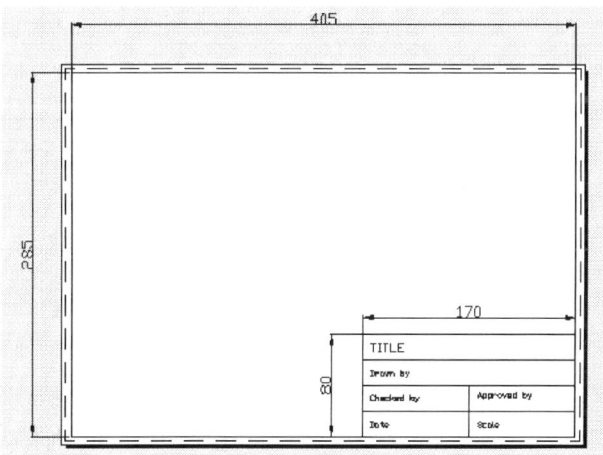

- Create a viewport inside the title block.

Creating Templates

After specifying the required settings in a drawing file, you can save those settings for the future use. You can do so by creating a template. Template files have settings such as units, limits, and layers already created, which will increase your productivity. In previous sections, you have configured various settings, such as layers, colors, linetypes and plotting settings. Now, you will create a template file containing all of these settings and the title block that you have created.

- On the **Quick Access toolbar**, click the **Save** button; the **Save Drawing As** dialog appears.
- In the **Save Drawing As** dialog, set **Files of type** to **AutoCAD Drawing Template (*.dwt).**
- Enter **ISOA3** in the **File name** box and click **Save**.
- In the **Template Options** dialog, enter **ISO-A3 Horizontal layout with title block** in the **Description** box.
- Click **OK** to close the dialog and save the template file.

Plotting/Printing the drawing

- Click the **New** button.
- Select **ISOA3**. A new drawing will be started with the selected template.
- Open the **Layer Properties Manager**; you will notice that the layers saved in the template file are loaded automatically.
- Close the **Layer Properties Manager**.

- Create a drawing, as shown below.

- Click the **Layout 1** tab to activate the paper space.
- Double-click inside the viewport to activate the model space.
- Set the **Viewport Scale** to 1:1 on the status bar.
- Use the **Pan** tool and position the drawing in the center of the view port.
- Double-click outside the viewport to activate the paper space.
- Hide the viewport frame by freezing the **Viewport** layer.

- Click the **Plot** button on the **Quick Access Toolbar**; the **Plot** dialog appears.

- Make sure that the options in this dialog are

same as that you specified while creating the template.

- Click the **Preview** button located at the bottom left corner; the preview window appears.
- Click the **Zoom Original** button to fit the drawing to the window.

- Examine print preview for the desired output and click the **Plot** button; the drawing will be plotted.

- Save and close the drawing file.

Exporting to PDF

The drawing can be exported to the PDF or DWF formats.

- On the ribbon, click **Output > Export DWF/PDF > Export to PDF Options** .

- On the **Export to PDF Options** dialog, set the Vector quality, Raster image quality, line merge control, and Data options.

The options in the **Data** section help you to include layer information, hyperlinks, and create bookmarks. Also, you can capture fonts used in the drawing.

- Click **OK**.
- On the ribbon, click **Output > Export DWF/PDF > Export > PDF** .

- On the **Save As PDF** dialog, select a **PDF Preset** to specify the PDF quality.

- Examine the options in the **Output Controls** section, Export, and Page Setup.

- Specify the location of the PDF file and click **Save**. A bubble appears on the status bar after exporting the PDF file.

- Open the PDF file in a PDF viewer and notice the layers, bookmarks, hyperlinks in the drawing. Also, you can find any text in

the drawing using the text search option in the PDF viewer.

Publishing a 2D Drawing to a Browser

AutoCAD 2017 allows you to publish a drawing to a web browser so that you can view it without any application installed on your device. To publish drawing to a web browser, follow the steps given next:

- Click **Application Menu > Publish > Design Views**.

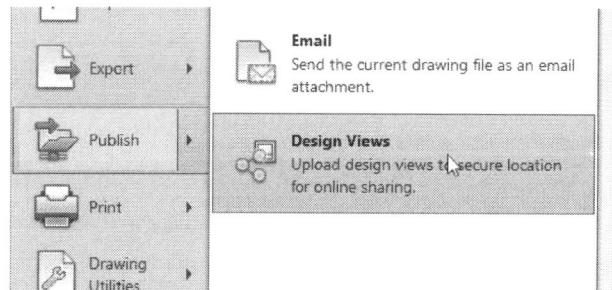

The **Autodesk Sign In** dialog appears, if have no signed into your Autodesk account.

- Enter your Autodesk ID and password, and then click **Sign in**.

The **DesignShare – Publish Options** dialog appears.

- Select the appropriate option from the **DesignShare – Publish Options** dialog.

DesignShare - Publish Options   ✕

Your design will be published to a secure location for online
viewing and sharing. How do you want to do this?

→ Publish and display in my browser now
   Your browser will open and display the design. This might take several
   minutes.

→ Publish and notify me when complete
   A notification bubble will display on your status bar when the
   processing is complete.

☐ Always perform my current choice   Cancel

About design views

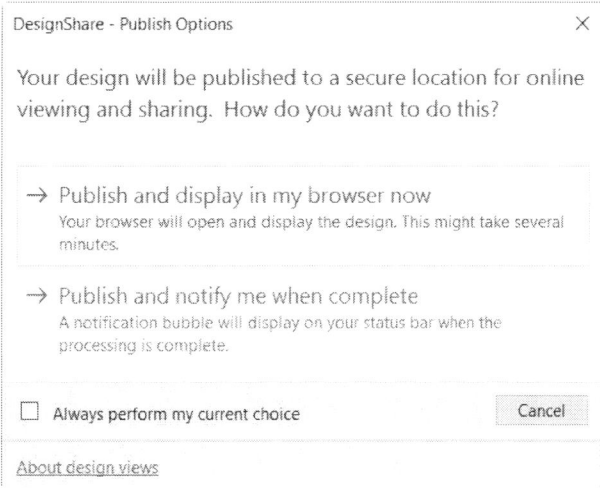

The drawing will be published and opened in the A360 Viewer. You can sign into A360 using you Autodesk ID and share the link of the drawing.

Exercise

Create and plot the drawing as shown in figure.

Chapter 12: 3D Modeling Basics

In this chapter, you will learn to do the following:

- **Create boxes, cylinders, wedges, cones, pyramids, spheres, and torus**
- **Create User Coordinate Systems**
- **Work with Dynamic UCS**
- **Change the View Style of objects**
- **Create Viewports in model space**
- **Create walls using the Polysolid tool**
- **Change the view orientation**
- **Create extruded, revolved, swept, lofted, and press-pulled objects**
- **Perform Boolean operations**
- **Align objects**
- **Create spiral and helical curves**

Introduction

In AutoCAD, you can create three types of 3D models: surfaces, solids, and meshes. Solids are used to create 3D models of engineering components and assemblies, surfaces are used to create complex shapes such as plastic parts, and meshes are used for games and movies. Solids are three-dimensional models of actual objects that possess physical properties such as mass properties, center of gravity, surface area, moments of inertia, and so on. Surfaces are construction features without any thickness. They do not possess any physical properties. Meshes are similar to solids without mass and volume properties. In this chapter, you will learn the basics of 3D modeling such as creating, navigating and visualizing solid models.

3D Modeling Workspaces in AutoCAD

In AutoCAD, there are separate workspaces created to work on 3D models. In these workspaces, the tools are organized into ribbon tabs, menus, toolbars, and palettes to perform a specific task in 3D modeling. You can activate these workspaces by using the **Workspace** drop-down located on the **Quick Access Toolbar**, or by using the **Workspace Switching** menu on the status bar. You can also start an AutoCAD session directly in the 3D Modeling workspace using the **acad3D.dwt, acadiso3D.dwt, acad -Named Plot Styles3D,** or **acadISO-Named Plot Styles3D** templates.

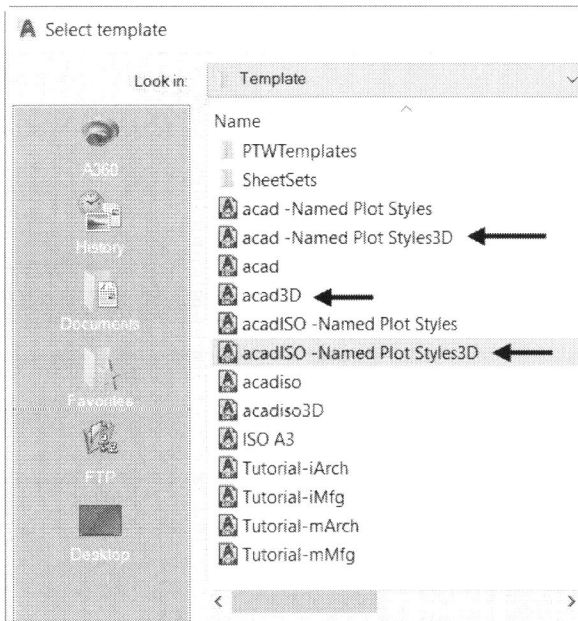

There are two workspaces of 3D modeling: **3D Basics** and **3D Modeling**. The **3D Basics** workspace has commonly used tools, whereas the **3D Modeling** workspace includes all the tools required for creating 3D models.

The 3D Modeling Workspace

Activating the **3D Modeling** workspace either by using the template or from the **Workspace** drop-down displays the screen as shown below. It contains the ribbon and tools related to 3D modeling. By default, the **Home** tab is activated in the ribbon. From this tab, you can access the tools for creating and editing solids and meshes, modifying the model display, working with coordinate systems, sectioning 3D models and so on.

There are some additional tabs such as **Solid**, **Surface**, **Mesh**, and **Render**. The **Solid** tab contains tools to create solid models; the **Surface** and **Mesh** tabs are used to create surface models and complex shapes; the **Visualize** tab is used for creating realistic images of solid and surface models.

The **ViewCube** can be used to modify the view of the model quickly and easily. It is located at the top right corner of the graphics window. Using the ViewCube, you can switch between the standard and isometric views, rotate the model, switch to the **Home** view of the model, and create a new user coordinate system. You can also change the way the ViewCube functions by using the **ViewCube Settings** dialog. Right-click on the ViewCube, and then select the **ViewCube Settings** option; the **ViewCube Settings** dialog will be opened.

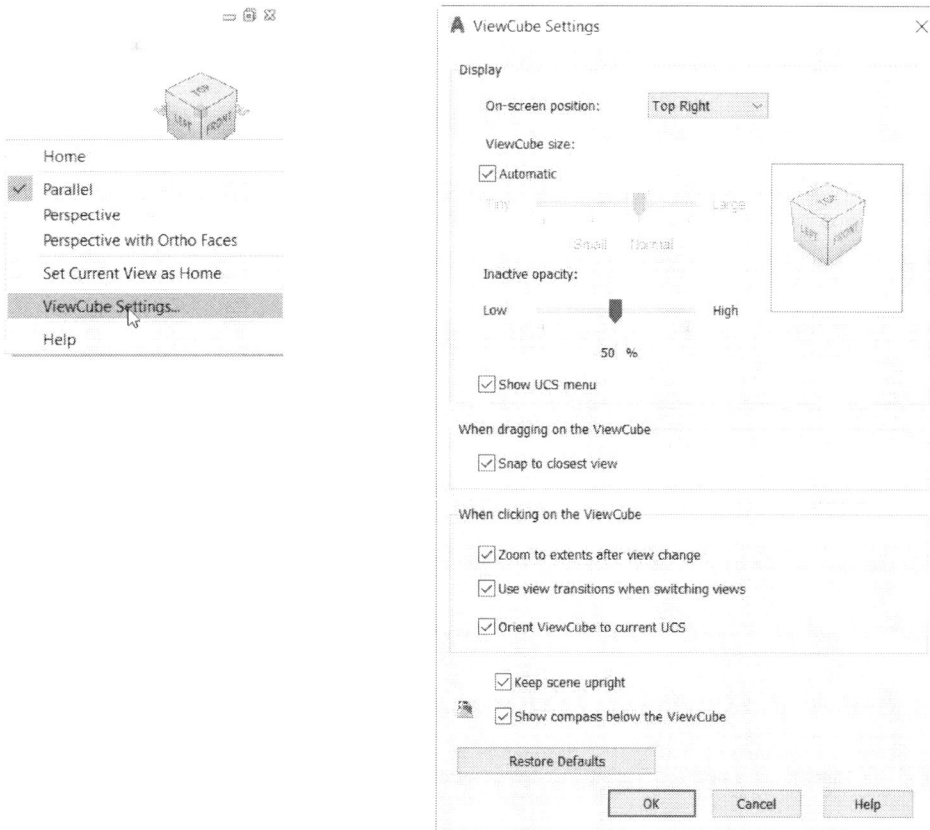

You can also modify the model view by using the In-canvas controls. In addition to that, you also change the view style of the model and control the display of other tools in the graphics window using the In-canvas controls.

[−][Custom View][Realistic]

Custom Model Views ▸
Top
Bottom
Left
Right
Front
Back
SW Isometric
SE Isometric
NE Isometric
NW Isometric
View Manager...
Parallel
✓ Perspective

[−][Custom View][Realistic]

Custom Visual Styles ▸
2D Wireframe
Conceptual
Hidden
✓ Realistic
Shaded
Shaded with edges
Shades of Gray
Sketchy
Wireframe
X-ray
Visual Styles Manager...

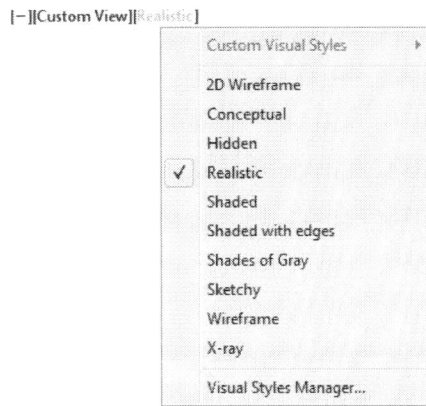

Now, you will create 3D models using the tools available in AutoCAD.

The Box tool

The **Box** tool is used to create boxes having six rectangular or square faces. It is most commonly used tool as many 3D objects are made of boxes.

- Click the **AutoCAD 2017** icon on your desktop.
- On the Quick Access Toolbar, click the New icon.
- On the **Select Template** dialog, click **acadiso3D**, and then click **Open**. A new file will be started in the **3D Modeling** workspace.
- Click **Home > Modeling > Box** on the ribbon or type **BOX** in the command line; the message, "Specify the first corner" appears in the command line.

- Pick an arbitrary point in the graphics window; the message, "Specify the other corner" appears in the command line.
- Ensure that the **Dynamic Input** icon is active on the status bar. You will notice the two value boxes to specify the length and width of the box.
- Type 100 in the length box and press the TAB key.
- Type 70 in the width box and press ENTER.
- Move the pointer upward, type 60 as height and press ENTER; the box will be created as shown.
- Click **Zoom > Zoom All** on the Navigation Bar.
- On the In-canvas controls, click **View Style Controls > Shades of Grey**.

- Right click on the **Home** icon above the ViewCube and select **Parallel**.

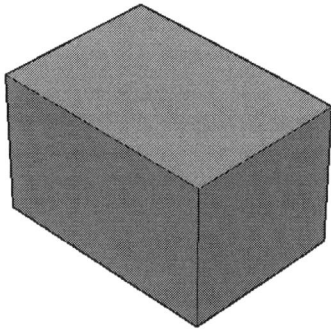

Creating the User Coordinate System

User Coordinate Systems assist you while creating 3D models. They are used to create construction planes on which you can add additional features to the model. Various methods to create User coordinate systems are discussed next.

Example1:

- On the status bar, click the **Customization** button and select **Dynamic UCS** from the menu. Also, select **3D Object Snap** from the menu.

- Deactivate the **Dynamic UCS** icon on the status bar. You will learn about this option later in this chapter.

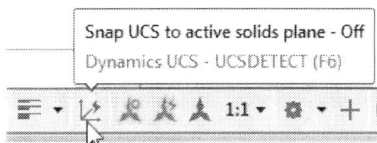

- Click **Home > Coordinates > UCS** on the ribbon; the UCS is attached to the pointer and the message, "Specify the origin of UCS" appears.

- Activate the **3D Object Snap** on the status bar.

- Select the vertex point on the top left corner of the box as shown below; the message, "Specify point X-axis or <accept>:"appears in the command line.

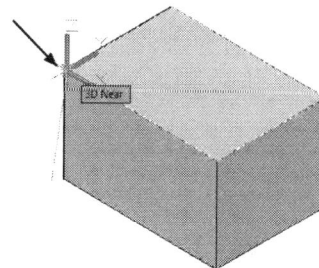

- Press ENTER to accept the orientation of the UCS as shown below.

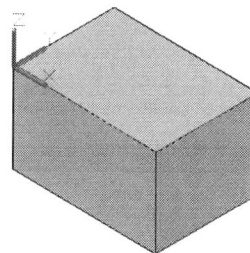

Creating a Wedge

When you slice a box diagonally, it results in a wedge. A wedge has five faces, three rectangular and two triangular.

- Click **Home > Modeling > Primitives drop-down > Wedge** on the ribbon or type **WE** in the command line and press ENTER; the message, "Specify first corner or [Center]" appears in the command line.

- Select the endpoint of the top face of the box as shown in figure; the message, "Specify other corner or [Cube Length]:" appears in the command line.

- On the Status bar, click the down arrow next to the **3D Object Snap** icon, and select **Midpoint on edge**.

- Select the midpoint of the front edge of the box as shown below.

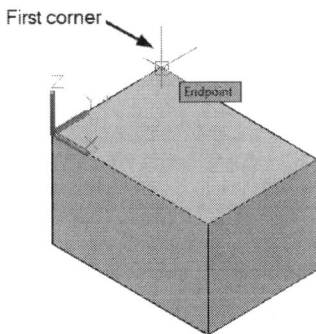

- Move the pointer upward and enter 40 as the height; the wedge will be created, as shown below.

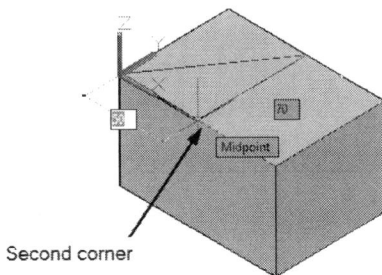

Example2: (Creating UCS by selecting 3-points)

 You can create a UCS by selecting three points. The first point will be the origin of the UCS, the second point will define the X axis, and the third point defines the Y-axis.

- Click **Home > Coordinates > 3 Point** on the ribbon; the UCS is attached to the pointer and the message, "Specify new origin point <0,0,0>:" appears.

- Select the lower endpoint of the wedge as shown in figure.

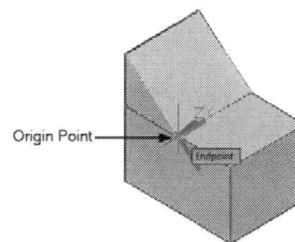

- Move the pointer toward right and select the other endpoint of the bottom edge of the wedge, as shown in figure.

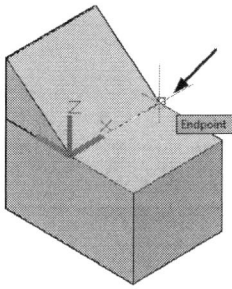

- Move the pointer along the diagonal edge of the wedge and select the endpoint on the top edge as shown below; the UCS will be created and aligned to the inclined face of the wedge.

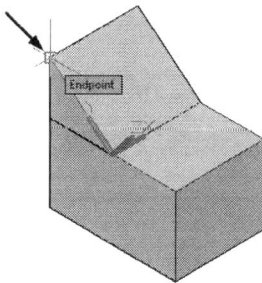

Creating a Cylinder

Cylinders are commonly used features after boxes. In AutoCAD, you can create cylinders easily by using the **Cylinder** tool. You can create a circular or elliptical cylinder by using this tool.

- Click **Home > View > View Style drop-down > Wireframe** on the ribbon; the view style of the model will be changed to wireframe.

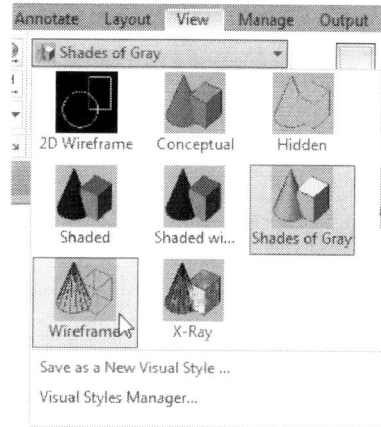

- On the Status bar, click the down arrow next to the **3D Object Snap** and select the **Center of face** option, if not already selected.
- Click **Home > Modeling > Primitives drop-down > Cylinder** on the ribbon or type **CYL** in the command line.
- Specify the center point of the cylinder on the inclined face of the wedge.

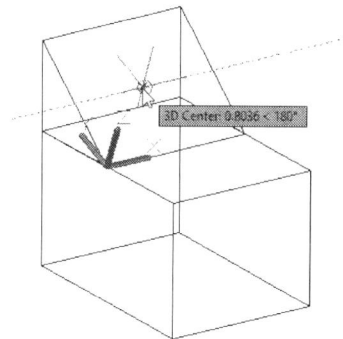

- Type 20 as the base radius and press ENTER.
- Move the pointer upward; you will notice that the pointer moves along the Z-axis of the UCS.
- Type 25 as height and press ENTER; the cylinder will be created as shown below.

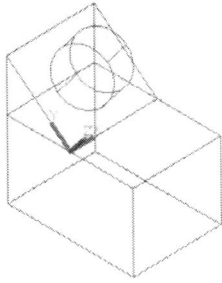

Example 3: (Returning to previous position of the UCS)

- Click **Home > Coordinates > UCS, Previous** on the ribbon; the UCS will return to its previous position.

Example 4: (Creating a UCS by specifying its origin)

- Click **Home > Coordinates > Origin** on the ribbon; the UCS will be attached to the pointer.
- Select the lower left corner point of the box; the UCS will be placed at that point. Note that the orientation will not change.

Example 5: (Rotating the UCS about X, Y, and Z axes)

You can rotate a UCS about X, Y, or Z axes by using the drop-down available in the **Coordinates** panel, as shown below.

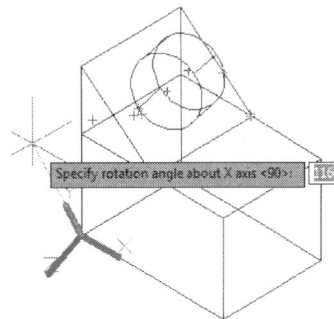

- Click the **X** option from the drop-down shown in the above figure; the message, "Specify rotation angle about X axis <90>:" appears in the command line. Also, a rubber band line originating from the Y axis is attached to the pointer.
- Rotate the pointer and pick a point to specify the rotation angle. You can also type-in the rotation angle in the dynamic input or command line.
- Similarly, you can rotate the UCS about the Y and Z axes using the respective options from the drop-down.

Example 6: (Creating the UCS by specifying the Z-axis)

Using the **Z-Axis Vector** tool, you can create a UCS by specifying its Z-axis.

- Click **Home > Coordinates > Z-Axis Vector** on the ribbon.

- Select the bottom right endpoint as the origin; the message, "Specify point on positive portion of Z-axis:" appears in the command line. Also, a rubber band line originating from the Z-axis is attached to the pointer. Now, as you move the pointer, you will notice that the Z-axis also moves.

- Move the pointer and select the left endpoint of the bottom edge as shown below; the Z-axis will be aligned to the bottom edge.

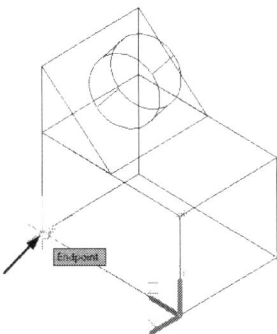

Example 7: (Creating UCS parallel to the screen)

Using the **View** tool in the **Coordinates** panel, you can create a UCS which is parallel to the screen.

- Click **Home > Coordinates > View** on the ribbon; the XY plane of the UCS will become parallel to the screen. The UCS origin will not change. This option is useful if you want to use the current view and add a title block, or any other annotation.

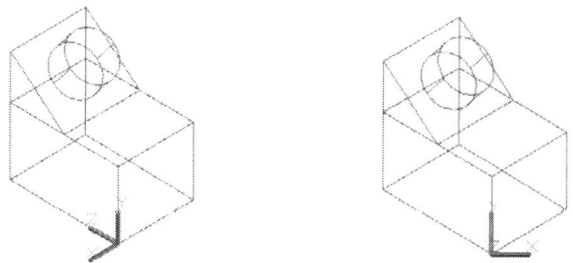

Example 8: (Creating UCS aligned to an object)

You can create a UCS aligned to an object. The origin of the UCS will be aligned to the nearest endpoint of the object.

- Click **Home > Coordinates > View > Object** on the ribbon; the message, "Select object to align UCS:" appears in the command line.

- Select the cylindrical object from the model; the UCS will be aligned to it.

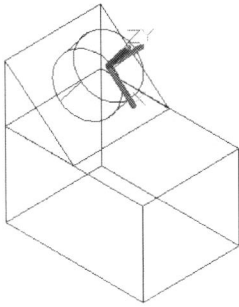

Example 9: (Creating UCS aligned to face)

You can align a UCS to a planar or curved face of a model using the **Face** tool.

- Click **Home > Coordinates >Face** on the ribbon; the message, "Select face of solid, surface, or mesh:" appears in the command line.

- Move the pointer over the faces of the model; you will notice that the UCS is displayed on the faces.

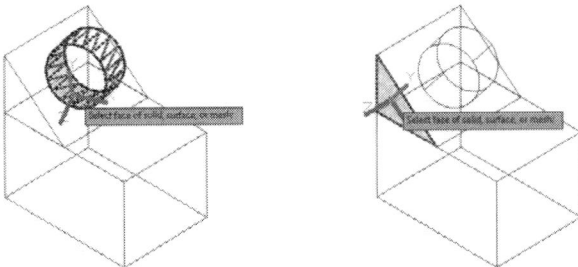

- Select the top face of the box; the message, "Enter an option [Next/Xflip/Yflip] <accept>:" appears in the command line. If you select the **Next** option, the adjacent face will be highlighted. The **Xflip** option is used to rotate the UCS 180 degrees about the X axis. The **Yflip** option is used to rotate the UCS 180 degrees about the Y axis.

- Press ENTER to accept; the UCS will be aligned to the selected face.

Using Dynamic User Coordinate System

In the previous section, you have learned to create various types of static user coordinate systems. They are active until you define another user coordinate system. You can also create dynamic user coordinate systems. A Dynamic User Coordinate System is a temporary UCS that appears automatically when you place your pointer over the face of a 3D solid object. Note that the Dynamic User Coordinate appears only when you use tools which create objects directly (For example, drawing tools and primitive tools). In order to create a Dynamic UCS, you need to activate the **Dynamic UCS** option on the status bar.

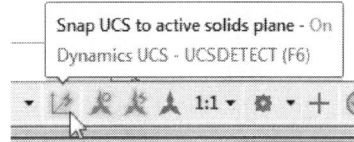

- Click the **Cylinder** button on the **Modeling** panel.

- Ensure that the **Dynamic UCS** button is active on the status bar.

- Move the pointer over the faces of the model; they will be highlighted.

- Click on the front face of the box and create the cylinder as shown below.

3D from the **Setup** drop-down. Click the **OK** button; four tiled view-ports are displayed in the screen. You can notice that each viewport has a different view and a different UCS. Click inside any viewport to activate it and perform any operation. To return to single viewport, click the **Restore Viewports** button on the **Model Viewports** panel; the currently active viewport will fill the screen area.

Model Space Viewports for 3D Modeling

While creating 3D models, it is useful to have a look at your model from several different orientations at the same time. For this purpose, you need to create different viewports in model space. You can create multiple viewports in model space using the **Viewport Configuration** drop-down available in the **Model Viewports** panel of the **View** tab. This can also be done by using the **Viewports** dialog. To load this dialog, click **Visualize > Model Viewports > Named**; the **Viewports** dialog appears. In the dialog, select the **New Viewports** tab and then select **Four: Equal** from the **Standard viewports** list. Next, select

Creating Other Primitive Shapes

In AutoCAD, there are set of tools to create basic geometric shapes. In earlier sections, you have learned to create boxes, wedges, and cylinders. Now, you will learn to create other primitive shapes.

Creating Cones

Creating a cone is similar to creating a cylinder. It

has a similar shape compared to a cylinder; but it is tapered on one side.

Example 1:

- To create a cone, click **Home > Modeling > Primitives drop-down > Cone** ⬠ Cone on the ribbon; the message, "Specify center point of base or [3P/2P/Ttr/Elliptical]:" appears in the command line.

- Pick an arbitrary point from the graphics window; the message, "Specify base radius or [Diameter]:" appears.

- Type a radius value in the command line and press ENTER. You can also select the **Diameter** option to specify the diameter of the base.

- Move the pointer in vertical direction and pick a point to specify the height of the cone. You can also type-in the height value in the command line and press ENTER; the cone will be created.

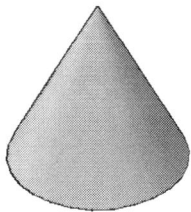

Example 2:

- Type **CONE** in the command line and press ENTER.

- Select the **Elliptical** option from the command line; the message, "Specify endpoint of first axis or [Center]:" appears in the command line.

- Pick a point to specify the end point of the first axis.

- Move the pointer and click specify the other end

point of the first axis. You can also type-in the length of the first axis and press ENTER; the message, "Specify endpoint of second axis:" appears.

- Pick a point or type-in the radius value to specify the second axis.

- Move the pointer upward and pick a point to specify the height. You can also enter the value of height in the command line or **Dynamic Input** box.

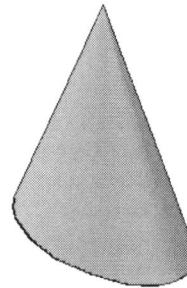

Example 3:

- Click **Solid > Primitive > Primitive drop-down > Cone** on the ribbon.

- Select the center point and specify the base radius as 20; the message, "Specify height or [2Point/Axis endpoint/Top radius]" appears in the command line.

- Select the **Top radius** option from the command line; the message, "Specify top radius:" appears.

- Type 10 as the top radius value and press ENTER.

- Move the pointer upward and enter 40 as the height.

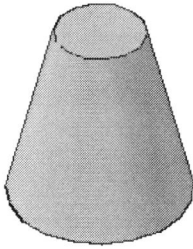

Creating a Sphere

- Click **Home > Modeling > Primitives drop-down > Sphere** on the ribbon.
- Specify the center point of the sphere.
- Move the pointer outward and enter the radius value. You can also select the **Diameter** option to specify the diameter of the sphere.

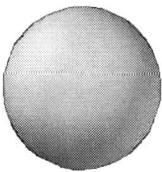

Creating a Torus

Torus is a donut shaped solid primitive. To create a torus, you need to specify center of the torus, radius or diameter of torus, and radius or diameter of the tube.

- Click **Home > Modeling > Primitives drop-down >Torus** on the ribbon or type **TOR** in the command line and press ENTER.
- Specify the center point of the torus.
- Move the pointer outward and enter the radius of the torus. You can also select the **Diameter** option to specify the diameter of the torus.

- Type the tube radius and press ENTER; the torus will be created.

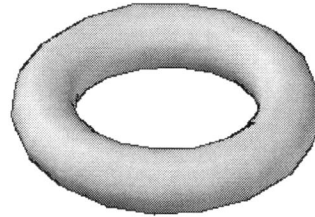

Creating a Pyramid

Pyramids are similar to cones except that the base of the pyramid is not circular in shape.

- To create a pyramid, click **Home > Modeling > Primitives drop-down > Pyramid** on the ribbon or type **PYR** in the command line and press ENTER.
- Specify the center point of the base. The base of pyramid is a polygon. The method to create a polygon is already discussed in Chapter 2.
- After creating the base, move the pointer in vertical direction and pick a point to specify the height of the pyramid. You can also type the value of the height and press ENTER; the pyramid will be created.

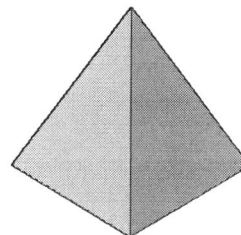

The other options displayed in the command line while creating the pyramid are same as in the **Cone** tool.

Using the Polysolid tool

The **Polysolid** tool is used to create a 3D wall. It can also be used to convert a line, polyline, arc, or a circle to a wall. The **Polysolid** tool is similar to **Polyline** tool except that you create a rectangular shaped wall that has a pre-defined height and width.

- Click **Home > Modeling > Polysolid** on the ribbon; the message, "Specify start point or [Object/Height/Width/Justify] <Object>:" appears in the command line.

- Activate the **Ortho Mode** on the status bar.

- Pick an arbitrary point in the graphics window and move the pointer in the X-direction.

- Type 200 in the command line and press ENTER; a 3D wall of 200 length is created.

- Select the **Arc** option from the command line and move the pointer in the Y-direction.

- Type 100 as the arc diameter and press ENTER.

- Select the **Line** option from the command line and move the pointer in the –X-direction.

- Type 100 and press ENTER.

- Move the pointer in the Y-direction and enter 150 as the wall length.

- Move the pointer in –X-direction and enter 100 as the wall length.

- Select the **Close** option from the command line; the wall will be closed.

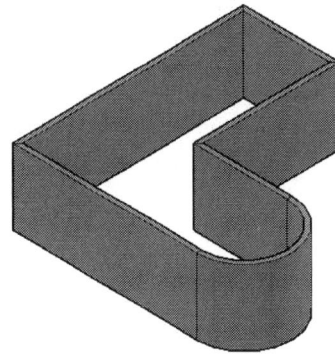

Using the Extrude tool

The **Extrude** tool is used to add a third dimension (height) to an existing 2D shape. If you extrude a closed shape such as circle and closed polylines, a solid is created. If you extrude an open sketch such as lines and arcs, a surface is created.

Example 1:

- Start a new AutoCAD file in **3D Modeling** workspace.

- Click **Home > View > 3D Navigation > Front** on the ribbon; the front view will become parallel to the screen.

- Click **Home > Draw > Polyline** on the ribbon and create the sketch as shown below.

- Select **SE Isometric** from the **In-canvas controls**; the view orientation will be changed South east Isometric.

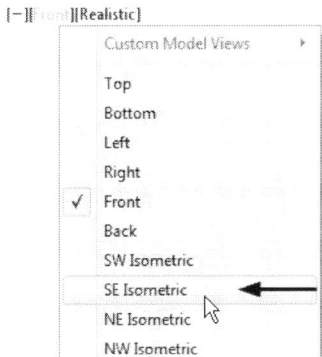

- Click **Home > Modeling > Extrude.**
- Select the polyline sketch and press Enter.
- Move the pointer toward right.
- Type **100** in the command line or **Dynamic Input** box and press ENTER; the polyline sketch will be extruded.

Example 2:

- Open a new AutoCAD file in **3D Modeling** Workspace.
- Click **Home > View > 3D Navigation > Top** on the ribbon; the view will become parallel to the screen.

- Click **Home > Draw > Line** on the ribbon and create the sketch as shown below.

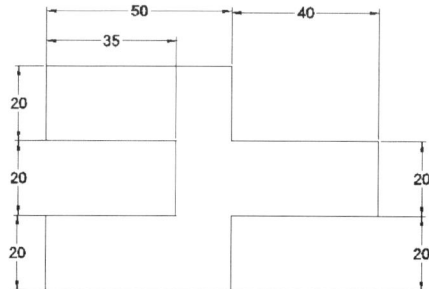

- Click **Home > View > 3D Navigation >SE Isometric** on the ribbon; the view orientation will be changed to south east Isometric.
- Expand the **Draw** panel of the **Home** tab and click the **Region** button.

- Press and drag a window and select all the objects of the sketch.
- Press ENTER; the sketch will be converted into a region. Now, you can extrude the region to create a solid. If you try to extrude the lines without creating a region, it will result in a surface.

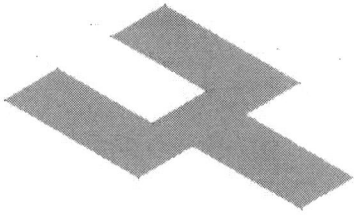

- Click **Solid > Solid > Extrude** on the ribbon.

  🔲 Extrude

  - Select the region and press ENTER; the message, "Specify height of extrusion or [Direction/Path/Taper angle/Expression]:" appears in the command line.

- Select the **Taper angle** option from the command line.

- Type 5 as the taper angle and press ENTER.

- Move the pointer upward, type 40 in the command line and press ENTER; the extruded solid will be created with a taper.

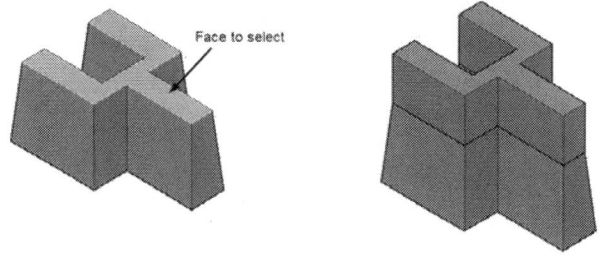

Example 3:

- Type **EXT** in the command line and press ENTER.

- Press and hold the CTRL key on and select the top face of the model.

- Press ENTER and move the pointer upward.

- Type 25 as the extrusion height and press ENTER; the extruded solid will be created.

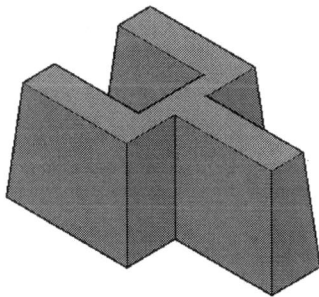

Using the Revolve tool

The **Revolve** tool is used to revolve an open or closed 2D sketch about a selected axis. If you revolve a closed profile such as a polyline sketch, polygon, circle, or a sketch region, a solid object is created. An open profile results in a surface. The sketch is deleted after revolving it. If you want to retain the sketch, you need set the **DELOBJ** system variable to 0.

- Open a new file in **3D Modeling** workspace.

- Set the view orientation to front and create the sketch using the **Line** tool.

- Convert the sketch into region using the **Region** tool.

- Click **Solid > Solid > Revolve** on the ribbon or type REV in the command line.
- Select the sketch region and press ENTER; the message, "Specify axis start point or define axis by [Object/X/Y/Z] <Object>:" appears in the command line.
- Select the **Object** option from the command line and select the vertical line created at an offset; the message, "Specify angle of revolution or [STart angle/Reverse/EXpression] <360>:" appears.
- Press ENTER to specify 360 as the revolution angle.

Using the Sweep tool

 The **Sweep** tool is used to create a new solid or surface by sweeping a closed or open planar profile along an open or closed 2D or 3D

path. The procedure to create a solid by using the **Sweep** tool is discussed next.

Example:

- Open a new file in **3D Modeling** workspace.
- Set the view orientation to **Front** and create the sketch using the **Polyline** tool.

- Use the **Fillet** tool and apply fillets of 25 mm radius.

- Change the view orientation to SE Isometric.
- Click **Home > Coordinates > Z-Axis Vector** on the ribbon.
- Select the endpoint of the top vertical line as the UCS origin and align the Z-axis to it.

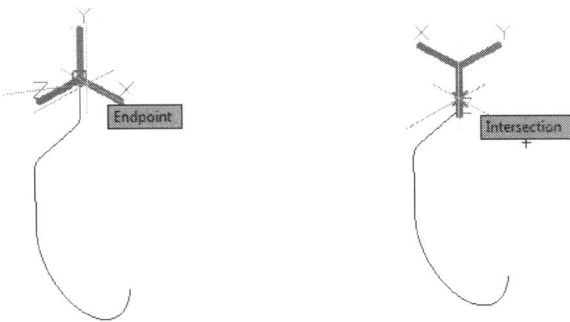

- Click the **Circle** button on the **Draw** panel.
- Select the end point of the vertical line to specify the center point of the circle. Specify 5 mm as radius of the circle.
- Click the **UCS, World** button on the **Coordinates** panel; the User Coordinate System will be set to World Coordinate System (0,0,0).
- Click **Home > Modeling > Solids drop-down > Sweep** on the ribbon.

- Select the circle as the profile and press ENTER; the message, "Select sweep path or [Alignment/Base point/Scale/Twist]:" appears in the command line.

The **Alignment** option aligns the profile perpendicular to the direction of the sweep path. By default, the profile is aligned to the path.

The **Base point** specifies the base point of the profile. By, default, the center of the profile is used as the

base point. You can select any other point on the profile to define the base point.

The **Scale** option scales the profile along the path.

The **Twist** option twists the profile as it is swept along the length of the path.

- Select the path to create the swept solid object.

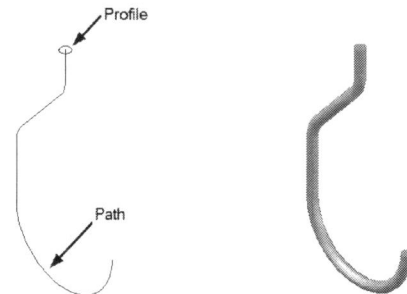

Using the Loft tool

Using the **Loft** tool, you can create a solid or surface by selecting a series of cross sections. The selected cross sections will define the shape of the lofted solid.

Example 1:

- Create three circles as shown below. The diameters and center point locations are given in the table.

Circle Center points (Absolute Coordinates)	Circle Diameters
0,0,0	Ø50
0,0,70	Ø100
0,0,140	Ø50

- Click **Home > Modeling > Solids drop-down > Loft** on the ribbon or type **LOFT** in the command line and press ENTER.

- Select the cross-sections one by one; the preview of the lofted solid appears.

- Press ENTER to accept the selection; the message, "Enter an option [Guides/Path/Cross sections only/Settings] <Cross sections only>:"appears in the command line.

- Select the **Settings** option from the command line; the **Loft Settings** dialog appears. In this dialog, the **Smooth Fit**

option creates a smooth connection between the cross-sections. If you select the **Ruled** option, the lofted solid or surface has sharp edges.

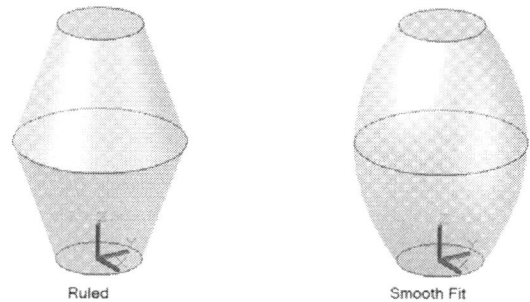

The **Normal to** option creates a solid or surface normal to the cross-section. You can select the loft solid or surface to be normal to **All cross sections**, or **Start Cross Section** or **End Cross Section** or **Start and End Cross Sections**.

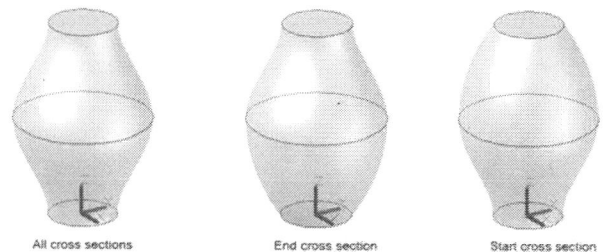

The **Draft angles** option defines the draft angle and magnitude at start and end cross sections. The draft angle is the beginning direction of the loft surface. If you set the draft angle to 90 degrees, the loft surface starts vertically from the cross section and the 0-draft angle starts loft surface horizontally. The Magnitude is the relative distance up to which the loft surface will follow the draft angle before it bends.

The **Close surface or solid** option connects the start and end section of the lofted object.

- Select the **Normal to** option and select **All cross sections**. Click **OK**; the loft solid will be created as shown below.

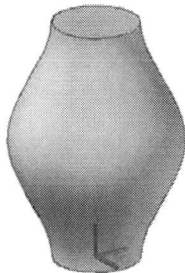

Using the Presspull tool

The **Presspull** tool is used to create and modify solid models with a greater ease and speed. It can be used to accomplish two types of operations: extruding closed 2D shapes and add or remove material from a solid object based on whether you "pull" or "push" the extrusion.

- Start a new file.

- Create two layers called **Sketch** and **Solid**. Make the **Sketch** layer as current.
- Set the view orientation to **Right** and draw the sketch as shown below.

- Change the view orientation to SE Isometric.
- Ensure that the **Dynamic Input** is activate
- Set the **Solid** layer are current.
- Click **Home > Modeling > Presspull** on the ribbon.
- Click inside the bottom region of the sketch and move the pointer backwards. Type 60 in the Dynamic input box and press ENTER; the extruded feature will be created.

- Click in the region enclosed by the larger circle and extrude it up to 64 mm distance.

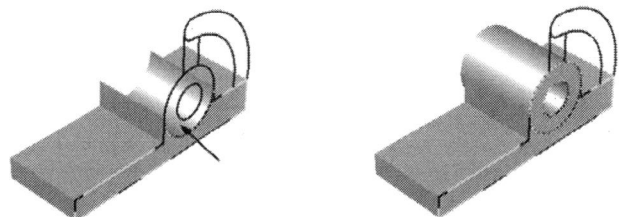

- Press and hold the CTRL key and select the front face of the cylindrical object. Move the pointer forward. Type 4 in the dynamic input box and press ENTER.

- Click in the curved slot region and move the pointer backward; the message, "Specify extrusion height or [Multiple]:" appears in the command line.

- Select the **Multiple** option from the command line and click in the region enclosed by the two vertical lines.

- Right-click and move the pointer backwards. Type **12** in the dynamic input box and press ENTER.

- Press and hold the CTRL key and select the front face of the slot and move the pointer

forward. Type 4 in the dynamic input box and press ENTER.

- Set the **Sketch** layer as current.

- Click the **Circle** button on the **Draw** panel.

- Press and hold the SHIFT key. Right-click and select the **Center** option from the shortcut menu.

- Select the center point of the slot end cap and create a circle of 4 mm radius.

- Click **Home > Modify > Array drop-down > Path Array** on the ribbon.

- Select the circle created in the previous step and press ENTER.

- Select the arc as the path curve; the preview of the path array is displayed.

- In the **Array Creation** tab, set the **Between** value to 25; the item count is automatically adjusted.

- Click the **Close Array** button on the ribbon; the polar array is created.

- Activate the **Presspull** command.
- Click in any one of the circles and select the **Multiple** option from the command line.
- Click inside rest of the circles of the polar array. Right-click to accept.
- Move the pointer backward and click; holes will be created as shown in figure.
- Turn Off the **Sketch** layer; the sketches will be hidden.

- Click the **Orbit** button on the **Navigation Bar**.
- Press and drag the left mouse button to rotate the model.

Performing Boolean Operations

Boolean operations are performed to add two or more solids together, subtract a single solid or group of solids from another, or form a common portion when two solids are combined. You must have at least two solids in order to perform a Boolean operation. There are three tools available to perform Boolean Operations- **Union**, **Subtract**, and **Intersect**. These tools are discussed next.

The Union tool

The **Union** tool joins two or more solids together into a single solid. For example, when you try to select the complete model, its individual objects are selected. But, after performing the Union operation, all the solid objects are combined together and act as one object.

- To perform the Union operation, click **Solid > Boolean > Union** on the ribbon.

- Click the left mouse button and create a selection window across the model; all the objects of the model will be selected.
- Press ENTER; all the solid objects of the model will be combined.

Now, when you select an individual object, the complete model will be selected.

The Subtract tool

The **Subtract** tool is used to subtract one or more solid objects from another object.

- Create two concentric circles of 240 and 100 mm diameter.

- Use the **Presspull** tool and extrude up to 250 mm distance.
- Set the view orientation to **Right** and create a cylinder of 100 mm diameter and 250 mm length.
- Change the view orientation to **SE Isometric**.
- Expand the **Modify** panel and click the **Align** button.

- Select the horizontal cylinder and press ENTER; the message, "Specify first source point:" appears in the command line.
- Press and hold the SHIFT key. Right-click and select the **Center** option.
- Select the center point of the front face of the horizontal cylinder; the message, "Specify first destination point:" appears in the command line.
- Press and hold the SHIFT key. Right-click and select the **Quadrant** option.
- Select the quadrant point of the outer circle on the top face of the hollow cylinder.

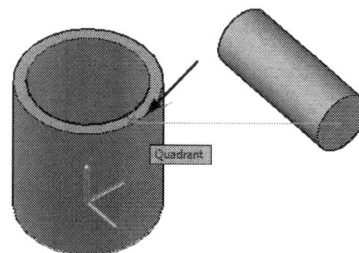

- Press ENTER; the horizontal cylinder will be aligned with hollow cylinder.

- Click **Solid > Boolean > Subtract** on the ribbon; the message, "Select solids, surfaces, and regions to subtract from" appears above the command line.
- Select the hollow cylinder and press ENTER; the message, "Select solids, surfaces, and regions to subtract" appears above the command line.
- Select the horizontal cylinder and press ENTER; it will be subtracted from the hollow cylinder as shown below.

The Intersect tool

The **Intersect** tool is used to create a composite solid by finding common volume shared by the selected objects.

- Start a new file.

- Set the view orientation to **Front** and create the sketch as shown below.

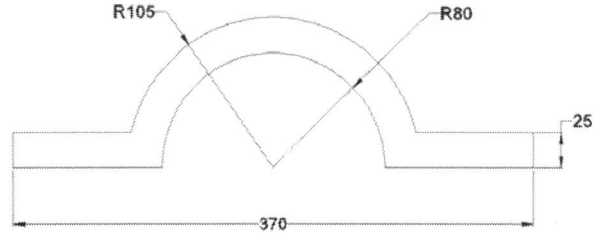

- Use the **Presspull** tool and extrude the sketch up to 150 mm distance.

- Set the view orientation to Top and create the sketch as shown below.

- Use the **Presspull** tool and extrude the view up to 200 mm height as shown below.

- Change the View style to **Wireframe**.
- Deactivate the **3D Object Snap** option on the status bar.
- Type **DS** in the command line and press ENTER; the **Drafting Settings** dialog appears.
- Click the **Object Snap** tab and **Clear All** the **Object Snap** modes.
- Now, select the **Quadrant** and **Midpoint** options and click **OK**.

- Type **AL** in the command line and press ENTER.

- Select the second extrusion and press ENTER; the message, "Specify first source point:" appears.
- Select the point on the source object as shown below; the message, "Specify first destination point:" appears.
- Select the point on the destination object as shown below; the message, "Specify second source point:" appears.

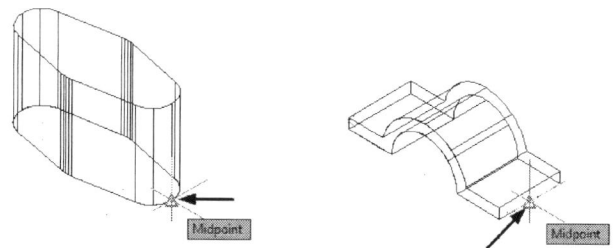

- Select another point on the source object, as shown below; the message, "Specify second destination point:" appears.
- Select another point on the destination object, as shown below; the message, "Specify third source point or <continue>:" appears.

- Press ENTER to continue; the message, "Scale objects based on alignment points? [Yes/No] <N>:" appears.
- Select the **NO** option; the two objects will be aligned.
- Change the **View style** to **Shade of Gray**.

[−][SE Isometric][Wireframe]

- Click **Solid > Boolean > Intersect** on the ribbon.
- Select the two objects and press ENTER; the intersection object will created as shown below.

Using the Helix tool

The **Helix** tool is used to create a spiral or helix object. You can use this helix object as a path for a swept solid object.

Example 1:

- Start a new file.
- Expand the **Draw** panel in the **Home** tab and click the **Helix** button.

Helix
Creates a 2D spiral or 3D spring

- Type 0,0 as the center point of the helix and press ENTER; the message, "Specify base radius or [Diameter]:" appears in the command line.
- Type 50 and press ENTER; the message, "Specify top radius or [Diameter] <50.0000>:" appears.
- Type 0 and press ENTER; the message, "Specify helix height or [Axis endpoint/Turns/turn Height/tWist] <1.0000>:" appears.
- Select the **Turns** option from the command line.
- Type 8 as number of turns and press ENTER; the message, "Specify helix height or [Axis endpoint/Turns/turn Height/tWist] <1.0000>:" appears.
- Type 0 as the height and press ENTER; the spiral curve will be created as shown in figure.

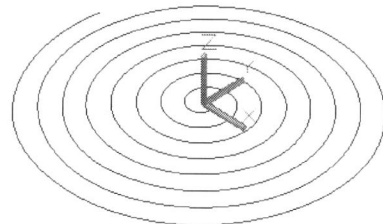

Example 2:

- Start a new file.

- Type HELIX in the command line and press ENTER.
- Type 0, 0 as the center point of the helix.
- Type 50 as the base radius and press ENTER.
- Press ENTER to accept 50 as the top radius.
- Select the **turn Height** option from the command line.
- Type 20 as the turn height (pitch) and press ENTER.
- Type 200 as the total height of the helix and press ENTER; the helix will be created as shown in figure.

Exercises

Create 3D models using the drawing views and dimensions.

Chapter 13: Solid Editing & generating 2D views

In this chapter, you will learn to do the following:

- **Move objects**
- **Create 3D Arrays**
- **Mirror objects in 3D space**
- **Fillet edges**
- **Taper faces of the solid object**
- **Offset faces**
- **Rotate objects**
- **Create 3D Polylines**
- **Shell objects**
- **Chamfer edges**
- **Create Live sections**
- **Generate 2D views of a 3D model**
- **Create section and detailed views**

Introduction

In the previous chapter, you have learnt to create simple solid objects. Now, you will learn to use solid editing tools to create complex models. You will also learn to generate orthographic views of 3D models.

Using the Move tool

The **Move** tool that you used in 2D drawings can also be used in 3D modeling. You can change the position of an object using the **Move** tool. The application of this tool in 3D modeling is discussed next.

Example:

- Start a new file in the **3D Modeling** workspace.
- Select **Front** from the **3D Navigation** drop-down of the **View** panel.
- Create the sketch on the front view and presspull it up to 100 mm distance.

- Create a cylinder of 20 mm diameter and 20 mm height.

- Type **M** in the command line and press ENTER; the **Move** tool is activated.
- Select the cylinder and press ENTER.
- Select the center point of the cylinder to

define the base point.

- Select the end point of the base object; the cylinder will be aligned to it.

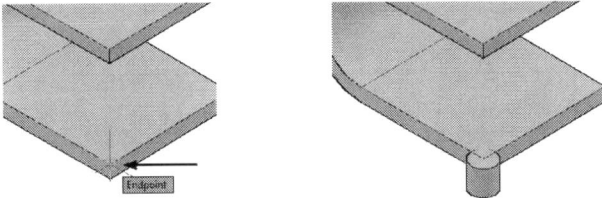

Using the 3D Move tool

The **3D Move** tool is similar to the **Move** tool. You can use this tool to move objects in 3D space. By default, the **3D Move** tool is activated and the **Move gizmo** is displayed when you select an object. You can use the **Move gizmo** to move the object along a particular axis.

- Select the cylinder to display the **Move gizmo** tool.
- Select the X-axis (Red arrow) of the gizmo and move the pointer backwards.
- Type 20 and press ENTER; the cylinder will be moved through 20 mm distance along the X-axis.

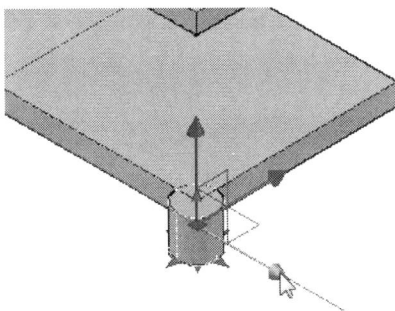

- Select the Y-axis (Green arrow) of the gizmo

and move the pointer toward right.

- Type 20 and press ENTER; the cylinder will be moved as shown below.

Using the 3D Array tool

The **3D Array** tool is used to create Rectangular and polar arrays. You can create a rectangular array by specifying the item count and distance along the X, Y and Z directions. For creating the 3D polar array, you must select any 3D axis to rotate about.

Example 1 (Rectangular Array)

- Type **3DARRAY** in the command line and press ENTER.
- Select the cylinder from the model and press ENTER; the message, "Enter the type of array [Rectangular/Polar] <R>:" appears in the command line.
- Select the **Rectangular** option from the command line; the message, "Enter the number of rows (---) <1>:" appears.
- Type 2 and press ENTER; the message, "Enter the number of columns (| | |) <1>:" appears.
- Type 2 and press ENTER; the message, "Enter the number of levels (...) <1>:" appears.
- Type 2 and press ENTER; the message, "Specify the distance between rows (---):" appears.
- Type 60 and press ENTER; the message,

"Specify the distance between columns (| | |):" appears.

- Type -40 and press ENTER; the message, "Specify the distance between levels (...):" appears.

- Type 80 and press ENTER; the rectangular array will be created as shown below.

- Type **SU** in the command line and press ENTER; the **Subtract** tool will be activated.

- Select the base object and press ENTER; the message, "Select solids, surfaces, and regions to subtract" appears.

- All the cylinders and press ENTER; holes will be created on the model.

Base object

Using the 3D Align tool

The **3D Align** tool aligns one solid with another. It translates and rotates the object to align with the

destination object. You need to select three points on the source object and destination object to align them together. An example of **3D Align** tool is given next.

Example 2:

- Start AutoCAD in **3D Modeling** workspace.

- Select **Front** from the **3D Navigation** drop-down in the **View** panel. Create the solid object as shown below. The extrusion distance is 40 mm.

- Select **Front** from the **3D Navigation** drop-down in the **View** panel. Draw the sketch as shown below and extrude it up to 12 mm using the **Presspull** tool.

- Deactivate the **3D Object Snap** button on the status bar.

- Type **DS** in the command line and press ENTER; the **Drafting Settings** dialog appears.

- Click the **Object Snap** tab and **Clear All** the **Object Snap** modes.

- Now, select the **Endpoint** option and click **OK**.

- Click **Home > Modify > 3D Align** on the ribbon.

- Select the second solid object from the graphics window and press ENTER; the message, "Specify base point or [Copy]:" appears in the command line.

- Select the **Copy** option from the command line.

- Select three end points on the source object as shown below.

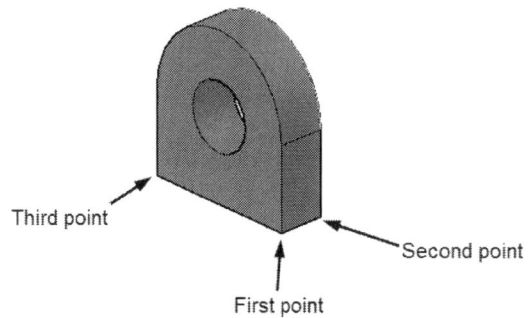

- Select three end points on the destination object as shown below; a copy of the source object will be aligned to the destination object.

- Activate the **Ortho Mode** button on the status bar.

- Type **3DALIGN** in the command line and press ENTER.

- Select the object, which you have aligned in the previous step. Press ENTER to accept the selection.

- Select the base point on the object as shown in figure; the message, "Specify second point or [Continue] <C>:" appears in the command line.

- Select the **Continue** option from the command line; the message, "Specify first destination point:" appears in the command line.

- Select the endpoint on the destination object as shown below.

- Move the pointer along the X-direction and select the endpoint as shown in figure; the message, "Specify third destination point or [eXit] <X>:" appears in the command line.

- Select the **eXit** option from the command line; the source object will be aligned as shown below.

Using the 3D Mirror tool

The **3D Mirror** tool is similar to the **Mirror** tool. Using the **Mirror** tool, you can create mirrored replica of an object in a 2D drawing. The objects are mirrored about an axis lying on a plane. But, with the **3D Mirror** tool, you need to define a plane about which the object will be mirrored. The **3D Mirror** tool provides many options to define the mirror plane.

- Click **Home > Modify > 3D Mirror** on the ribbon.

3D Mirror

Creates a mirrored copy of se plane

- Select the object to be mirrored from the

model and press ENTER; the message, "Specify first point of mirror plane (3 points)" appears above the command line.

Object to mirror

The **3points** option is selected by default to create the mirror plane. You need to specify three points to create the mirror plane. The mirror plane will pass through the selected points.

- Select the first and second point of the mirror plane as shown below.

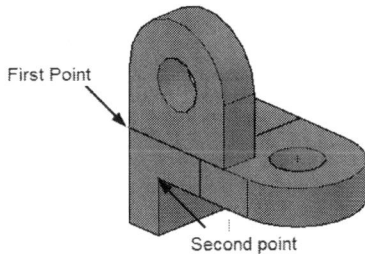

First Point

Second point

- Click the **Orbit** button on the **Navigation Bar** and rotate the model as shown below.

- Right-click and select **Exit** from the shortcut menu.
- Select the third point to define the mirror

plane; the message, "Delete source objects? [Yes/No] <N>:" appears in the command line.

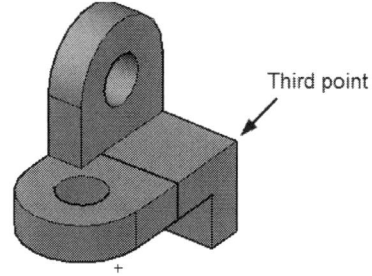

Third point

- Select the **No** option from the command line; the object will be mirrored.

- Click the down arrow next to the **Object Snap** icon on the status bar and select **Center**.
- Type **3DMIRROR** in the command line and press ENTER.
- Select the object to be mirror from the model and press ENTER.

- Select the **XY** option from the command line; the message, "Specify point on XY plane <0,0,0>:" appears in the command line.

The **XY** option creates plane parallel to the XY plane. You need to specify a point at which the plane parallel to the XY plane will be created.

- Select the center point of the horizontal hole to define the mirror plane; the message, "Delete source objects? [Yes/No] <N>:" appears in the command line.

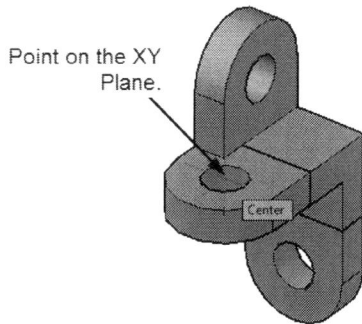

- Select the **No** option; the object will be mirrored, as shown below.

- Click the **Union** button on the **Solid Editing** panel and select all the object of the model.
- Press ENTER; the objects will be combined into a single object.
- Change the view to SE Isometric.

Using the Fillet Edge tool

The **Fillet Edge** tool is used to create rounds (convex corners) or fillets (concave corners) on solid objects, just as in 2D drawings. When you create a fillet or round, a cylinder is created automatically and the Boolean operation is performed to subtract or add it to the solid object.

- Click **Solid > Solid Editing > Fillet Edge** on the ribbon (or) type **FILLETEDGE** in the command line and press ENTER; the message, "Select an edge or [Chain/Loop/Radius]:"

- Select the **Chain** option from the command line; the message, "Select an edge chain or [Edge/Radius]:" appears.
- Select the edges from the model, as shown below; you will notice that a chain of edges is selected.

- Select the **Radius** option from the command line; the message, "Enter fillet radius or [Expression] <1.0000>:" appears.
- Type 2 in the command line and press ENTER.
- Press ENTER; the message, "Press Enter to accept the fillet or [Radius]:"appears. Also, a grip displayed on the fillets. You can use this grip to dynamically change the fillet radius.

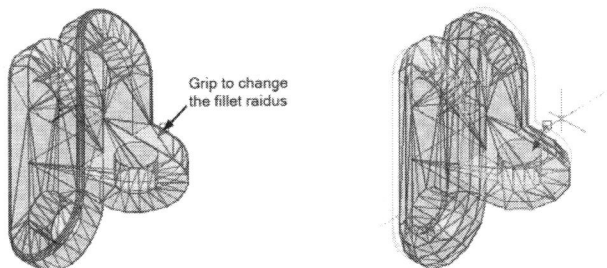

- Press ENTER to create rounds as shown in figure.

- Click the **Fillet Edge** button on the **Solid Editing** panel.
- Select the **Loop** option from the command line

and select the edge from the model, as shown in figure; the edges on the front face of the model are highlighted. Also the message, "Enter an option [Accept/Next] <Accept>:" appears in the command line.

- Select the **Next** option from the command line; the edges on the side face will be highlighted.
- Select the **Accept** button; rounds and fillets are displayed on the side face.

- Likewise, select the round edge as shown in figure and select the **Next** option from the command line; the edges on the bottom face of the model will be highlighted.
- Click the **Orbit** button on the **Navigation Bar** and rotate the model.
- Select the **Accept** option to view rounds and fillets on the bottom face.
- Select the **Radius** option and type 2. Press ENTER to accept.

- Press ENTER twice to create rounds as shown in figure.

- Similarly, create fillets on remaining edges by using the **Chain** option.

- Save and close the file.

Using the Taper Faces tool

The **Taper Faces** tool is used to taper faces. You can use this tool to change the angle of planar or curved faces.

Example 3:

In this example, you will create a polysolid and taper the outer face.

- Start a new AutoCAD file.
- Select **Front** from the **3D Navigation** drop-down on the **Views** panel.
- Create a hollow cylinder with inner and outer diameter as 140 and 150, respectively. The cylinder height is 50.

- Click **Solid > Solid Editing > Taper Faces** on the ribbon.

- Select the outer cylindrical face of the polysolid and press ENTER to accept; the message, "Specify the base point:" appears in the command line.
- Press and hold the SHIFT key and right-click to display the shortcut menu. Select the **Center** option from the shortcut menu.
- Move the pointer over the circular edge on the front face; the center point of the circular edge will be highlighted.
- Select the center point of the circular edge.
- Move the pointer along the Z-direction and click to specify the axis of the taper; the message,

"Specify the taper angle:" appears in the command line.

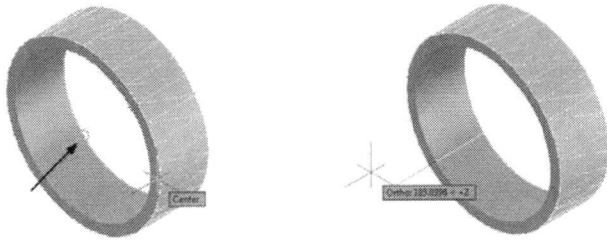

- Type 10 as the taper angle and press ENTER; the outer cylindrical face of the polysolid will be tapered as shown in figure.

- Press Esc

Using the Offset Faces tool

The **Offset Faces** tool is used to make parallel copy of faces of a 3D object.

- Click **Solid > Solid Editing > Faces drop-down > Offset Faces** on the ribbon.

- Select the front face of the model and press ENTER; the message, "Specify the offset distance:" appears in the command line.
- Type -20 in the command line and press ENTER; the face will be offset.

- Press Esc.
- Create a cylinder of 40 mm diameter and 30 mm length at the center of the polysolid.

- Create a truncated cone with the following dimensions.

  Base radius: 8 mm

  Top radius: 5 mm

  Height: 65mm

Using the 3D Rotate tool

The **3D Rotate** tool is used to rotate objects about an axis. You can define the axis of rotation by using the **Rotate Gizmo** tool. The **Rotate**

Gizmo tool will be displayed when you activate the **3D Rotate** tool and select an object.

- Click **Home > Modify > 3D Rotate** on the ribbon.

- Select the truncated cone and press ENTER; the **Rotate Gizmo** tool will be displayed.
- Select the center point of the front face as the base point; the **Rotate Gizmo** tool will be moved to the selected point.

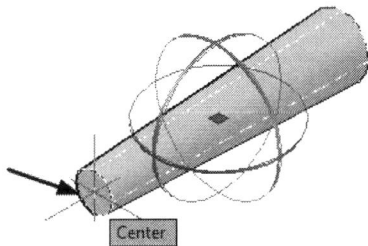

- Select the Z axis (Blue ring) of the **Rotate Gizmo**; an axis line is displayed along the Z-axis.
- Type **270** as the rotation angle and press ENTER; the cone will be rotated by 270 degrees.

- Click the **Move** button on the **Modify** panel and select the cone. Press ENTER to accept.
- Select the base point and the destination point as shown below; the cone will be placed at the destination point.

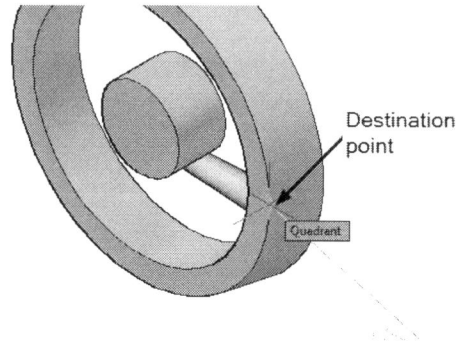

- Select the cone; the **Move Gizmo** tool will be displayed on it.
- Select the Y-axis (Green arrow) of the **Move Gizmo** tool and move the pointer toward right.
- Type 22 in the command line and press ENTER; the cone will be moved through 22 mm.

Using the 3D Polyline tool

The **3D Polyline** tool is similar to the **Polyline** tool, except that you can create a polyline by specifying coordinate points in three dimensions. Also, you can only create straight lines using this tool.

- Change the **Visual Style** of the model to **Wireframe**.
- Click **Home > Draw > 3D Polyline** on the ribbon.

- Select the center point on the front face on the cylindrical object.
- Move the pointer toward right and select the center point on the back face of the cylindrical object.

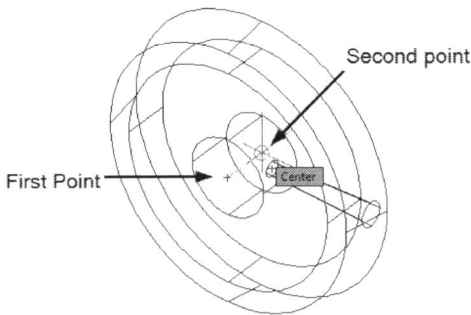

- Press ENTER; the 3D polyline will be created.

Creating a 3D Polar Array

You can create a 3D polar array by using the **Polar** option of the **3DARRAY** command. This option is similar to the 2D **Polar Array** tool. The only difference between these two tools is that you need to specify an axis of rotation in 3D polar array, whereas in 2D Polar array you need to specify an axis point. The axis of rotation in 3D polar array can be specified by selecting two points. This allows you to create a 3D polar array about any axis in the 3D workspace.

- Type **3A** in the command line and press ENTER.
- Select the truncated cone from the model and press ENTER.

- Select the **Polar** option from the command line; the message, "Enter the number of items in the array:" appears.
- Type 6 in the command line and press ENTER; the message, "Specify the angle to fill (+=ccw, - =cw) <360>:" appears in the command line.

  Type + and press ENTER to create the polar array in counter clockwise direction and type – to create it in the clockwise direction.

- Press ENTER to accept 360 as the fill angle; the message, "Rotate arrayed objects? [Yes/No] <Y>:" appears in the command line.
- Select the **Yes** option from the command line; the message, "Specify center point of array:" appears.
- Select the first and second points of the axis as shown in figure; the polar will be created.

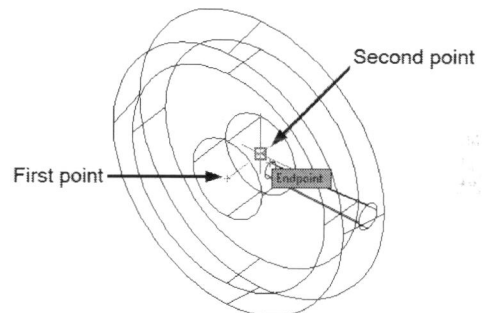

- Change the **Visual Style** to the **Shades of Grey**.
- Perform the **Union** operation to combine all the objects.

Using the Shell tool

The **Shell** tool converts a solid object into a thin walled hollow object. You need to first select the object to be shelled, and then select the faces to be removed and enter the thickness of the walls.

- Click **Solid > Solid Editing > Shell** on the ribbon.
- Select the solid model; the message, "Remove faces or [Undo/Add/ALL]:" appears.
- Select the front face of the cylindrical object.
- Press and hold the SHIFT key, and then press the middle mouse button on drag; the model will be rotated.
- Select the back face of the cylindrical object.

Face to remove

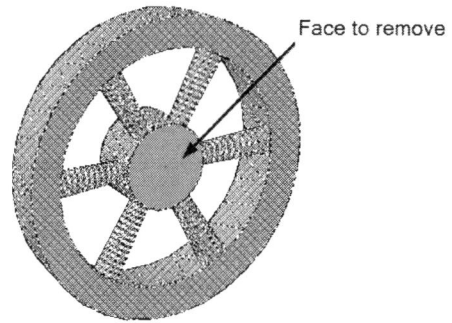

Face to remove

- Press ENTER; the message, "Enter the shell offset distance:" appears.
- Type 10 in the command line and press ENTER; the cylindrical object will be shelled.
- Select the **eXit** option from the command line.

Using the Chamfer Edge tool

The **Chamfer Edge** tool is used to bevel sharp edges of a solid object. When you chamfer an edge, a wedge is created automatically and the Boolean operation is performed to subtract it from the solid object.

- Click **Solid > Solid Editing > Chamfer Edge** on the ribbon.

- Select the outer circular edge of the cylindrical object.
- Select the **Distance** option from the command line; the message, "Specify Distance1 or [Expression] <1.0000>:" appears.
- Type 4 in the command line and press ENTER; you will notice that preview of the chamfer changes. Also, the message, "Specify Distance2 or [Expression] <1.0000>:" appears in the command line.
- Type 2 in the command line and press ENTER.
- Press ENTER twice to the chamfer, as shown in figure.

Using the Section Plane tool

The **Section Plane** tool is creates a translucent cutting plane passing through a solid object to show the inside portion of it. This tool is very useful when the inside portion of the solid is not visible. You can move this cutting plane dynamically to view the inside portion at different locations of the solid.

- To create a section plane, click **Solid > Section > Section Plane** on the ribbon; the message, "Select face or any point to locate

section line or [Draw section/Orthographic]:" appears.

- Select the **Orthographic** option from the command line.
- Select **Right**.

Using the Live Section tool

The **Live Section** tool is used to make one side of the section plane invisible or visible. When you create a section plane by selecting plane, one side of the section plane will be invisible automatically. However, when you create a section plane by selecting points, you need to use the **Live Section** tool to make the one side invisible. Click **Solid > Section > Live Section** on the ribbon. Next, select the section plane; one side of the section plane will be hidden or unhidden as shown in figure.

- Save the file as **Example 3**.

Creating Drawing Views

In Chapter 5, you have learned to create multi view drawings using the standard projection techniques. Now, you will learn to automatically generate views of a 3D model.

Setting the Drafting Standard

Before you start generating the drawing views of 3D model, you need to specify the drafting standard. This defines the way the views will be generated. To specify the drafting standard, click **Home > View > Drafting Standard (inclined arrow)** on the ribbon; the **Drafting Standard** dialog appears.

- In the **Drafting Standard** dialog, set the **Projection type** to **Third angle.**

- Examine the other options in the dialog, as they are self-explanatory.

- Click the **OK** button.

Creating a Base View

Base view will be the first view of the drawing. It can be any view (front, top, right, left, bottom, back) of the model. But commonly, the front or top views of the model are generated first.

- Open the **Example 3.dwg**, if it is not already opened.
- To generate the base view of the model, click **Home > View > Base > From Model Space** on the ribbon; the message, "Select objects or [Entire model] <Entire model>:" appears in the command line.

- Select the **Entire model** option from the command line; the model in the model space will be selected and the message, "Enter new or existing layout name to make current or [?] <Layout1>:" appears in the command line.
- Press ENTER to select **Layout 1**; the base view will be attached to the pointer and the message, "Specify location of base view or [Type/sElect/Orientation/Hidden lines/Scale/Visibility] <Type>:" appears in the command line. Also, the **Drawing View Creation** tab appears in the ribbon.

- Specify the location of the view in the paper space, as shown below.

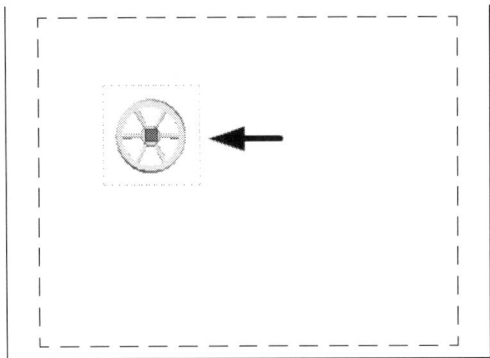

- In the **Drawing View Creation** tab, set the **Orientation** to **Front**.
- Select the **Visible Lines** option from the **Hidden Lines** drop-down.

- Set the **Scale** in the **Appearance** panel to **1:4**.
- Click the **OK** button on the **Create** panel to create the base view; a projected view will be attached to the pointer and you will be asked to specify its location. You will learn to create projected views in the next section.
- Press ENTER to exit the command.

Creating a Projected View

A projected view can be created from an existing view. It can be an orthographic view or isometric view generated by projecting from a base view or any other existing view.

- To create a projected view, click **Layout > Create View > Projected** on the ribbon, and then select the base view from the **Layout 1**; the projected view will be attached to the pointer.
- Move the pointer downward and specify the location of the projected view, as shown below.

- Move the pointer diagonally toward top-right corner and place the isometric view as shown below.

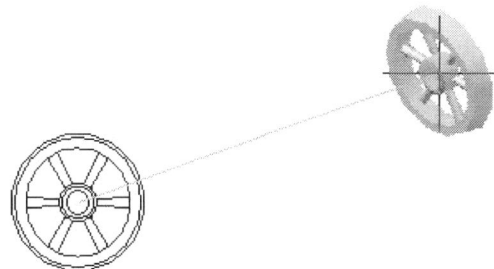

- Select the **eXit** option from the command line to exit the command.

Creating Section Views

In Chapter 8, you have learned to create section views manually. Now, you will learn to generate section views automatically from a 3D model. You can create different types of section views using the tools available in the **Section** drop-down in the **Create Views** panel.

Creating the Section View Style

Section View Style defines the display of the section view and the cutting plane. To create a section view style, click **Layout > Styles and Standards > Section View Style** on the ribbon; the **Section View Style Manager** dialog appears. Click the **New** button in the **Section View Style Manager** dialog; the **Create New Section View Style** dialog appears. Type **Example** in the **New Style Name** box and click **Continue**; the **New Section View Style** dialog appears. In this dialog, click the **Cutting Plane** tab and select the **Show cutting plane lines** option.

Click the **Hatch** tab and set the **Hatch Scale** to **0.5** and click **OK**. Click the **Set current** button on the **Section View Style Manager** dialog and click **Close**.

Creating a Full Section View

To create a full section view, click **Layout > Create Views > Section > Full** on the ribbon. Next, select the base view from the layout. After selecting the base view, you need to specify the start and end points of the cutting plane. Select the start point of the cutting plane by as shown below. Move the pointer vertically upward and specify the end point of the cutting plane.

Move the pointer toward right and click to specify the location of the section view. Select the **eXit** option to create the section view.

A-A (1:4)

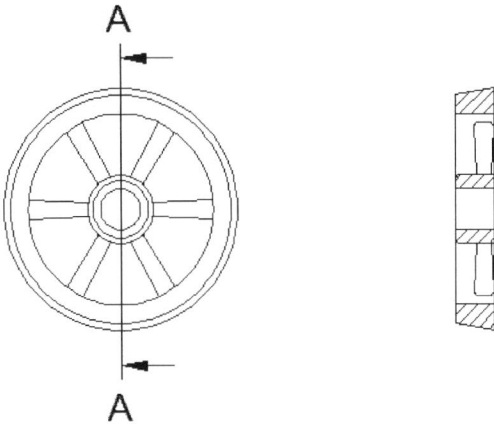

Creating a Detailed View

A detailed view is created to enlarge and view small portions of a drawing.

- To create a detailed view, click **Layout > Create Views > Detail > Circular** on the ribbon; the message, "Select parent view" appears in the command line.

- Select the section view from the layout; the message, "Specify center point or [Hidden

Exercises

Create 3D models using the drawing views and dimensions.

lines/Scale/Visibility/Boundary/model Edge/Annotation] <Boundary>:" appears in the command line.

- Select a point on the section view, as shown below; the message, "Specify size of boundary or [Rectangular/Undo]:" appears in the command line.

- Draw a circle similar to the one shown below.

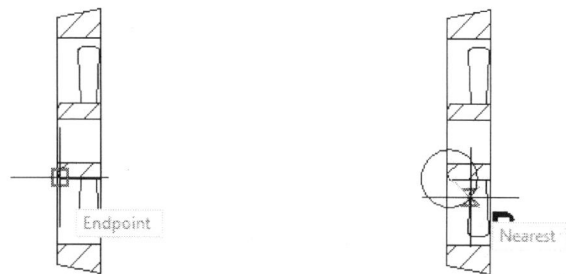

- Next, place the detail view on the lower right corner of the layout.

- Select the **Smooth with border** button on the **Model Edge** panel of the **Detail View Creation** tab.

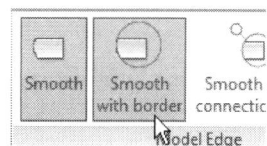

- Click **Detail View Creation > Create > OK** on the ribbon; the detail view will be created.

R50

32

4X Ø10 THRU

10

R30

32

R10

R16

21

104

8 HOLES Ø16
EQUI-SPACED ON 90 PCD

Ø130

PIPE I.D.=50 mm
PIPE O.D.=60 mm

500

20

250

500

R35

250

20

400

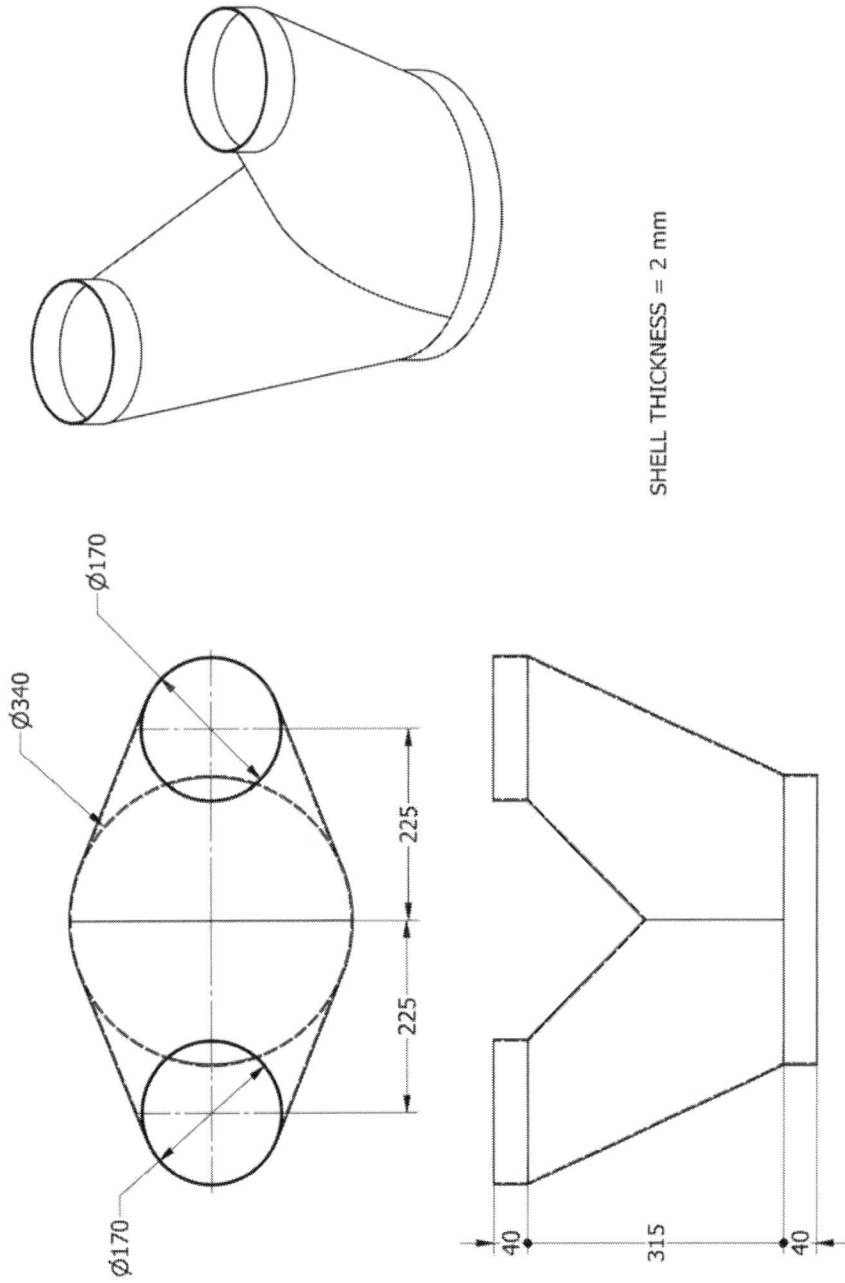

SHELL THICKNESS = 2 mm

Ø170

Ø340

Ø170

225

225

40

315

40

Chapter 14: Creating Architectural Drawings

In this chapter, you will learn to do the following:

- **Defining Settings for Architectural Drawings**

- **Creating Inner Walls**

- **Creating Openings and Doors**

- **Creating Kitchen Fixtures**

- **Creating Bathroom Fixtures**

- **Adding Furniture using Blocks**

- **Adding Windows**

- **Arranging Objects of the drawing in Layers**

- **Creating Grid Lines**

- **Adding Dimensions**

Introduction

In this chapter, you will learn to create architectural drawing shown below.

Creating Outer Walls

- Start **AutoCAD 2017** and click **Get Started > Templates > acad.dwt**.

- Set the **Workspace** to **Drafting & Annotation**.

  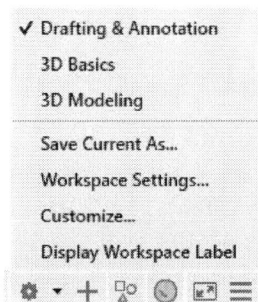

- Type UN in the command line and press Enter.

- On the **Drawing Units** dialog, select **Type > Architectural**.

- Select **Precision > 0-01/16**.

- Set the **Insertion Scale** to **Inches**, and click **OK**.

- Type LIMITS in the command line and press Enter.

- Press Enter to accept 0, 0 as the lower limit.

- Type 100', 80' in the command line and press Enter. The program sets the upper limit of the drawing.

- Turn OFF the grid.

- Double-click the middle mouse button to zoom extents.

- On the Status bar, turn ON the **Ortho Mode** icon.

- On the ribbon, click **Home > Draw > Line**, and then select an arbitrary point. This defines the start point of the line.

- Move the pointer horizontally and type-in 412 in the Dynamic Input box. Press Enter.

- Move the pointer vertically and type-in 338 in the Dynamic Input box. Press Enter.

- Move the pointer onto the starting point of the drawing, and then move it upwards.

You will notice that a dotted line appears.

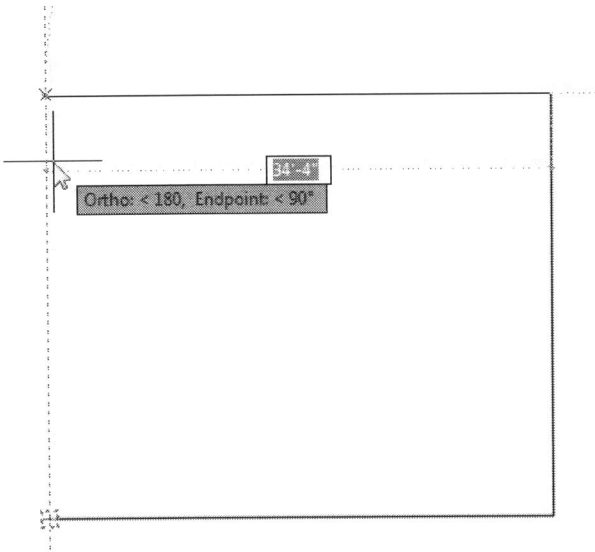

- Click to create a horizontal line. You will notice that the horizontal line is of same length.
- Click the right mouse button and select **Close**.

- On the ribbon, click **Home > Modify > Offset**.
- Type-in 6 as offset distance and press Enter.
- Select the left vertical line of the drawing.
- Move the pointer inside the drawing and click to create an offset line.

- Likewise, offset the other lines, as shown below.

- On the Navigation Bar, click **Zoom > Zoom Window**.

  - ✓ Zoom Extents
  - Zoom Window
  - Zoom Previous
  - Zoom Realtime
  - Zoom All
  - Zoom Dynamic
  - Zoom Scale
  - Zoom Center
  - Zoom Object
  - Zoom In
  - Zoom Out

- Create a window on the top left corner of the drawing. The corner portion will be zoomed in.

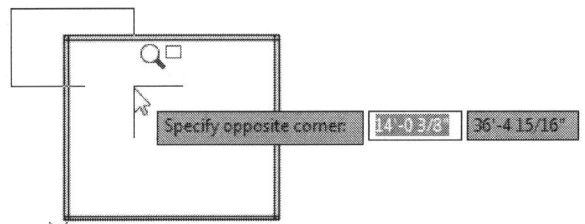

- On the ribbon, click **Home > Modify > Fillet**.
- Select the **Radius** option on the command line, and then type-in 0. Press Enter.

- Select the inner offset lines, as shown below.

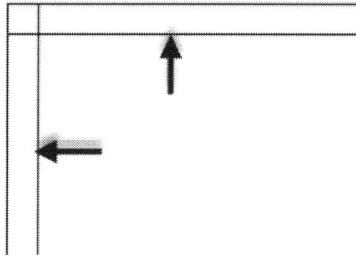

- Press Enter to activate the Fillet command, again.
- Select the inner offset line at the top right corner.
- Likewise, fillet the other corners.

- Save the drawing. Make sure that you save the drawing after each section.

Creating Inner Walls

- Activate the **Offset** command and type-in **130** in the command line, and then press Enter.
- Select the inner line of the right side wall and click inside the drawing.
- Press Esc.

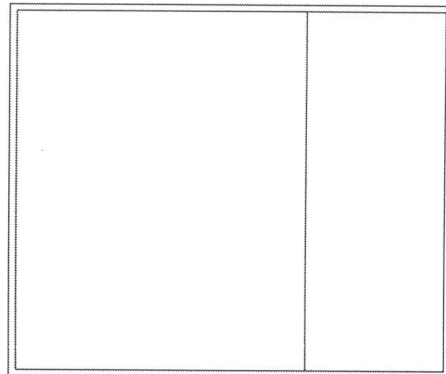

- Select the new offset line. You will notice that three grips are displayed on the line.
- Click the right mouse button and select **Copy Selection**.

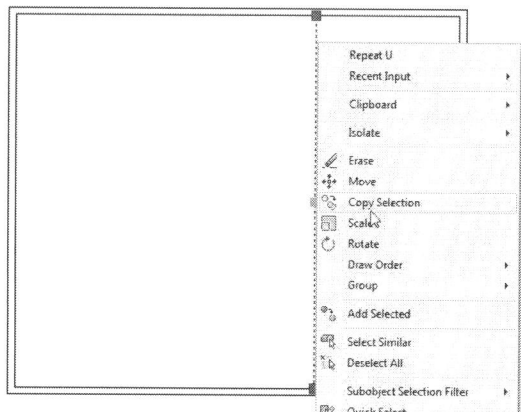

- Select the endpoint of the selected line as base point.
- Move the pointer toward left and type-in 4, and then press Enter. A new line is created

and another line is attached to the pointer.

- Move the pointer toward left and type-in 118, and then press Enter.

- Move the pointer toward left and type-in 122, and then press Enter.
- Press Esc to come out of the **Copy** command.

- Likewise, create horizontal offset lines, as shown below.

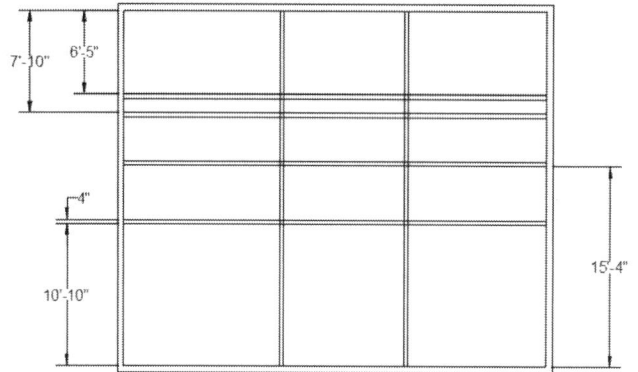

- On the ribbon, click **Home > Modify > Trim**.
- Press Enter to select all the elements of the drawing as cutting elements.
- Click on the lines at the locations shown below.

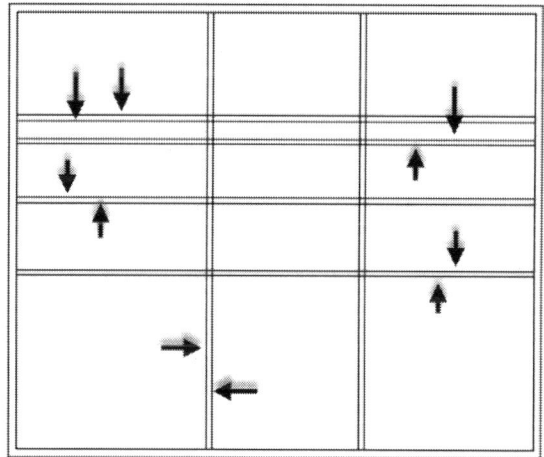

- Create a selection window, as shown below.

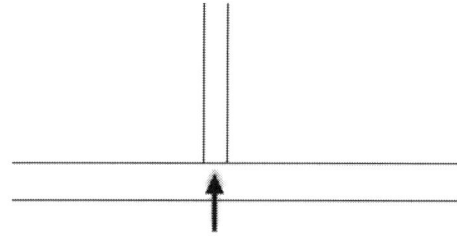

- Trim the unwanted portions, as shown below.

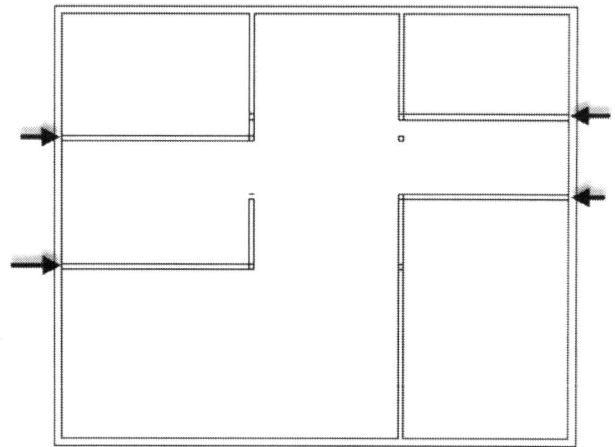

- Zoom to the top portion of the drawing by rotating the mouse scroll in the forward direction.

- Select the portion of the horizontal line that lies between the lines of the inner wall. The selected portions will be trimmed.

- Trim the unwanted portions at the corners.

- Press and hold the mouse scroll wheel and drag downwards until the lower portion of the drawing is visible.

- Trim the unwanted portion, as shown below.

other corner point.

- Press Esc to deactivate the **Trim** command.
- Select the unwanted portion and press Delete.

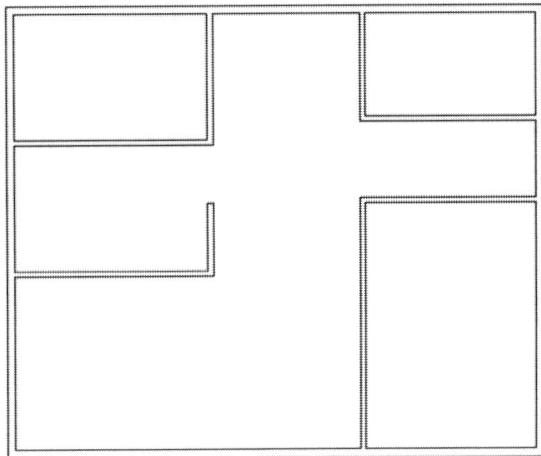

- Deactivate the **Line** command and select the new line.
- Select the middle point of the new line and move pointer toward right.
- Type-in 6 and press Enter.

- Activate the **Offset** command, and specify 32 as the offset distance.
- Select the new line and move rightwards, and then click.

Creating Openings and Doors

- Activate the **Line** command select the corner of the inner wall, as shown below.
- Move the pointer downward and select the

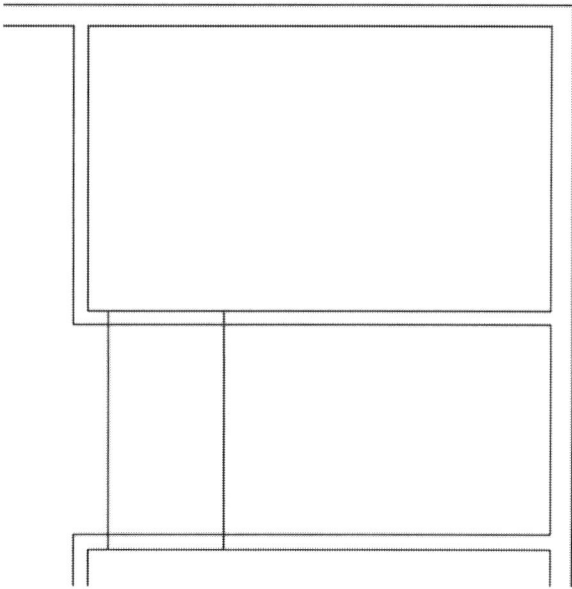

- Activate the **Trim** command and trim the unwanted portions.

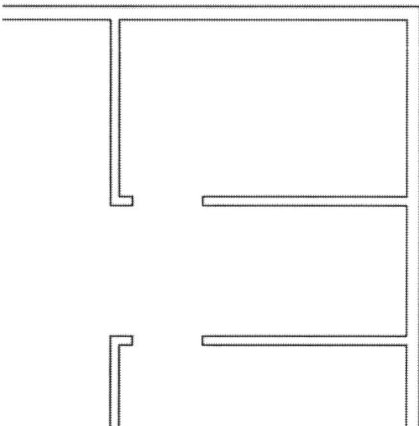

- Likewise, create other openings, as shown below.

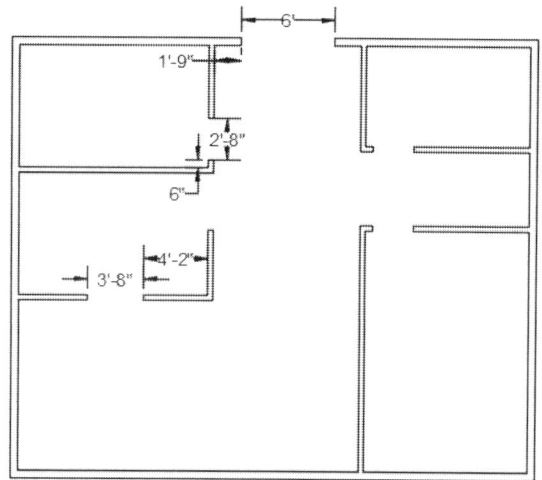

- On the ribbon, click **Home > Draw > Rectangle**.

- Select the endpoint of the opening, as shown below.

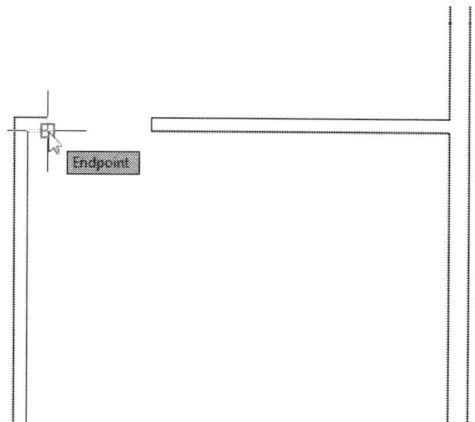

- Select **Dimensions** from the command line.

- Type-in 1 and press Enter. This defines the length of the rectangle.

- Type-in 32 and press Enter. This defines the width of the rectangle.

- Move the pointer down and click to create the door. Now, you need to create the door swing.

base point.

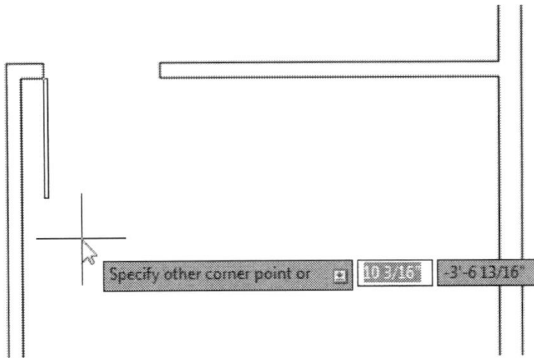

- On the ribbon, click **Home > Draw > Arc drop-down > Start Center End**.

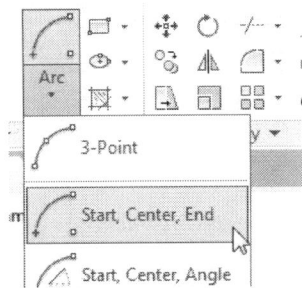

- Select the start, center, and end of the arc in the sequence shown below.

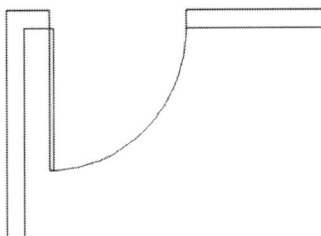

- Select the door and door swing.
- Click the right mouse button and select **Copy Selection**.
- Select the corner point of the rectangle as

- Select the corner points of openings, as shown below.

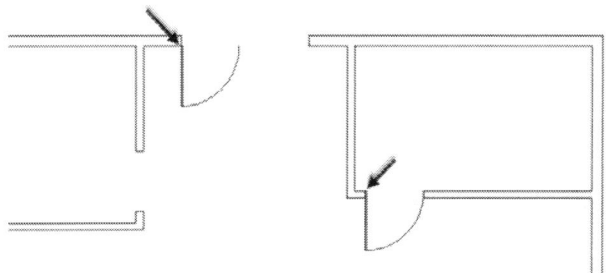

- Press Esc to deactivate the **Copy** command.
- On the ribbon, click **Home > Modify > Mirror**, and then select the door and swing of the bathroom. Press Enter to accept the selection.
- Define the mirror line my selecting the points, as shown below.

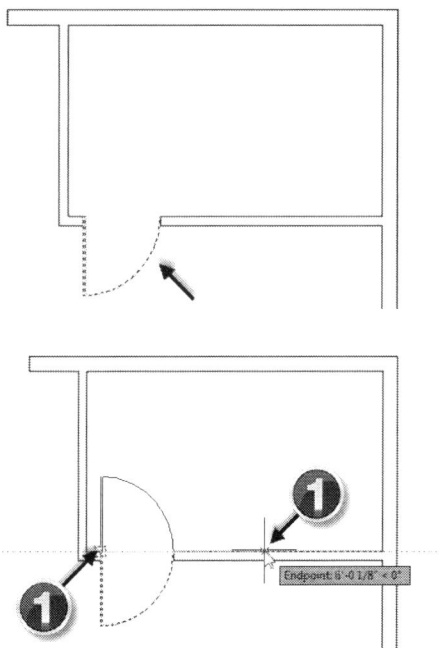

This defines the reference length of the objects. Now, you need to define the length up to which you want to scale the objects.

- Type-in 36 and press Enter. The objects will be scaled.

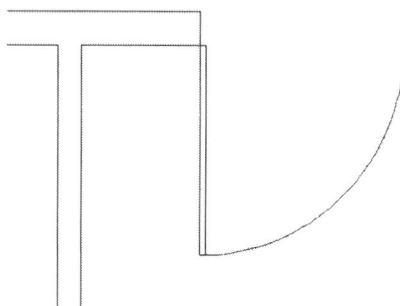

- Select **Yes** from the command line. This deletes the original object.

- On the ribbon, click **Home > Modify > Scale**, and then select the door & swing at the main entrance. Press Enter.

- Select the base point, as shown below.

- Activate the **Mirror** command and select the door & swing at the entrance. Press Enter to accept the selection.

- Define the mirror line by selecting the points, as shown below.

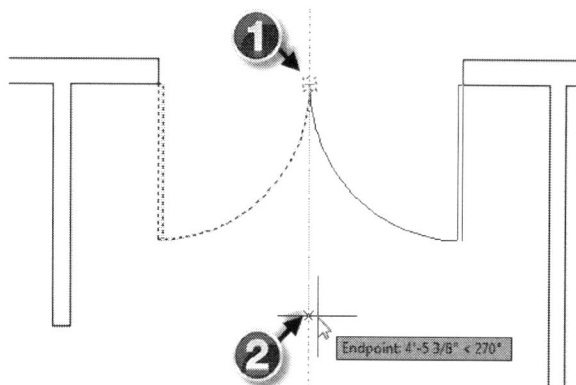

- Select the **Reference** option from the command line.

- Select the two endpoints, as shown below.

- Select **No** from the command line. This

keeps the original object.

- Copy the door & swing of the bathroom and place at the opening, as shown below.
- Press Esc.

- On the ribbon, click **Home > Modify > Rotate**, and then select the copied object.
- Rotate the objects by selecting the base point and typing 90 as the rotation angle.

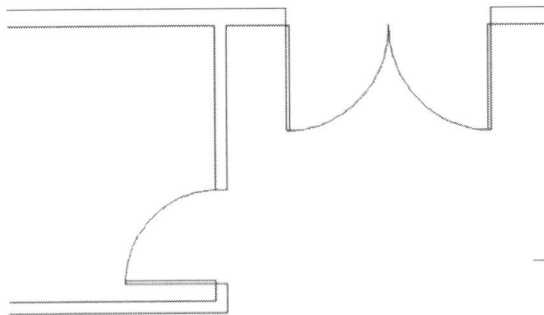

- Create an opening on the rear side of the plan, as shown below.

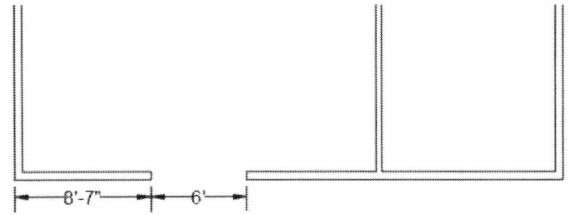

Now, you will create sliding door in the opening.

- Activate the **Rectangle** command and select the corner point of the opening, as shown below.

- Select the **Dimensions** option from the command line.
- Specify 37 and 2 as length and width of the rectangle, respectively.
- Move the pointer upward and click to create the rectangle.

- Type **M** in the command line and press Enter. Select the rectangle, and then press Enter.
- Select its lower left corner point to define the base point. Move the pointer upward and type-in 1 in the command line, and then press Enter.

- On the ribbon, click **Home > Modify >**

Explode, and select the rectangle. Press Enter to explode the rectangle.

- Activate the **Offset** command and specify 2 as the offset distance.

- Offset the left and right vertical lines of the rectangle.

- Click the down arrow next to the **Object Snap** icon on the status bar, and then select **Midpoint** from the flyout.

- Activate the **Line** command and select the midpoints of the offset lines. This creates a line connecting the offset lines. This creates one part of the sliding door.

- Press Esc to deactivate the line command.

- Type-in CO in the command line and press Enter.

- Drag a selection window covering all the elements of the sliding door. Press Enter.

- Select the lower left corner of the sliding door as base point.

- Move the pointer and select the endpoint of the offset line, as shown.

- Press Esc to deactivate the **Copy** command.

Now, you need to draw thresholds on the door openings.

- Zoom to the front door area using the **Zoom Window** tool.

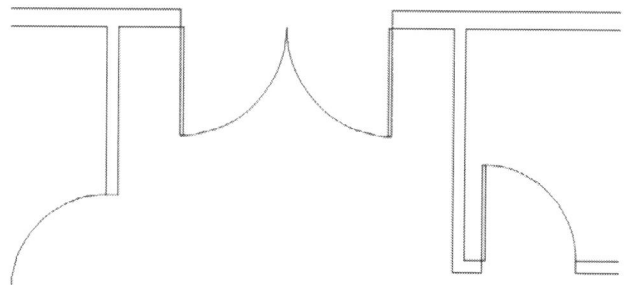

- On the status bar, click the down arrow next to the **Object Snap** button and make sure that **Endpoint**, **Nearest** and **Perpendicular** options are selected.

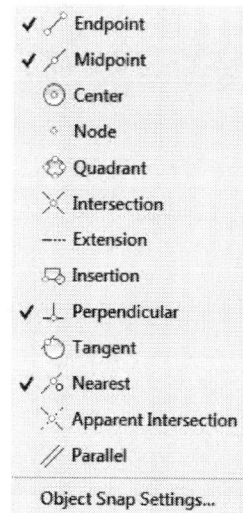

- Type-in L in the command line and press Enter.

- Press and hold Shift key and click the right mouse button.

303

- Select **From** from the shortcut menu and click the endpoint of the door opening, as shown below.
- Move the point on the horizontal line and type-in 3, and then press Enter. This defines the start point of the line at 3 distance from the endpoint.

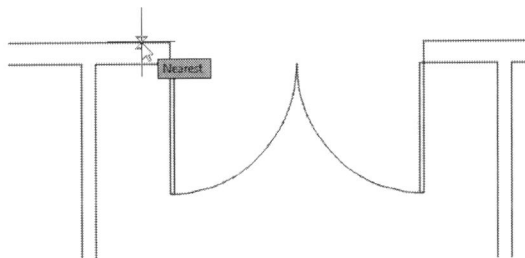

- Move the pointer up and type-in 2, and then press Enter.
- Move the pointer toward right and type-in 78, and then press Enter.
- Move the pointer downward and type-in 2, and then press Enter.

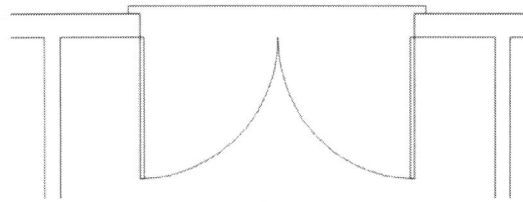

- Press Esc to deactivate the **Line** command.
- Likewise, create a threshold on the sliding glass door.

Creating Kitchen Fixtures

- Zoom to the kitchen area by using the **Zoom Window** tool.

- Activate the **Offset** command, and specify 26 as the offset distance.
- Offset the lines shown below.

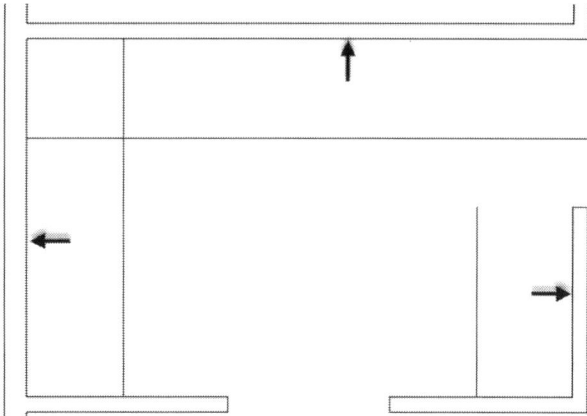

- Trim the unwanted portions.

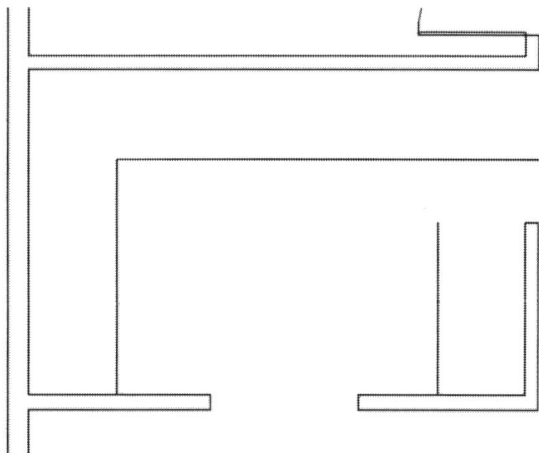

- Create another offset line at 54 distance, and then trim the unwanted elements.

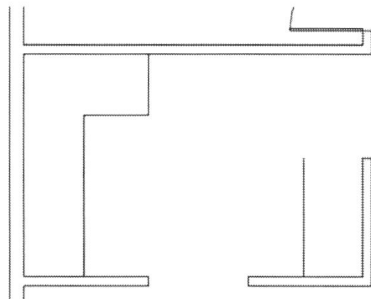

- Create another line, as shown below.

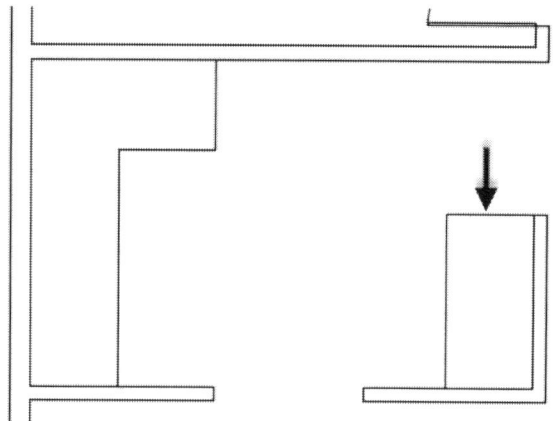

Now, you have finished drawing the counters. You need to draw refrigerator, stove, and sink.

- Type-in REC in the command line and press Enter. This activates the **Rectangle** command.

- Select the corner point of the counter.

- Select the **Dimensions** option from the command line.

- Specify 28 as length and width of the rectangle. Move the pointer toward right and click to create the rectangle.

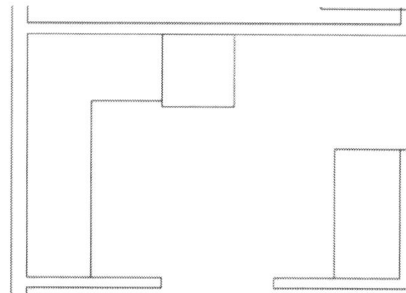

- Use the **Move** command to move the rectangle 2 rightwards and downwards.

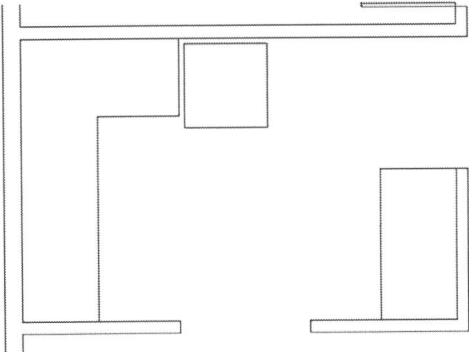

- Create the outline of the stove using the **Line** command.

Now, you need to create the sink.

- Use the **Offset** command and create offset lines, as shown below.

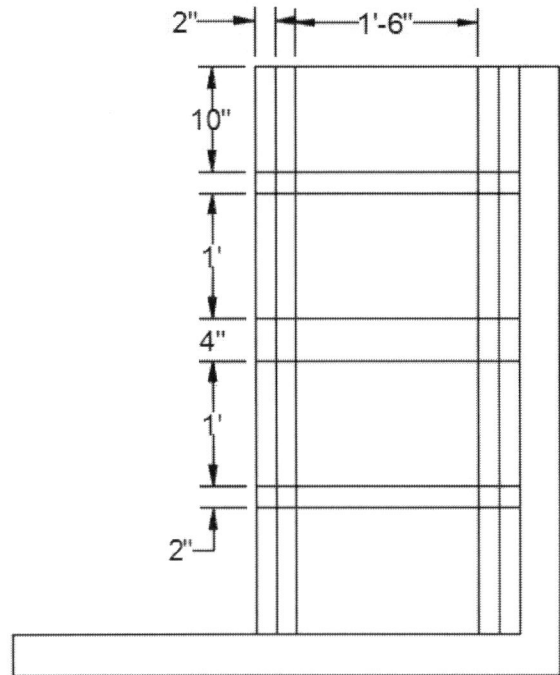

- Trim the unwanted elements, as shown below.

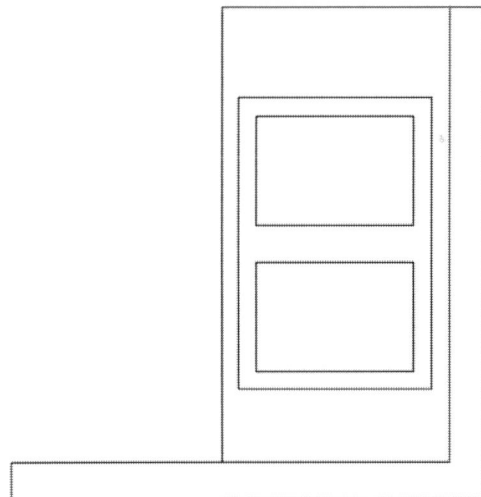

- Fillet the corners, as shown below.

- Activate the **Circle** command and hover the pointer on the midpoints of the sink edges and move, as shown below.

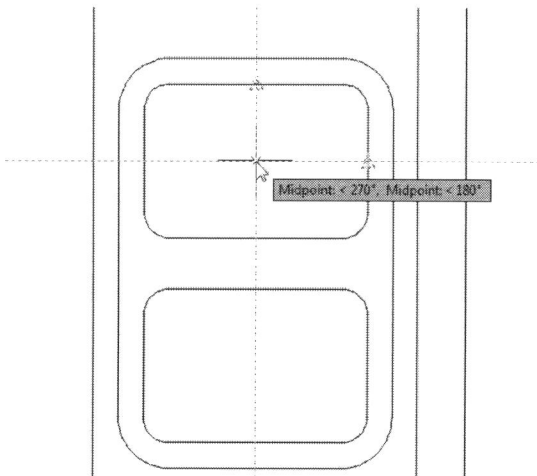

- Create the circles at the intersection points of the trace lines.

Creating Bathroom Fixtures

- Zoom into the bathroom area and create offset lines, as shown below.

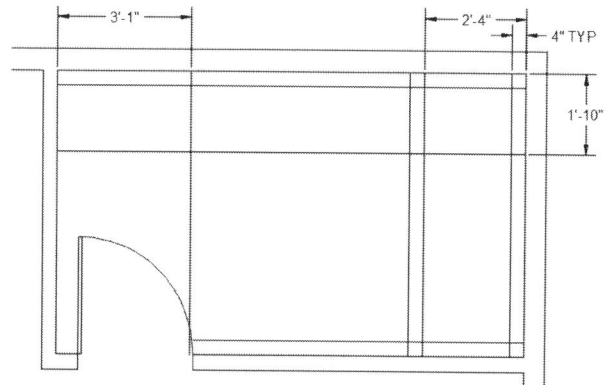

- Trim the unwanted elements, as shown below.

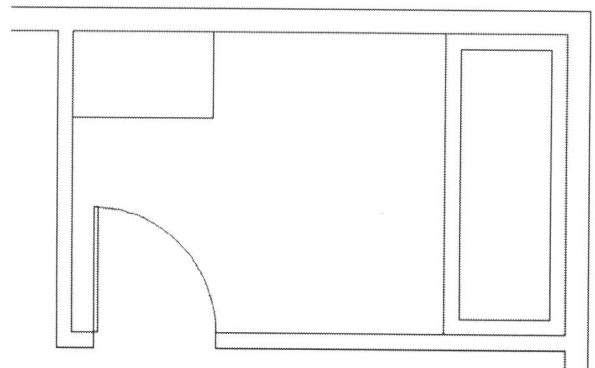

- Fillet the corners, as shown below. The fillet radius is 4.

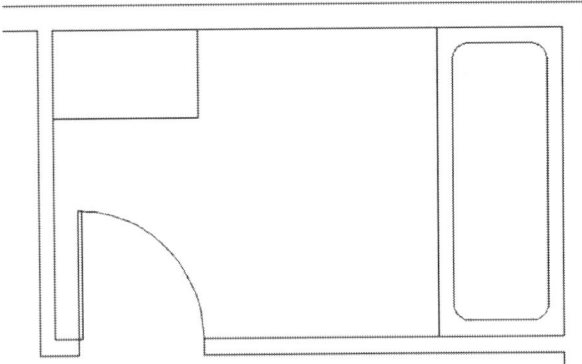

- On the ribbon, click **Home > Draw > Ellipse drop-down > Center**.

- Hover the pointer on the midpoints of the vertical and horizontal lines, as shown below.
- Move the pointer and click at the intersection point of the trace lines.

- Move the pointer toward right and type-in 10, and then press Enter. This defines the major radius of the ellipse.

- Move the pointer downward and type-in 5, and then press Enter. This defines the minor radius of the ellipse.

- Likewise, create another ellipse of 11 major radius and 7 minor radius.

- Select the outer ellipse, and then click on the center point of the ellipse.
- Move the pointer up and type-in 1, and then press Enter. The outer ellipse moves up.

- Activate the **Rectangle** command and create a 22 x 9 rectangle, as shown below.

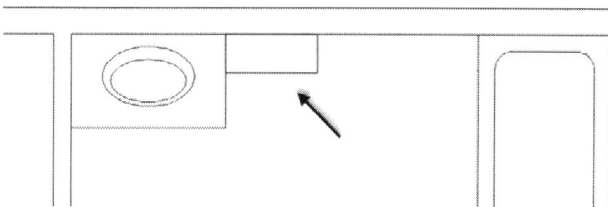

- Move the rectangle up to 19.5 rightwards and 1 downwards.

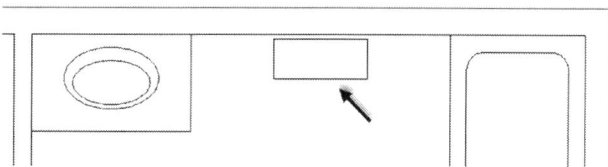

- On the ribbon, click **Home > Draw > Ellipse drop-down > Axis, End**.

- Select the midpoint of the lower horizontal

line of the rectangle.

- Move the pointer downward and type-in 18, and then press Enter.

- Type-in 6 as the minor radius and press Enter.

Adding Furniture using Blocks

- Type **DC** and press Enter. This opens the **Design Center** palette.

- On the **Design Center** palette, click the **Home** button. This opens the folder in which all the samples are located.

- In the **Design Center** palette, expand the **Sample** folder and go to **en-us > Design Center > Home –Space Planner.dwg**.

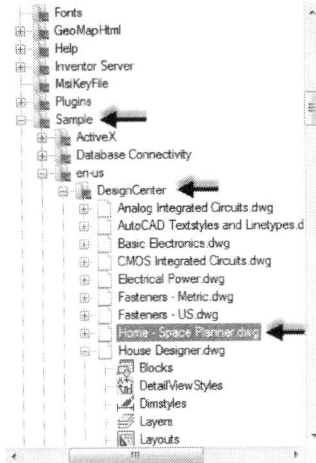

- Double-click the **Blocks** icon. This displays all the blocks available in the selected drawing file.

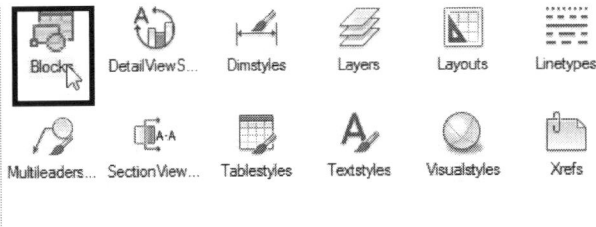

- Click and drag the highlighted blocks into the graphics window.

- Close the **Design Center** palette.
- Select the Dining set block, and then click on the point located at its center.
- Move the block and place it at the location shown below.

- Activate the **Rectangle** command and select the corner point of the bedroom.

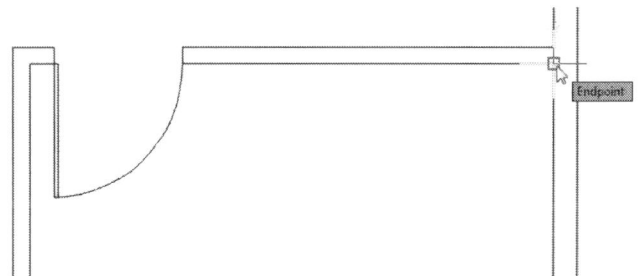

- Select the **Dimensions** option from the command line, and then specify 90 and 27.5 as length and width of the rectangle, respectively.
- Move the pointer downward and click create the rectangle.

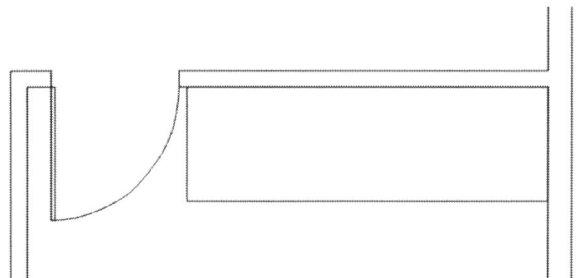

- Create another rectangle by selecting the corner points, as shown below.

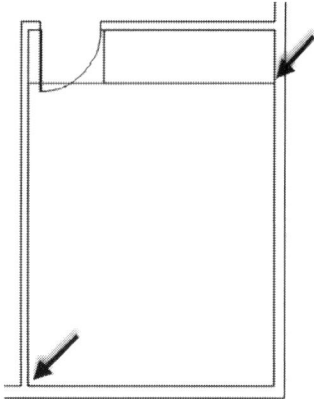

- Offset the rectangle 47.5 inwards.

- Delete the original rectangle.

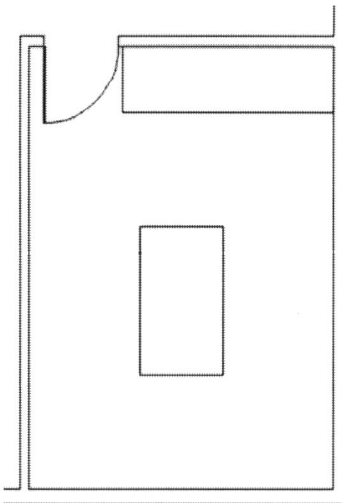

- Rotate the bed by **90** degrees.

- Activate the **Move** command and select the bed. Press Enter to accept the selection.

- Select the top left corner of the bed to define the base point.

- Select the top left corner of the offset rectangle to define the destination point.

- Delete the offset rectangle.

Adding Windows

- Use the **Line** command and create the window, as shown below.

- On the ribbon, click **Insert > Block Definition > Create Block**.

- On the **Block Definition** dialog, type-in **Window** in the **Name** box.

- Click the **Select Objects** button and select all

the elements of the window by dragging a selection window.

- Press Enter.
- Click the **Pick point** button and select the lower left corner of the window.

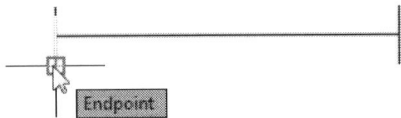

- On the dialog, check the **Open in block editor** option and click **OK**. This creates the block and opens it in the **Block Editor**.
- In the **Block Editor** window, activate **Authoring Palettes**, if inactive.

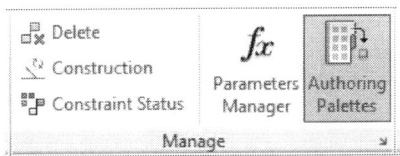

- On **Authoring Palettes**, click the **Parameters** tab and select the **Linear** command.

- Click the endpoints of the horizontal line to define the linear parameter between them.

- On **Authoring Palettes**, click the **Actions** tab and select the **Stretch** command.

- Select the **Distance1** parameter.
- Select the right endpoint of the horizontal line. This defines the point that can be used to stretch the block.

- Create a window around the selected endpoint.

- Select the horizontal and right vertical line, and then press Enter. This defines the elements that can be stretched.

- On the **Block Editor** ribbon tab, click **Open/Save > Test Block**. The **Test Block**

Window appears.

- Select the block and click the arrow grip. Drag the pointer to stretch the block.

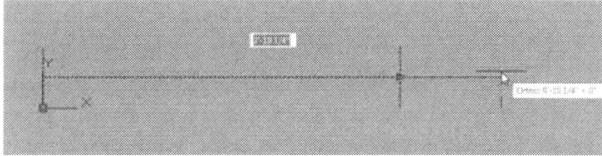

- On the ribbon, click the **Close Test Block** button.

- Click the **Save Block** button on the **Open/Save** panel.

- Click the **Close Block Editor** button on the **Close** panel. This closes the **Block Editor** window. Now, you need to place the windows.

- On the ribbon, click **Insert > Block > Insert > Window**.

- Press and hold the Shift key and right click.

- Select **From**.

- Select the lower right corner of the bedroom.

- Move the pointer on the horizontal wall and type-in 95, and then press Enter. The **Window** block will be placed at the specified location.

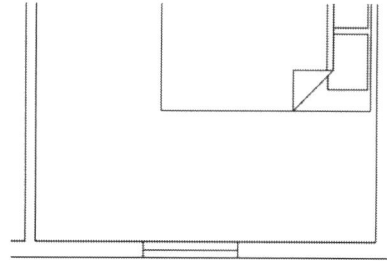

- Select the **Window** block and drag the arrow grip.

- Type-in 54 and press Enter. This changes the window size to 54.

- On the ribbon, click **Insert > Block > Insert > Window**.

- Select the **Rotate** option from the command line.

- Type-in **90** and press Enter.

- Place the **Window** block on the kitchen wall, as shown below.

Arranging Objects of the drawing in Layers

- Likewise, place the window blocks, as shown below.

- On the ribbon, click the **Home > Layers > Layer Properties**. This displays the Layer Properties Manager.

- On the Layer Properties Manager, click the **New Layer** button.

Current layer: 0

- Type **Wall** in the layer **Name** box and press Enter.

- Create another layer, and then type-in Door. Press Enter.

- Likewise, create other layers and define the layer properties, as shown below. Refer to Chapter 3 to learn more about layers.

S...	Name	O...	Fre...	L...	Color	Linetype	Lineweight
✓	0	♀	☼	🔓	■ white	Continuous	—— Default
▱	Counter	♀	☼	🔓	■ red	Continuous	—— Default
▱	Defpoints	♀	☼	🔓	■ white	Continuous	—— Default
▱	Dimensions	♀	☼	🔓	■ 8	Continuous	—— Default
▱	Door	♀	☼	🔓	□ yellow	Continuous	—— Default
▱	Fixtures	♀	☼	🔓	■ magenta	Continuous	—— Default
▱	Furniture	♀	☼	🔓	□ 9	Continuous	—— Default
▱	Grid	♀	☼	🔓	□ 9	DASHED	—— Default
▱	Roof	♀	☼	🔓	■ white	DASHED	—— Default
▱	Section Line	♀	☼	🔓	■ white	PHANTOM	—— Default
▱	Stairs	♀	☼	🔓	■ blue	Continuous	—— Default
▱	Text	♀	☼	🔓	■ white	Continuous	—— Default
▱	Wall	♀	☼	🔓	■ green	Continuous	—— Default
▱	Window	♀	☼	🔓	■ white	Continuous	—— Default

- Close the Layer Properties Manager.

- Select the Dining set, cupboard, and bed.

- On the ribbon, click **Home > Layers > Layer drop-down > Furniture**. The selected objects will be transferred to the Furniture layer.

click the bulb symbols associated to Door, Window, Fixtures Furniture, and Counter layers. This will hide corresponding layers.

- Press Esc to deselect the selected objects.
- Likewise, transfer the other objects to their respective layers.

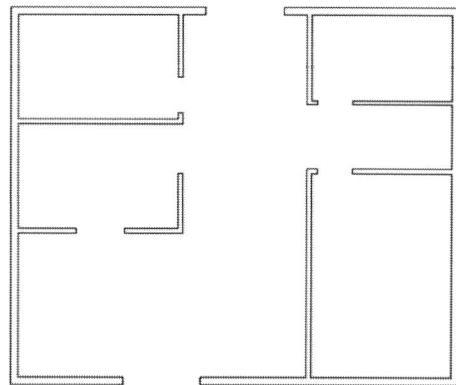

- Create a selection window and select all the walls.
- On the ribbon, click **Home > Layers > Layer drop-down > Wall**. All the walls will be transferred to the **Wall** layer.

- Open the Layer Properties Manager and

- Now, turn ON the hidden layers by clicking the bulb symbols.

Creating Grid Lines

- On the ribbon, click **Home > Layers > Layer drop-down > Grid**. The Grid layer becomes active.

- Activate the **Line** command.
- Press and hold the Shift key and right-click, and then select the **Mid Between 2 Points** option.
- Select the endpoints of the wall, as shown below.

- Move the point upward and click to draw vertical line of arbitrary length.

- Select the line to display grips on it.
- Click the lower end grip and drag the pointer to increase the length of line.
- Activate the **Offset** command and offset the grid line up to 406.
- Create other grid lines, as shown below.

- Create a new layer called **Grid Bubbles** and make it current.

- Create a circle of 12 diameter.
- On the ribbon, click **Insert > Block Definition > Define Attributes**.

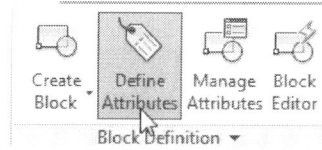

- On the **Attribute Definition** dialog, type-in GRIDBUBBLE in the **Tag** box and select **Justification > Middle center**.
- Type-in 6″ in the **Text height** box and click **OK**.
- Select the center point of the circle. The attribute text will be place at it center.

GRIDBUBBLE

- On the ribbon, click **Insert > Block Definition > Create Block**.
- Type-in Grid bubble in the **Name** box and click the **Select objects** button.
- Draw a crossing window to select the circle and attribute. Press Enter to accept the selection.
- Check the **Pick point** option under the **Base point** section.
- Select the lower quadrant point of the circle to define the base point of the block.

- Uncheck the **Open in block editor** option and click **OK**.
- On the ribbon, click **Insert > Block > Insert > Grid bubble**.

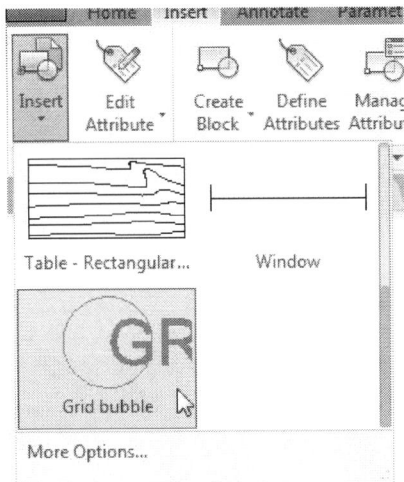

- Select the top endpoint of the first vertical grid line. The **Edit Attributes** dialog pops up.
- Type-in **A** in the GRIDBUBBLE box and click **OK**.

- Likewise, add other grid bubbles to the vertical grid lines.

- Create another block with name Vertical

Grid bubble. Make sure that you select the right quadrant point of the circle as the base point.

- Insert the vertical grid bubbles, as shown below.

Adding Dimensions

- On the ribbon, click **Home > Layers > Layer drop-down > Dimensions** to make it current.
- Type **D** in the command line and press Enter.
- On the **Dimension Style Manager** dialog, select the **Standard** dimension style and click the **New** button.
- Type-in Floor Plan in the **New Style Name** box and click **Continue**.
- Click the **Primary Units** tab and select **Unit format > Architectural**.

- Set **Precision** to **0'-01/16"**.

- Set **Fraction format** to **Horizontal**.

- Under the **Zero Suppression** section, uncheck the **0 inches** option.

- Click the **Symbol and Arrows** tab.

- Under the **Arrowhead** section, select **First > Architectural tick**. The second arrowhead is automatically changed to **Architectural tick**.

- Select **Leader > Closed Filled** and enter 1/4' in the **Arrow Size** box.

- Click the **Lines** tab and set **Extend beyond dim lines** and **Offset from origin** to 3".

- Click the **Text** tab and **Text height** to 6".

- In the **Text placement** section, set the following settings.
  Vertical-Centered
  Horizontal-Centered
  View Direction-Left-to-Right

- In the **Text alignment** section, select the **Aligned with dimension line** option.

- Click the **Fit** tab, and select **Either text or arrows (best fit)** option from the **Fit Options** section.

- In the **Text placement** section, select the **Over dimension line, without Leader** option.

- Click **OK** and click **Set Current** on the **Dimension Style Manager**. Click **Close**.

- On the ribbon, click **Annotate > Dimensions > Dimension**.

- Select the points on the vertical grid lines, as shown below.

- Move the pointer and click to locate the dimension.

- On the ribbon, click **Annotate > Dimensions > Continue**. You will notice that a dimension is attached to the pointer

- Move the pointer and click on next grid line.

- Likewise, move the pointer and click on the next grid line.

- Activate the **Dimension** command create the overall horizontal dimension.

- Likewise, add vertical dimensions to the grid lines.

- Complete adding dimensions to the drawing, as shown below.

- Save and close the drawing.

Exercise

Part 2: Autodesk Inventor Basics

Chapter 1: Getting Started with Autodesk Inventor 2017

This tutorial book brings in the most commonly used features of the Autodesk Inventor.

In this chapter, you will:

- Understand the Inventor terminology
- Start a new file
- Understand the User Interface
- Understand different environments in Inventor

In this chapter, you will learn some of the most commonly used features of Autodesk Inventor. In addition, you will learn about the user interface.

In Autodesk Inventor, you create 3D parts and use them to create 2D drawings and 3D assemblies.

Inventor is Feature Based. Features are shapes that are combined to build a part. You can modify these shapes individually.

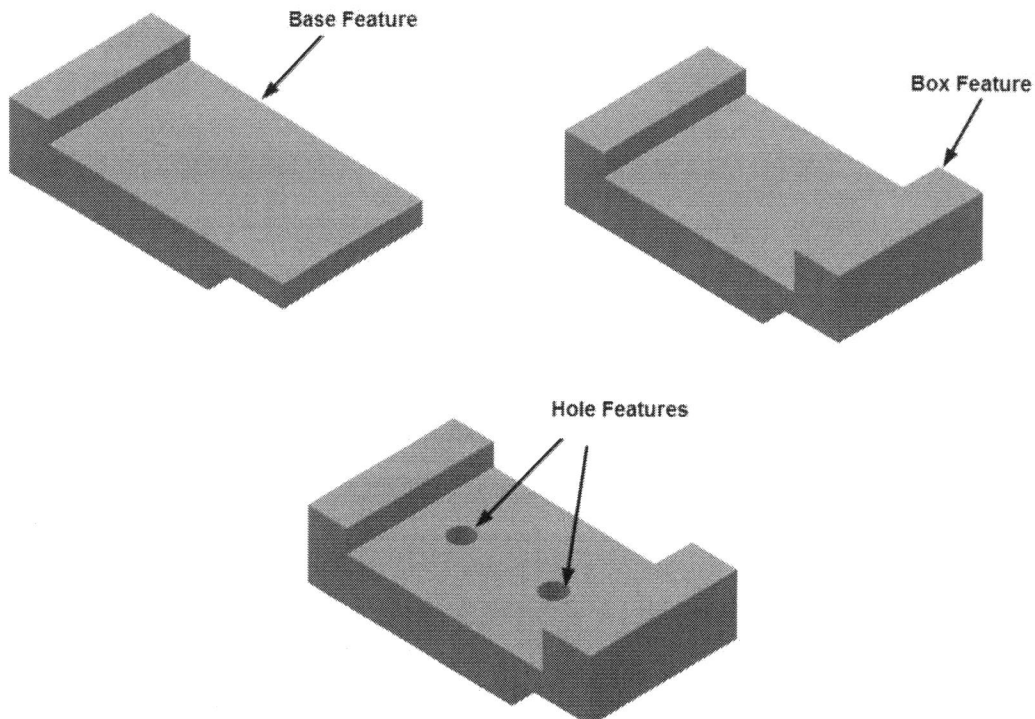

Most of the features are sketch-based. A sketch is a 2D profile and can be extruded, revolved, or swept along a path to create features.

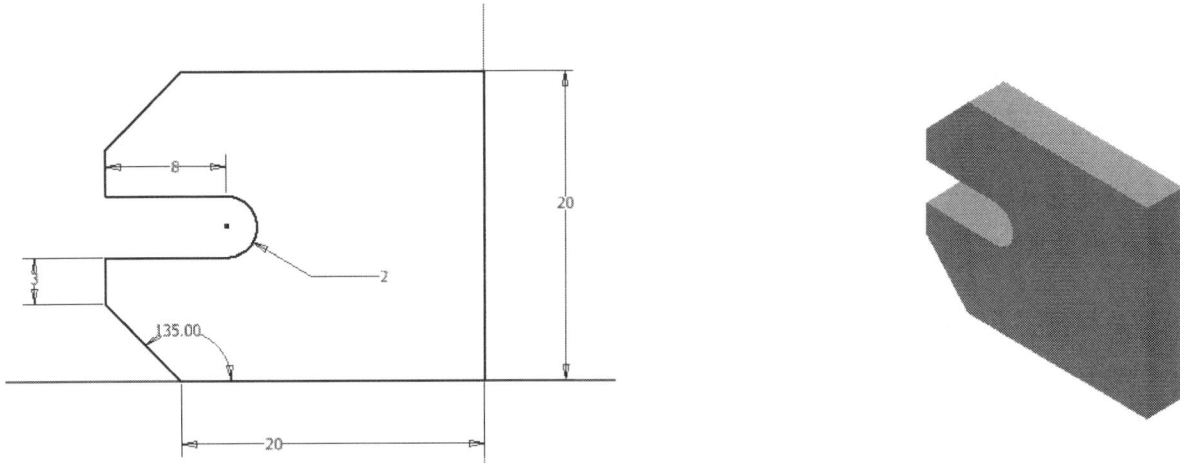

Inventor is parametric in nature. You can specify standard parameters between the elements. Changing these parameters changes the size and shape of the part. For example, see the design of the body of a flange before and after modifying the parameters of its features.

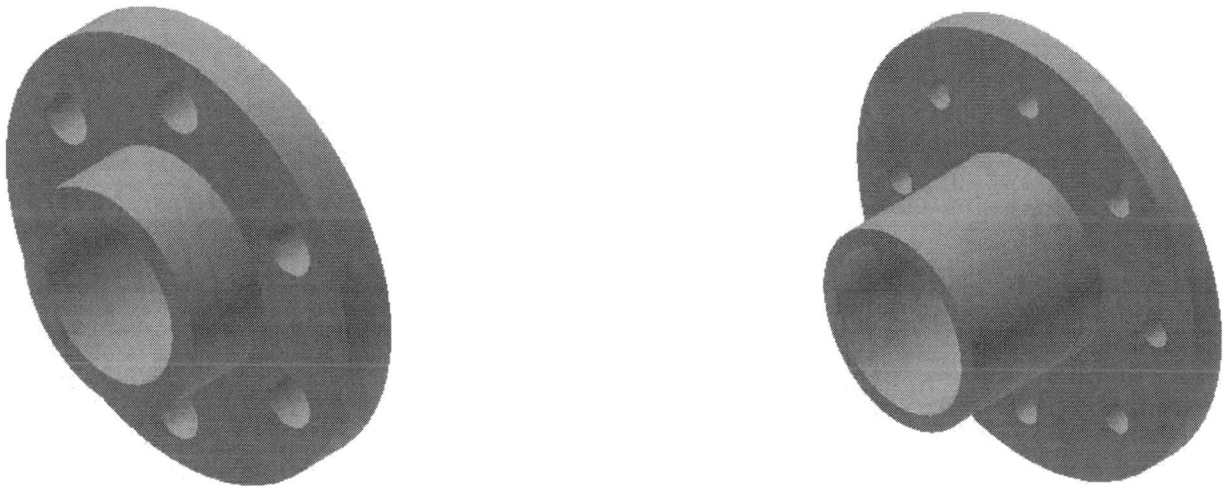

Starting Autodesk Inventor

- Click the **Start** button on the Windows taskbar.
- Click **All Programs**.
- Click **Autodesk > Autodesk Inventor 2017 > Autodesk Inventor 2017**.
- On the ribbon, click **Get Started > Launch > New**.
- On the **Create New File** dialog, click the Templates folder located at the top left corner. You can also select the **Metric** folder to view various metric templates.
- In the **Part – Create 2D and 3D objects** section, click the **Standard.ipt** icon.
- Click **Create** to start a new part file.

Notice these important features of the Inventor window.

User Interface

Various components of the user interface are discussed next.

Ribbon

Ribbon is located at the top of the window. It consists of various tabs. When you click on a tab, a set of tools appear. These tools are arranged in panels. You can select the required tool from this panel. The following sections explain the various tabs of the ribbon available in Autodesk Inventor.

The Get Started ribbon tab

This ribbon tab contains the tools such as **New**, **Open**, **Projects** and so on.

The 3D Model ribbon tab

This ribbon tab contains the tools to create 3D features, planes, surfaces, and so on.

The View ribbon tab

This ribbon tab contains the tools to modify the display of the model and user interface.

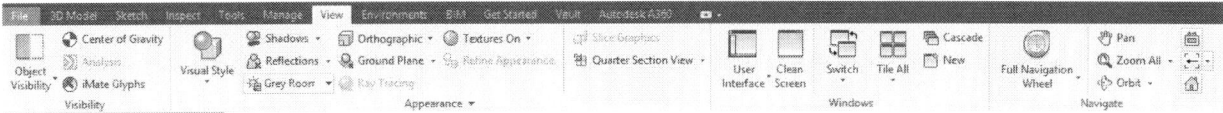

The Inspect ribbon tab

This ribbon tab has tools to measure the objects. It also has analysis tools to analyze the draft, curvature, surface and so on.

Sketch ribbon tab

This ribbon tab contains all the sketch tools.

Assemble ribbon tab

This ribbon tab contains the tools to create an assembly. It is available in an assembly file.

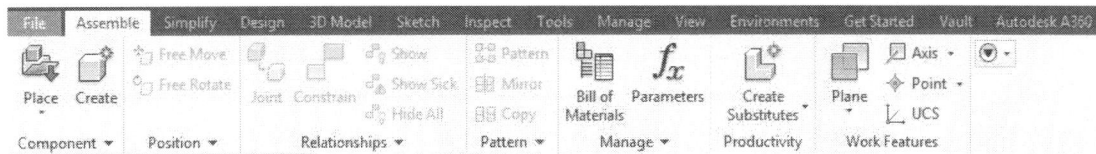

Presentation ribbon tab

This tab contains the tools to create the exploded views of an assembly. It also has the tools to create presentations, assembly instructions, and animation of an assembly.

Drawing Environment ribbon tabs

In the Drawing Environment, you can create print-ready drawings of a 3D model. The ribbon tabs in this environment contain tools to create 2D drawings.

The Sheet Metal ribbon tab

The tools in this tab are used to create sheet metal components.

File Menu

This appears when you click on the **File** tab located at the top left corner. This menu contains the options to open, print, export, manage, save, and close a file.

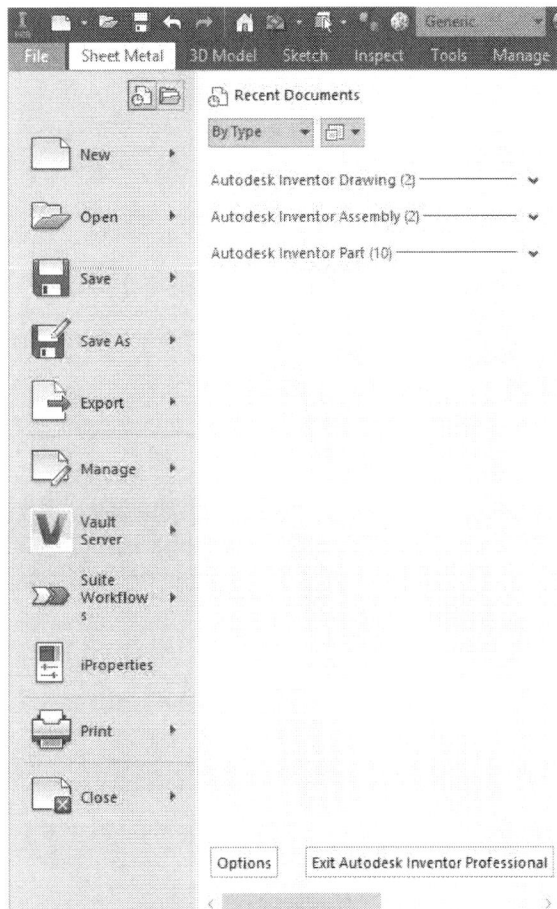

Quick Access Toolbar

This is available at the top left of the window. It contains the tools such as **New**, **Save**, **Open,** and so on.

You can customize this toolbar by clicking the down arrow at the right side of this toolbar.

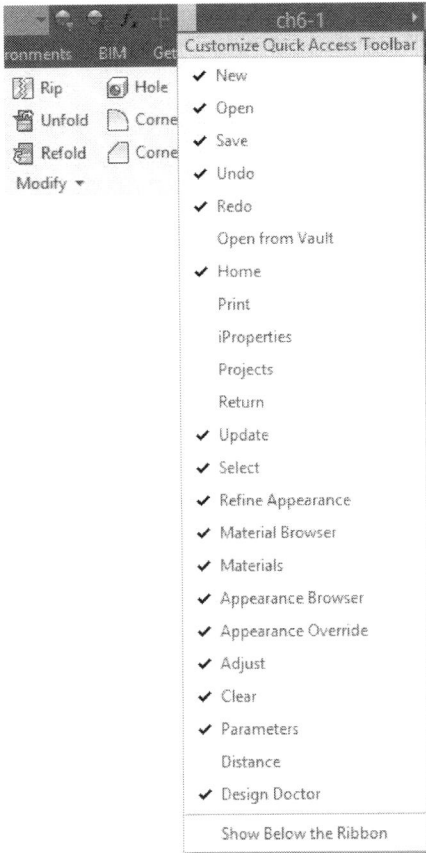

Browser window

This is located at the left side of the window. It contains the list of operations carried in an Autodesk Inventor file.

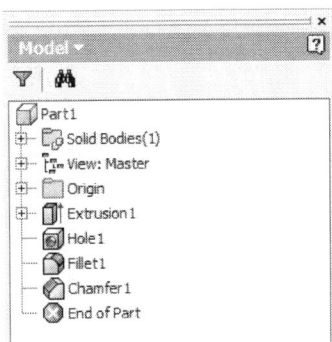

Status bar

This is available below the Browser window. It displays the prompts and the actions taken while using the tools.

Navigation Bar

This is located at the right side of the window. It contains the tools to zoom, rotate, pan, or look at a face of the model.

View Cube

It is located at the top right corner of the graphics window. It is used to set the view orientation of the model.

Shortcut Menus and Marking Menus

When you click the right mouse button, a shortcut menu along with a marking menu appears. A shortcut menu contains a list of some important options. The marking menu contains important tools. It allows you to access the tools quickly. You can customize the marking menu (add or remove tools).

Dialogs

When you activate any tool in Autodesk Inventor, the dialog related to it appears. It consists of various options, which help you to complete the operation. The following figure shows the components of the dialog.

Customizing the Ribbon, Shortcut Keys, and Marking Menus

To customize the ribbon, shortcut keys, or marking menu, click **Tools > Options > Customize** on the ribbon. On the **Customize** dialog, use the tabs to customize the ribbon or marking menu, or shortcut keys.

For example, to add a command to the ribbon, select the command from the list on the left side of the dialog and click the **Add** $\boxed{>>}$ button. If you want to remove a command from the ribbon, then select it from the right-side list and click the **Remove** $\boxed{<<}$ button. Click **OK** to make the changes to effect.

To add or remove panels from the ribbon, click the **Show Panels** icon located at the right-side of the ribbon and check/uncheck the options on the fly out.

Color Settings

To change the background color of the window, click **Tools > Options > Application Options** on the ribbon. On the **Application Options** dialog, click the **Colors** tab on the dialog. Set the **Background** value to **1 Color** to change the background to plain. Select the required color scheme from the **Color Scheme** group. Click **OK**.

Chapter 2: Part Modeling Basics

This chapter takes you through the creation of your first Inventor model. You create simple parts:

In this chapter, you will:

- Create Sketches
- Create a base feature
- Add another feature to it
- Create revolved features
- Create cylindrical features
- Create box features
- Apply draft

TUTORIAL 1

This tutorial takes you through the creation of your first Inventor model. You will create the Disc of an Old ham coupling:

Creating a New Project

1. Start **Autodesk Inventor 2017** by clicking the **Autodesk Inventor 2017** icon on your desktop.

2. To create a new project, click **Get Started > Launch > Projects** on the ribbon.

3. Click the **New** button on the **Projects** dialog.

4. On the **Inventor project wizard** dialog, select **New Single User Project** and click the **Next** button.

5. Enter **Oldham Coupling** in the **Name** field.

6. Enter C:\Users\Username\Documents\Inventor\Oldham Coupling\ in the **Project(Workspace) Folder** box and click **Next**.

7. Click **Finish**.

8. Click **OK** on the **Inventor Project Editor** dialog.

9. Click **Done**.

Starting a New Part File

1. To start a new part file, click **Get Started > Launch > New** on the ribbon.

2. On the **Create New File** dialog, click the **Templates** folder located the top right corner.

3. Click the **Standard.ipt** icon located under the **Part – Create 2D and 3D Objects** section.

4. Click the **Create** button on the **Create New File** dialog.

A new model window appears.

Starting a Sketch

1. To start a new sketch, click **3D Model > Sketch > Start 2D Sketch** on the ribbon.

2. Click on the **XY Plane**. The sketch starts.

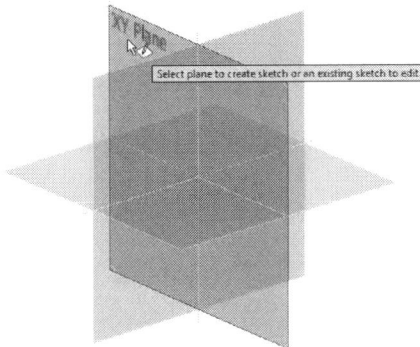

The first feature is an extruded feature from a sketched circular profile. You will begin by sketching the circle.

3. On the ribbon click **Sketch > Create > Circle > Circle Center Point**.

4. Move the cursor to the sketch origin, and then click on it.

5. Drag the cursor and click to create a circle.

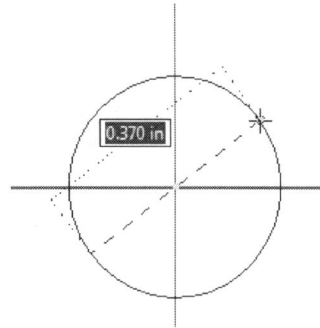

6. Press **ESC** to deactivate the tool.

Adding Dimensions

In this section, you will specify the size of the sketched circle by adding dimensions. As you add dimensions, the sketch can attain any one of the following states:

Fully Constrained sketch: In a fully constrained sketch, the positions of all the entities are fully described by dimensions, constraints, or both. In a fully constrained sketch, all the entities are dark blue color.

Under Constrained sketch: Additional dimensions, constraints, or both are needed to completely specify the geometry. In this state, you can drag under constrained sketch entities to modify the sketch. An under constrained sketch entity is in black color.

If you add any more dimensions to a fully constrained sketch, a message box will appear showing that dimension over constraints the sketch. In addition, it prompts you to convert the dimension into a driven dimension. Click **Accept** to convert the unwanted dimension into a driven dimension.

1. On the ribbon, click **Sketch > Constrain > Dimension**.

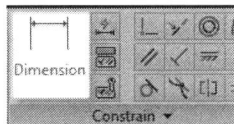

2. Select the circle and click; the **Edit Dimension** box appears.

3. Enter **4** in the **Edit Dimension** box and click the green check.

4. Press **Esc** to deactivate the **Dimension** tool.

You can also create dimensions while creating the sketch objects. To do this, enter the dimension values in the boxes displayed while sketching.

5. To display the entire circle at full size and to center it in the graphics area, use one of the following methods:

   - Click **Zoom All** on the **Navigate Bar**.
   - Click **View > Navigate > Zoom All** on the ribbon.

6. Click **Finish Sketch** on the **Exit** panel.

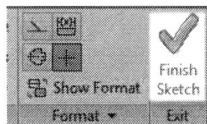

7. Click **Zoom All** on the **Navigate Bar.**

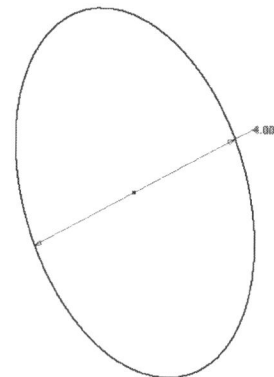

Creating the Base Feature

The first feature in any part is called a base feature. You now create this feature by extruding the sketched circle.

1. On the ribbon, click **3D Model > Create > Extrude.**

2. Type-in 0.4 in the **Distance** box attached to extrusion.

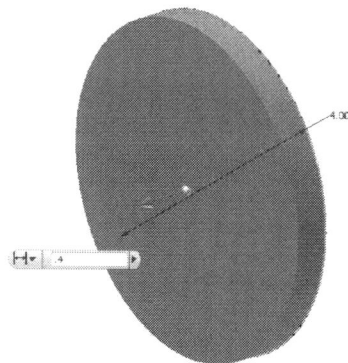

3. Place the pointer on the handle attached to the extruded feature.

4. Click **OK** to create the extrusion.

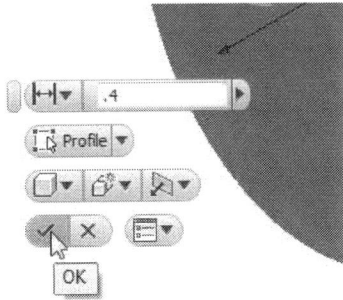

Notice the new feature, **Extrude 1**, in the **Browser window**.

To magnify a model in the graphics area, you can use the zoom tools available on the **Zoom** drop-down in the **Navigate** panel of the **View** tab.

Click **Zoom All** to display the part full size in the current window.

Click **Zoom Window**, and then drag the pointer to create a rectangle; the area in the rectangle zooms to fill the window.

Click **Zoom**, and then drag the pointer. Dragging up zooms out; dragging down zooms in.

Click on a vertex, an edge, or a feature, and then click **Zoom Selected**; the selected item zooms to fill the window.

To display the part in different modes, select the options in the **Visual Style** drop-down on the **Appearance** panel of the **View** tab.

Realistic

Shaded

Shaded With Edges

Shaded with Hidden Edges

Monochrome

Wireframe

Watercolor

Wireframe with Hidden Edges

Wireframe with Visible Edges Only

Sketch Illustration

Technical Illustration

The default display mode for parts and assemblies is **Shaded**. You may change the display mode whenever you want.

Adding an Extruded Feature

To create additional features on the part, you need to draw sketches on the model faces or planes, and then extrude them.

1. On the ribbon, click **View > Appearance > Visual Style > Wireframe**.

2. On the ribbon, click **3D Model > Sketch > Start 2D Sketch**.

3. Click on the front face of the part.

4. Click **Line** on the **Create** panel.

5. Click on the circular edge to specify the first point of the line.

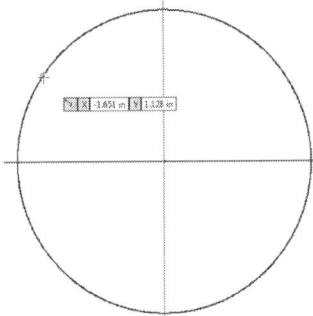

6. Move the cursor towards right.

7. Click on the other side of the circular edge; a line is drawn.

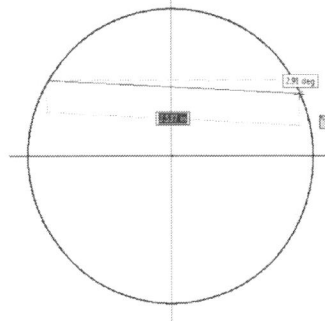

8. Draw another line below the previous line.

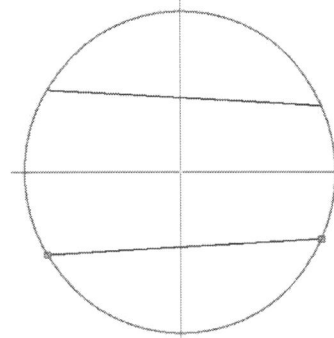

9. On the ribbon, click **Sketch > Constrain > Horizontal Constraint**.

10. Select the two lines to make them horizontal.

11. On the ribbon, click **Sketch > Constrain > Equal**.

12. Select the two horizontal lines to make them equal.

13. Click **Dimension** on the **Constrain** panel.

14. Select the two horizontal lines.

15. Move the cursor toward right and click to locate the dimension; the **Edit Dimension** box appears.

16. Enter **0.472** in the **Edit Dimension** box and click the green check.

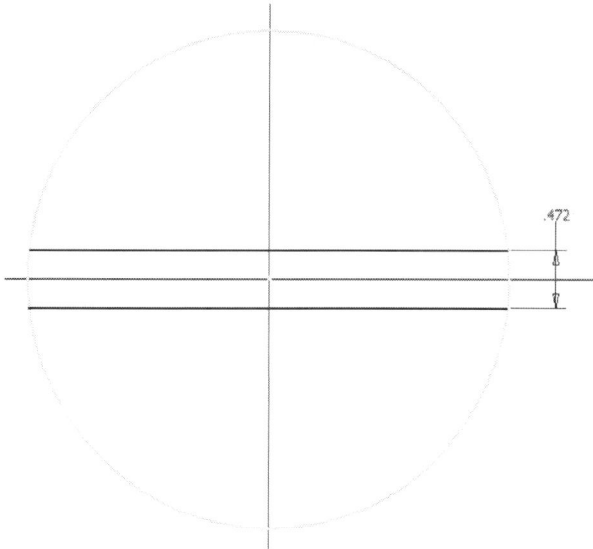

17. Click **Finish Sketch** on the **Exit** panel.

18. Click on the sketch, and then click **Create Extrude** on the **Mini Toolbar**; the **Extrude** dialog appears.

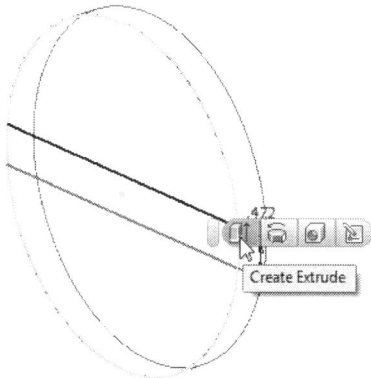

19. Click in the region bounded by the two horizontal lines.

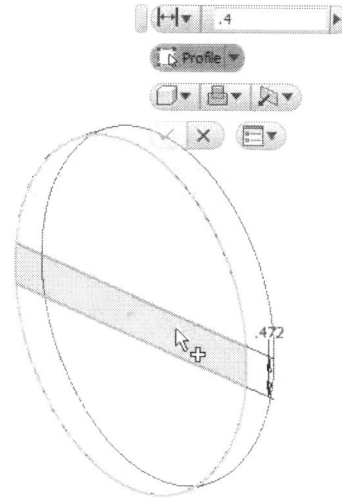

20. Enter **0.4** in the **Distance1** box.

21. Click **OK** ✔ to create the extrusion.

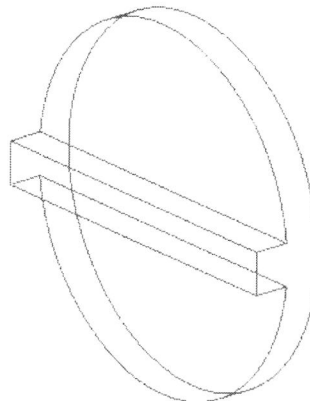

*You can reuse the sketch of an already existing feature. To do this, expand the feature in the Browser Window, right click on the sketch, and select **Share Sketch** from the shortcut menu. You will notice that the sketch is visible in the graphics window. You can also unshare the sketch by right clicking on it and selecting **Unshare**.*

Adding another Extruded Feature

1. Click **Start 2D Sketch** on the **Sketch** panel of the **3D Model** ribbon tab.

2. Use the **Free Orbit** button from the **Navigate Bar** to rotate the model such that the back face of the part is visible.

3. Right click and select **OK**.

4. Click on the back face of the part.

5. Click **Line** ⟋ on the **Create** panel.

6. Draw two lines, as shown below.

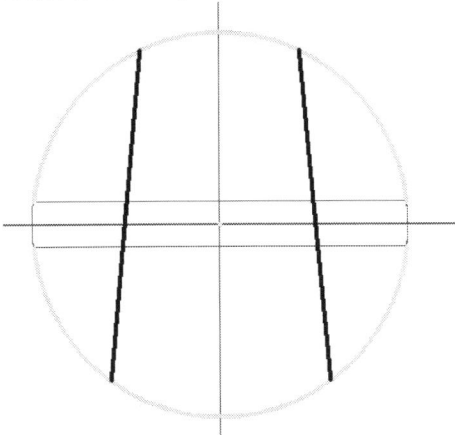

> You can specify a point using various point snap options. To do this, activate a sketching tool, right click and select **Point Snaps**; a list of point snaps appears. Now, you can select only the specified point snap.

7. On the ribbon, click **Sketch > Constrain > Vertical Constraint** ⫲ .

8. Select the two lines to make them vertical.

9. On the ribbon, click **Sketch > Constrain > Equal** ═ .

10. Select the two vertical lines to make them equal.

11. Create a dimension of 0.472in between the vertical lines.

Note: Ensure that the end points of the lines coincide with the circular edge. You can use the **Coincident** constraint to make them coincident with each other.

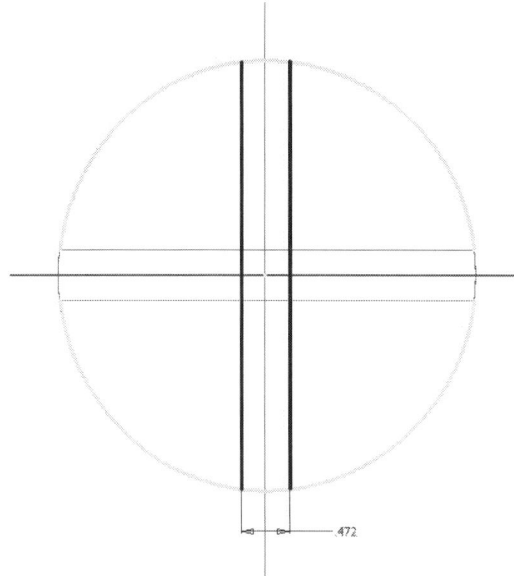

12. Click **Finish Sketch**.

13. On the ribbon, click **3D Model > Create > Extrude**.

14. Click inside the region enclosed by two lines, if they are not already selected.

15. Type 0.4 in the **Distance1** box on the Mini toolbar and click **OK**.

   To move the part view, click **Pan** 🖑 on **Navigate Bar**, and then drag the part to move it in the graphics area.

16. On the ribbon, click **View > Appearance > Visual Style > Shaded with Edges**.

17. On the ribbon, click **View > Navigate > Home View** 🏠 .

Saving the Part

1. Click **Save** 🖫 on the **Quick Access Toolbar**.

2. On the **Save As** dialog, type-in **Disc** in the **File name** box.

3. Click **Save** to save the file.

4. Click **File Menu > Close**.

Note:
*.ipt is the file extension for all the files that you create in the Part environment of Autodesk Inventor.

TUTORIAL 2

In this tutorial, you create a flange by performing the following:

- Creating a revolved feature
- Creating a cut features
- Adding fillets

Starting a New Part File

1. To start a new part file, click the **Part** icon on the Home screen.

Sketching a Revolve Profile

You create the base feature of the flange by revolving a profile around a centerline.

1. Click **3D Model > Sketch > Start 2D Sketch** on the ribbon.

2. Select the YZ plane.

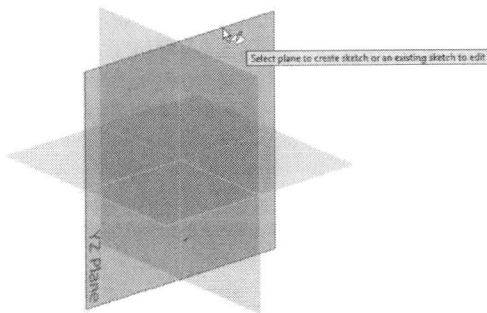

3. Click **Line** on the **Create** panel.

4. Create a sketch similar to that shown in figure.

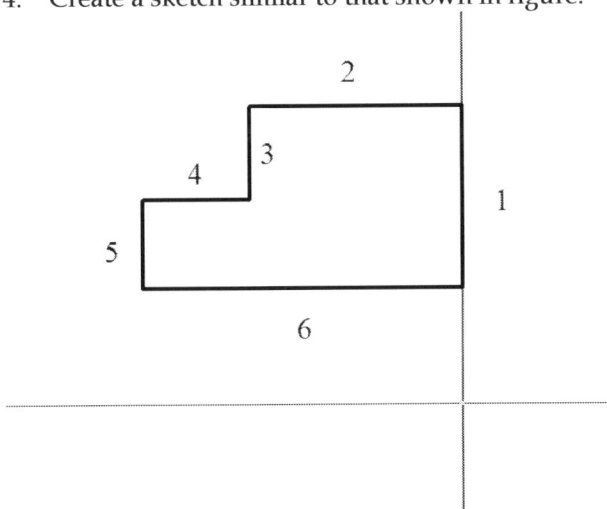

5. On the ribbon, click **Sketch > Format > Centerline**.

6. Click **Line** on the **Create** panel.

7. Create a centerline, as shown below.

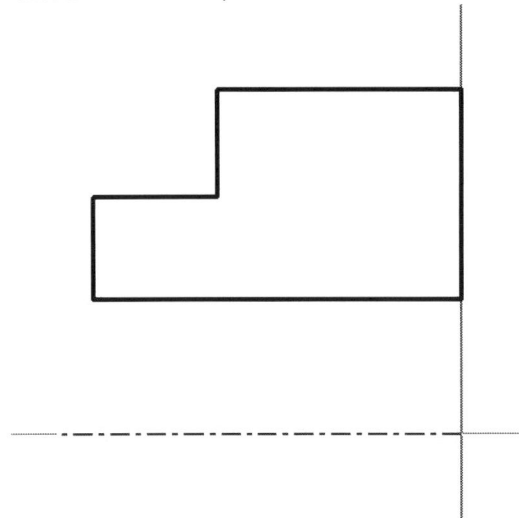

8. Click **Fix** on the **Constrain** panel.

9. Select the Line 1.

10. Click **Dimension** on the **Constrain** panel.

11. Select the centerline and Line 2; a dimension appears.

12. Move the pointer horizontally toward right and click to place the dimension.

13. Place the dimension and enter **4** in the **Edit Dimension** box.

14. Click the green check on the **Edit Dimension** dialog.

15. Select the centerline and Line 4; a dimension appears.

16. Move the pointer horizontally toward left and click to place the dimension.

17. Enter **2.4** in the **Edit Dimension** box.

18. Click the green check on the **Edit Dimension** dialog.

19. Select the centerline and Line 6; a dimension appears.

20. Move the pointer horizontally toward left and click to place the dimension.

21. Enter **1.2** in the **Edit Dimension** box.

22. Click the green check ✓ on the **Edit Dimension** dialog.

23. Create a dimension between the Line 1 and Line 3.

24. Set the dimension value to 0.8 inches.

25. Create a dimension between Line 1 and Line 5.

26. Set the dimension value to 2 inches.

📝 *You can display all the constraints by right clicking and selecting* **Show All Constraints** *option. You can hide all the constraints by right clicking and selecting the* **Hide All Constraints** *option.*

27. Right-click and select **Finish 2D Sketch**.

Creating the Revolved Feature

1. On the ribbon, click **3D Model > Create > Revolve** (or) right-click and select **Revolve** from the Marking menu.

2. Set **Extents** to **Full** on the Mini toolbar.

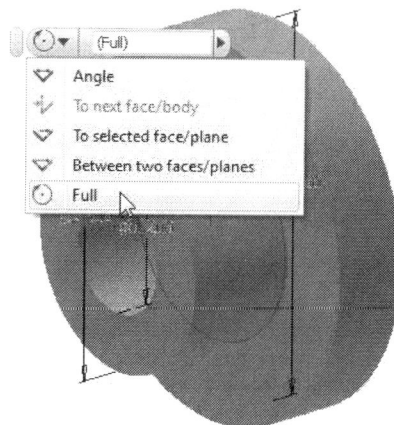

3. Place the pointer on the Mini toolbar and click **OK** ✓ to create the revolved feature.

Creating the Cut feature

1. On the Navigation pane, click the **Orbit** icon.

2. Press and hold the left mouse button and drag the mouse; the model is rotated.

3. Rotate the model such that its back face is visible.

4. Right click and select **OK**.

5. On the **3D Model** tab of the ribbon, click the **Show Panels** icon located at the right corner, and then check the **Primitives** option from the drop-down.

The **Primitives** panel is added to the ribbon.

6. On the ribbon, click **3D Model > Primitives > Primitive drop-down > Box** on the **Primitives** panel.

7. Click the back face of the part; the sketch starts.

8. Select the origin to define the center point.

9. Move the cursor diagonally toward right.

10. Enter 4.1 in the horizontal dimension box.

11. Press Tab key and enter 0.472 in the vertical dimension box.

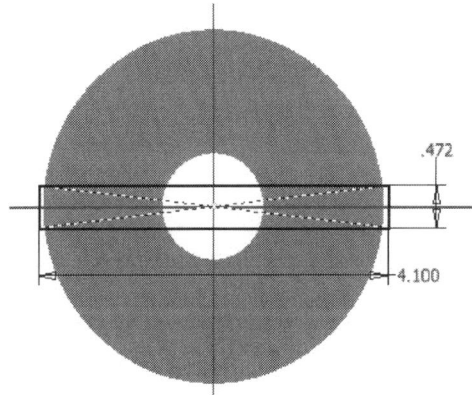

12. Press the Enter key; the **Extrude** dialog appears.

13. Expand the **Extrude** dialog by clicking the down arrow ▼ button.

14. Click the **Cut** 🖶 button on the **Extrude** dialog.

15. Enter 0.4 in the **Distance** box.

16. Click **OK** to create the cut feature.

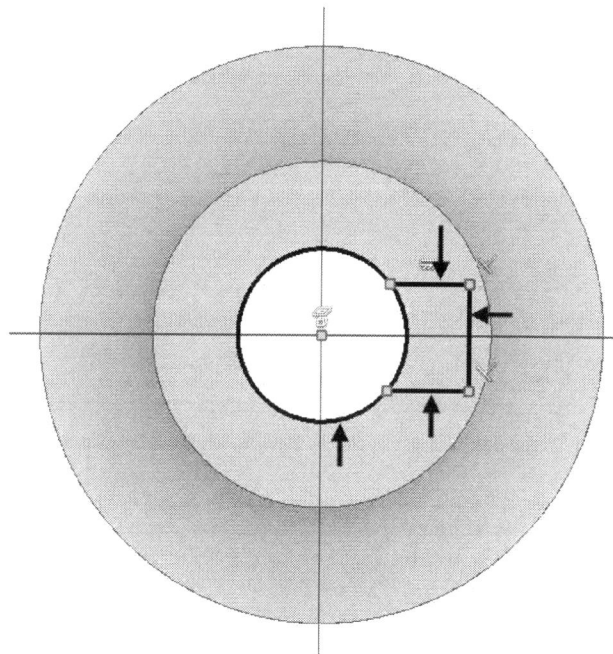

Creating another Cut feature

1. Click the Home icon located at the tope left corner of the ViewCube.

2. Create a sketch on the front face of the base feature.

- On the ribbon, click **3D Model > Sketch > Start 2D Sketch**.

- Select the front face of the model.

- Draw three lines and the circle, as shown in figure.

- Apply the **Horizontal** constraint to the horizontal lines, if not applied already.
- Apply the **Equal** constraint between the horizontal lines.
- Ensure that the endpoints of the horizontal line coincide with the circle.
- Apply dimension of 0.236 to the vertical line.
- Apply dimension of 0.118 to horizontal line.
- Apply dimension of the 1.2 diameter to the circle.

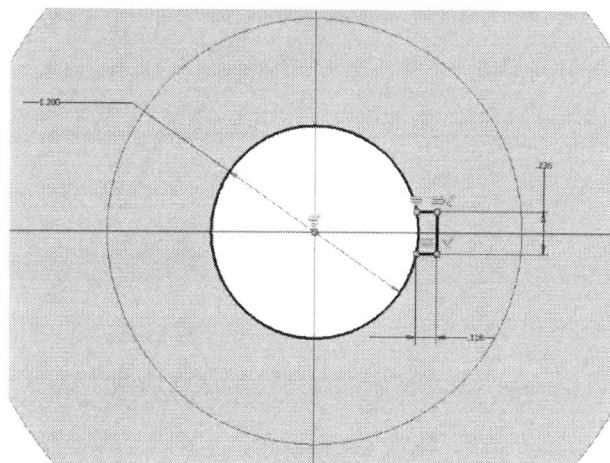

- On the ribbon, click **Sketch > Modify > Trim**.
- Click on the circle to trim it.

3. Finish the sketch.

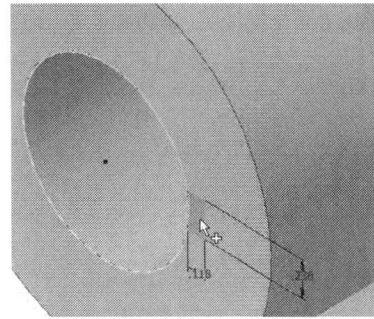 *You can hide or display the sketch dimensions. To do this, go to* **View > Visibility > Object Visibility** *and check the* **Sketch Dimensions** *option.*

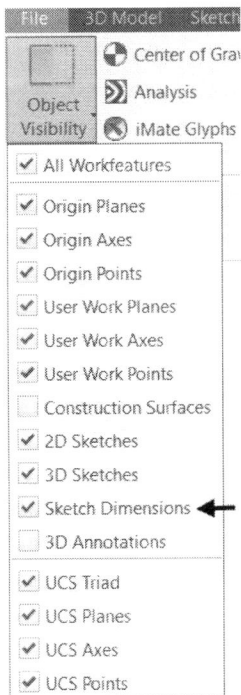

4. Click **Extrude** on the **Create** panel of the **3D Model**.

5. Click in the region enclosed by the three lines and the arc.

6. Select **All** from the **Extents** drop-down.

7. Click the **Cut** button on the **Extrude** dialog.

8. Click **OK** to create the cut feature.

Adding a Fillet

1. On the ribbon, click **3D Model > Modify > Fillet** (or) right-click and select **Fillet** from the Marking menu.

2. Click on the inner circular edge and set **Radius** as 0.2.

3. Click **OK** ✓ to add the fillet.

Saving the Part

1. Click **Save** 🖫 on the **Quick Access Toolbar**.

2. On the **Save As** dialog, type-in **Flange** in the **File name** box.

3. Click **Save** to save the file.

4. Click **File Menu > Close**.

TUTORIAL 3

In this tutorial, you create the Shaft by performing the following:

- Creating a cylindrical feature
- Creating a cut feature

Starting a New Part File

1. On the ribbon, click **Get Started > Launch > New** 🗋.

2. On the **Create New File** dialog, select **Standard.ipt**.

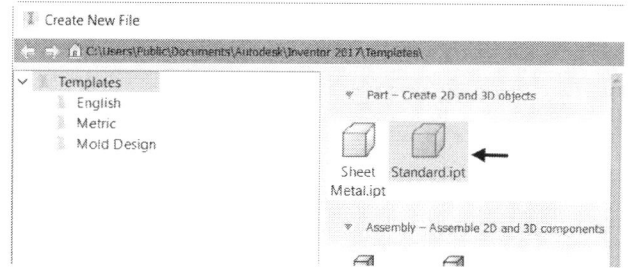

3. Click **Create**.

Creating the Cylindrical Feature

1. On the ribbon, click **Primitives > Primitive drop-down > Cylinder**.

2. Click on the XY plane to select it; the sketch starts.

3. Click at the origin and move the cursor outward.

4. Enter 1.2 in the box attached to the circle.

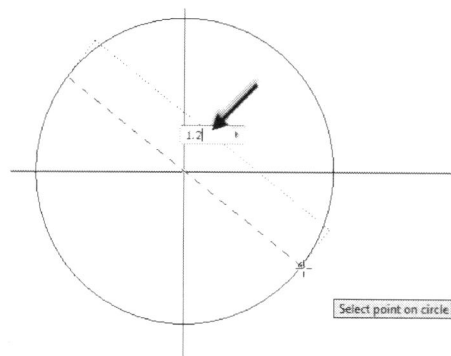

5. Press Enter key; the **Extrude** dialog appears.

6. Enter **4** in the **Distance** box.

7. Click **OK** to create the cylinder.

Creating Cut feature

1. Create a sketch on the front face of the base feature.
   - On the ribbon, click **3D Model > Sketch > Start 2D Sketch**.
   - Select the front face of the cylinder.
   - On the ribbon, click **Sketch > Create > Line**.
   - Draw three lines, as shown.

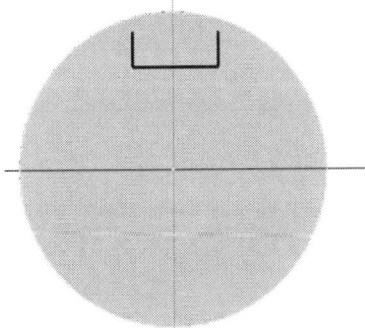

   - Apply the **Coincident** constraint between the end points of the vertical lines and the circular edge.
   - Add dimensions to the sketch.

2. Finish the sketch.

3. Click **Extrude** on the **Create** panel.

4. Click in the region enclosed by the sketch.

5. Click the **Cut** button on the **Extrude** dialog.

6. Set **Distance** to **2.165**.

7. Click **OK** to create the cut feature.

Saving the Part

1. Click **Save** on the **Quick Access Toolbar**; the **Save As** dialog appears.

2. Type-in **Shaft** in the **File name** box.

3. Click **Save** to save the file.

4. Click **File Menu > Close**.

TUTORIAL 4

In this tutorial, you create a Key by performing the following:

- Creating an Extruded feature
- Applying draft

Start Extruded feature

1. Start a new part file using the **Standard.ipt** template.

2. On the ribbon, **Primitives > Primitive** drop-down **> Box**.

3. Select the XY plane.

4. Create the sketch, as shown in figure.

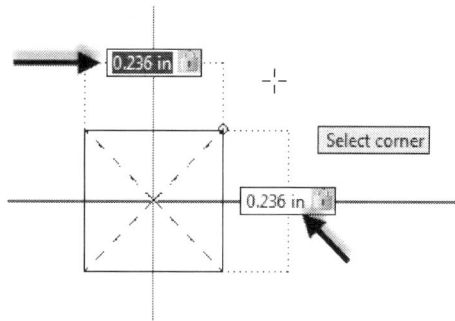

5. Press ENTER.

6. Enter 2 in the **Distance** box.

7. Click **OK** to create the extrusion.

Applying Draft

1. On the ribbon, click **3D Model > Modify > Draft**.

2. Select the **Fixed Plane** option.

3. Select front face as the fixed face.

4. Select the top face as the face to be draft.

5. Set **Draft Angle** to **1**.
6. Click the **Flip pull direction** button on the **Face Draft** dialog.

7. Click **OK** to create the draft.

Saving the Part

1. Click **Save** on the **Quick Access Toolbar**; the **Save As** dialog appears.

2. Type-in **Key** in the **File name** box.

3. Click **Save** to save the file.

4. Click **File Menu > Close**.

Chapter 3: Assembly Basics

In this chapter, you will:

- Add Components to assembly
- Apply constraints between components
- Check Degrees of Freedom
- Check Interference
- Create exploded view of the assembly

TUTORIAL 1

This tutorial takes you through the creation of your first assembly. You create the Oldham coupling assembly:

PARTS LIST		
ITEM	PART NUMBER	QTY
1	Disc	1
2	Flange	2
3	Shaft	2
4	Key	2

There are two ways of creating any assembly model.

- Top-Down Approach
- Bottom-Up Approach

Top-Down Approach
The assembly file is created first and components are created in that file.

Bottom-Up Approach
The components are created first, and then added to the assembly file. In this tutorial, you will create the assembly using this approach.

Starting a New Assembly File
To start a new assembly file, click the **Assembly** icon on the Home screen.

Inserting the Base Component
1. To insert the base component, click **Assemble > Component > Place** on the ribbon.

2. Browse to the project folder and double-click on **Flange.ipt**.

3. Right-click and select **Place Grounded at Origin**; the component is placed at the origin.

4. Right-click and select **OK**.

Adding the second component
1. To insert the second component, right-click and select **Place Component**; the **Place Component** dialog appears.

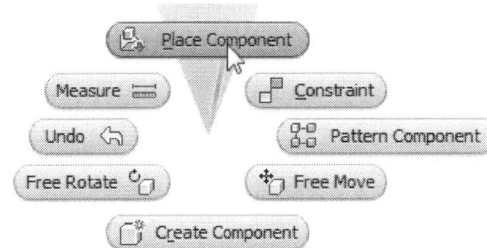

2. Browse to the project folder and double-click on **Shaft.ipt**.

3. Click in the window to place the component.

4. Right-click and select **OK**.

Applying Constraints
After adding the components to the assembly environment, you need to apply constraints between

354

them. By applying constraints, you establish relationships between components.

1. To apply constraints, click **Assemble > Relationships > Constrain** on the ribbon.

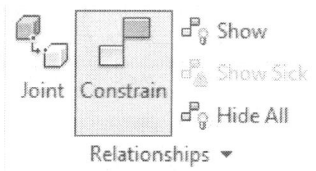

The **Place Constraint** dialog appears on the screen.

Different assembly constraints that can be applied using this dialog are given next.

Mate: Using this constraint, you can make two planar faces coplanar to each other.

Mate Solution

Note that if you set the **Solution** to **Flush**, the faces will point in the same direction.

Flush Solution

You can also align the centerlines of the cylindrical faces.

Angle: Applies the angle constraint between two components.

Tangent: This constraint is used to apply a tangent relation between two faces.

Positive Angle

Negative Angle

30.00 deg

-30.00 deg

Positive Angle

Negative Angle

30.00 deg

-30.00 deg

Positive Angle

Negative Angle

First face

Second face

Outside solution

Inside Solution

Insert: This constraint is used to make two cylindrical faces coaxial. In addition, the planar faces of the cylindrical components will be on the same plane.

First selection

Second selection

Opposed solution

Aligned solution

Symmetry: This constraint is used to position the two components symmetrically about a plane.

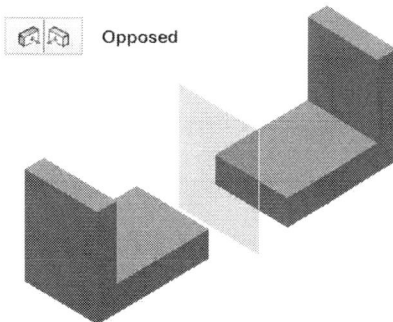

First face

Second face

Symmetry Plane

Opposed

Aligned

2. On the **Place Constraints** dialog, under the **Type** group, click the **Mate** icon.

3. Click on the cylindrical face of the Shaft.

4. Click on the inner cylindrical face of the Flange.

5. Click the **Apply** button.

6. Ensure that the **Mate** icon is selected in the **Type** group.

7. Click on the front face of the shaft.

8. Rotate the model.

9. Click on the slot face of the flange, as shown in figure.

10. Click the **Flush** button on the **Place Constraint** dialog.

11. Click **Apply**. The front face of the Shaft and the slot face of the Flange are aligned.

12. Ensure that the **Mate** button is selected in the **Type** group.

13. Expand **Flange: 1** in the Browser window.

14. Select the XZ Plane of the Flange.

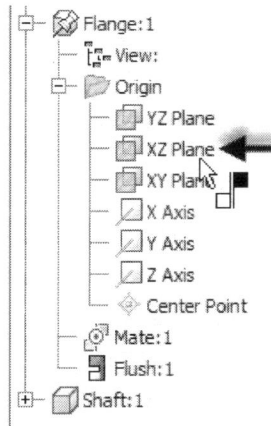

15. Expand **Shaft: 1** and select the YZ plane of the Shaft.

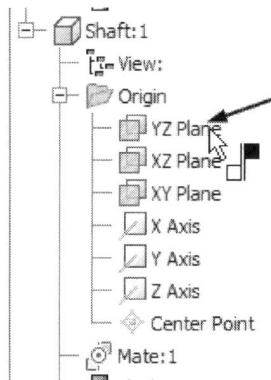

16. Click the **Flush** button on the **Place Constraint** dialog.

17. Click **OK** to assemble the components.

Adding the Third Component

1. To insert the third component, click **Assemble > Component > Place** on the ribbon.

2. Go to the project folder and double-click on **Key.ipt**.

3. Click in the graphics window to place the key.

4. Right-click and click **OK**.

5. Right-click on **Flange: 1** in the Browser window.

6. Click **Visibility** on the shortcut menu; the Flange is hidden.

7. Click **Constrain** on the **Relationships** panel.

8. Click **Mate** on the **Place Constraint** dialog.

9. Select **Mate** from the **Solution** group.

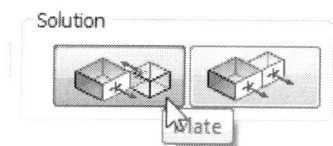

10. Click the right mouse button on the side face of the key and click **Select Other** on the shortcut menu.

11. Select the bottom face of the Key from the flyout.

12. Select the flat face of the slot.

Face to be selected

13. Click the **Apply** button. The bottom face of the key is aligned with the flat face of the slot.

14. Click the **Mate** icon on the **Place Constraint** dialog.

15. Select **Flush** from the **Solution** group.

16. Select the front face of the Key and back face of the Shaft, as shown.

17. Click **Apply** on the dialog; the mate is applied.

Now, you need to check whether the parts are fully constrained or not.

18. Click **View > Visibility > Degrees of Freedom** on the ribbon.

You will notice that an arrow appears pointing in the upward (or downward) direction. This means that the Key is not constrained in the Z-direction.

You must apply one more constraint to constrain the key.

19. Click **Constrain** on the **Relationships** panel of the **Assemble** ribbon tab.

20. Click the **Mate** icon the dialog.

21. Select **Flush** from the **Solution** group.

22. Expand the **Origin** node of the **Assembly** in the **Browser window** and select **XZ Plane**.

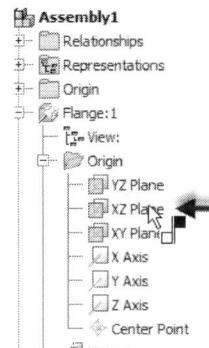

23. Expand the **Key: 1** node in the **Browser window** and select **YZ Plane**.

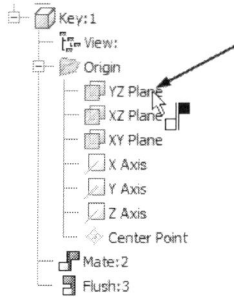

24. Click **OK**. The mate is applied between the two planes.

Now, you need to turn-on the display of the Flange.

25. Right-click on the **Flange** in the **Browser window** and select **Visibility**; the **Flange** appears.

Checking the Interference

1. Click **Inspect > Interference > Analyze Interference** on the Ribbon. The **Interference Analysis** dialog appears.

2. Select the Flange and Shaft as **Set #1**.

3. Click the **Define Set #2** button.

4. Select the Key as **Set # 2**.

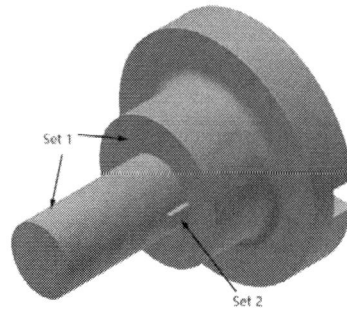

5. Click **OK**; the message box appears showing that there are no interferences.

Saving the Assembly

1. Click **Save** on the **Quick Access Toolbar**; the **Save As** dialog appears.

2. Type-in **Flange_subassembly** in the **File name box.**

3. Go to the project folder.

4. Click **Save** to save the file.

5. Click **File Menu > Close**.

Starting the Main assembly

1. On the ribbon, click **Get Started > Launch > New**.

2. On the **Create New File** dialog, click the **Standard.iam** icon.

Standard.iam

3. Click **Create** to start a new assembly.

Adding Disc to the Assembly

1. Click **Assemble > Component > Place** on the ribbon.

2. Go to the project folder and double-click on **Disc.ipt**.

3. Right-click and select **Place Grounded at Origin**; the component is placed at the origin.

4. Right-click and select **OK**.

Placing the Sub-assembly

1. To insert the sub-assembly, click the **Place** button on the **Component** panel of the ribbon.

2. Go to the project folder and double-click on **Flange_subassembly.iam**.

3. Click in the window to place the flange sub assembly.

4. Right-click and click **OK**.

Adding Constraints

1. Click **Constrain** on the **Relationships** panel of the **Assemble** ribbon.

2. Click the **Insert** button on the **Place Constraint** dialog.

3. Select **Opposed** from the **Solution** group.

4. Click on the circular edge of the Flange.

5. Click on the circular edge of the Disc.

6. Click **OK** on the dialog.

Next, you have to move the subassembly away from the Disc to apply other constraints.

7. Click **Free Move** on the **Position** panel.

8. Select the flange subassembly and move it.

9. Click the **Constrain** button on the **Relationships** panel.

10. Click **Mate** on the **Place Constraints** dialog.

11. Select **Mate** from the **Solution** group.

12. Click the **View > Navigate > Orbit** on the ribbon.

13. Press and hold the left mouse button and drag the cursor toward left.

14. Release the mouse button, right click, and select **OK**.

15. Click on the face on the Flange, as shown in figure.

16. Click on the face on the Disc as shown in figure.

17. Click **OK** on the dialog.

Placing the second instance of the Sub-assembly

1. Insert another instance of the Flange subassembly.

2. Apply the **Insert** and **Mate** constraints.

Saving the Assembly

1. Click **Save** on the **Quick Access Toolbar**; the **Save As** dialog appears.

2. Type-in **Oldham_coupling** in the **File name box.**

3. Click **Save** to save the file.

4. Click **File Menu > Close**.

Tutorial 2

In this tutorial, you create the exploded view of the assembly:

Starting a New Presentation File

1. On the Home screen, click the **Presentation** icon (or) click **Get Started > Launch > New**, and then select the **Standard.ipn** template from the **Create New File** dialog.

The **Insert** dialog appears.

2. On the **Insert** dialog, go to the project folder and double-click on the **Oldham Coupling.iam** file.

The Presentation Environment appears, as shown.

Creating a Storyboard Animation

1. In the **Model** tree, double-click on **Scene1** and type **Explosion**.

Before creating an exploded view, you need to take a look at the Storyboard displayed at the bottom of the window. The Storyboard has the Scratch Zone located at the left side of the timeline. Also, notice that the play marker is displayed at 0 seconds in the timeline.

2. Click in the Scratch Zone area and notice that the play marker is displayed inside it.

   Now, the changes made to the assembly in the Scratch Zone will be the starting point of the exploded animation. You can change the orientation of the assembly, hide a component, or change the opacity of the component. Use the **Capture Camera** tool on the **Camera** panel to set the camera position for the animation.

3. Click the **Tweak Components** button on the **Component** panel of the **Presentation** ribbon tab. The mini toolbar appears with different options, as shown.

   Notice that the default duration for a tweak is 2.500 s. You can type a new value in the **Duration** box available on the Mini toolbar.

4. Select **Component** from the Selection Filter drop-down of Mini toolbar.

5. Select the **All Components** from the Tracelines drop-down. This will create tracelines of all exploded components.

6. Select the Flange subassembly from the graphics window. The manipulator appears on the assembly.

   Now, you must specify the direction along which the sub-assembly will be exploded.

7. Click the Z axis of the manipulator.

8. Type 4 in the Z box attached to the manipulator.

9. Click **OK** on the Mini toolbar.

10. Right click in the graphics window and select **Tweak Components** from the Marking menu.

11. Select **Component** from the Selection filter drop-down on the Mini toolbar.

12. Click on the Z axis of the manipulator.

13. Type -4 in the Z box attached to the manipulator, and click **Apply**.

14. Click the **Tweak Components** button on the **Component** panel of the **Presentation** ribbon tab.

15. On the Mini Toolbar, select **Part** from the drop-down, as shown.

16. Click on the Z axis of the manipulator.

17. Type 4 in the box attached to the manipulator, and then press Enter.

18. Click the **OK** on the Mini Toolbar.

19. Activate the **Tweak Components** command.

20. Zoom into the flange and click on the key, as shown.

21. Click on the Z axis of the manipulator.

22. Type -3.15 in the box attached to the manipulator and press Enter.

18. Likewise, explode the other flange subassembly and its parts in the opposite direction. The explosion distances are same.

Animating the Explosion

1. To play animation of the explosion, click the **Play Current Storyboard** button on the Storyboard.

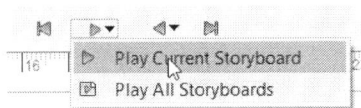

2. Click the **Reverse Play Current Storyboard** button on the Storyboard.

    You can publish the animation video using the **Video** tool available on the **Publish** panel.

3. Make sure that the play marker is at 0 secs on the timeline.

4. On the ribbon, click **Presentation** tab > **Publish** panel > **Video** .

5. On the **Publish to Video** dialog, select **Current Storyboard** option from the **Publish Scope** section.

    You can also select **Current Storyboard Range** and specify the

6. On the **Publish to Video** dialog, click the folder icon and specify **the project folder as the File Location.**

7. Set the **File Format** to **WMV File (*.wmv)**.

8. Check the **Reverse** option to reverse the animation.

9. Leave the other default settings and click **OK; Publish Video Progress dialog appears.**

    A message box appears that the video has been published.

10. Click **OK** on the message box.

Taking the Snapshot of the Explosion

1. Click and drag the play marker on the timeline to 15 seconds.

    You can capture the snapshot of the current position of the assembly using the **New Snapshot View** tool.

2. On the ribbon, click **Presentation** tab > **Workshop** panel > **New Snapshot View** .

The snapshot appears in the Snapshot Views window. Notice that playmarker on the snapshot. It indicates that the snapshot is dependent on the storyboard.

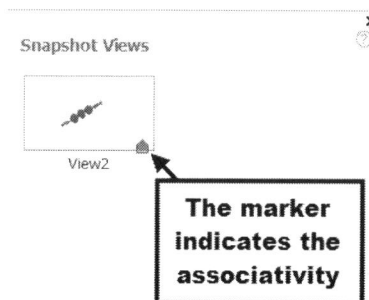

For example, if you make changes to the assembly at the position of the playmarker where the snapshot was taken, the Update View symbol appears on the snapshot view. You need to click on the Update View symbol to update the snapshot.

3. Click **Save** on the **Quick Access Toolbar**; the **Save As** dialog appears.

4. Type-in **Oldham_coupling** in the **File name box.**

5. Go to the project folder.

6. Click **Save** to save the file.

7. Click **OK**.

8. Click **File Menu > Close**.

Chapter 4: Creating Drawings

In this chapter, you will generate 2D drawings of the parts and assemblies.

In this chapter, you will:

- Insert standard views of a part model
- Create centerlines and centermarks
- Retrieve model dimensions
- Add additional dimensions and annotations
- Create Custom Sheet Formats and Templates
- Insert exploded view of the assembly
- Insert a bill of materials of the assembly
- Apply balloons to the assembly

TUTORIAL 1

In this tutorial, you will create the drawing of Flange.ipt file created in the second chapter.

Starting a New Drawing File

1. To start a new drawing, click the **Drawing** icon on the Home screen.

Editing the Drawing Sheet

1. To edit the drawing sheet, right-click on **Sheet:1** in the **Browser window** and select **Edit Sheet** from the shortcut menu.

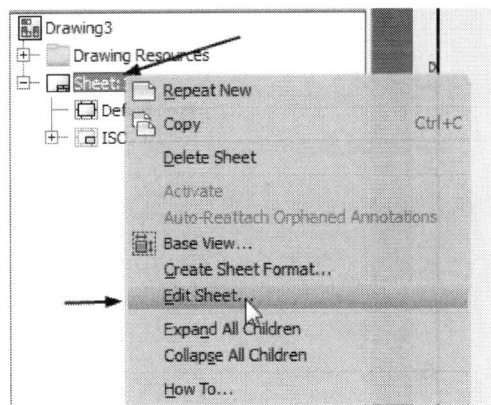

2. On the **Edit Sheet** dialog, set **Size** to **B**.

3. Click **OK**.

The drawing views in this tutorial are created in the Third Angle Projection. If you want to change the type of projection, then following the steps given next:

4. Click **Manage > Styles and Standards > Style Editor** on the ribbon.

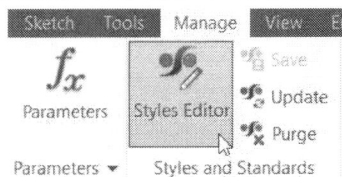

5. On the **Style and Standard Editor** dialog, specify the settings shown in figure.

6. Click **Save and Close**.

Generating the Base View

1. To generate the base view, click **Place views > Create > Base** on the ribbon.

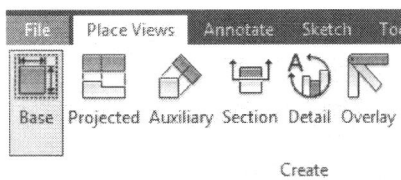

2. On the **Drawing View** dialog, click **Open existing file** .

3. On the **Open** dialog, browse to the project folder.

4. Set **Files of type** to **Inventor Files (*.ipt, *.iam, *.ipn)**, and then double-click on **Flange.ipt**.

5. Set the **Style** to **Hidden Line** .

6. Set **Scale** to **1:1**.

7. Click on the preview, drag, and place it at the left side on the drawing sheet, as shown.

8. Click **OK** on the dialog.

Generating the Section View

1. To create the section view, click **Place Views > Create > Section** on the ribbon.

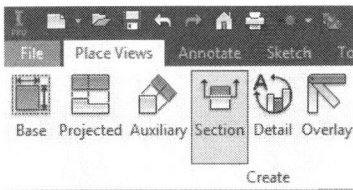

2. Select the base view.

3. Place the cursor on the top quadrant point of the circular edge, as shown.

4. Move the pointer upward and notice the dotted line.

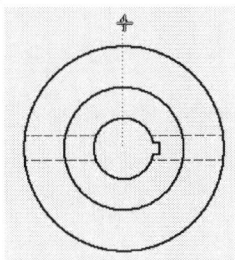

5. Click on the dotted line and move the cursor vertically downwards.

6. Click outside the bottom portion of the view, as shown.

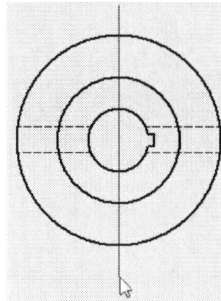

7. Right-click and select **Continue**.

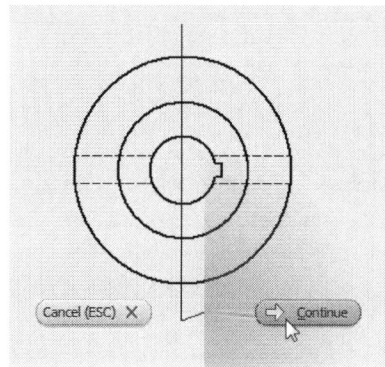

8. Move the cursor toward right and click to place the section view.

Creating the Detailed View

Now, you have to create the detailed view of the keyway, which is displayed, in the front view.

1. To create the detailed view, click **Place Views > Create > Detail** on the ribbon.

2. Select the base view.

3. On the **Detail View** dialog, specify the settings, as shown next.

4. Specify the center point and boundary point of the detail view, as shown in figure.

5. Place the detail view below the base view.

DETAIL B
SCALE 2 : 1

Creating Centermarks and Centerlines

1. To create a center mark, click **Annotate > Symbols > Center Mark** on the ribbon.

2. Click on the outer circle of the base view.

3. To create a centerline, click **Annotate > Symbols > Centerline Bisector** on the ribbon.

4. Click on the inner horizontal edges of the section view.

SECTION A-A   SECTION A-A
SCALE 1 : 1   SCALE 1 : 1

Retrieving Dimensions

Now, you will retrieve the dimensions that were applied to the model while creating it.

1. To retrieve dimensions, click **Annotate > Dimension > Retrieve** on the ribbon.

The **Retrieve Dimension** dialog appears.

2. Select the section view from the drawing sheet.

3. Click the **Select Dimensions** button on the dialog.

Now, you must select the dimensions to retrieve.

4. Drag a window on the section view to select all the dimensions.

SECTION A-A
SCALE 1 : 1

5. Click **Select Features** under the **Select Source** group.

6. Click **OK** to retrieve feature dimensions.

SECTION A-A
SCALE 1 : 1

7. Click **Annotate > Dimension > Arrange** on the ribbon.

8. Drag a selection box and select all the dimensions of the section view.

SECTION A-A
SCALE 1 : 1

SECTION A-A
SCALE 1 : 1

9. Click the right-mouse button and select **OK**.

SECTION A-A
SCALE 1 : 1

10. Select the unwanted dimensions and press Delete.

SECTION A-A
SCALE 1 : 1

11. Click and drag the dimensions to arrange them properly.

Adding additional dimensions

1. To add dimensions, click **Annotate > Dimension > Dimension** on the ribbon.

2. Select the center hole on the base view.

3. Right-click and select **Dimension Type > Diameter**.

4. Place the dimension, as shown in figure. The **Edit Dimension** dialog appears.

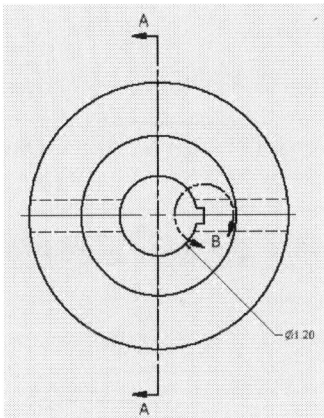

5. Click **OK**.

6. Create the dimensions on the detail view, as shown in figure.

DETAIL B
SCALE 2 : 1

Populating the Title Block

1. To populate the title block, click **File Menu > iProperties**.

2. On the **Flange iProperties** dialog, click the tabs one-by-one and type-in data in respective fields.

3. Click **Apply** and **Close**.

Saving the Drawing

1. Click **Save** on the **Quick Access Toolbar**; the **Save As** dialog appears.

2. Type-in **Flange** in the **File Name** box.

3. Go to the project folder.

4. Click **Save** to save the file.

5. Click **File Menu > Close**.

TUTORIAL 2

In this tutorial, you will create a custom template, and then use it to create a new drawing.

Creating New Sheet Format

1. On the ribbon, click **Get Started > Launch > New**.

2. On the **Create New File** dialog, click the **Standard.idw** icon.

Standard.idw

3. Click **Create** to start a new drawing file.

4. To edit the drawing sheet, right-click on **Sheet:1** in the **Browser window** and select **Edit Sheet** from the shortcut menu.

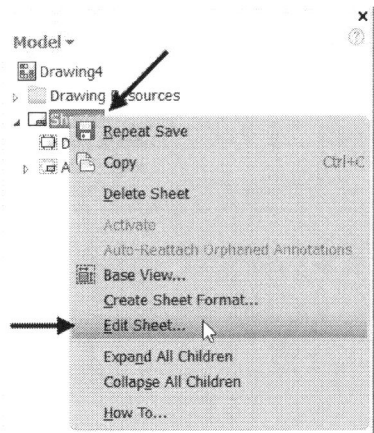

5. On the **Edit Sheet** dialog, set **Size** to **B**.

   Under the **Orientation** section, you can change the orientation of the title block as well as the sheet orientation.

6. Click **OK**.

7. In the **Browser window**, expand the **Drawing Resources > Sheet Formats** folder to view different sheet formats available. Now, you will add a new sheet format to this folder.

8. Click the right mouse button on the **Borders** folder and select **Define New Border**.

   Now, you can create a new border using the sketch tools available in the **Sketch** tab.

9. Click **Finish Sketch** on the **Sketch** tab of the ribbon.

10. On the **Border** dialog, click **Discard**.

11. In the Browser window, click the right mouse button on the **Borders** folder and select **Define New Zone Border**.

12. On the **Default Drawing Border Parameters** dialog, type-in **4** in the **Vertical Zones** box and click **OK**.

13. Click **Finish Sketch** on the **Sketch** tab of the ribbon.

14. On the **Border** dialog, type-in **4-Zone Border** and click **Save**.

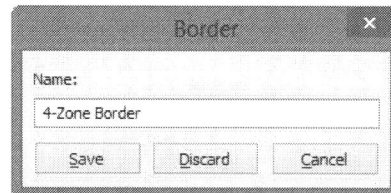

15. Expand the **Title Blocks** folder and click the right mouse button on **ANSI-Large**.

16. Select **Edit** from shortcut menu.

17. On the **Sketch** tab of the ribbon, click **Insert > Image**.

18. Draw a rectangle in the **Company** cell of the title block. This defines the image size and location.

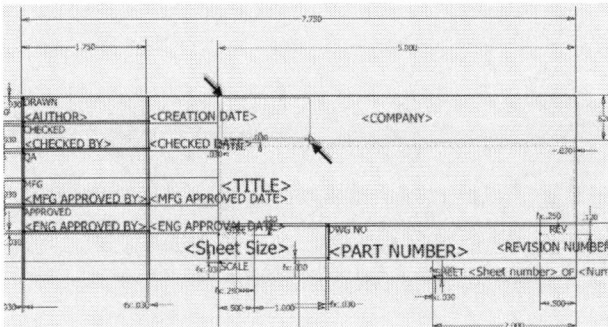

19. Go to the location of your company logo or any other image location. You must ensure that the image is located inside the project folder.

20. Select the image file and click **Open**. This will insert the image into the title block.

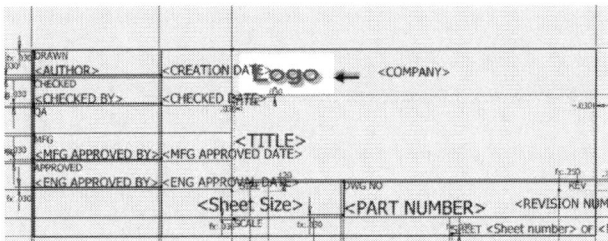

21. Click **Finish Sketch** on the ribbon.

22. Click **Save As** on the **Save Edits** dialog.

23. Type-in **ANSI-Logo** in the **Title Block** dialog.

24. Click **Save**.

25. In the Browser window, expand **Sheet:1** and click the right mouse button on **Default Border**.

26. Select **Delete** from the shortcut menu.

27. Expand the **Borders** folder and click the right mouse button on **4-Zone Border**.

28. Select **Insert** from the shortcut menu.

29. Click **OK** on the **Edit Drawing Border Parameters** dialog.

30. Expand **Sheet:1** and click the right mouse button on **ANSI-Large**.

31. Select **Delete** from the shortcut menu.

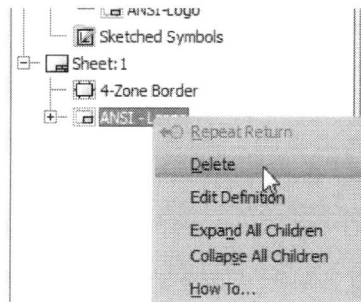

32. Expand the **Title Blocks** folder and click the right mouse button on **ANSI-Logo**.

33. Select **Insert** from the shortcut menu to insert the title block.

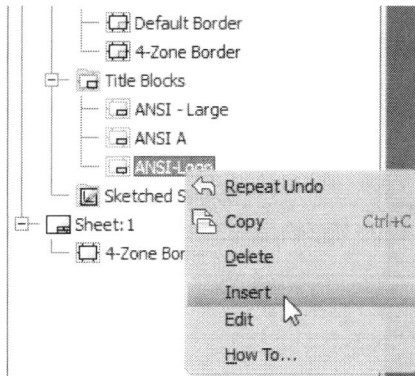

34. Click the right mouse button on **Sheet:1** and select **Create Sheet Format**.

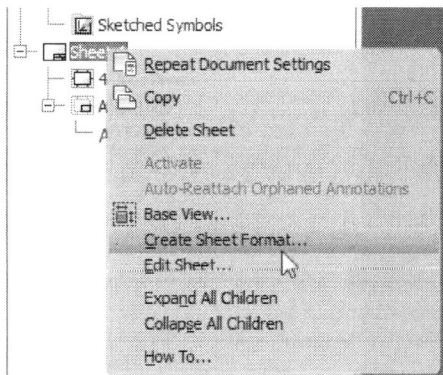

35. Type-in **Custom Sheet** in the **Create Sheet Format** dialog, and then click **OK**.

You will notice that the new sheet format is listed in the **Sheet Formats** folder.

Creating a Custom Template

1. On the ribbon, click **Tools > Options > Document Settings**.

On **Document Settings** dialog, you can define the standard, sheet color, drawing view settings, and sketch settings.

2. Leave the default settings on this dialog and click **Close**.

3. In the Browser window, expand the **Sheet Formats** folder and double-click on **Custom Format**.

4. Click the right mouse button on **Sheet: 2** and select **Delete Sheet** from the shortcut menu.

5. Click **OK**.

6. On the ribbon, click **Manage > Styles and Standards > Styles Editor**.

7. On the **Style and Standard Editor** dialog, select **Dimension > Default (ANSI)**.

8. Click the **New** button located at the top of the dialog.

9. Type-in **Custom Standard** in the **New Local Style** dialog, and then click **OK**.

10. Click the **Units** tab and set **Precision** to **3.123**.

11. Click **Save and Close**.

12. On the **File Menu**, click **Save As > Save Copy As Template**. This will take you to the templates folder on your drive.

13. Type-in **Custom Template** in the **File name** box.

14. Click **Save**.

15. Close the drawing file without saving it.

Starting a Drawing using the Custom template

1. On the ribbon, click **Get Started > Launch > New**.

2. On the **Create New File** dialog, click the **Custom Standard.idw** icon.

Custom
Template.idw

3. Click **Create** and **OK** to start a new drawing file.

Generating the Drawing Views

1. To generate views, click **Place views > Create > Base** on the ribbon.

2. On the **Drawing View** dialog, click **Open existing file** .

3. Go to the project folder and double-click on **Disc.ipt**.

4. Select **Front** from the ViewCube displayed on the sheet.

5. Set **Scale** to **1:1**.

6. Click and drag the view to top-center of the drawing sheet.

7. Move the cursor downwards and click to place the projected view.

8. Right-click and select **OK**.

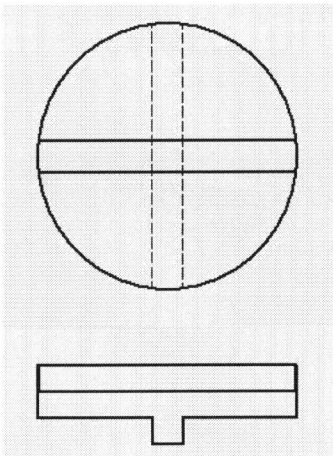

Adding Dimensions

1. On the ribbon, click **Annotate > Dimension > Dimension**.

2. On the ribbon, click **Annotate > Format > Select Style > Custom Standard**.

3. Select the circular edge on the base view.

4. Right-click and select **Dimension Type > Diameter**.

5. Click to place the dimension.

6. Click **OK**.

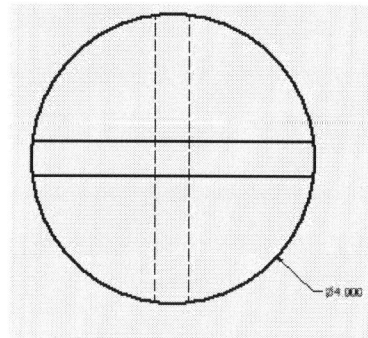

7. Select the horizontal edges on the base view.

8. Move the pointer toward right and click to place the dimension.

9. Click **OK** on the **Edit Dimension** dialog.

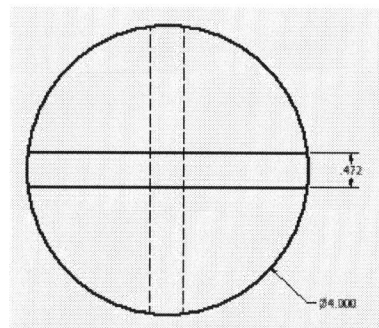

10. Add other dimensions to drawing.

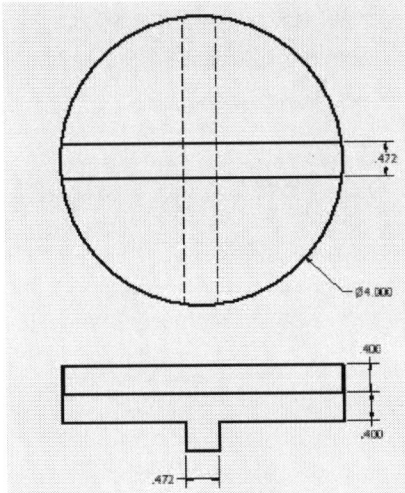

11. Right-click and select **OK** to deactivate the **Dimension** tool.

12. Save and close the drawing file.

TUTORIAL 3

In this tutorial, you will create the drawing of Oldham coupling assembly created in the previous chapter.

Creating a New Drawing File

1. On the ribbon, click **Get Started > Launch > New**.

2. On the **Create New File** dialog, click the **Custom Standard.idw** icon.

Custom
Template.idw

3. Click **Create** and **OK** to start a new drawing file.

Generating Base View

1. To generate the base view, click **Place views >**

   Create > Base on the ribbon; the **Drawing View** dialog appears.

2. Click **Open existing file** on this dialog; the **Open** dialog appears.

3. Go to the project folder and double-click on **Oldham_Coupling.iam**.

4. Click the **Home** icon located above the ViewCube.

5. Set **Scale** to **1/2**.

6. Click and drag the view at top left corner.

7. Right-click and select **OK**.

Generating the Exploded View

1. To generate the base view, click **Place views > Create > Base** on the ribbon; the **Drawing View** dialog appears.

2. Click **Open existing file** on this dialog; the **Open** dialog appears.

3. Go to the project folder and double-click on **Oldham_Coupling.ipn**.

4. Click the **Home** icon located above the ViewCube.

5. Set **Scale** to **1/2**.

6. Click and drag the view to the center of the drawing sheet.

7. Right-click and select **OK**.

Configuring the Parts list settings

1. Click **Manage > Styles and Standards > Style Editor** on the ribbon; the **Style and Standard Editor** dialog appears.

2. Expand the **Parts List** node and select **Parts List (ANSI)**.

3. Click the **Column Chooser** button under the **Default Columns Settings** group; the **Parts List Column Chooser** dialog appears.

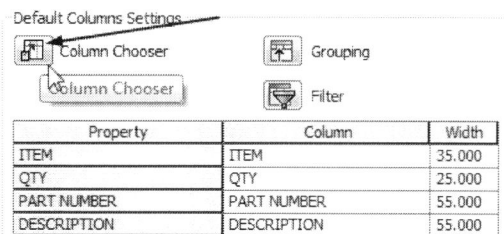

4. On this dialog, select **DESCRIPTION** from the **Selected Properties** list and click the **Remove** button.

5. Select **PART NUMBER** from the **Selected Properties** list and click **Move Up**.

6. Click **OK**.

7. Click **Save and Close**.

Creating the Parts list

1. To create a parts list, click **Annotate > Table > Parts List** on the ribbon; the **Parts List** dialog appears.

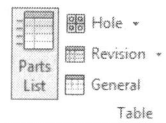

2. Select the exploded view from the drawing sheet.

3. Select **Parts Only** from the **BOM View** drop-down under the **BOM Settings and Properties** group.

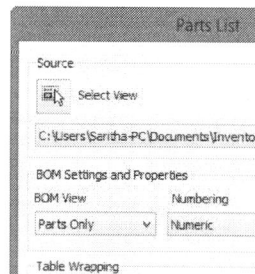

4. Click **OK** twice.

5. Place the part list above the title block.

PARTS LIST		
ITEM	PART NUMBER	QTY
1	Disc	1
2	Flange	2
3	Shaft	2
4	Key	2

Creating Balloons

1. To create balloons, click **Annotate > Table > Balloon > Auto Balloon** on the ribbon; the **Auto-Balloon** dialog appears.

5. Click **OK**.

6. Click **File Menu > Close**.

2. Select the exploded view from the drawing sheet.

3. Select all the parts in the exploded view.

4. Select **Horizontal** from the **Placement** group.

5. Click the **Select Placement** button in the **Placement** group.

6. Click above the exploded view.

7. Click **OK** to place the balloons.

Saving the Drawing

1. Click **Save** on the **Quick Access Toolbar**; the **Save As** dialog appears.

2. Type-in **Oldham_Coupling** in the **File Name** box.

3. Go to the project folder.

4. Click **Save** to save the file.

Chapter 5: Additional Modeling Tools

In this chapter, you create models using additional modeling tools. You will learn to:

- Create slots
- Create circular patterns
- Create holes
- Create chamfers
- Create shells
- Create rib features
- Create coils
- Create a loft feature
- Create an emboss feature
- Create a thread
- Create a sweep feature
- Create a grill feature
- Create a replace faces
- Create a face fillet
- Create a variable fillet
- Create a boss feature
- Create a lip feature

TUTORIAL 1

In this tutorial, you create the model shown in figure:

Creating the First Feature

1. Create a new project with the name **Autodesk Inventor 2017 Basics Tutorial** (See Chapter 2,

Tutorial 1, Creating New Project section to learn how to create a new project).

2. Open a new Inventor part file using the **Standard.ipt** template (See Chapter 2, Tutorial 3, Starting a New Part File section).

3. Click the **Start 2D sketch** button on the ribbon, and select the XY Plane.

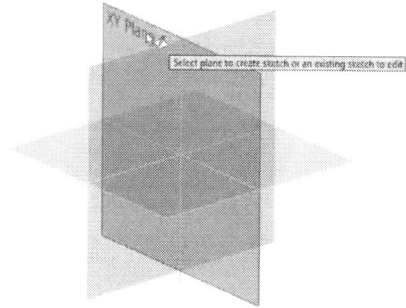

4. Click the **Circle Center Point** button and draw a circle (See Chapter 2, Tutorial 1, Starting a Sketch section to learn how to create a new project).

5. Click the **Line** button.

6. Specify a point at top left outside the circle.

7. Move the pointer horizontally and notice the Horizontal constraint symbol.

8. Click outside the circle. Press Esc to deactivate the **Line** tool.

9. Click the **Trim** button on the **Modify** panel.
10. Click on the portions of the sketch, as shown below.

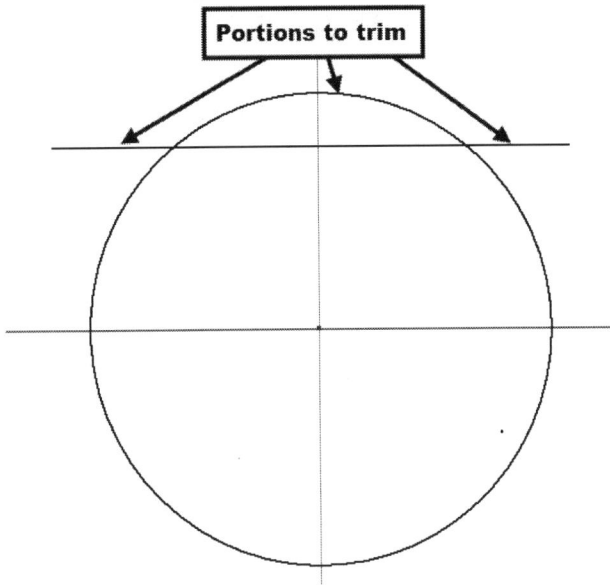

Portions to trim

11. Apply dimensions to the sketch (Radius=0.63, vertical length=1.102). To apply the vertical length dimension, activate the **Dimension** tool and select the horizontal line. Move the pointer downward and place the cursor on the bottom quadrant point of the arc. Click when the symbol $\overrightarrow{\circ}$ appears. Move the pointer toward left and click to place the dimension.

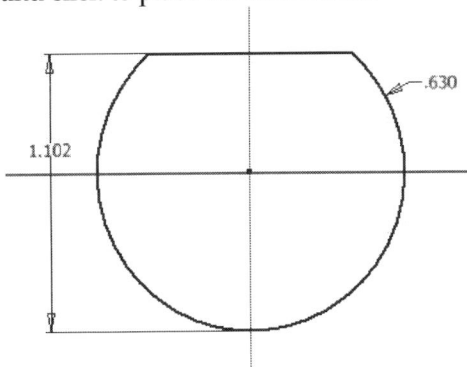

12. Click **Rectangle > Slot Center Point Arc** on the **Create** panel.

13. Select the origin as the center point.

14. Move the cursor outside and click in the first quadrant of the circle to specify the start point of the slot arc.

15. Move the cursor and click in the fourth quadrant of the circle to specify the end point of the slot arc.

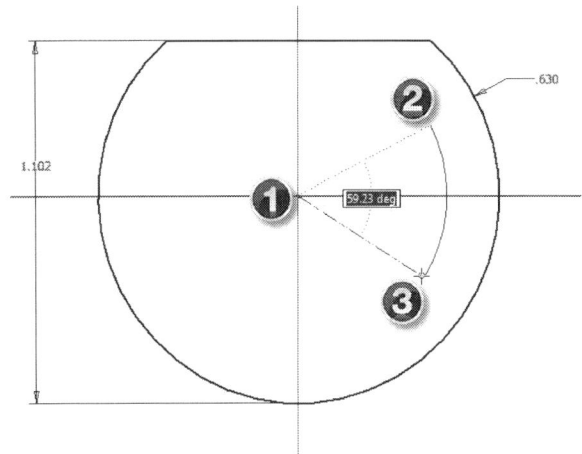

16. Move the cursor outward from the arc and click.

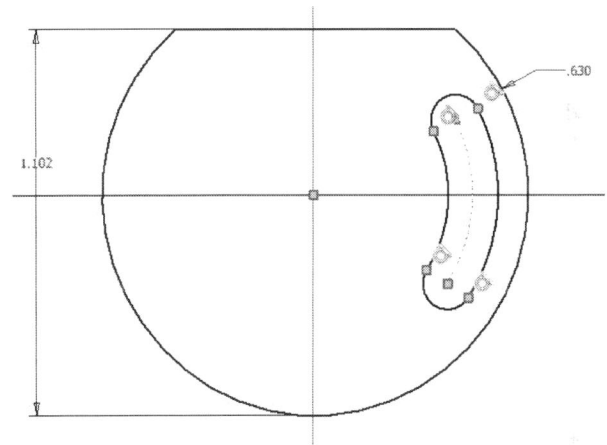

17. Click the **Dimension** button on the **Constrain** panel.

18. Select the start point of the slot arc.

19. Select the center point of the slot arc.

20. Select the end point of the slot arc.

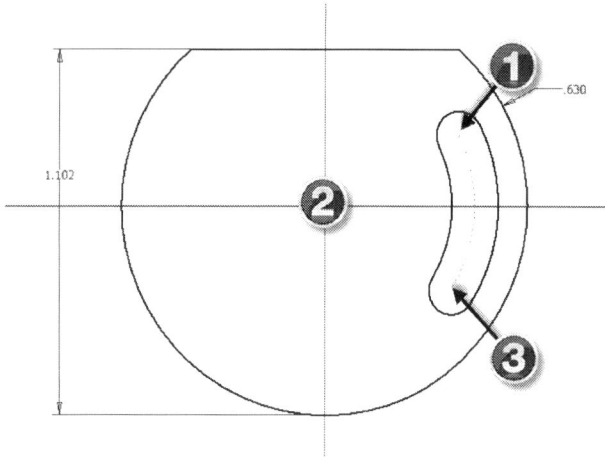

21. Place the angular dimension of the slot; the **Edit Dimension** box appears.

22. Enter **30** in the **Edit Dimension** box and click the green check.

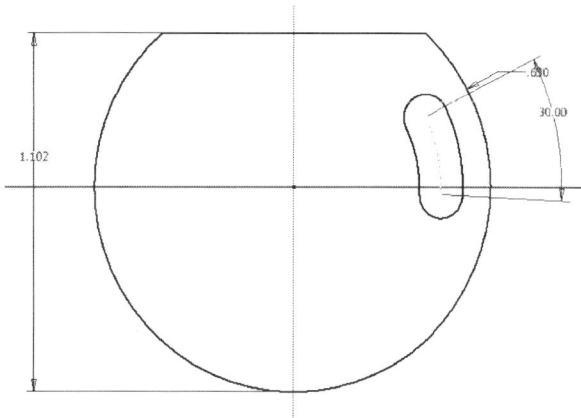

23. Click the **Construction** button on the **Format** panel.

24. Click the **Line** button on the **Create** panel.

25. Draw a horizontal line passing through the origin.

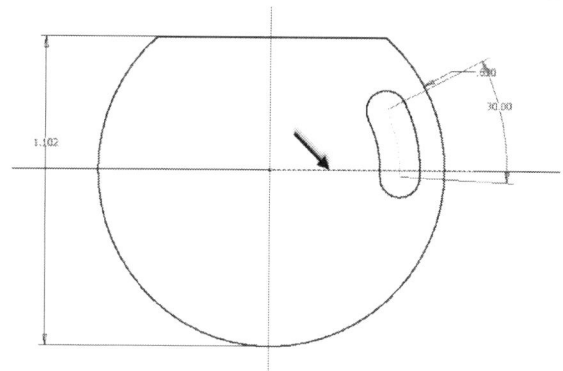

26. Click the **Symmetric** button on the **Constrain** panel.

27. Select the end caps of the slot.

28. Select the construction line; the slot is made symmetric about the construction line.

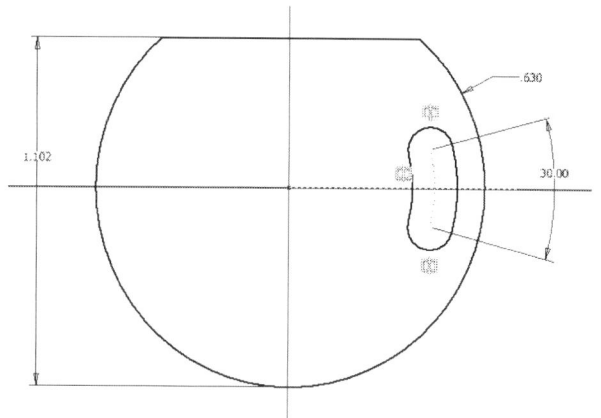

29. Apply other dimensions to the slot.

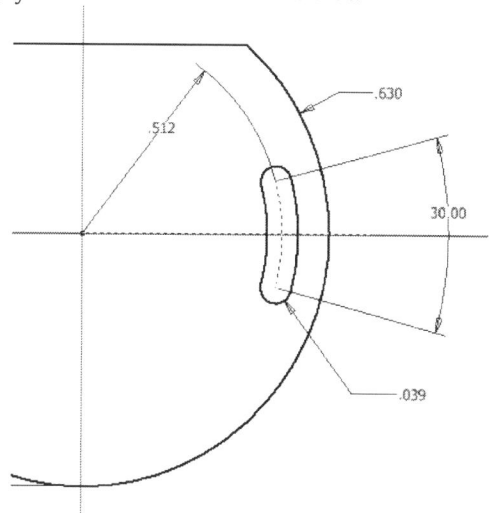

30. Click the **Circular Pattern** button on the **Pattern**

panel; the **Circular Pattern** dialog appears.

31. Select all the elements of the slot by creating a selection window.

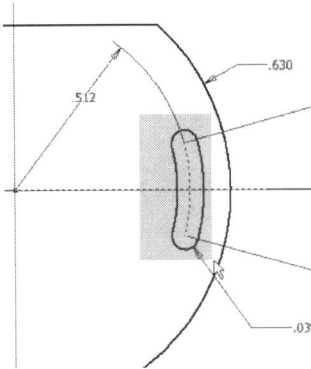

32. Click the cursor button located on the right-side on the dialog.

33. Select the origin point of the sketch axis point.

34. Enter **4** in the **Count** box and **180** in the **Angle** box.

35. Click the **Flip** button.

The preview of the circular pattern appears.

36. Click **OK** to create the circular pattern.

37. Click the **Finish Sketch** button on the ribbon.

38. Extrude the sketch up to 0.236 distance (See Chapter 2, Tutorial 1, Creating the Base Feature section to learn how to create a new project).

Adding the Second feature

1. Create a sketch on the back face of the model (use the Orbit tool available on the Navigate bar to rotate the model).

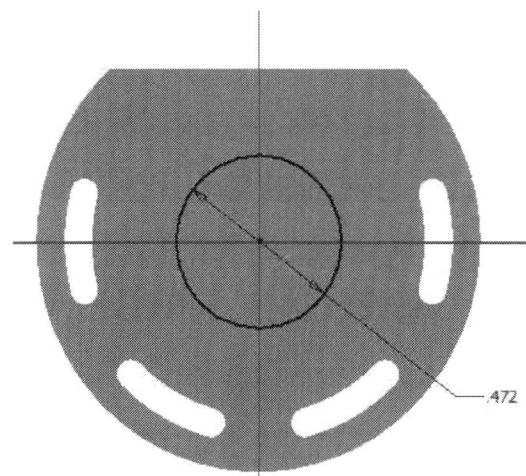

2. Extrude the sketch up to 0.078 distance.

Creating a Counterbore Hole

In this section, you will create a counterbore hole concentric to the cylindrical face.

1. Click the **Hole** button on the **Modify** panel; the **Hole** dialog appears.

2. Set the parameters in the **Hole** dialog, as shown in figure.

3. Click on the front face of the model; the preview of the hole appears.

Now, you need to specify the concentric reference.

4. Select the cylindrical face of the model; the hole is made concentric to the model.

5. Click **OK** on the dialog; the counterbore hole is created.

Creating a Threaded hole

In this section, you will create a hole using a sketch point.

1. Click the **Start 2D Sketch** button and select front face of the model.

2. Click the **Point** button on the **Create** panel.

3. Place the point on the front face of the model.

4. Click the **Horizontal** button on the **Constrain** panel.

5. Select the point and sketch origin; the point

becomes horizontal to the origin.

6. Create a horizontal dimension of 0.354 between point and origin.

7. Click **Finish Sketch**.

8. Click the **Hole** button on the **Modify** panel; the **Hole** dialog appears.

9. On the **Hole** dialog, set **Placement** to **From Sketch**.

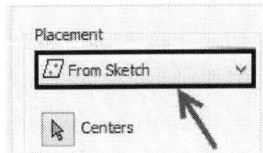

10. Select the **Counterbore** option.

11. Set the **Counterbore Diameter** to 0.118.

12. Set the **Counterbore Depth** to 0.039.

13. Select the **Tapped Hole** option.

14. Set the **Thread Type** to **ANSI Unified Screw Threads**.

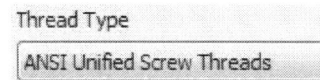

15. Set the **Size** to **0.073**.

16. Set the **Designation** to **1-64 UNC**.

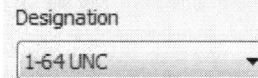

17. Select the **Full Depth** option.

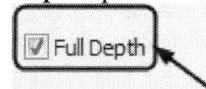

18. Set the **Direction** to **Right Hand**.

19. Click **OK** to create the hole.

Creating a Circular Pattern

1. Click the **Circular Pattern** button on the **Pattern** panel; the **Circular Pattern** dialog appears.

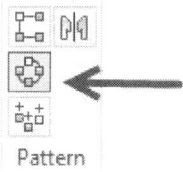

2. Select the threaded hole created in the previous section.

3. Click the **Rotation Axis** button on the dialog.

4. Select the outer cylindrical face of the model.

5. Enter **6** in the **Occurrence** box and **360** in the **Angle** box.

6. Click **OK** to create the circular pattern.

Creating Chamfers

1. Click the **Chamfer** button on the **Modify** panel.

2. Click the **Distance and Angle** button on the dialog.

3. Select the cylindrical face of the counterbore hole located at the center.

Face selected

4. Select the circular edge of the counterbore hole.

5. Enter 0.039 in the **Distance** box and 30 in the **Angle** box.

6. Click **OK** to create the chamfer.

7. Save the model and close it.

TUTORIAL 2

In this tutorial, you will create the model shown in figure.

Creating the first feature

1. Open a new Inventor part file using the **Standard.ipt** template (See Chapter 2, Tutorial 3, Starting a New Part File section).

2. On the ribbon, click **3D Model > Sketch > Start 2D Sketch** .

3. Select the YZ plane.

4. Draw an L-shaped sketch using the **Line** tool and dimension it.

5. Click the **Offset** button on the **Modify** panel.

6. Select the sketch and specify the offset position.

7. Click the **Line** button and draw lines closing the offset sketch.

8. Add the offset dimension to the sketch.

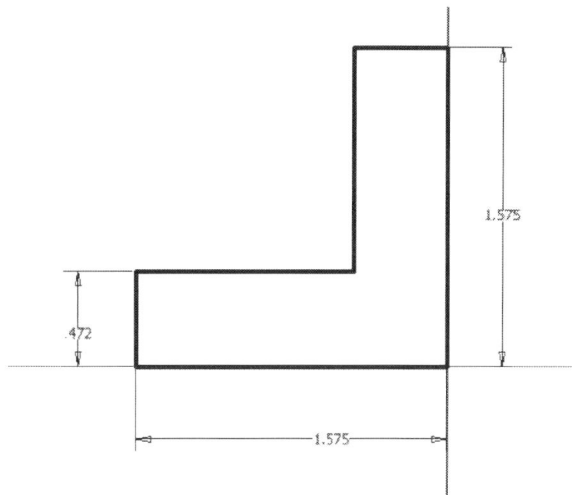

9. Click **Finish Sketch**.

10. Click **3D Model > Create > Extrude** on the ribbon.

11. Select the **Symmetric** option from the Mini toolbar.

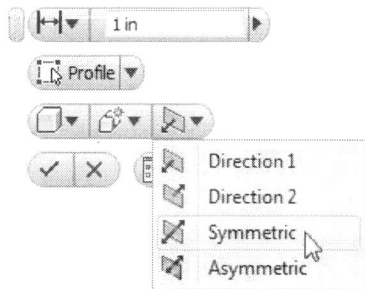

12. Set the **Distance** to 1.575.

13. Click **OK** to create the first feature.

Creating the Shell feature

You can create a shell feature by removing a face of the model and applying thickness to other faces.

1. Click **3D Model > Modify > Shell** on the ribbon; the **Shell** dialog appears.

2. Set **Thickness** to 0.197.

Now, you need to select the faces to remove.

3. Select the top face and the back face of the model.

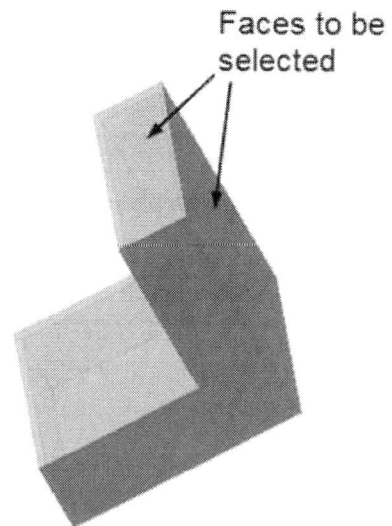

Faces to be selected

4. Select the front face and the bottom face of the model.

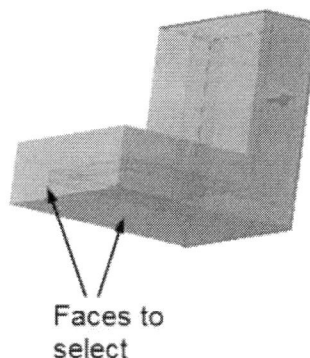

Faces to select

5. Click **OK** to shell the model.

Creating the Third feature

1. Click **3D Model > Sketch > Start 2D Sketch** on the ribbon.

2. Select the front face of the model.

3. Click **Sketch > Create > Rectangle** drop-down > **Slot Center to Center** on the ribbon.

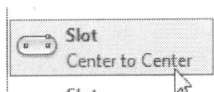

4. Draw a slot by selecting the first, second, and third points.

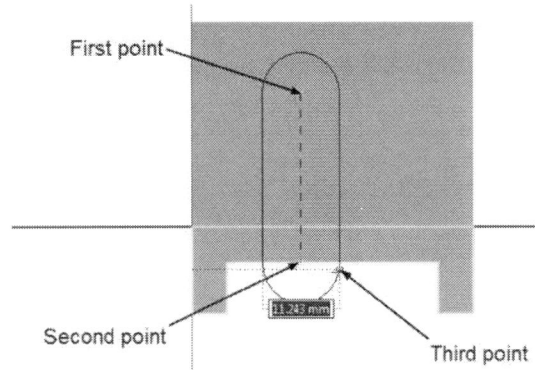

5. Apply dimensions to the slot.

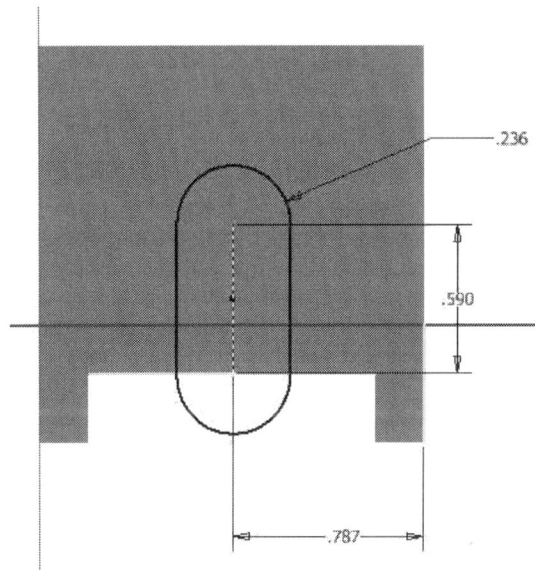

6. Click **Finish Sketch**.

7. Click **3D Model > Create > Extrude** on the ribbon.

8. Select the sketch.

9. Select the **To** option from the **Extents** drop-down.

10. Select the back face of the model.

11. Click the **Join** button on the dialog.

12. Click **OK** to create the feature.

Creating a Cut Feature

1. Create the sketch on the front face of the model, as shown below.

2. Finish the sketch.

3. Click **3D Model > Create > Extrude** on the ribbon.

4. Select the sketch.

5. Select the **All** option from the **Extents** drop-down.

6. Click the **Cut** button on the dialog.

7. Click **OK** to create the cut feature.

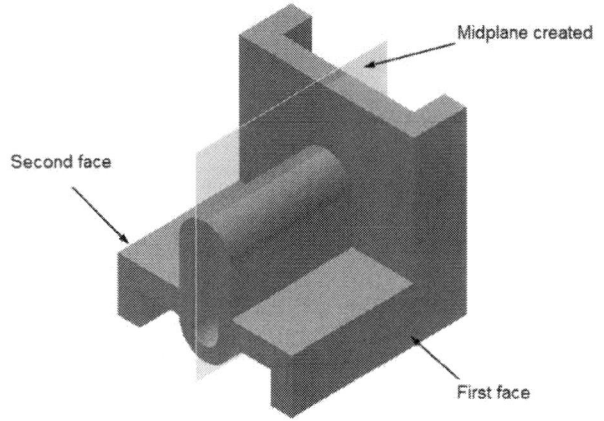

Creating the Rib Feature

In this section, you will create a rib feature at the middle of the model. To do this, you must create a mid-plane.

1. To create a mid-plane, click **3D Model > Work Features > Plane > Midplane between Two Parallel Planes** on the ribbon.

2. Select the right face of the model.

3. Select the left face of the model; the midplane is created.

4. Click **3D Model > Sketch > Start 2D Sketch** on the ribbon.

5. Select the mid plane.

6. Click the **Slice Graphics** button at the bottom of the window.

7. Click **Sketch > Create > Project Geometry > Project Cut Edges** on the ribbon; the edges cut by the sketch plane are projected.

8. Draw the sketch, as shown below.

9. Finish the sketch.

10. Click **3D Model > Create > Rib** ⬆ on the ribbon; the **Rib** dialog appears.

11. Select the sketch.

12. Click the **Parallel to Sketch** 🔲 button on the dialog.

13. Click the **Direction 1** 🔲 button.

14. Set **Thickness** to 0.197.

15. Click the **To Next** 🔲 button.

16. Click the **Symmetric** 🔲 button below the **Thickness** box.

17. Click **OK** to create the rib feature.

18. To hide the midplane, select it and right-click.

19. Click **Visibility** on the Marking Menu; the plane will be hidden.

20. Save the model and close it.

TUTORIAL 3

In this tutorial, you will create a helical spring using the **Coil** tool.

Creating the Coil

1. Open a new Inventor file using the **Standard.ipt** template (See Chapter 2, Tutorial 3, Starting a New Part File section).

2. Click the **Start 2D sketch** button on the ribbon, and select the XY Plane.

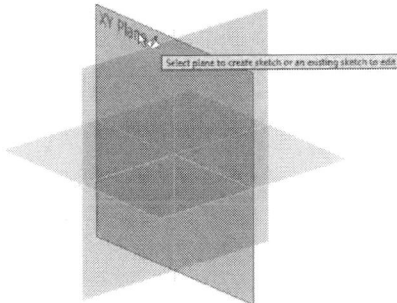

3. Click the **Circle Center Point** button.

4. Select a point on the left portion of the horizontal axis.

5. Move the cursor outward and click to create a circle.

6. On the ribbon, click **Sketch > Format > Centerline**.

7. Click the **Line** button.

8. Select the origin point of the sketch, move the cursor upward, and click to create a centreline.

9. On the ribbon, click **Sketch > Constrain > Dimension**.

10. Add the diameter dimension to the circle, as shown.

11. Select the centreline and circle.

12. Move the pointer downward and click.

13. Type 1.575 and press Enter.

14. Finish the sketch.

15. To create a coil, click **3D Model > Create > Coil** on the ribbon; the **Coil** dialog appears.

In addition, the profile is automatically selected. Now, you need to select the axis of the coil.

16. Select the centerline as the axis. Click the **Reverse Axis** button on the **Coil** dialog, if the coil preview is downwards.

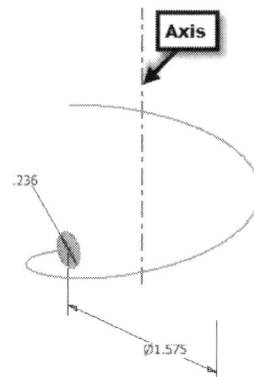

17. Click the **Coil Size** tab on the dialog.

18. In the **Coil Size** tab, specify the settings as given next.

Part 2: Autodesk Inventor Basics

19. Click the **Coil Ends** tab on the dialog.

20. Specify the settings in the **Coil Ends** tab, as given next.

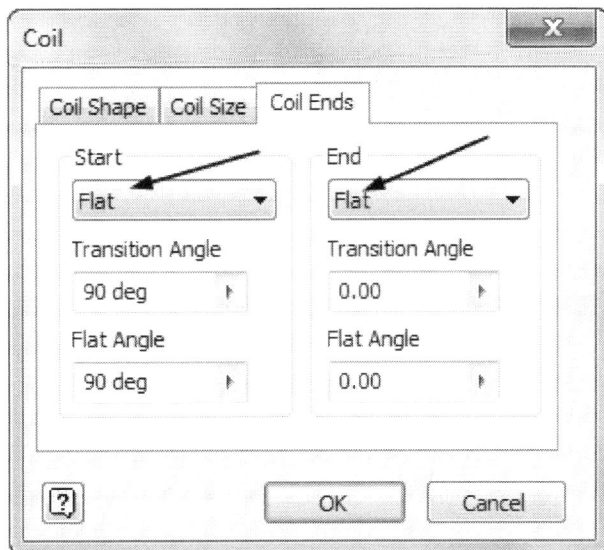

21. Click **OK** to create the coil.

22. Save the model as **Coil.ipt** and close the file.

TUTORIAL 4

In this tutorial, you create a shampoo bottle using the **Loft**, **Extrude**, and **Coil** tools.

Creating the First Section and Rails

To create a swept feature, you need to create sections and guide curves.

1. Open a new Part file (See Chapter 2, Tutorial 3, Starting a New Part File section).

2. Click **3D Model > Sketch > Start 2D Sketch** on the ribbon.

399

3. Select the XZ plane.

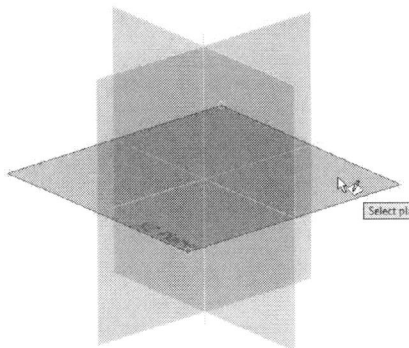

4. Click **Sketch > Create > Circle > Ellipse** on the ribbon.

5. Draw the ellipse by selecting the points, as shown.

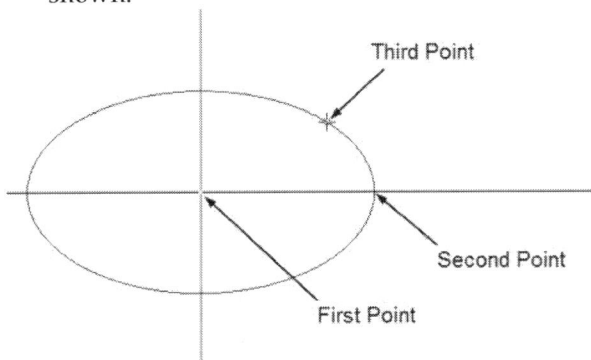

6. On the ribbon, click **Sketch > Constrain > Dimension**.

7. Select the ellipse, move the cursor downward, and click.

8. Type 1.968 and press Enter.

9. Select the ellipse, move the cursor toward left, and click.

10. Type 0.984 and press Enter.

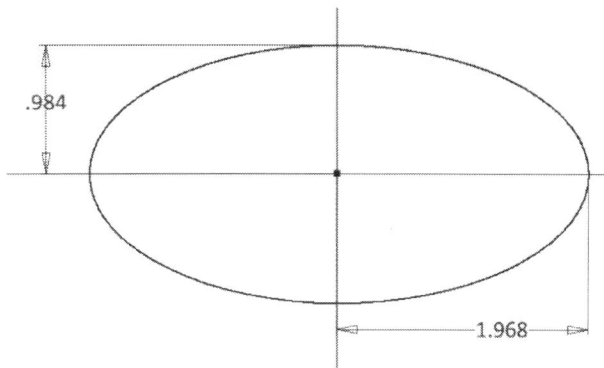

11. Click **Finish Sketch**.

12. Click **3D Model > Sketch > Start 2D Sketch** on the ribbon.

13. Select the YZ plane from the graphics window.

14. Click **Sketch > Create > Line> Spline Interpolation** on the ribbon.

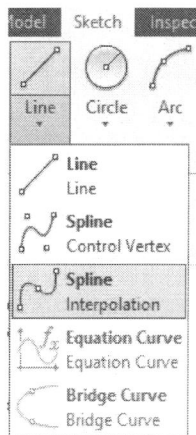

15. Select a point on the horizontal axis of the sketch; a rubber band curve is attached to the cursor

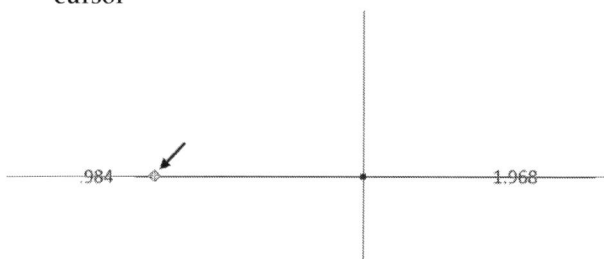

16. Move the cursor up and specify the second point of the spline; a curve is attached to cursor.

17. Likewise, specify the other points of the spline, as shown.

18. Click the right mouse button and select **Create**. The spline will be similar to the one shown in figure.

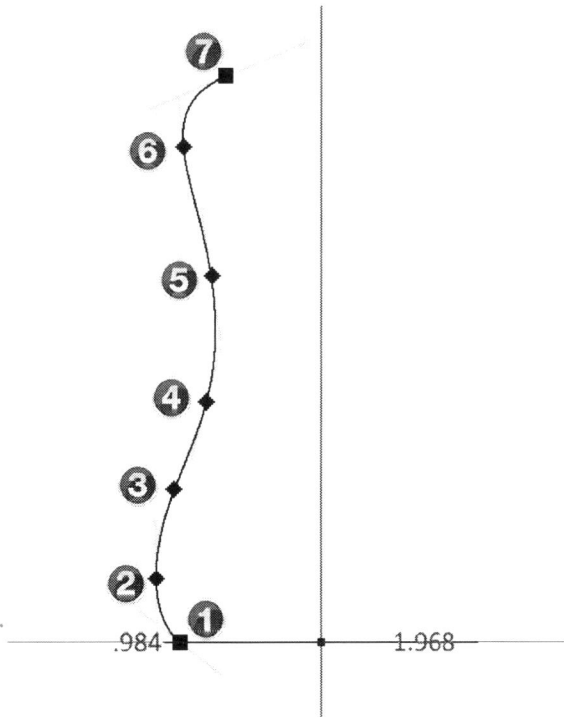

19. Right click and select **Line** from the Marking Menu.

20. On the ribbon, click **Sketch > Format > Construction**.

21. Select the origin point of the sketch, move the pointer vertically upward and click to create a vertical construction line.

22. On the ribbon, click **Sketch > Constrain > Vertical**.

23. Select the lower end points of the vertical construction line and the spline.

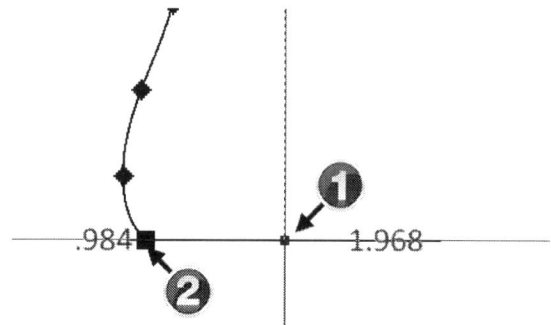

24. On the ribbon, click **Sketch > Constrain > Dimension**.

25. Select the lower end points of the construction line and spline.

26. Move the cursor downward and click.

27. Type the 1.968 in the Edit Dimension box and press Enter.

Points to select

.984   1.968

⊢ 1.771 ⊣

Edit Dimension : d4   ✕

1.968   >   ✓

28. Select the second point of the spline and the construction line.

29. Move the cursor and click to place the dimension.

30. Type 2.362 in the **Edit Dimension** box and press Enter.

Selections

2.241

.984   Edit Dimension : d5   ✕   1.968

2.362   >   ✓

1.968

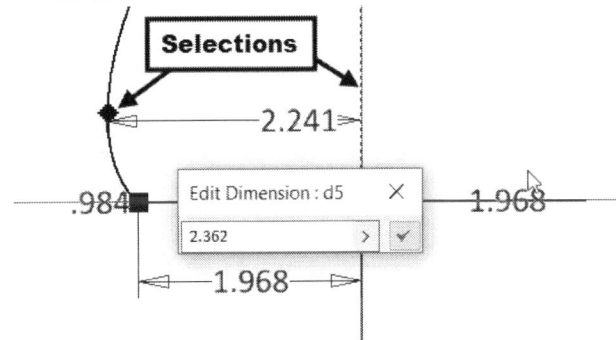

31. Apply the other horizontal dimensions to the spline, as shown in figure.

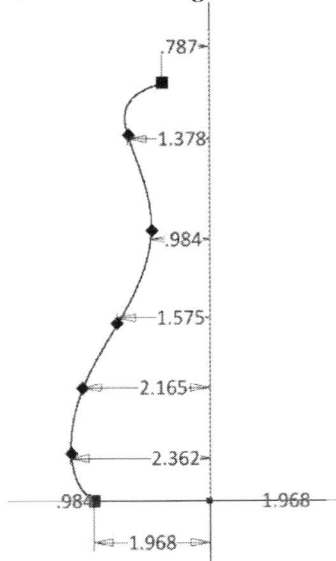

.787
1.378
.984
1.575
2.165
2.362
.98   1.968
1.968

32. Select the origin point of the sketch and the top end point of the spline.

33. Move the pointer toward right and click.

34. Type 8.858 in the **Edit Dimension** box and press Enter.

.787
1.378
.984

Points to select   6.867

Edit Dimension : d11   ✕

8.858   >   ✓

1.575
2.165
2.362
.984   1.968
1.968

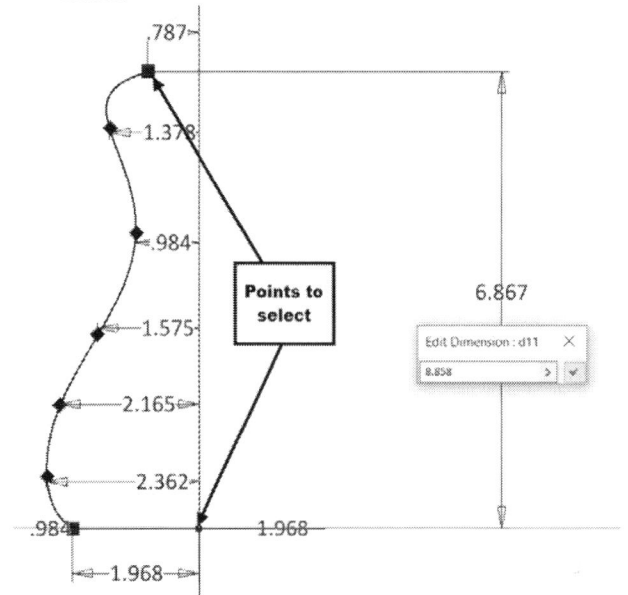

35. Likewise, create other dimensions, as shown.

.787
1.378
.984
4.921   1.575   6.102   8.858
2.165   7.677
3.740   2.362
2.362
.98   1.968
1.968

36. Click **Sketch > Pattern > Mirror** 🔲🔲 on the ribbon; the **Mirror** dialog appears.

37. Select the spline. Make sure that you select the curve and not the points.

38. Click **Mirror line** on the **Mirror** dialog, and then select the construction line.

39. Click **Apply**, and then click **Done**.

40. Click **Finish Sketch**.

Creating the second section

1. Click **3D Model > Work Features > Plane > Offset from Plane** on the ribbon.

2. Select the XZ plane from the Browser window.

3. Enter **8.858** in the **Distance** box.

4. Click **OK** ✔.

5. On the ribbon, click the **3D Model > Sketch > Start 2D Sketch**.

6. Select the newly created datum plane.

7. Right click and select **Center Point Circle** from the Marking Menu.

8. Select the origin point, move the cursor outside, and click to create a circle.

9. Right click and select **OK**.

10. Right click and select **General Dimension** from the Marking Menu.

11. Select the circle, move the cursor outward, and click.

12. Type 1.574 and press Enter.

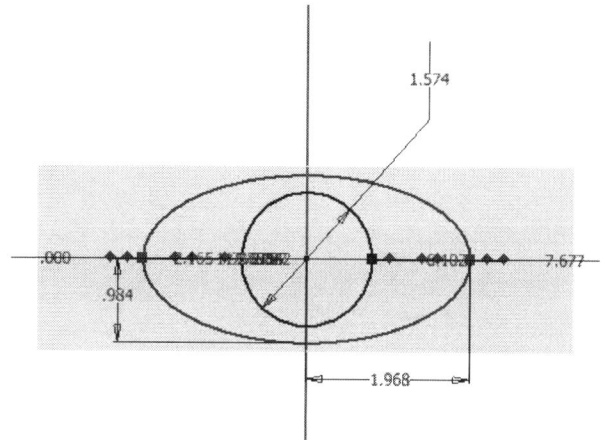

13. Click **Finish Sketch** on the ribbon.

Creating the Loft feature

1. To create a loft feature, click **3D Model > Create > Loft** ⬙ on the ribbon; the **Loft** dialog appears.

2. Select the **Rails** option from the dialog.

3. Click **Click to add** in the **Sections** group and select the circle.

First Section

Rail 1

Rail 2

Second Section

4. Select the ellipse.

5. Click **Click to add** in the **Rails** group.

6. Select the first rail.

7. Select the second rail.

8. Click **OK** to create the loft feature.

Creating the Extruded feature

1. Right click and select **New Sketch** from the Marking Menu.

2. Select the plane locate at the top of the sweep feature.

3. Right click and select **Center Point Circle** from the Marking Menu.

4. Select the origin point, move the cursor outside, and click to create a circle.

5. Right click and select **OK**.

6. Right click and select **General Dimension** from the Marking Menu.

7. Select the circle, move the cursor outward, and click.

8. Type 1.574 and press Enter.

9. Click **Finish Sketch** on the ribbon.

10. Click the **Extrude** button on the **Create** panel.

11. Extrude the circle up to 1 in.

Creating the Emboss feature

1. Click **3D Model > Work Features > Plane > Offset from Plane** on the ribbon.

2. Select the YZ plane from the Browser window.

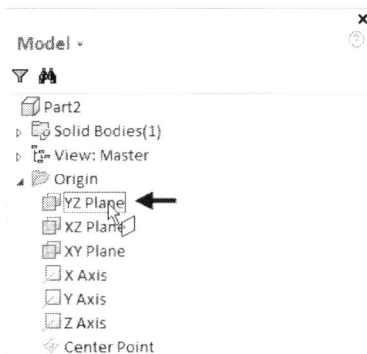

3. Enter **2** in the **Distance** box and click **OK** ✔.

4. Click **3D Model > Sketch > Start 2D Sketch** on the ribbon.

5. Select the newly created datum plane.

6. Click **Sketch > Create > Circle > Ellipse** ⊙ on the ribbon.

7. Draw the ellipse by selecting the points, as shown.

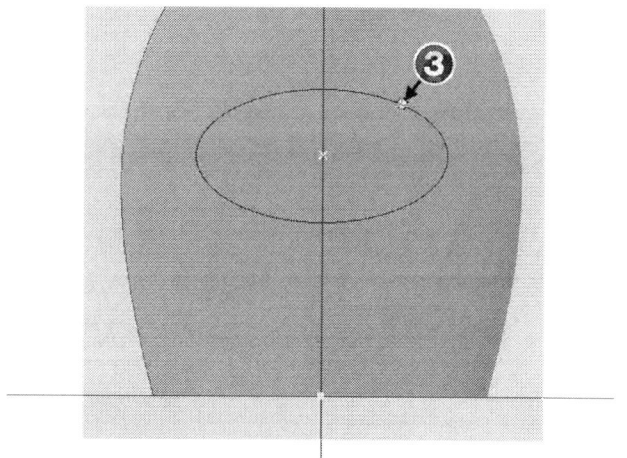

8. On the ribbon, click **Sketch > Constrain > Dimension**.

9. Select the ellipse, move the cursor downward, and click.

10. Type 2 and press Enter.

11. Select the ellipse, move the cursor toward left, and click.

12. Type 1.35 and press Enter.

13. Select the origin point of the sketch and the center point of the ellipse.

14. Move the cursor toward left and click to place the dimension between the selected point.

15. Type 2.55 and press Enter.

16. Right click and select **Create Line** from the Marking Menu.

17. Right click and select **Construction** from the Marking Menu.

18. Select the origin point of the sketch and the center point of the ellipse.

19. Right click and select **OK**; a construction line is created between the sketch origin and the ellipse. Also, the sketch is fully-constrained.

20. Click **Finish Sketch**.

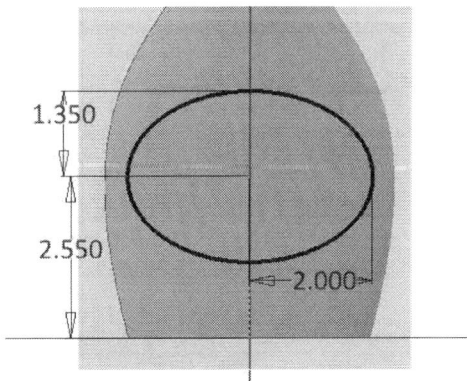

21. Click **3D Model > Create > Emboss** on the ribbon; the **Emboss** dialog appears.

22. Select the sketch, if not already selected.

23. Click the **Engrave from Face** button on the dialog.

24. Set the **Depth** to 0.125.

25. Click **OK** to create the embossed feature.

Mirroring the Emboss feature

1. Click **3D Model > Pattern > Mirror** on the ribbon.

2. Select the emboss feature from the model geometry.

3. On the **Mirror** dialog, click the **Mirror Plane** button, and then select the YZ Plane from the Browser window.

4. Click **OK** to mirror the emboss feature.

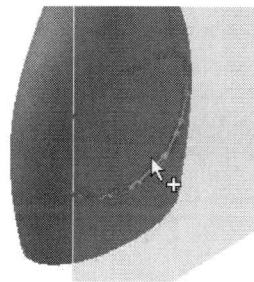

Creating Fillets

1. Click **3D Model > Modify > Fillet** on the ribbon; the **Fillet** dialog appears.

2. Click on the bottom and top edges of the swept feature.

3. Set **Radius** to 0.2.

4. Click **Click to add** on the Fillet dialog.

5. Set **Radius** to 0.04.

6. Select the edges of the emboss features, and click **OK**.

Shelling the Model

1. Click **3D Model > Modify > Shell** on the ribbon; the **Shell** dialog appears.

2. Set **Thickness** to 0.03.

3. Select the top face of the cylindrical feature.

4. Click **OK** to create the shell.

Adding Threads

1. Select the YZ Plane, and then click **Create Sketch**.

2. Click the **Slice Graphics** icon located at the bottom of the window.

3. On the ribbon, click **Sketch > Create > Line**.

4. Right click and select **Centerline** from the Marking Menu.

5. Select the origin point of the sketch, move the cursor vertically upward and click to create a vertical centreline. Press Esc.

6. Deactivate the Centerline icon on the **Format** panel.

7. Right click and select **Create Line** from the Marking Menu.

8. Right click and select **Construction** from the Marking Menu.

9. Create a horizontal construction line, as shown.

10. Deactivate the **Construction** icon on the **Format** panel of the **Sketch** ribbon tab.

11. On the ribbon, click **Sketch > Create > Line**.

12. Create a closed profile, as shown.

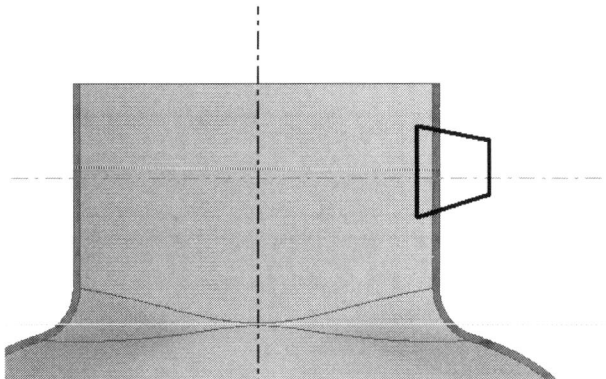

13. On the ribbon, click **Sketch > Constrain > Symmetric** ⊡ .

14. Select the two inclined lines of the sketch, and then select the construction line; the two inclined lines are made symmetric about the construction line.

15. Click the **Dimension** button on the **Constrain** panel.

16. Select the two inclined lines, move the cursor horizontally toward left and click.

17. Type 60 in the **Edit Dimension** box and press Enter.

18.
19. Draw the thread profile.

20. On the ribbon, click **Sketch > Create > Fillet** ⬡ .
21. Type 0.04 in the **2D Fillet** box.
22. Make sure that the **Equal** ⁼ button is active on the **2D Fillet** box.
23. Select the two corners of the sketch, as shown.

24. Close the **2D Fillet** dialog box.

25. Click **Finish Sketch** on the ribbon.

26. On the ribbon, click **3D Model > Create > Coil** ; the closed profile of the sketch is selected, automatically.

27. Select the axis of the coil.

28. On the dialog, click the **Coil Size** tab and select **Type > Pitch and Revolution**.

29. Type-in **0.275** and **2** in the **Pitch** and **Revolution** boxes, respectively.

30. Click **OK**.

31. In the Browser Window, right click on the YZ Plane, and then select **New Sketch**.

32. On the ribbon, click **Sketch > Create > Project Cut Edges > Project Geometry** .

33. Select the edges of the end face of the thread.

34. Draw a straight line connecting the end points of the projected elements.

35. Click **Finish Sketch**.

36. Activate the **Revolve** tool and click on the vertical line of the sketch.

37. On the dialog, select **Extents > Angle**, and then type-in **100** in the **Angle1** box.

38. Click the **Direction 1** button.

39. Click **OK**.

40. Likewise, blend the other end of the thread. Note that you need the reverse the direction of revolution.

41. Save the model.

TUTORIAL 5

In this tutorial, you create a chair, as shown.

Creating a 3D Sketch

1. Open a new Inventor file using the Standard.ipt template (See Chapter 2, Tutorial 3, Starting a New Part File section).

2. Click the **Home** icon located above the ViewCube. This changes the view orientation to Home.

3. On the ribbon, click **3D Model > Sketch > Start**

2D Sketch > Start 3D Sketch.

4. On the **3D Sketch** tab of the ribbon, click **Draw > Line**.

5. Expand the **Draw** panel on the ribbon and activate the **Precise Input** option.

6. On the **Precise Input** toolbar, click the **Reset to Origin** button.

7. Select the **Relative** option from the drop-down available on the **Precise Input** toolbar.

8. On the **Precise Input** toolbar, click in the X box and type 0.

9. Press the Tab key and type 0 in the Y box.

10. Likewise, type 0 in the Z box.

11. Press Enter to specify the first point.

12. Type-in 12 in the **X** box and press Tab on your keyboard.

13. Likewise, type-in 0 in the **Y** and **Z** boxes. Press Enter to specify the second point.

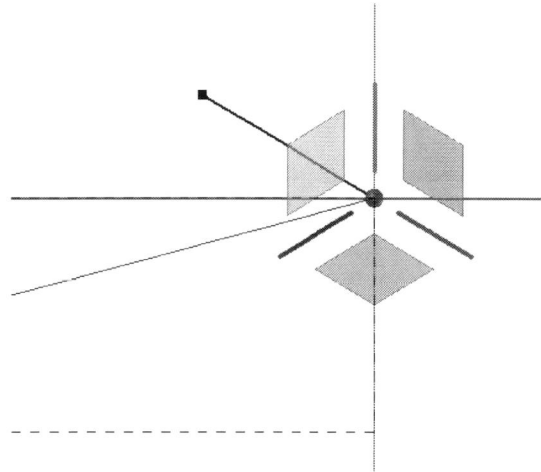

14. Type-in 0, 0, and 20 in the X, Y, and Z boxes, respectively. Press Enter.

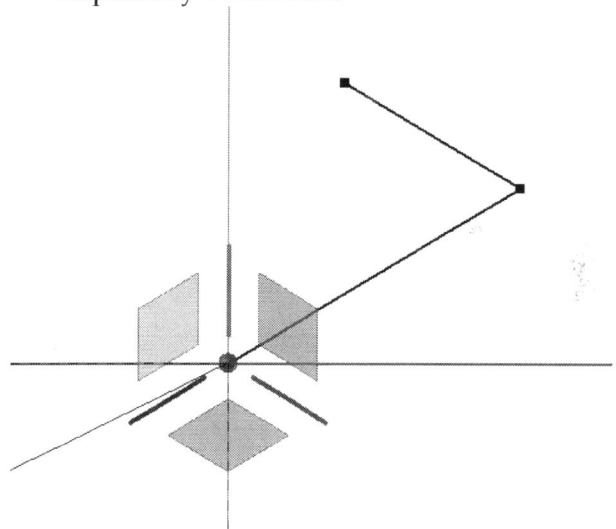

15. Type-in 0,18, 0 in the X, Y, and Z boxes, respectively. Press Enter.

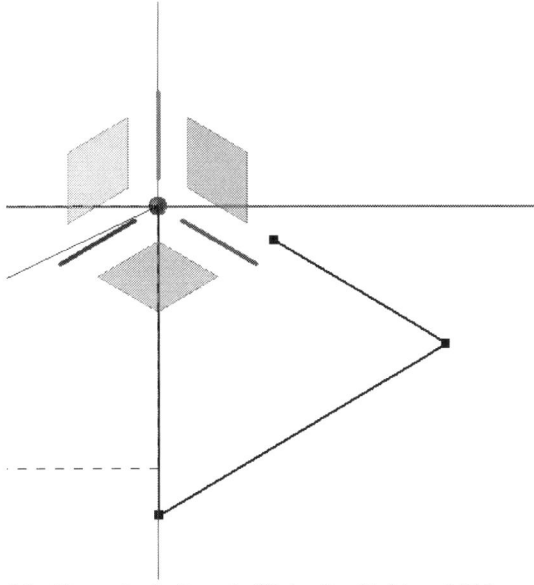

16. Type-in 0, 0 and -22 in the X, Y and Z boxes, respectively. Press Enter.

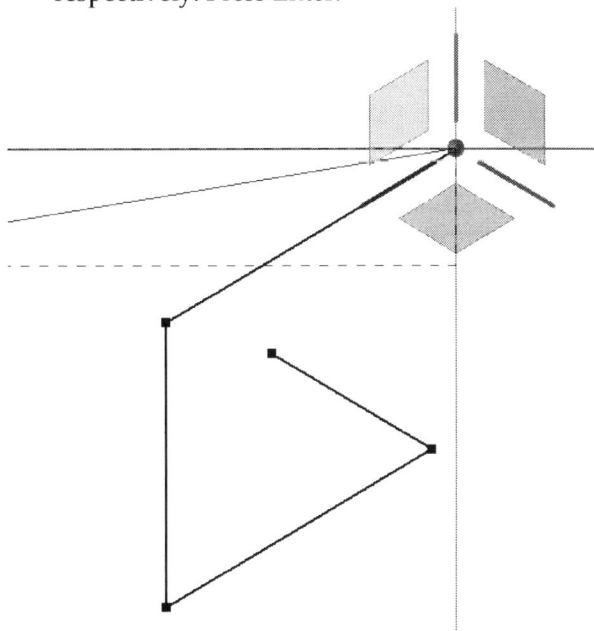

17. Type-in 0, 18, and 0 in the X, Y, and Z boxes, respectively. Press Enter.

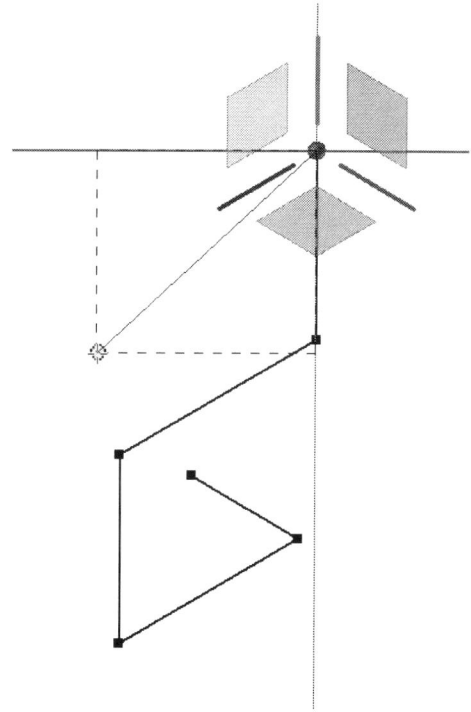

18. Type-in -12, 0, and 0 in the X, Y, and Z boxes, respectively. Press Enter.

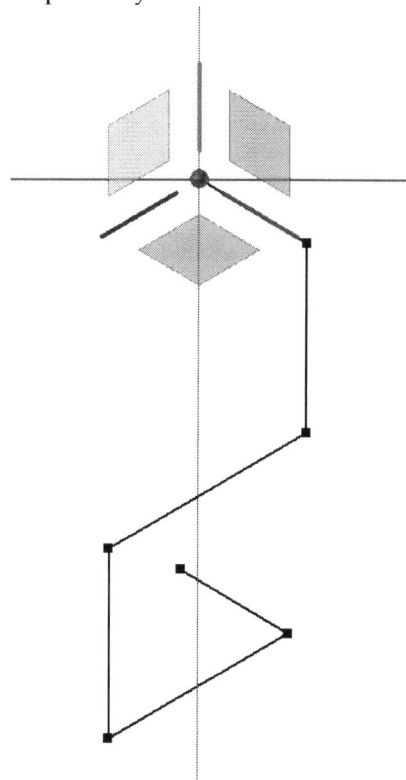

19. Click the right mouse button and select **OK**.

20. On the **3D Sketch** tab of the ribbon, click **Pattern > Mirror**.

21. Drag a selection box and select all the sketch elements.

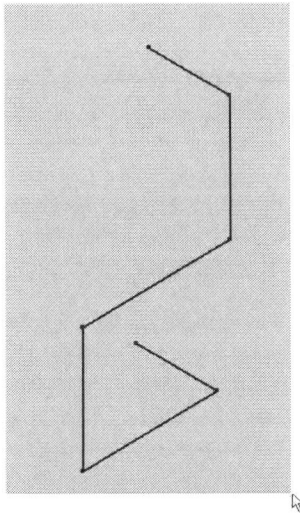

22. Click the **Mirror Plane** button on the dialog, and then select YZ Plane from the Browser window.

23. Click **Apply** and **Done** on the dialog.

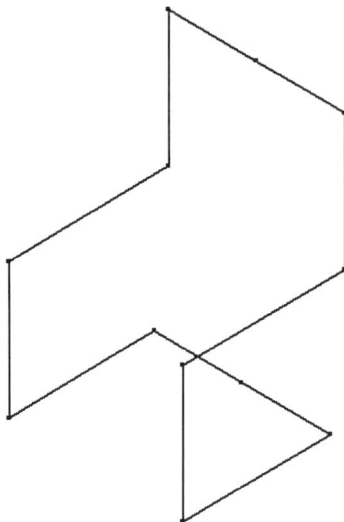

24. On the ribbon, click **3D Sketch > Draw > Bend**.

25. Type-in 3 in the **Bend** dialog and select the intersecting lines, as shown in figure.

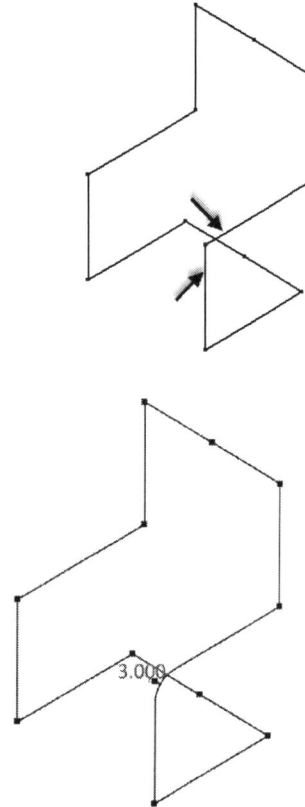

26. Likewise, bend the other corners of the 3D sketch.

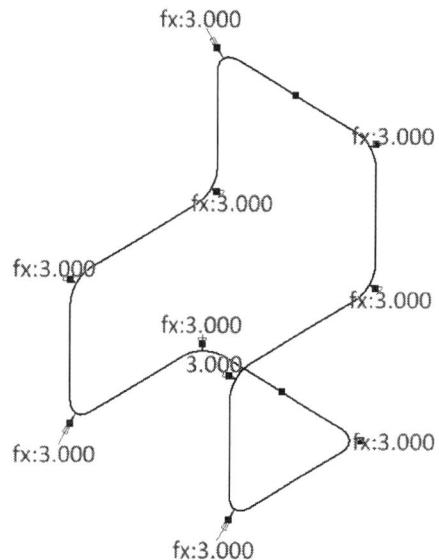

27. Click the right mouse button and select **OK**.

28. On the ribbon, click **3D Sketch > Constrain > Fix** 🔒 .

29. Select the origin point of the sketch.

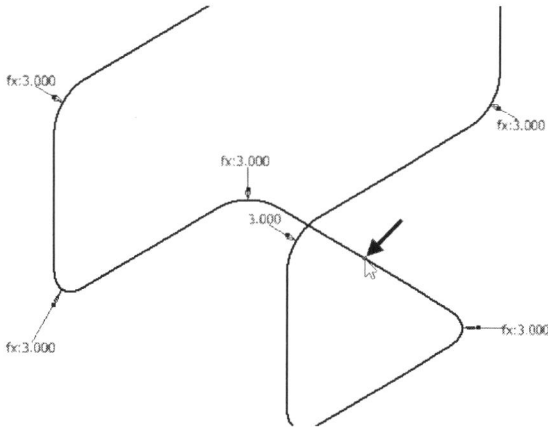

30. Add dimensions to fully define the sketch.

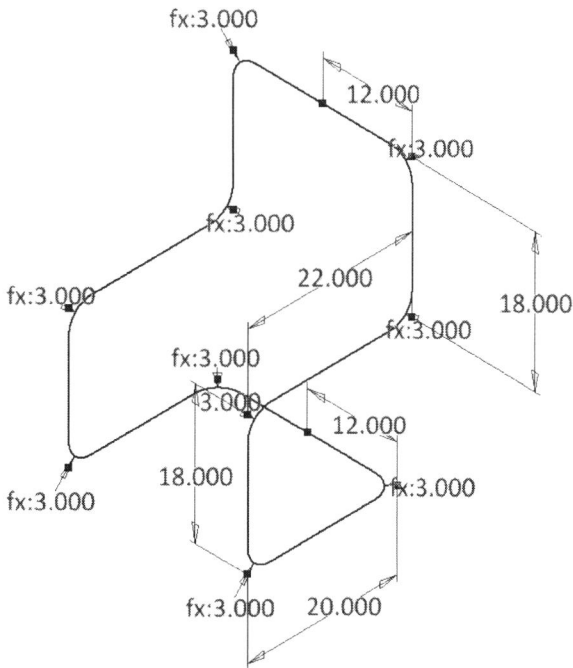

31. Click **Finish Sketch** on the ribbon.

32. On ribbon, click **3D Model > Work Features > Plane > Normal to Axis through Point**.

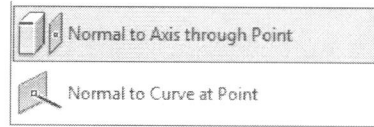

33. Click on the horizontal line of the sketch and its end point.

34. Click **3D Model > Sketch > Start 2D Sketch** on the ribbon.

35. Select the newly created plane.

36. Create two concentric circles of 1.250 and 1 diameters.

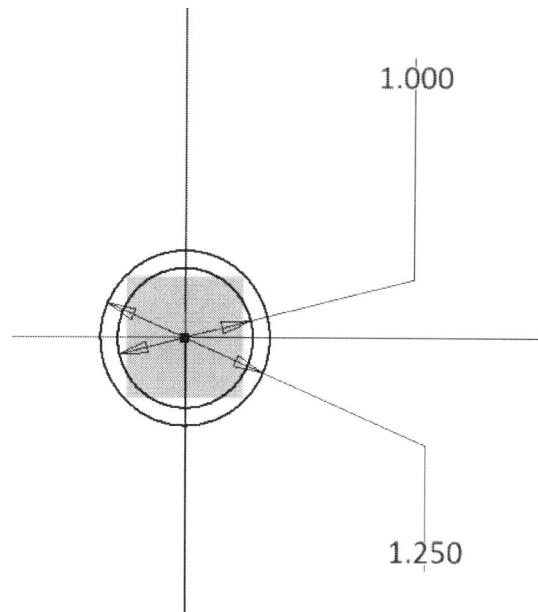

37. Add dimensions from the sketch origin to position the circles.

38. Click **Finish Sketch**.

Creating the Sweep feature

1. On the ribbon, click **3D Model > Create > Sweep**.

2. Zoom into the circular sketch and click in the outer loop.

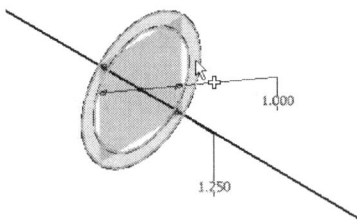

3. Click on the 3D sketch to define the sweep path.

4. Click **OK** to sweep the profile.

5. Start a sketch on the YZ Plane.

6. Click the **Slice Graphics** icon at the bottom of the graphics window.

7. Draw two concentric circles and dimension them.

8. Click **Finish Sketch.**

9. Activate the **Extrude** tool and click in the outer loop of the sketch.

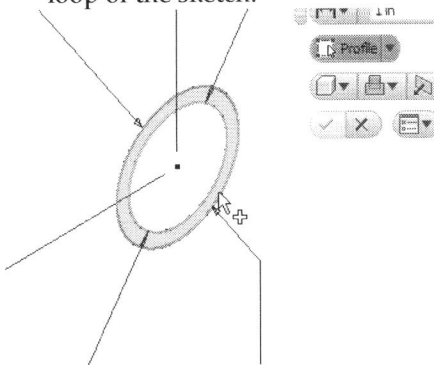

10. On the **Extrude** dialog, select **Extents > Between**.

11. Click on the tubes on both sides of the sketch.

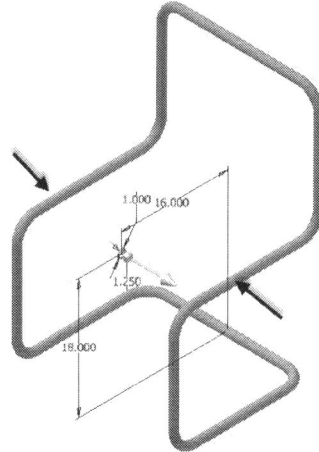

12. On the **Extrude** dialog, uncheck the **Check to terminate feature on the extended face** options.

This will avoid the extruded feature from terminating on the extended portion of the selected surface.

13. Click **OK** to extrude the sketch.

Creating the Along Curve pattern

1. On the Browser window, click the right mouse

button on the **3D Sketch** and select **Visibility**; the 3D sketch is displayed.

2. On the ribbon, click **3D Model > Pattern > Rectangular Pattern**.

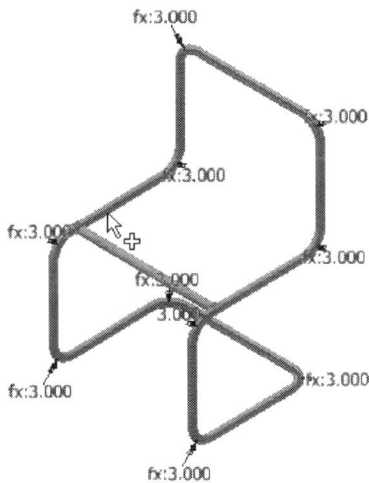

3. Click on the extrude feature.

4. On the **Rectangular Pattern** dialog, click the **Direction 1** button, and then click on the **3D sketch**.

5. Type-in **3** and **23** in the **Column Count** and **Column Spacing** boxes, respectively.

6. Select **Spacing > Distance** from the drop-down menu.

7. Click the double-arrow button located at the bottom of the dialog. This expands the dialog.

8. Set the **Orientation** to **Direction 1**.

9. Click **OK** to pattern the extruded feature.

10. On the Browser window, click the right mouse button on the 3D sketch and select **Visibility**. This hides the 3D sketch.

Creating the Freeform feature

1. On the ribbon, click **3D Model > Work Features > Plane**.

2. On the **Browser window**, click the XZ Plane. A plane appears on the XZ Plane.

3. Click on top portion of the extruded feature. A plane appears tangent to the extruded feature.

4. Start a sketch on the new plane.

5. Place a point on the sketch plane and add dimensions to position it.

6. Click **Finish Sketch**.

7. On the ribbon, click **3D Model > Freeform > Box**.

8. Select the plane tangent to the extruded feature.

9. Select the sketch point to define the location of the freeform box.

10. Click and drag the side-arrow of the freeform box.

11. Click and drag the front arrow of the freeform box.

12. Click and drag the top arrow to increase the height of the freeform box.

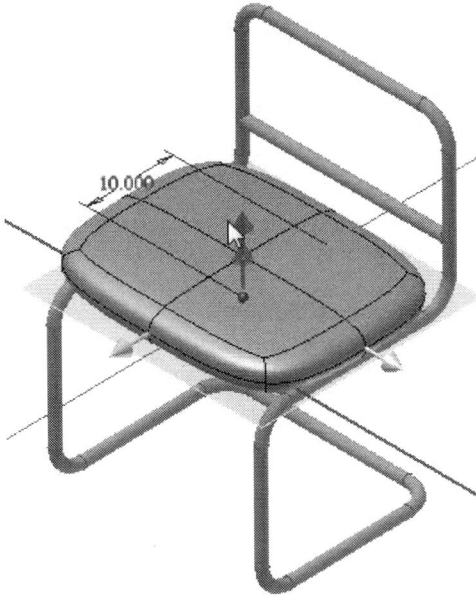

13. On the **Box** dialog, type-in 4, 1, and 2 in the **Faces** boxes, respectively.

14. Click **OK** to create the freeform shape.

Editing the Freeform Shape

1. On the ribbon, click **Freeform > Edit > Edit Form** .

2. Hold the Ctrl key and click on top faces of the freeform shape.

3. Click on the arrow pointing upwards.

4. Drag it downwards.

5. Click **OK** on the dialog.

6. On the ribbon, click **Freeform > Edit > Edit Form** .

7. Hold the Ctrl key and click on the two edges at the front.

8. Drag the vertical arrow downwards.

9. Click **OK** on the **Edit Form** dialog.

10. Click **Finish Freeform** on the ribbon.

Create another Freeform box

1. On the ribbon, click **3D Model > Work Features > Plane** .

2. On the Browser window, click the XY Plane.

3. Click on the vertical portion of the sweep feature to create a plane tangent to it.

4. Start a sketch on the new plane.

5. Place a point and add dimensions to it.

6. Click **Finish Sketch**.

7. Activate the Freeform **Box** tool.

8. Select the new plane and click on the sketch point.

9. On the **Box** dialog, type-in 27, 16, and 3 in the **Length**, **Width**, and **Height** boxes, respectively.

10. Click **OK**, and then click **Finish Freeform**.

11. Save and close the file.

TUTORIAL 6

In this tutorial, you create a bolt.

Start a new part file

1. Start a new part file using the **Standard.ipt** template (See Chapter 2, Tutorial 3, Starting a New Part File section).

2. On the ribbon, click **3D Model > Primitives > Primitive drop-down > Cylinder**.

3. Click on the YZ Plane.

4. Click the origin point of the sketch to define the center point of the circle.

5. Move the pointer and type-in 0.75 in the box, and then press Enter.

6. Type-in 3 in the **Distance** box and press Enter.

Creating the second feature

1. Start a sketch on the YZ Plane.

```
⬚ Part1
 ▷ 🗂 Solid Bodies(1)
 ▷ ┇ View: Master
 ⬚ 🗁 Origin
     ⬚ YZ Plane    ⬅
     ⬚ XZ Plane
     ⬚ XY Plane
     ⬚ X Axis
     ⬚ Y Axis
     ⬚ Z Axis
     ◇ Center Point
 ▷ ⬚ Extrusion1
     ◉ End of Part
```

2.   On the ribbon, click **Sketch > Create >
     Rectangle** drop-down > **Polygon**.

```
〰 Three Point Arc
◠ Slot
+  Center Point Arc
⬠ Polygon
□  Polygon          ▷
```

3.   Click the sketch origin.

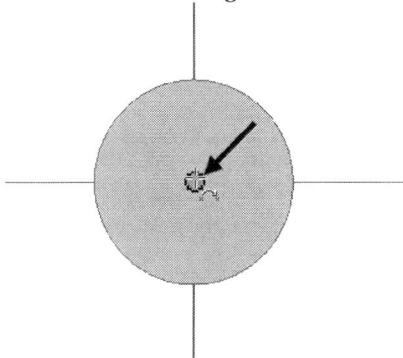

4.   Type-in 6 in the **Polygon** dialog.

```
Polygon          ✕
⬡ ⬡    6    ⟩
?      Done
```

5.   Move the pointer vertically upward. You will
     notice that a dotted trace line appears between
     the origin point and the pointer.

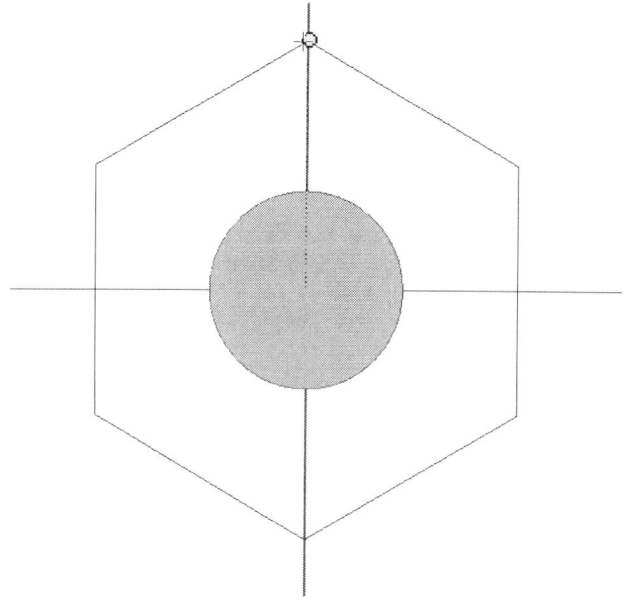

6.   Click to create the polygon.

7.   Click **Done** on the dialog.

8.   On the ribbon, click the **Sketch > Format >
     Construction** ⟋.

9.   Activate the **Line** tool and select the vertices of
     the polygon.

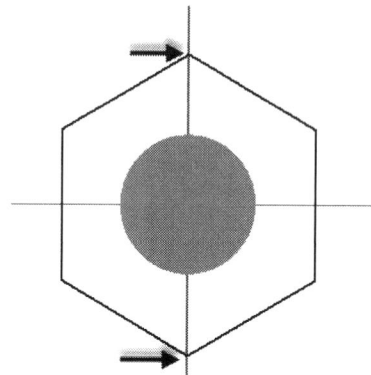

10. Activate the **Dimension** tool and create a
     dimension, as in figure.

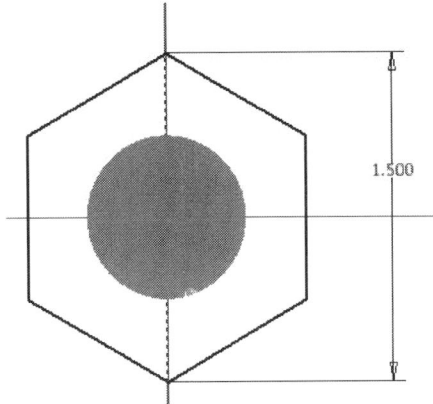

11. Finish the sketch.

12. Activate the **Extrude** tool and select the sketch, if not already selected.

13. On the **Extrude** dialog, type-in 0.5 in the **Distance** box.

14. Use the **Direction 1** or **Direction 2** buttons to make sure that the polygon is extruded toward left.

15. Click **OK**.

Adding Threads

1. On the ribbon, click **3D Model > Modify > Thread**.

2. Click on the cylindrical face of the model geometry.

3. On the **Thread** dialog, uncheck the **Full Length** option and type-in **1.5** in the **Length** box.

4. Click the **Specification** tab to specify the thread settings.

5. Click **OK** to add the thread.

Creating iParts

The iParts feature allow you to design a part with different variations, sizes, materials and other attributes. Now, you will create different variations of the bolt created in the previous section.

1. On the ribbon, click **Manage > Parameters > Parameters**. This opens the **Parameters** dialog.

2. On the **Parameters** dialog, click in the first cell of

the **Model Parameters** table, and type-in **Diameter**.

3. Likewise, change the names of other parameters.

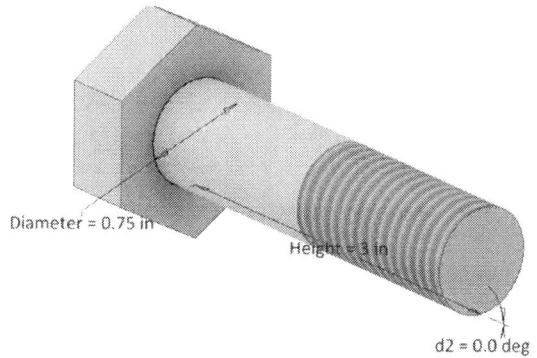

4. Click **Done** on the **Parameters** dialog.

5. Click the right mouse button in the graphics window and select **Dimension Display > Expression**.

6. On the Browser window, click the right mouse button on the **Extrusion1** and select **Show Dimensions**. You will notice that the dimensions are shown along with the names.

Diameter = 0.75 in
Height = 3 in
d2 = 0.0 deg

7. On the ribbon, click **Manage > Author > Create iPart**.

This opens the **iPart Author** dialog. In this dialog, you will define the parameters to create other versions of the model geometry.

The table at the bottom of this dialog shows the parameters for the iPart factory. You will notice that the renamed parameters are automatically added to the table. If you want to add more parameters to the table, then select them from the section located at the left side. Click the arrow button pointing towards right. Likewise, if you want to remove a parameter from the table, then select it from the right side section and click the arrow pointing toward left.

8. Now, click the right mouse button on the table and select **Insert Row**. Notice that a new row is added to the table.

	Member	Part Number	Diameter	Height
1	Part2-01	Part2-01	0.75 in	3 in
	Insert Row			
	Delete Row			

9. Likewise, insert another row.

	Member	Part Number	Diameter	Height	Headsize	Headwidth	Threadwidth
1	Part1-01	Part1-01	0.75 in	3 in	1.5 in	0.5 in	1.5 in
2	Part1-02	Part1-02	0.75 in	3 in	1.5 in	0.5 in	1.5 in
3	Part1-03	Part1-03	0.75 in	3 in	1.5 in	0.5 in	1.5 in

10. In the second row of the table, type-in new values (5, 0.75, and 3) in the Height, Headwidth, and Threadlength boxes. This creates the second version of the bolt.

	Member	Part Number	Diameter	Height	Headsize	Headwidth	Threadlength
1	Part2-01	Part2-01	0.75 in	3 in	1.5 in	0.5 in	1.5 in
2	Part2-03	Part2-03	0.75 in	5	1.5 in	0.75	3
3	Part2-02	Part2-02	0.75 in	3 in	1.5 in	0.5 in	1.5 in

11. In the third row of the table, type-in new values in (2, 0.75, and 3) the Headsize, Headwidth, and Threadlength boxes. This creates the third version of the bolt.

	Member	Part Number	Diameter	Height	Headsize	Headwidth	Threadlength
1	Part2-01	Part2-01	0.75 in	3 in	1.5 in	0.5 in	1.5 in
2	Part2-03	Part2-03	0.75 in	5	1.5 in	0.75 in	3
3	Part2-02	Part2-02	0.75 in	3 in	2	0.75 in	3

Now, you have to set the default version of the bolt.

12. Click the right mouse button on the third row of the table and select **Set As Default Row**.

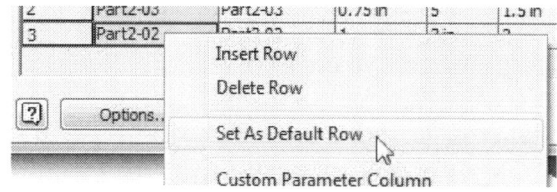

2	Part2-03	Part2-03	0.75 in	5	1.5 in
3	Part2-02				

Insert Row
Delete Row
Set As Default Row
Custom Parameter Column

Options..

13. Click **OK** to close the dialog. Notice that the default version of the bolt changes.

In the Bowser Bar, you will notice that the **Table** item is added.

14. Expand the **Table** item in the Browser Window to view the different variations of the iPart. Notice that the activated version of the iPart is designated by a check mark.

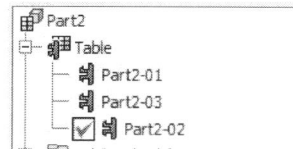

- Part2
  - Table
    - Part2-01
    - Part2-03
    - ☑ Part2-02

15. Double-click on any other version of the iPart to activate it.

- Part2
  - Table
    - Part2-01
    - ☑ Part2-03
    - Part2-02

If you want to make changes to any version of the bolt, then click the right mouse button on it and select **Edit table**.

If you want to edit the table using a spreadsheet, then click the right mouse button on **Table** and select **Edit via Spreadsheet**. Click **OK** on the message box.

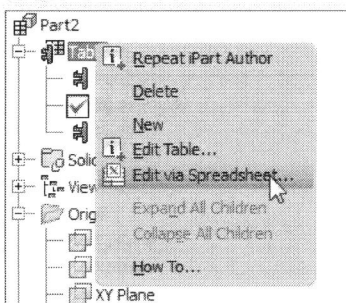

Now, modify the values in the spreadsheet and close it. A message pops up asking you to save the changes. Click **Yes** to save the changes.

	A	B	C	D	E	F	G	H
1	Member	Part Num	Diameter	Height	Headsize	Headwidt	Threadler	Thread1
2	Part2-01	Part2-01	0.75 in	3 in	1.5 in	0.5 in	1.5 in	Compute
3	Part2-03	Part2-03	0.75 in	5	1.5 in	0.75 in	3	Compute
4	Part2-02	Part2-02	0.75 in	3 in	2	0.75 in	3	Compute

If you want to save anyone of the iPart versions as a separate part file, then click the right mouse button on it and select **Generate Files**.

16. Save and close the file.

TUTORIAL 7

In this tutorial, you create a plastic casing.

Creating the First Feature

1. Open a new Autodesk Inventor part file using the **Standard.ipt** template (See Chapter 2, Tutorial 3, Starting a New Part File section).

2. On the ribbon, click **3D Model > Sketch > Start 2D Sketch**.

3. Select the XZ Plane.

4. On the ribbon, click Sketch > Create > Line.

5. Click in the second quadrant, move the cursor horizontally toward right, and then click to create a horizontal line, as shown.

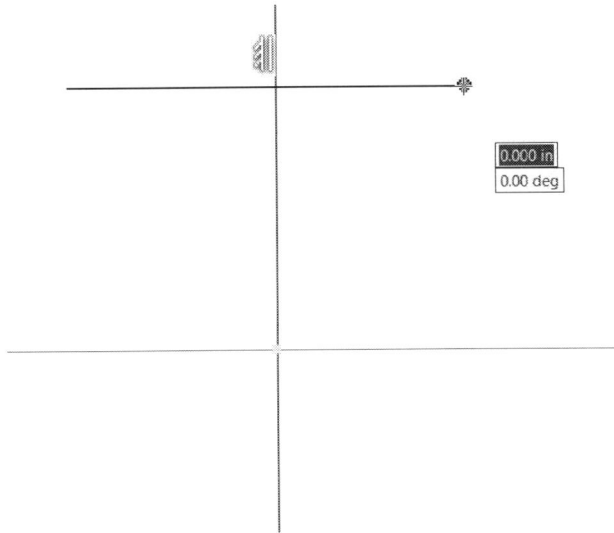

6. On the ribbon, click **Sketch > Create > Arc drop-down > Arc Three Point**.

7. Select the right endpoint of the horizontal line.
8. Move the cursor vertically downwards and click to define the second point.
9. Move the pointer towards right and click on the horizontal axis line.

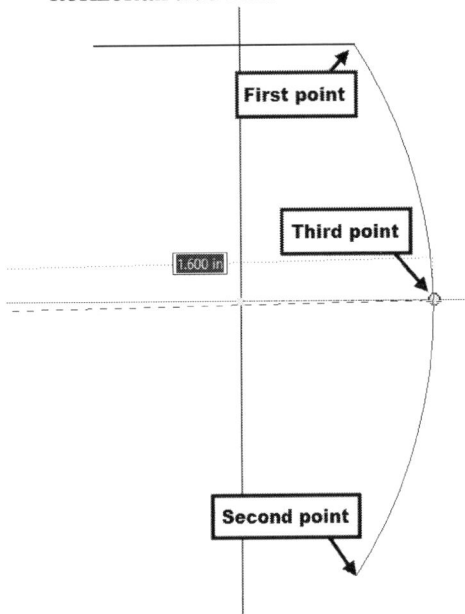

10. Likewise, create another three-point arc and horizontal line, as shown.

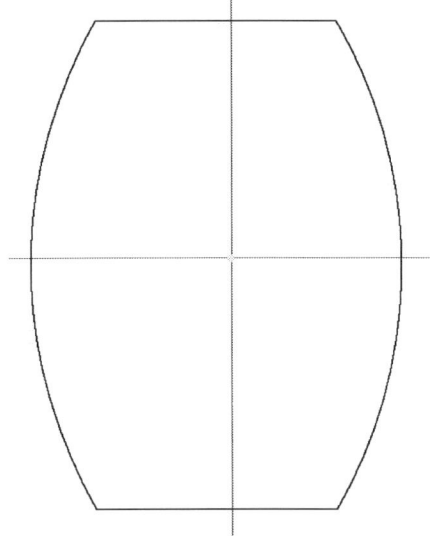

11. Create a vertical construction from the origin point.

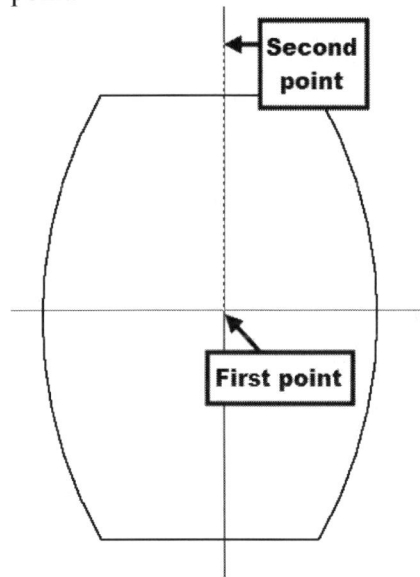

12. On the ribbon, click **Sketch > Constrain > Symmetric** ⬚.
13. Select the two arcs and the construction

14. Likewise, create a horizontal construction line from the origin point, and then make the two horizontal lines symmetric about it.

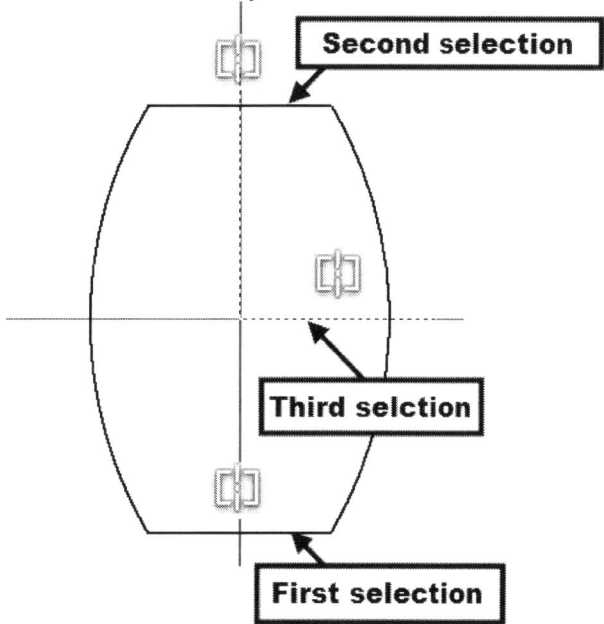

15. Add dimensions to the sketch. Also, add the Vertical constrain between the origin and center point of the arc.

16. Click **Finish Sketch**.

17. Click the **3D Model > Create > Extrude** on the ribbon; the **Extrude** dialog appears.

18. Set the **Distance** to 3.15.

19. Click the **More** tab and set the **Taper** angle to -10.

20. Click the **OK** button.

Creating the Extruded surface

1. Click **3D Model > Sketch > Start 2D Sketch** on the ribbon, and then select the XY Plane.

2. Click the **Slice Graphics** button at the bottom of the window or press **F7** on the keyboard.

3. Click **Sketch > Create > Line > Spline Interpolation** on the ribbon.

4. Create a spline, as shown in figure (See Chapter 5, Tutorial 4, Creating the First Section and Rails section).

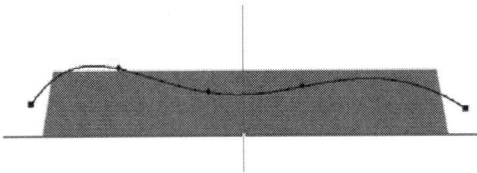

5. Apply dimensions to the spline, as shown below.

6. Click **Finish Sketch**.

7. Click the **Extrude** button.

8. Select the sketch, if not already selected.

9. On the **Extrude** dialog, set the **Output** type to **Surface**.

10. Set the **Extents** type to **Distance**.

26. Select the **Symmetric** button.

27. Extrude the sketch up to 17 in distance.

Replacing the top face of the model with the surface

1. On the **Surface** panel of the **3D Model** ribbon, click the **Replace Face** button; the **Replace Face** dialog appears.

Now, you need to select the face to be replaced.

2. Select the top face of the model.

Next, you need to select the replacement face or surface.

3. Click the **New Faces** button on the dialog and select the extruded surface.

 You can also use a solid face to replace an existing face.

4. Click **OK** to replace the top face with a surface.

5. Hide the extruded surface by clicking the right mouse button on it in the Browser Window and un-checking **Visibility**.

Creating a Face fillet

1. Click the **Fillet** button on the **Modify** panel.

2. Click the **Face Fillet** button on the **Fillet** dialog.

3. Select the top surface as the first face and the inclined front face as the second face.

4. Set the **Radius** to 1.5 and click the **OK** button to create the face fillet.

5. Likewise, apply a face fillet of 1.5 radius between top surface and the back inclined face of the model.

Creating a Variable Radius fillet

1. Click the **Fillet** button on the **Modify** panel.

2. Click the **Variable** tab on the **Fillet** dialog.

3. Select the curved edge on the model; the preview of the fillet appears.

4. Select a point on the fillet, as shown in figure.

5. Select another point the fillet, as shown in figure.

6. Set the radii of the **Start**, **End**, **Point 1** and **Point 2** as shown below.

Point	Radius	Position
Start	.6	0.0
End	.6	1.0
Point 1	1	0.0000
Point 2	.8	0.9103

You can also specify the fillet continuity type. By default, the **Tangent Fillet** type is specified.

6. Select **Smooth (G2) Fillet** type.

7. Make sure that the **Smooth radius transition** option is checked.

8. Click **OK** to create the variable fillet.

Mirroring the fillet.

9. Click the **Mirror** button on the **Pattern** panel; the **Mirror** dialog appears.

10. Select the variable radius fillet from the model.

11. Click the **Mirror Plane** button on the dialog.

12. Select the **XY Plane** from the Browser window.

13. Click **OK** to mirror the fillet.

Shelling the Model

1. Click the **Shell** button on the **Modify** panel; the **Shell** dialog appears.

2. Click the **Inside** button on the dialog and set the **Thickness** to 0.2 in.

3. Rotate the model and select the bottom face.

4. Click **OK**.

Creating the Boss Features

1. Click **3D Model > Sketch > Start 2D Sketch** on the ribbon and select the bottom face of the model.

2. Activate **Construction** ⟍ button on the **Format** panel.

3. On the ribbon, click **Sketch > Create > Rectangle drop-down > Rectangle Two Point Center**.

4. Select the origin point of the sketch.

5. Move the cursor outward and click to create the rectangle.

6. Apply dimensions to the rectangle.

7. Click the **Point** button on the **Create** panel.

8. Place four points at corners of the rectangle.

9. Click **Finish Sketch**.

Now, you will create bosses by selecting the points created in the sketch.

10. On the ribbon, click the **Show Panels** ⟐ button located at the right side, and then select **Plastic Part** from the menu.

11. Click the **Boss** button on the **Plastic Part** panel; the **Boss** dialog appears.

12. Click the **Thread** button on the dialog.

13. Select the **From Sketch** option from the **Placement** group.

14. Select the points located on the corners of the rectangle, if not already selected; the bosses are placed at the selected points.

15. Click the **Thread** tab and specify the parameters, as shown below.

16. Click the **Ribs** tab and check the **Stiffening Ribs** option.

17. Set the rib parameters, as shown next.

18. Expand the **Fillet options**.

19. Specify the fillet options, as shown below.

20. Click **OK** to create the bosses with ribs.

Creating the Lip feature

1. Click the **Lip** ⊒ button on the **Plastic Part** panel of the ribbon; the **Lip** dialog appears.

2. Click the **Lip** button on the dialog.

3. Select the outer edge of the bottom face.

4. Click the **Guide Face** button on the dialog and select the bottom face of the model.

5. Click the **Lip** tab and set the parameters, as shown below.

6. Click **OK** to create the lip.

Creating the Grill Feature

1. Click the **Home** button located at the top of the VIewCube.

2. Click the corner point of the ViewCube, as shown.

3. On the ribbon, click **3D Model > Sketch >> Start 2D Sketch**.

4. Select the inclined face, as shown.

5. Create the sketch using the **Rectangle Two Point Center** and **Line** tools.

6. Click **Finish Sketch**.

7. Click the **Grill** button on the **Plastic Part** panel.

8. Select the rectangle as the boundary and set the **Boundary** parameters, as shown below.

9. Click the **Rib** tab and select the horizontal lines.

10. Set the rib parameters, as shown below.

11. Click **OK** to create the grill.

12. Save the model as Plastic Cover.ipt.

Creating Ruled Surface

1. Click **3D Model > Surface > Ruled Surface** on the ribbon and select the bottom edge of the model.

2. Click the **Normal** button on the **Ruled Surface** dialog.

    The preview of the ruled surface appears normal to the selected edge.

    You can click the **Alternate All Faces** button to change the direction of the ruled surface.

3. Type in 2 in the **Distance** box.

4. Click **OK** to create the ruled surface.

The ruled surface can be used as a parting split while creating a mold.

5. Close the part file without saving.

Chapter 6: Sheet Metal Modeling

This chapter will show you to:

- Create a face feature
- Create a Flange
- Create a Contour Flange
- Create a Corner Seam
- Create Punches
- Create a Bend Feature
- Create Corner Rounds
- Flat Pattern

TUTORIAL 1

In this tutorial, you create the sheet metal model shown in figure.

Starting a New Sheet metal File

1. To start a new sheet metal file, click **Get Started Launch > New** on the ribbon.

2. On the **Create New File** dialog, click the **Sheet Metal.ipt** icon, and then click **Create**.

Sheet
Metal.ipt

Setting the Parameters of the Sheet Metal part

1. To set the parameters, click **Sheet Metal > Setup > Sheet Metal Defaults** on the ribbon; the Sheet Metal Defaults dialog appears.

This dialog displays the default preferences of the sheet metal part such as sheet metal rule, thickness, material, and unfold rule. You can change these preferences as per your requirement.

2. To edit the sheet metal rule, click the **Edit Sheet Metal Rule** button on the dialog.

In the **Sheet** tab of the **Style and Standard Editor** dialog, you can set the sheet preferences such as sheet thickness, material, flat pattern bend angle representation, flat pattern punch representation and gap size.

3. In the **Sheet** tab, set the **Thickness** to 0.12 and leave all the default settings.

4. Click the **Bend** tab.

In the **Bend** tab of this dialog, you can set the bend preferences such as bend radius, bend relief shape and size, and bend transition.

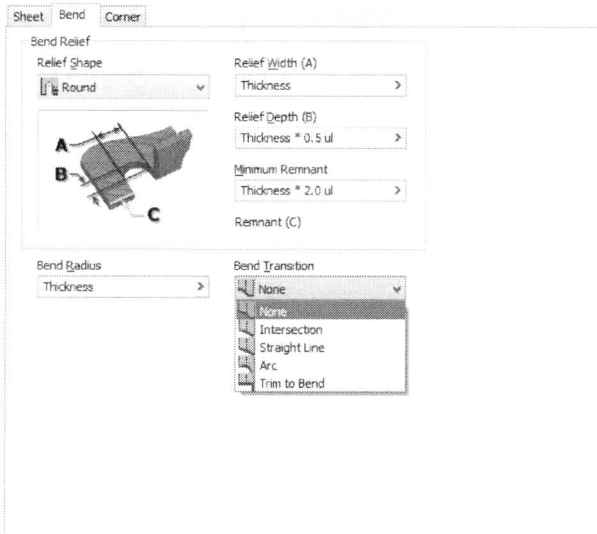

5. Set the **Relief Shape** to **Round**.

6. Click the **Corner** tab.

In the **Corner** tab, you can set the shape and size of the corner relief to be applied at the corners.

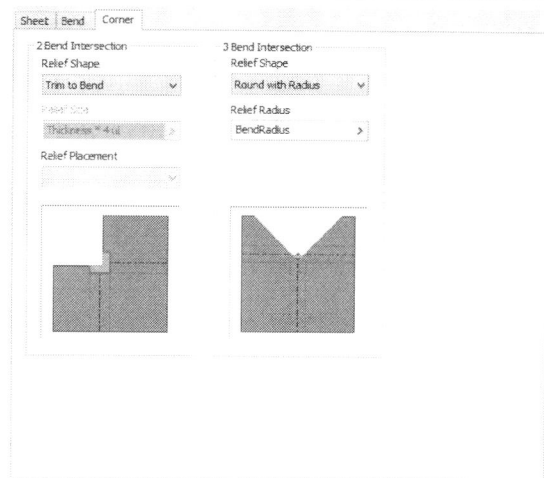

7. After setting the required preferences, click the **Save and Close** button.

The **Unfold Rule** option on the **Sheet Metal Defaults** dialog defines the folding/unfolding method of the sheet metal part. To modify or set a new Unfold Rule, click the **Edit Unfold Rule** button on the **Sheet Metal Defaults** dialog.

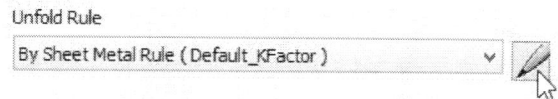

On the **Style and Standard Editor** dialog, select the required **Unfold Method**.

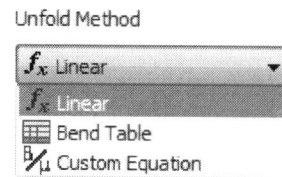

You can define the Unfold rule by selecting the **Linear** method (specifying the K factor), selecting a **Bend Table**, or entering a custom equation. Click **Save and Close** after setting the parameters.

8. Close the **Sheet Metal Defaults** dialog.

Creating the Base Feature

1. Create the sketch on the XZ Plane, as shown in figure (Use the **Rectangle Two Point Center** tool).

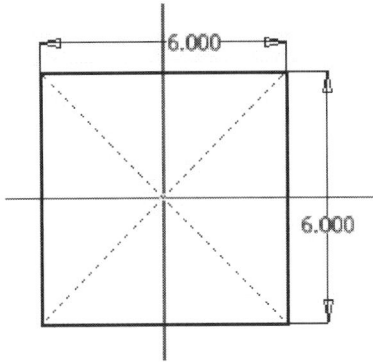

6.000

6.000

2. Click **Finish Sketch**.

3. To create the base component, click **Sheet Metal > Create > Face** on the ribbon; the **Face** dialog appears.

4. Click **OK** to create the tab feature.

Creating the flange

1. To create the flange, click **Sheet Metal > Create > Flange** on the ribbon; the **Flange** dialog appears.

2. Select the edge on the top face, as shown.

3. Set the **Distance** to 4.

Height Extents

Distance

4

4. Click on the **Bend from the intersection of the two outer faces** icon in the **Height Datum** section. This measures the flange height from the outer face.

Height Datum

5. Under the **Bend Position** section, click the **Inside of the Bend extents** icon.

Bend Position

6. Click **OK** to create the flange.

Creating the Contour Flange

1. Draw a sketch on the front face of the flange, as shown in figure.

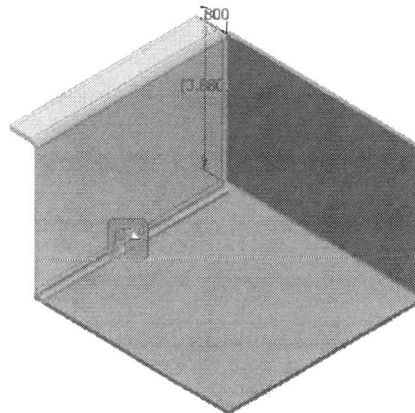

Edge to select

.800

(3.880)

2. Click **Finish Sketch**.

3. To create the contour flange, click **Sheet Metal > Create > Contour Flange** on the ribbon; the **Contour Flange** dialog appears.

4. Select the sketch from the model.

5. Select the edge on the left side of the top face; the contour flange preview appears.

6. Click **>>** located at the bottom of the dialog.

7. Select **Edge** from the **Type** drop-down.

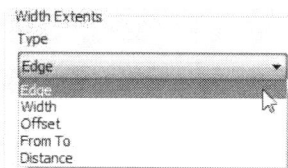

8. Click **OK** to create the contour flange.

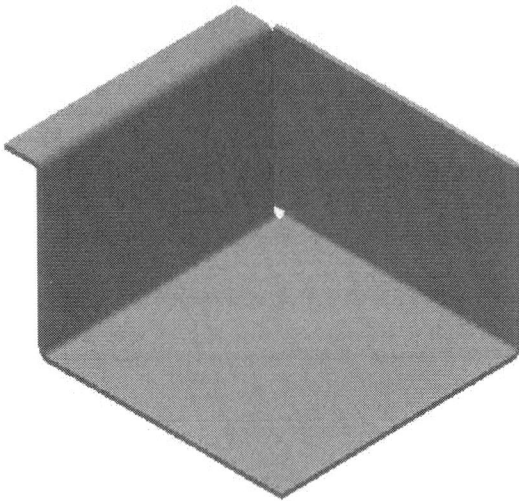

Creating the Corner Seam

1. To create the corner seam, click **Sheet Metal> Modify > Corner Seam** on the ribbon; the **Corner Seam** dialog appears.

2. Rotate the model.

3. Select the two edges forming the corner.

4. Set the parameters in the **Shape** tab of the dialog, as shown.

5. Click the **Bend** tab and make sure that the **Default** option is selected in the **Bend Transition** drop-down.

6. Click the **Corner** tab and set the **Relief Shape** to **Round**.

You can also apply other types of relief using the options in the **Relief Shape** drop-down.

7. Click **OK**.

Creating a Sheet Metal Punch iFeature

1. Open a new sheet metal file using the **Sheet Metal.ipt** template.

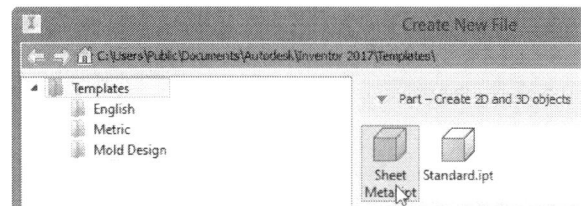

2. Create a sheet metal face of the dimensions 4x4.

3. Click **Manage > Parameters > Parameters** f_x on the ribbon; the **Parameters** dialog appears.

4. Select the **User Parameters** row and click the **Add Numeric** button on the dialog. This adds a new row.

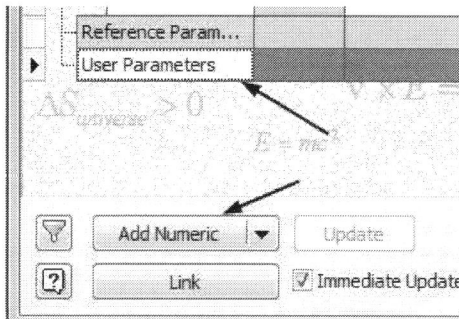

5. Enter **Diameter** in the new row.

6. Set **Unit Type** to **in** and type-in 0.04 in the **Equation** box.

7. Likewise, create a parameter named **Length** and specify its values, as shown below.

8. Click **Done**.

9. Click **Sheet Metal > Sketch > Start 2D Sketch** on the ribbon.

10. Select the top face of the base feature.

11. On the ribbon, click **Sketch > Create > Rectangle drop-down > Slot Center to Center**.

12. Click to define the first center point of the slot.

13. Move the cursor horizontally and click to define the second center point of the slot.

14. Move the cursor outward and click to define the slot radius.

15. Click **Dimension** on the **Constrain** panel and select the round end of the slot.

16. Click to display the **Edit Dimension** box.

17. Click the arrow button on the box and select **List Parameters** from the shortcut menu; the **Parameters** list appears.

18. Select **Diameter** from the list and click the green check on the **Edit Dimension** box.

443

19. Likewise, dimension the horizontal line of the slot and set the parameter to **Length**.

20. Click the **Point** button on the **Create** panel and place it at the center of the slot.

21. Delete any projected edges (yellow lines) from the sketch.

22. Click **Finish Sketch**.

23. Click **Sheet Metal > Modify > Cut** on the ribbon; the **Cut** dialog appears.

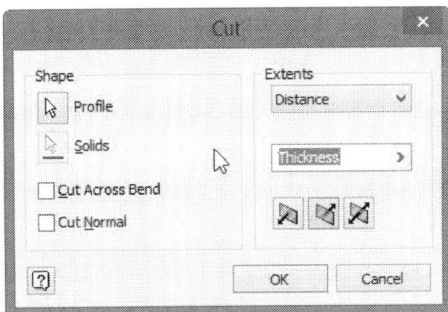

24. Accept the default values and click **OK** to create the cut feature.

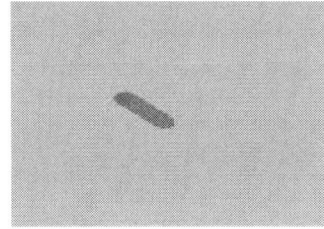

25. Click **Manage > Author > Extract iFeature** on the ribbon; the **Extract iFeature** dialog appears.

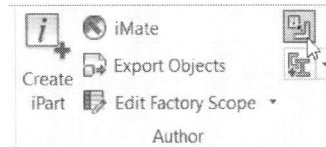

26. On the dialog, select **Type > Sheet Metal Punch iFeature**.

27. Select the cut feature from the model geometry or from the Browser window. The parameters of the cut feature appear in the **Extract iFeature** dialog.

Next, you must set the **Size Parameters** of the iFeature.

28. Set the **Limit** of the **Diameter** value to **Range**. The **Specify Range** dialog appears.

29. Set the values in the **Specify Range** dialog, as shown below and click **OK**.

Greater than or equal to infinity

Specify Range: Diameter

| 0.04 in | —∞ ≤ ▼ | 0.04 in | ≤ ∞ ▼ | 0.04 in |
| Minimum | | Default | | Maximum |

[?]   OK   Cancel

Less than or equal to infinity

Specify Range: Thickness

| 0.120 in | —∞ ≤ ▼ | 0.02 | ≤ ∞ ▼ | 0.120 in |
| Minimum | | Default | | Maximum |

[?]   OK   Cancel

Next, you need to select the center point of the slot. This point will be used while placing the slot.

30. Set the **Limit** of the **Length** value to **List**. The **List Values** dialog appears.

31. Click on **Click here to add value** and enter 0.2 as value.

32. Likewise, type-in values in the **List Values** dialog, as shown below.

36. Click the **Select Sketch** button on the **Extract iFeature** dialog.

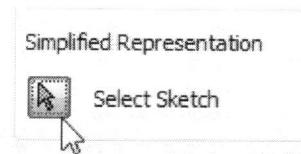

Simplified Representation

[cursor] Select Sketch

37. Select the sketch of the cut feature from the Browser window.

List Values: Length

| Value |
| 0.2 in |
| 0.25 in |
| 0.3 in |
| 0.35 in |
| 0.4 in |
| 0.45 in |

Default

0.12 in ▼

[?]   OK   Cancel

Part2
  Folded Model
    View: Master
    Origin
    Face1
    Cut1
      Sketch2
    End of Fold

38. Click **Save** on the dialog; the **Save As** dialog appears.

39. Browse to the **Punches** folder and enter **Custom slot** in the **File name** box.

33. Click **OK**.

34. Set the **Limit** of the **Thickness** value to **Range**. The **Specify Range** dialog appears.

35. Set the values in the **Specify Range** dialog, as shown below. Next, click **OK**.

Save in: Catalog

Name
  Geometric Shapes
  Pockets and bosses
  Punches ◄——
  Slots

40. Click **Save** and **Yes**.

41. Click **File Menu > Save**.

42. Save the sheet metal part file as Custom slot.

43. Switch to the sheet metal file of the current tutorial.

Creating a Punched feature

1. Start a sketch on the top face of the base sheet.
2. On the ribbon, click **Sketch > Create > Point**.
3. Place a point and add dimensions to it, as shown below.

4. Click **Finish Sketch**.

5. To create the punch, click **Sheet Metal > Modify > Punch Tool** on the ribbon; the **PunchTool Directory** dialog appears.

6. Select Custom slot.ide from the dialog and click **Open**; the **PunchTool** dialog appears.

7. Click the **Size** tab on the **PunchTool** dialog.

8. Set **Length** to 0.45 and **Diameter** to 0.1.

9. Click **Refresh** to preview the slot.

10. Click **Finish** to create the slot.

Edge to be selected

Note: If the slot is not oriented as shown in figure, then click the **Geometry** tab on the **PunchTool** dialog and type-in **90** in the **Angle** box.

Creating the Rectangular Pattern

1. Click **Sheet Metal > Pattern > Rectangular Pattern** on the ribbon. The **Rectangular Pattern** dialog appears.

2. Select the slot feature.

 You can also select multiple solid bodies from the graphics window using the **Pattern Solids** *option.*

3. Click the **Direction 1** button on the dialog.

4. Select the edge of the base feature, as shown below.

5. Select **Spacing** from the drop-down located in the **Direction 1** group.

6. Specify **Column Count** as 5.

7. Specify **Column Span** as 0.6.

8. Click the **Direction 2** button on the dialog.

9. Select the edge on the base feature, as shown below.

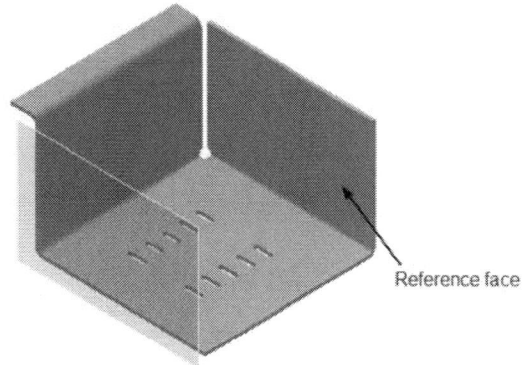

Reference face

2. Create a sketch on the new work plane.

10. Click the **Flip** [icon] button in the **Direction 2** section to make sure the arrow is pointed toward right.

11. Select **Spacing** from the drop-down located in the **Direction 2** group.

12. Specify **Column Count** as **2**.

13. Specify **Column Span** as 2.

14. Click **OK** to create the pattern.

1.380

.400

1.200

.800

3. Click **Finish Sketch**.

4. Click **Sheet Metal > Create > Face** on the ribbon and create a face feature.

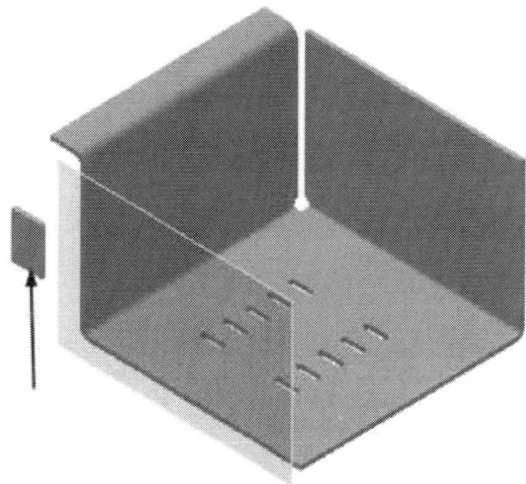

Creating the Bend Feature

1. Create a plane parallel to the front face of the flange feature. The offset distance is 6.3.

5. Click **Sheet Metal > Create > Bend** on the ribbon. The **Bend** dialog appears.

6. Select the edges from the model, as shown below.

7. Make sure the **Bend Extension** is set to perpendicular.

8. Click **OK** to create the bend feature.

9. Hide the work plane (Right-click on it and uncheck **Visibilty**).

Applying a corner round

1. To apply a corner round, click **Sheet Metal > Modify > Corner Round** on the ribbon; the **Corner Round** dialog appears.

2. Set the **Radius** value to 0.2.

3. Set the **Select Mode** to **Feature**.

4. Select the face feature from the model.

5. Click **OK** to apply the rounds.

Creating Countersink holes

1. Click **Sheet Metal > Modify > Hole** on the ribbon; the **Hole** dialog appears.

2. Set the **Placement** method to **Concentric**.

3. Set the hole type to **Countersink**.

4. Set the other parameters on the dialog, as shown below.

5. Click on the face of the flange, as shown below.

6. Select the corner round as the concentric reference.

7. Click **Apply**.

8. Again, click on the flange face and select the other corner round as the concentric reference.

9. Click **OK** to create the countersink.

Creating Hem features

1. To create the hem feature, click **Sheet Metal > Create > Hem** on the ribbon; the **Hem** dialog appears.

2. Set the **Type** to **Single**.

3. Select the edge of the contour flange, as shown below.

4. Leave the default settings of the dialog and click **OK** to create the hem.

Mirroring the Features

1. Click **Mirror** on the **Pattern** panel; the **Mirror** dialog appears.

2. Click **>>** at the bottom of the dialog and make sure the **Creation Method** is set to **Identical**.

3. Select the features from the Browser window, as shown below.

4. Click the **Mirror Plane** button on the dialog and select the YZ Plane from the Browser window.

5. Click **OK** to mirror the feature.

6. Create a corner seam between the mirrored counter flange and flange.

Creating the Flat Pattern

1. To create a flat pattern, click **Sheet Metal > Flat Pattern > Flat Pattern** on the ribbon.

You can set the order in which the bends will be annotation.

2. Click the **Bend Order Annotation** button on the **Manage** panel. The order in which the bends will be annotated is displayed.

3. To change the order of the bend annotation, click on the balloon displayed on the bend. The **Bend Order Edit** dialog appears.

4. Select the **Bend Number** check box and enter a new number in the box.

5. Click **OK** to change the order.

6. To switch back to the folded view of the model, click **Go to Folded Part** on the **Folded Part** panel.

7. Save the sheet metal part.

Creating 2D Drawing of the sheet metal part

1. On the Quick Access toolbar, click the **New** button.

2. On the **Create New File** dialog, double-click on **Standard.idw**.

3. Activate the **Base View** tool.

4. Click Home icon on the ViewCube.

5. Leave the default settings on the Drawing View dialog and click **OK**.

6. Click and drag the drawing view to top right corner of the drawing sheet.

7. Likewise, create the front, and top views of the sheet metal part.

8. Activate the **Base View** tool and select **Sheet Metal View > Flat Pattern** on the **Drawing View** dialog.

9. Place the flat pattern view below the Isometric view.

10. To add bend notes to the flat pattern, click **Annotate > Feature Notes > Bend** on the ribbon.

11. Click the horizontal bend line on the flat pattern to add the bend note.

12. Likewise, select other bend lines on the flat pattern. You can also drag a selection box to select all the bend lines from the flat pattern view.

13. To add centerlines to the flat pattern view, click the right mouse button on it and select **Automated Centerlines**.

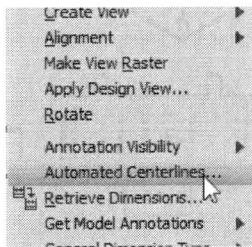

14. On the **Automated Centerlines** dialog, click the **Punches** button under the **Apply To** section.

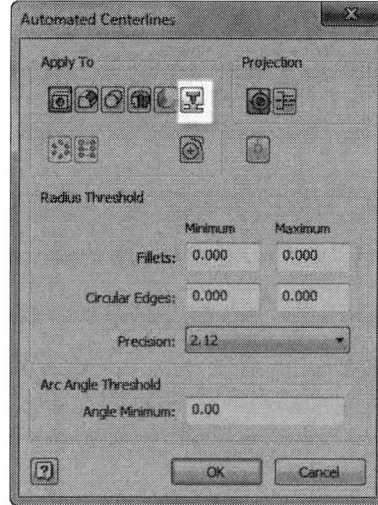

15. Click **OK** to add centerlines to the flat pattern view.

16. Likewise, add centerlines to other views on the drawing sheet.

17. To add a punch note, click **Annotate > Feature Notes > Punch** on the ribbon.

18. Zoom into the flat pattern view and click on the arc of the slot.

19. Move the pointer and click to create annotation.

90° R.12

DOWN 180°

UP

20. Use the **Retrieve Dimension** and **Dimension** tools to add dimensions to drawing.

21. Save and close the drawing and sheet metal part.

Chapter 7: Top-Down Assembly and Motion Simulation

In this chapter, you will learn to

- Create a top-down assembly
- Insert Fasteners using Design Accelerator
- Create assembly joints

TUTORIAL 1

In this tutorial, you will create the model shown in figure. You use top-down assembly approach to create this model.

Creating a New Assembly File

1. To create a new assembly, click **New Assembly** on the Home screen.

Creating a component in the Assembly

In a top-down assembly approach, you create components of an assembly directly in the assembly by using the **Create** tool.

1. Click **Create** on the **Component** panel. The **Create In-Place Component** dialog appears.

2. Enter **Base** in the **New Component Name** field.

3. In the **Create In-Place Component** dialog, set the **New File Location** to the current project folder.

4. Click the **Browse to New File Location** icon.

5. On the **Save As** dialog, click the **Create New Folder** icon.

6. Type **C07_Tut_01** as the name of the folder.

7. Double-click on the new folder and click **Save**.

8. Click **OK** on the **Create In-Place Component** dialog.

9. Expand the **Origin** folder in **Browser window** and select the **XZ Plane**. The **3D Model** tab is activated in the ribbon.

10. Click **Sketch > Start 2D Sketch** on the ribbon.

11. Select **XZ Plane**.

12. Create a sketch as shown below.

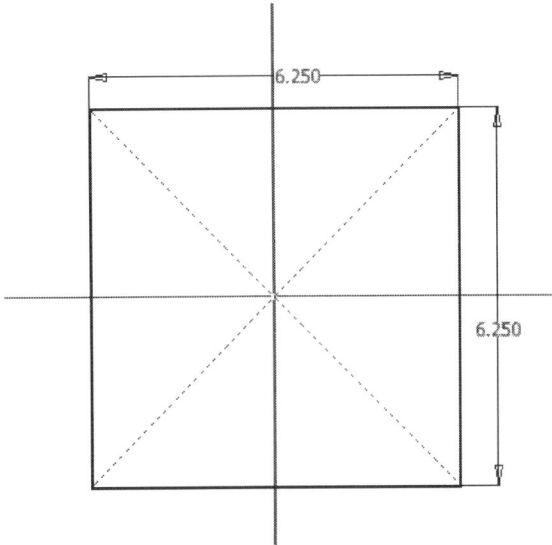

28. Click **Finish Sketch**.

29. Click **3D Model > Create > Extrude** on the ribbon and extrude the sketch up to 1.5 in.

30. Start a sketch on the top face and draw a circle of **2** in diameter.

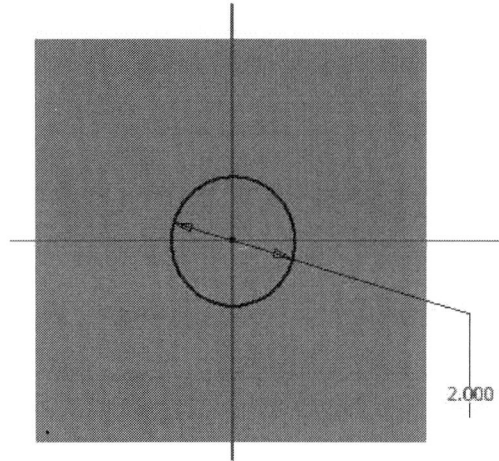

31. Click **Finish Sketch**

32. Extrude the sketch up to 3.75 in distance.

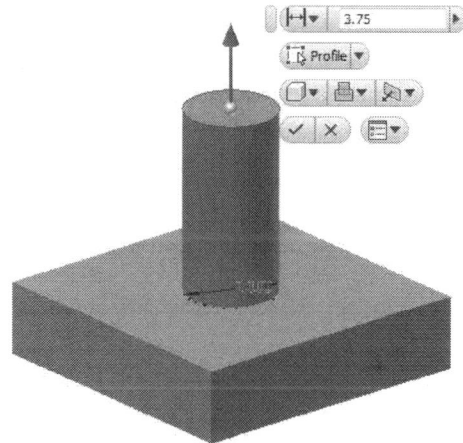

33. Create a counterbore hole on the second feature (See Chapter 5, Tutorial 1, Create a Counterbore Hole section). The following figure shows the dimensions of the counterbore hole.

34. Start a new sketch on the top face of the first feature.
35. Create a 3.5 diameter circle with the **Construction** button active.

36. On the ribbon, click **Sketch > Create > Point**.
37. Place a point on the circle, as shown.

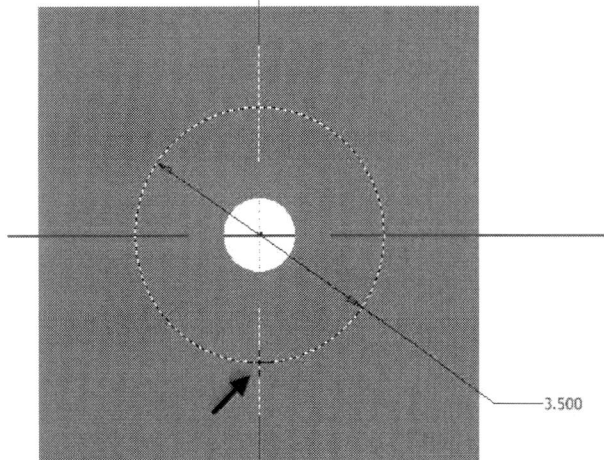

38. Click **Finish Sketch**.
39. On the ribbon, click **3D Model > Modify >**

Hole.

40. On the **Hole** dialog, specify the settings, as shown.

41. Make sure that the sketch point is selected.

42. Click **OK** to create the hole.
43. Create a circular pattern of the hole (See Chapter 5, Tutorial 1, Create a Circular Pattern).

44. Click the **Return** button on the ribbon.

Creating the Second Component of the Assembly

1. Click **Assemble > Component > Create** on the ribbon; the **Create In-Place Component** dialog appears.

2. Enter **Spacer** in the **New Component name** field.

3. Check **Constrain sketch plane to selected face or plane** option.

4. Click **OK**.

5. Select the top face of the Base.

6. Click **Sketch > Start 2D Sketch** on the ribbon.

7. Select top face of the Base.

8. On the ribbon, click **Sketch > Create > Project Geometry** and select the circular edges of the Base.

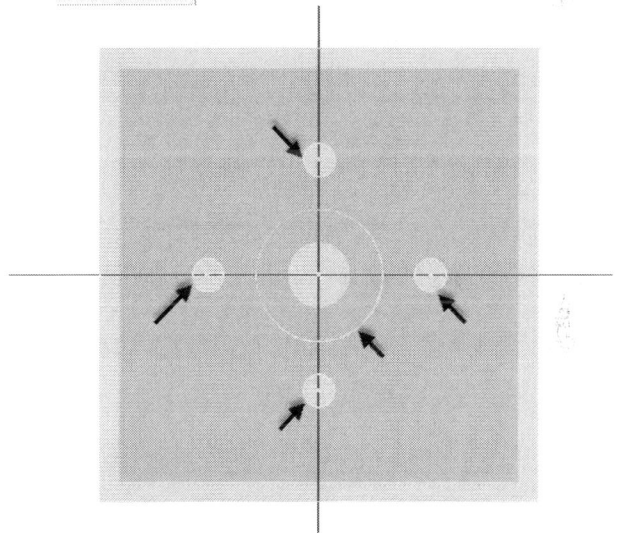

9. Draw a circle of 4.5 in diameter.

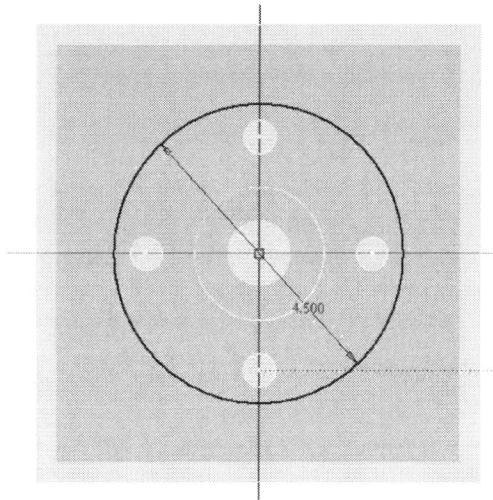

10. Click **Finish Sketch**.

11. Extrude the sketch up to 1.5 in.

12. Click **Return** on the ribbon.

Creating the third Component of the Assembly

1. Click **Assemble > Component > Create** on the ribbon; the **Create In-Place Component** dialog appears.

2. Enter **Shoulder Screw** in the **New Component name** field.

3. Check **Constrain sketch plane to selected face or plane** option.

4. Click **OK**.

5. Click on the top face of the Base.

6. Start a sketch on the YZ Plane.

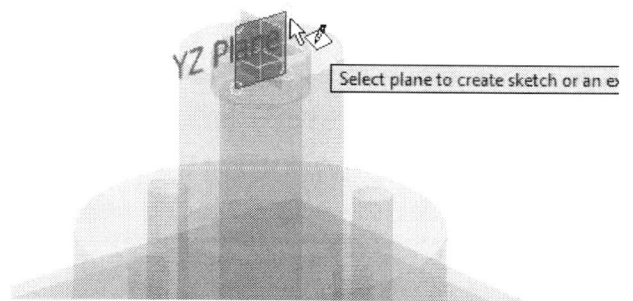

7. Draw a sketch, as shown in figure.

8. Click **Finish Sketch**.

9. Activate the **Revolve** tool and revolve the sketch.

10. Activate the **Chamfer** ⬭ tool and chamfer the edges, as shown in figure.

11. Activate the **Fillet** tool and round the edges, as shown in figure.

12. Click **Return** ↩⬤ on the ribbon.

13. Save the assembly.

Adding Bolt Connections to the assembly

1. On the ribbon, click **Design > Fasten > Bolt Connection**.

2. On the **Bolted Connection Component Generator** dialog, under the **Design** tab, select **Type > Through All**.

3. Select **Placement > Concentric**.

4. Select the top face of the Spacer.

5. Click on the hole to define the circular reference.

6. Rotate the model and click on the bottom face of the base. This defines the termination.

7. On the dialog, set the **Thread** type to **ANSI Unified Screw Threads**.

8. Make sure that the **Diameter** is set to **0.5** in.

9. On the dialog, click **Click to add a fastener**.

10. On the pop up dialog, set the **Standard** to **ANSI** and **Category** to **Hex Head Bolt**.

11. Select **Hex Bolt-Inch**. This adds a hex bolt to the list.

12. On the list, click **Click to add a fastener** below the Hex Bolt.

13. On the pop up dialog, scroll down and select **Plain Washer (Inch)**.

14. Click **Click to add a fastener** at the bottom of the list.

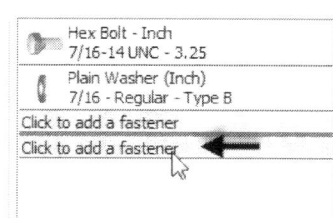

15. On the pop up dialog, scroll down and select **Plain Washer (Inch)**.

16. Click **Click to add a fastener** at the bottom of the list.

17. On the pop up dialog, set the **Category** to **Nuts** and select **Hex Nut –Inch**.

18. Click **OK** twice to add a bolt connection subassembly.

Patterning components in an assembly

1. On the ribbon, click **Assemble > Pattern > Pattern**.

2. Select the **Bolt connection** from the Browser window.

3. On the **Pattern Component** dialog, click the **Circular** tab and select the **Axis Direction** button.

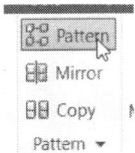

4. Click on the large cylindrical face of the Spacer to define the axis of the circular pattern.

5. On the dialog, type-in 4 and 90 in the **Circular Count** and **Circular Angle** boxes, respectively.

6. Click **OK** to pattern the bolt connection.

Applying the constraint to the components

1. On the ribbon, click **View > Visibility > Degrees of Freedom**.

2. On the ribbon, click **Assemble > Relationships > Constrain**.

3. On the dialog, click the **Mate** icon and click on the cylindrical faces of the Spacer and Base.

4. Click **Apply**.

5. Click on the cylindrical faces of the Shoulder Screw and Base.

6. Click **Apply**.

7. On the dialog, select **Flush** from the **Solution** section.

8. In the Browser Window, expand the **Origin** folder and select XY Plane.

9. Expand the **Origin** folder of the Shoulder Screw and select XZ Plane.

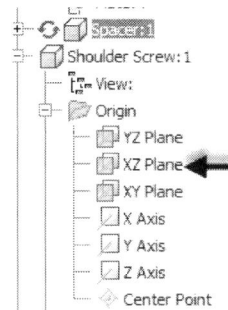

10. Click **OK** to fully-constrain the assembly.

11. Save the assembly and all its parts.

TUTORIAL 2

In this tutorial, you create a slider crank mechanism by applying Joints.

1. Create the **Slider Crank Assembly** folder inside the project folder.

2. Download the part files of the assembly from the companion website. Next, save the files in the **Slider Crank Assembly** folder.

3. Start a new assembly file using the **Standard.iam** template.

4. Click **Assemble > Component > Place** on the ribbon.

5. Browse to the **Slider Crank Assembly** folder and double-click on **Base**.

6. Right-click and select **Place Grounded at Origin**.

7. Right click and select **OK**.

8. Click **Assemble > Component > Place** on the ribbon.

9. Browse to the **Slider Crank Assembly** folder and select all the parts except the **Base**.

10. Click **Open** and click in the graphics window to place the parts.

11. Right click and select **OK**.

12. Click and drag the parts, if they are coinciding with each other.

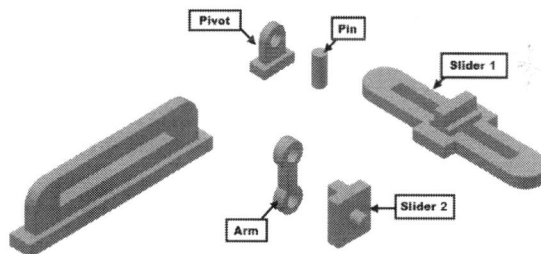

Creating the Slider Joint

1. Click **Assemble > Relationships > Joint** on the ribbon; the **Place Joint** dialog appears.

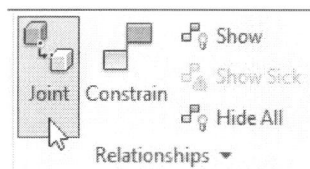

2. Set the **Type** to **Slider**.

Type
- Automatic
- Automatic
- Rigid
- Rotational
- Slider
- Cylindrical
- Planar
- Ball

3. Select the face on the Slider1, as shown below.

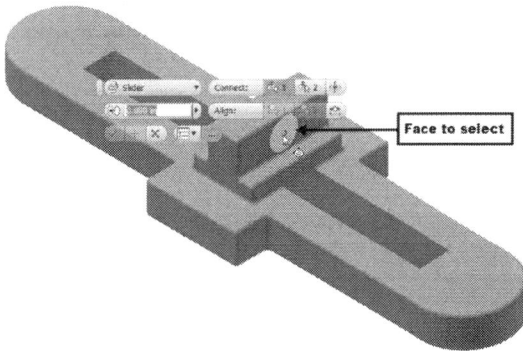

Face to select

4. Select the face on the Base, as shown below; the two faces are aligned.

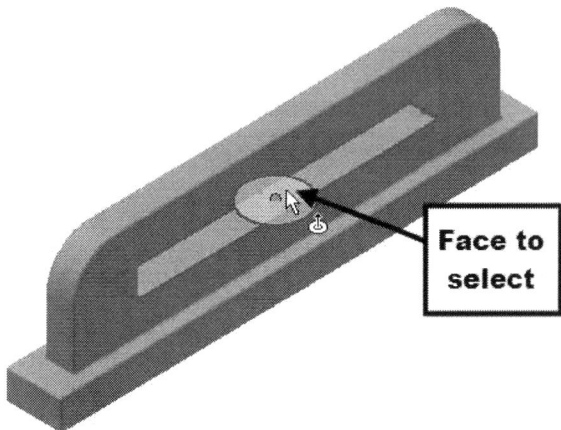

Face to select

5. On the dialog, click the **First Alignment** button.
6. Select the face of the Slider1, as shown.

Face to select

7. Select the face of the Base, as shown; the Slider 1 is aligned to the selected face.

Face to select

5. Click the **Limits** tab on the **Place Joint** dialog.

6. Check the **Start** and **End** options under the **Linear** group.

7. Set the **Start** value to 1.5 in and **End** to -1.5 in.

8. Click **OK**.

9. Select the Slider1 and drag the pointer; the Slider1 slides in the slot of the Base. Also, the slider motion is limited up to the end of the slot.

10. Click the corner of the ViewCube, as shown; the orientation of the assembly is changed.

11. Click **Assemble > Relationships > Joint** on

the ribbon.

12. On the dialog, set the **Type** to **Slider**.

13. Select the face on the Slider2, as shown below.

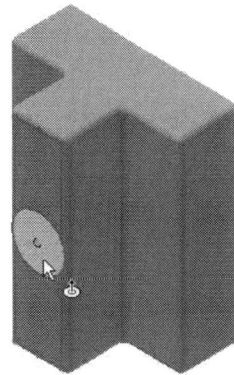

14. Select the right edge of the top face of the ViewCube; the orientation of the assembly changes.

15. Select the face on the Slider1, as shown below.

Face to select

Creating the Rotational Joint

1. Click **Assemble > Relationships > Joint** on the ribbon.

2. Set **Type** to **Rotational**.

Type

3. Select the circular edge of the arm, as shown below.

4. Select the circular edge of the Slider2.

6. Click the **Flip Component** button under the

Connect group.

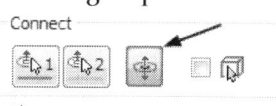

7. Click **OK**

Creating the Rigid Joint

1. Click **Assemble > Relationships > Joint** on the ribbon.

2. Set the **Type** to **Rigid**.

Type

3. Select the top face on the pin.

4. Click the on the corner point of the ViewCube, as shown.

5. Select the circular edge on the back face of the arm.

6. Click **OK**.

Adding more assembly joints

1. Create another rotational joint between the Pin and the Pivot.

Next, you need to constrain the Pivot by applying constraints.

2. Click the **Assemble** button on the **Relationships** panel.

10. On the **Assembly** mini toolbar, select **Mate – Flush** from the drop-down.

11. Select the bottom face of the Pivot, and then select the bottom face of the Base.

Face to
select

Face to
select

12. Click **Apply** (plus symbol on the mini toolbar).

13. Select the **XY Plane** of the Pivot and **XY Plane** of the Base from the **Browser window**.

14. Click **OK** (check mark on the mini toolbar).

Driving the joints

1. In the Browser window, expand Pivot and click the right mouse button on the **Rotational** joint.

2. Select **Drive** from the shortcut menu.

3. On the **Drive** dialog, type-in 0 and 360 in the

Start and **End** boxes, respectively.

4. Expand the dialog by clicking the double-arrow button located at the bottom. On the expanded dialog, you can define the settings such as drive adaptivity, collision detection, increment, repetition, and so on.

Drive (Rotational:2)

Angular (d12)   Position = (-82.10 deg)

Start   End   Pause Delay
0.00 deg   360.00 deg   0.000 s

☑ Minimize dialog during recording

OK   Cancel   <<

☐ Drive Adaptivity
☐ Collision Detection

Increment
◉ amount of value
○ total # of steps
1.00 deg

Repetitions
◉ Start/End
○ Start/End/Start
1.000 ul

Avi rate
10.000 ul

5. Click the **Record** button on the dialog. Specify the name and location of the video file. Click **Save** and **OK**.

6. On the dialog, click the **Forward** button to simulate the motion of the slider crank assembly.

7. Click **OK** to close the dialog.

8. Save and close the assembly and its parts.

Chapter 8: Dimensions and Annotations

In this chapter, you will learn to

- Create Centerlines and Centered Pattern
- Edit Hatch Pattern
- Apply Dimensions
- Place Hole callouts
- Place Leader Text
- Place Datum Feature
- Place Feature control frame
- Place Surface texture symbol
- Modify Title Block Information

TUTORIAL 1

In this tutorial, you create the drawing shown below.

1. Open a new drawing file using the **Standard.idw** template.

2. In the Browser Window, click the right mouse on Sheet:1 and select **Edit Sheet**.

3. On the **Edit Sheet** dialog, select **Size > A**, and then click **OK**.

4. Click **Place Views > Create > Base** on the ribbon.

5. Click **Open an existing file** button on the dialog.

6. Browse to the location of the Adapter Plate created in the Tutorial 1 of the Chapter 5. You can also download this file from the companion website and use it.

7. Select the Adapter Plate file and the click **Open**.

8. Set the **Scale** to 2:1.

9. Click the Front face on the ViewCube displayed in the drawing sheet.

10. Set the **Style** to **Hidden Line Removed**.

11. Click **OK** on the dialog.

12. Drag the view to the right-side of the drawing sheet.

13. Click **Place Views > Create > Section** on the ribbon.

14. Select the front view.

15. Draw the section line on the front view.

15. Right-click and select **Continue**.

16. Place the section view on the left side.

SECTION A-A
SCALE 2 : 1

Creating Centerlines and Centered Patterns

1. Click **Annotate > Symbols > Centerline Bisector** on the ribbon.

2. Select the parallel lines on the section view, as shown below; the centerline is created.

3. Click **Annotate > Symbols > Centered Pattern** on the ribbon.

4. Select the circle located at the center.

5. Select the center point of anyone of the counterbored holes.

6. Select the center points of other counterbored holes.

7. Click the right mouse button and select **Create**.

8. Likewise, create another centered pattern on the curved slots. Right-click and select **Create**.

9. Press Esc to deactivate the tool.

Editing the Hatch Pattern

1. Double-click on the hatch pattern of the section view; the **Edit Hatch Pattern** dialog appears.

You can select the required hatch pattern from the **Pattern** drop-down. If you select the **Other** option from this drop-down, the **Select Hatch Pattern** dialog appears. You can select a hatch pattern from this dialog or load a user-defined pattern by using

the **Load** option. Click **OK** after selecting the required hatch pattern.

2. Click **OK**.

Applying Dimensions

1. Click **Annotate > Dimension > Dimension** on the ribbon.

2. Select the center line on the slot located at the left.

3. Select the endpoint of the center line of the hole located at the center.

4. Move the pointer toward left and click.

5. Click **OK**.

6. Likewise, create another angular dimension, as shown below.

7. Create angular dimensions between the holes, and then between slots.

8. Dimension the pitch circle radius of the slots.

9. With the **Dimension** tool active, select the horizontal line of the front view and the lower quadrant point of the view.

10. Place the dimension on the right side. Click **OK**.

11. Click **Annotate > Feature Notes > Hole and Thread** on the ribbon.

12. Select the counterbore hole and place the hole callout, as shown below.

13. Add a pitch circle radius to counter holes.

14. Click **Leader Text** on the **Text** panel.

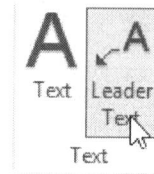

15. Select the slot end, as shown below.

16. Move the cursor away and click.

17. Right-click and select **Continue**; the **Format Text** dialog appears.

18. Enter the text shown below.

19. Click **OK**. Press Esc key.

20. Double-click on the section label below the section view.

21. On the **Format Text** dialog, select all the text and set the **Size** to **0.120**. Click **OK**.

22. Drag and place the section label on the top.

23. Click **Dimension** on the **Dimension** panel.

24. Select the lines, as shown below.

25. Move the pointer toward right and click to place the dimension.

26. On the dialog, click the **Precision and Tolerance** tab.

27. Set the **Tolerance Method** to **Limits/Fits - Show tolerance**.

28. Select **Hole > H7**.

29. Set the **Primary Unit** value to **3.123**.

30. Set the **Primary Tolerance** value to **3.123**.

31. Click **OK**.

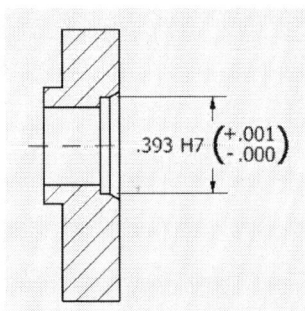

32. Likewise, apply the other dimensions, as shown below. You can also use the **Retrieve Dimensions** tool to create the dimensions.

Placing the Datum Feature

1. Click **Annotate > Symbols > Datum Feature** on the ribbon.

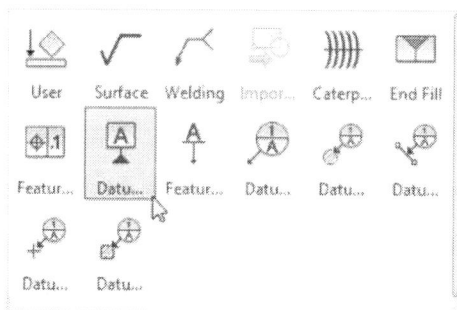

2. Select the extension line of the dimension, as shown below.

3. Move the cursor downward and click.

4. Move the cursor toward left and click; the **Format Text** dialog appears. Make sure that A is entered in the dialog.

5. Click **OK**.

6. Likewise, place a datum feature B, as shown below. Press Esc.

Placing the Feature Control Frame

1. Click **Annotate > Symbols > Feature Control Frame** on the ribbon.

2. Select a point on the line, as shown below.

3. Move the cursor horizontally toward right and click.

4. Right-click and select **Continue**; the **Feature Control Frame** dialog appears.

5. On the dialog, click the **Sym** button and select **Circular Run-out**.

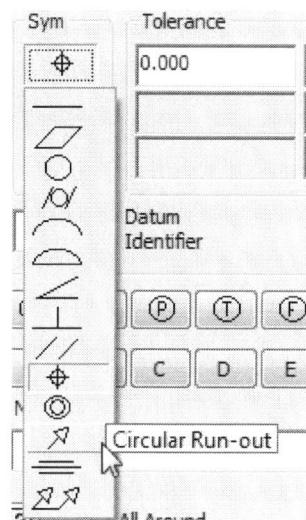

6. Enter 0.001 in the **Tolerance** box and **A** in the **Datum** box.

7. Click **OK**.

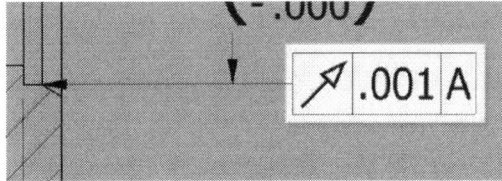

8. Right-click and select **Cancel**.

Placing the Surface Texture Symbols

1. Click **Annotate > Symbols > Surface Texture Symbol** on the ribbon.

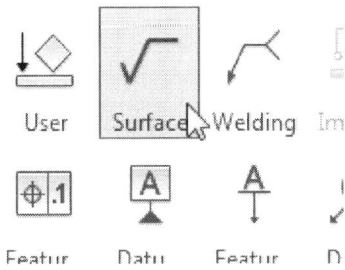

2. Click on the inner cylindrical face of the hole, as shown below.

3. Right-click and select **Continue**; the **Surface Texture** dialog appears.

4. Set the **Roughness Average - maximum** value to 63.

5. Click **OK**.

6. Right-click and select **Cancel**.

7. Apply the other annotations of the drawing. The final drawing is shown below.

3. Click **OK**.

4. Save the file.

5. To export the file to AutoCAD format, click **File Menu > Export > Export to DWG**.

6. Click **Save**.

7. Close the file.

Modifying the Title Block Information

1. Right-click on the **Adapter Plate** in the **Browser window**. Select **iProperties** from the shortcut menu.

2. Click the **Summary** tab and enter the information, as shown next.

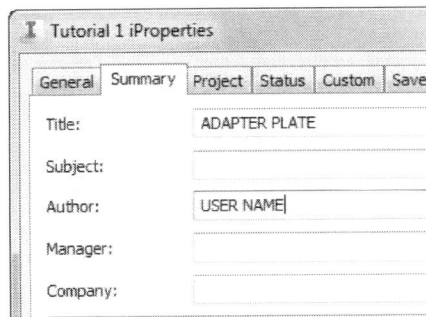

You can also update the Project information, drawing status and other custom information in the respective tabs.

Printed in Poland
by Amazon Fulfillment
Poland Sp. z o.o., Wrocław